Courage to Fly

Book #1 of the Courage Series

Courage to Fly

Julie Anne Kiley

Dedication

For Glyn,
Thank you for believing in me.
xxxx

Acknowledgements

I need to say some thank yous…

Firstly, to Glyn. Thank you for believing in me and not laughing when I told you I was writing a novel. Even after forty years I still love you more than ever. To Rian and Graeme – you are by far my greatest achievements – I'm so proud of you both.

To Zara for helping design the book cover.

To all of my friends, Jax and Nic, Lisa, Jacqui, Aly and Simon, everyone else (especially the dancing crew) who said they would read it if I ever got to the publishing stage…
well, here it is…

And finally, to the ladies that lunch, Gill, Glo, Joan, and Kathy for keeping me sane in a bonkers sort of way
what times we've had!

Thank you all

Jules

xxx

...Sometimes we need to spread our wings,
Sometimes we need to trust our hearts and take a leap of faith,
Sometimes we need the courage to fly...

Julie Anne Kiley

Prologue:

Mary – 19 years ago.

I regain consciousness to a distant buzzing sound. I'm dazed and confused, kneeling on the living room floor with the side of my face resting on the settee; my leaden arms hang limply by my sides and there's something wet on my face. My puffy eyes barely focus as I stare blankly at the wall.

The joints in my shoulder crack in protest as I tentatively raise a trembling hand to wipe away the sticky line of saliva trickling down my chin. An explosion of pain detonates, travelling from my neck, shooting bullets into my brain and burning fire along the length of my arm. "Ahh!" I croak through sore, swollen lips. A bubble of saliva pops at the corner of my mouth.

Squinting my eyes, I see my disembodied hand hovering at the side of my face. The polished nail on my little finger is hanging off; ripped to the cuticle, the delicate skin of the exposed nail bed is raw and bloody. When I touch my face, it's numb, like I've received a shot of Novocaine. Cautiously, I wipe my palm across my chin, sweeping away the spittle. When I look at my hand, it's streaked with red. My brow puckers in confusion as I try to piece together the sequence of events, which have me here, kneeling on the floor, battered, bloody and bruised.

Remaining in my hunched position, I attempt to gather my senses, knowing I need to muster the courage and energy to move my damaged body from its prone state and get away. This has to end now… it has to be the last time… I can't keep living like this.

As my other senses start to return, somewhere beneath the incessant buzzing sound, I can hear the baby crying and I know I need to get to her. Thankfully, it's not a high-pitched cry of fear and distress but a hiccupping, juddering cry. A cry that's starting to abate, as if it's been going on for a while but is now running its course. It's all the incentive I need for my mothering instinct to kick in. Gritting my teeth, angry at myself that I've once again allowed things to get this far, I start the painful process of moving.

Forcing myself to assess the damage, I perform a swift body assessment. My insteps are resting on the floor, rubbing against the carpet. Cautiously I wiggle my toes. Thankfully, there's some movement, and they don't appear to be broken or sprained. *"Oh, thank God!"* The relieved sigh leaves my lips before I can prevent it. I've pins and needles in the soles of my feet and my shins feel bruised but I can cope with that.

I vaguely register my dress is bunched up around my waist and I appear to have wet myself. But I know it's not urine. *"Shit!"* I rasp through my restricted larynx, the full chain of events gradually filtering back to me. I'm remembering.

Everything starts to unravel slowly at first, in convulsive, fast-forward flashes of motion, like an old movie; steadily increasing in speed until the whole sorry episode detonates into my unprepared brain like a nuclear explosion... *I can't stay here, I need to move... NOW!*

Lifting my head from the cushion, I inhale and hold my breath as the blood rushes to my brain, bright white flashing lights brand the backs of my eyes. Sudden shooting pains hammer into my temples as a tidal wave of nausea engulfs me. Swallowing hard, I force the feeling back in a desperate attempt not to vomit. My stomach clenches in objection but the sickly feeling quickly passes enough for me to move some more.

Ignoring the discomfort, I place my palms flat on the seat cushion in front of me, managing to lever myself so my bottom is resting on my heels, then using my arms to steady myself, I wait for a couple more seconds before cautiously turning my aching body around so my back rests against the couch. The sheer effort is exhausting, but I've done it.

Keeping my breathing shallow, to alleviate the pressure on my bruised ribs, I extend my cramping legs out in front of me. Blood immediately floods through the restricted limbs, turning the pins and needles in my feet into a paralyzing cramp. My toes spasm, spreading of their own volition while all I can do is bite my lip to keep from crying out. Whatever I do, I know I must keep as quiet as possible.

Slowly the cramp subsides and I force myself to take deeper breaths in an attempt to remain calm. Shaking my head at the beginning of a headache, I rub at my temples and the back of my neck to relieve the tension, groaning as the random distorted images persistently invade my mind.

No... you will not think of that...!

The deep breathing helps, the cramp in my legs and feet has finally gone, I think I can get up now. Looking round the room, I see the remnants of my shredded underwear bunched in an untidy heap, lying discarded beside the fireplace. My lovely new shoes lie like dead creatures against the skirting board. They've been flung against the wall with such violent force, there's a livid scar where they've torn the expensive wallpaper.

"*Christ!*" The clock on the mantelpiece says 9:35pm and I'm trembling uncontrollably.

The door between the dining room and the kitchen is open, and I can see all the way through to the bi-folding doors leading out onto the back-patio. It's dark outside and there's no moon. Used crockery, silverware and glasses - some still half full of stale liquid - are stacked on the black granite worktop next to the sink.

He's sitting at the kitchen table with a half empty bottle of whiskey in front of him, surrounded by the scattered remnants of party food. His head is tipped back and he appears to be looking directly above him, as if contemplating whether the kitchen ceiling needs a fresh coat of paint. I can't be sure but I think his eyes are closed. His position looks incredibly uncomfortable, as if he's sleeping; either that or he's passed out. *Perhaps I should move him so he doesn't end up with a stiff neck?*

His designer shirt's creased and half hanging out of his black Armani pants. His belt and trousers are undone and he's missing a shoe. The suit jacket has fallen to the floor and is lying beneath the chair. He won't be pleased when he wakes and finds I've not picked it up - he's particular about his clothes – I can't see the other shoe.

The baby's in her playpen in the corner of the kitchen. She's just about visible through the dining room archway. I thank my lucky stars she's no longer crying, but staring intently at me through the kitchen door with a silent knowing gaze; her eyes wide, her rosebud lips parted and wet. Her pale blonde hair is fluffy; ruffled into damp unruly curls, which cling in little wisps to her damp forehead. She must've been crying for some time. It's almost as if she understands the need for quiet just now.

I smile at her and she smiles back. "Hi baby," I whisper. My voice sounds hoarse, choked. I raise my finger to my lips and make a hushing sound. "Shhh now darling; Daddy's asleep and we need to be very quiet so he doesn't wake up. He's really tired."

I try to make my voice light and calm. Her deep brown eyes make the quick journey to where her Daddy sits at the table, his protective hands resting either side of his precious bottle. Then just as swiftly, she flicks them back to me. She smiles again but remains silent.

"Okay... time to get moving," I whisper encouragingly to myself under my breath.

Looking at my injured hand, my finger feels like it's on fire from where the nail's hanging off. With a silent count to three, using the couch for leverage, I haul my heavy, aching body up off the floor. I manage to lift myself up enough so eventually my bottom is resting on the settee, letting my shoulders sag against the back of the sofa.

Dropping my head into my hands I endeavour to calm my erratic breathing. The tops of my arms feel sore, like I've been lifting heavy weights. Subconsciously, I register I've achieved item number one of my mental check list.

Number one: Get off the floor – Tick.

Number two proves to be a bit easier, now the feeling has returned to my legs and feet.

Number two: Stand up – Tick.

Swaying as if I'm drunk, I wriggle, pulling my crumpled dress down to cover my modesty, keeping my right pinkie finger jutting out to the side so as not to cause any further damage.

I take a quick glance over at the baby. She's still watching me attentively but has, at last, sat down on the floor of the playpen. She looks drowsy. Her heavy eyes are fighting to stay open. She must be exhausted.

Checking the clock again, it's 9:37pm. Okay, that's two minutes to get off the floor and to my feet. I desperately need to speed up.

Number three: Move.

Number four: Get the baby.

Number five: Get the bags.

Number six: Get the hell out before he wakes up.

Stiffly I kick my feet into action and with a shambling, zombie-like walk across the room, I grab my shoes from under the window. Leaving my shredded underwear where it is and holding my breath, I tip-toe across the lounge towards the kitchen, desperate not to make a sound. The baby watches my approach and struggles to her feet, holding on to the side of the playpen for support.

"Okay, okay… Hey baby… Hi, sugar…" It's almost a silent prayer.

Once she's standing and steady, she raises her plump little arms to me so I can lift her out and sit her on my right hip.

"Hey there beautiful, come to mummy." Kissing the top of her sweaty little head, I resist the urge to squeeze her too tightly, burying my nose into her neck, inhaling deeply. She smells wonderful. It's a comforting mix of baby shampoo and her own unique baby smell. Instinctively, her little hands go for my shoes – she's helping! I pass them to her and she tucks them into her sides, under her arms as if they were a precious gift.

"Right Sugar, let's get going," I whisper. She nods her little head, her blonde curls bouncing up and down in agreement. Leaning into me, she wipes her runny nose on the shoulder of my designer dress and my lips form a sad smile at the normality of the tiny gesture.

Adrenalin is kicking in, the stiffness in my body's almost gone and I'm able to move more swiftly. Tip-toeing across the lounge and out into the hallway, I'm up to number five on my checklist.

Get the bags.

I'm unwilling to put the baby down so I balance her on my hip whilst wrestling the case out from the under-stair cupboard. My damaged finger is still stinging like a bitch but the sharp pain only increases the flow of adrenalin surging through my system.

The bags have been ready since I last spoke to a councillor. She recommended I pack the essentials in case this moment should ever arise. Once I have the small suitcase and holdall, I realise I don't have my handbag or my car keys. Leaving the case and holdall in the hall, I furtively return to the lounge.

I'm moving more confidently now, my courage growing with every positive step. If he wakes up… if he catches me… I can say I'm taking the baby to bed… and if he notices the bags, I'll say I'm going to the nursing home tomorrow to collect the rest of my Grandmother's belongings.

Yes, that sounds plausible.

Or, if he wakes up and says he's sorry - the emotion of the funeral got to him - promising he'll never do it again, I could stay, put the cases away and the baby to bed.

Playing happy families, Mary?

Foolishly, I realise I've invoked the bargaining game. I've always done this since I was a little girl.

'If the doorbell rings in the next 10 minutes it means I don't have to go to school tomorrow,' or *'if I can make it from my bedroom to the bathroom without touching the floor more than twice, it'll be chips for tea.'*

NO! Enough!... no bargaining... not this time.

Snapping myself out of it I search for my handbag. It's lying on the console table beside the TV. Thankfully, there's no sign of movement from the kitchen, so I check the clock again, 9:42pm; that's another five minutes gone. *"Jesus...Come on!"*

Rapidly I try to calculate how long he's been asleep. I think most of the people left at about 6:30'ish; that was when he opened the scotch. Then the hideousness began.

No! ... Stop thinking about it and MOVE!

Snatching up my bag I swiftly return to the hall. The baby still has hold of my shoes, quietly observing my actions. I methodically and calmly find my keys, opening the front door; just like we're on our way out to the supermarket. But the door catches on the jamb where the wood's swollen, forcing me to wrench it free, producing a familiar high-pitched scourging noise.

A glass shatters on the kitchen floor tiles and I freeze, listening for any further give-away sounds of movement, but I hear nothing.

12

Creeping into the now pitch-dark night, my bare feet crunch on the gravel driveway, and I scarcely feel the stabbing of the tiny pebbles. Pressing the key-fob to unlock my car the headlights flash twice in unison with the double hoot-hoot of the car horn, which echoes like a claxon in the night air, making me wince.

Opening the rear door, I strap the baby into her car seat, before returning to the house for the bags. "There you are, poppet. You wait here. Mummy won't be a minute," I whisper.

Quickly re-entering the house, I'm on high alert for any noise from the kitchen - not paying attention to what I'm doing - I reach for the suitcase, missing the handle; the remnant of my finger nail catches on the zip and rips off. *"Fuck!"* I swear under my breath shaking out my hand, hissing - that hurts. Sticking my injured finger into my mouth I suck away the bead of blood, trying to ignore the pain.

I can't afford this delay...

I strain my ears for any indication he's heard me, but the only sound is that of my own laboured breathing and the pounding of blood in my ears.

Grabbing the bags, I'm swiftly out of the door; not bothering to close it, taking long stalking strides, under the illusion it'll shorten the time it takes to get to my car. *"Shit, shit, shit!"* the curses come flying out in a hushed oath as I'm once again treading on every sharp stone on the gravel path. This time I feel every single one of them; it's like walking on broken glass.

Terror floods my system when I hear the screech of metal on tile; his chair scraping on the kitchen floor. He's awake!

Arriving at the car, the sudden rush of anxiety has me fumbling ineptly. I drop the holdall onto the pavement, snatching it up just as the sound of his commanding voice rings loudly, though the night.

"Mare!... Mary!... Mare? What the fuck?" He curses loudly as he collides with something, "shit ... *Mare, where the fuck, are*

13

you? Mare!" he bellows, his voice travelling clearly, angrily, permeating the silence of the cool night air.

Panicking, I struggle with the leather handles, flinging the bags into the car boot. My heart's hammering with fear, my eyes wide and staring into the darkness. I know he'll hear it close but I've no option. Quickly I slam the lid down and run to the driver's door.

Aware that he'll be moving, looking for his missing shoe, fastening his belt, tucking himself in, I know he won't come to the door in disarray - appearances are everything - silently, I start bargaining with myself again.

'If I can make it into the car before he gets to the lounge, we'll be free.'

I do.

'If he comes out of the house and is remorseful and loving, we'll go back and start over.'

He doesn't.

Sliding into the driver's seat I juggle franticly to get the key in the ignition. My hand's trembling so much it seems to take an age but eventually I manage it. Stamping my bare foot far too hard on the accelerator, the engine roars to life.

He's out of the front door now, careering down the driveway like a possessed madman; one shoe on, his untucked shirt flying behind him like a cape. *"Mare!* What the *fuck* do you think you're doing! Get out of the *fucking* car!" He hammers his fist on the car roof in utter rage.

Instinctively, I press the central locking, hearing the dull thunk as all four doors bolt down simultaneously, securing us both inside.

He's incensed. "You stupid, ugly, fat *cunt!*" His face is turning puce as he gets up close and personal at the driver's side window, his breath misting the glass as he yells his abuse. "Get out of the car... *NOW!*"

BANG, BANG!

His eyes are glazed with pure, unadulterated fury... I'm not getting out of the car. He starts to pull at his hair, spinning on the spot, not knowing what to do. I never disobey him. But this time... this time, it's different.

No more...

Along the avenue, the neighbour's lights go on, curtains start to twitch, but he keeps hollering like a maniac. He's pissed both at me and with the amount of alcohol he's consumed.

"*Mary,* I'm fucking warning you... get out of the *fucking* car!" He obviously thinks I'm going to follow orders... I'm not.

Action number six may have failed, but I'm determined that number seven won't.

Defiantly, I shift into reverse gear and slam my foot down, hard. The wheels spin, spitting up small stones as they battle for purchase on the loose gravel. Infuriated, he makes a desperate lunge for the door handle; it's snatched out of his grasp by the momentum of the moving car bumping down the pavement and into the road, causing him to stager backwards and shake out his stinging fist. The incredulous look of shock on his face is almost comical.

"*BASTARD!*" I hear him yell as he runs back inside the house.

Good! I hope that hurts...

Wasting no time, I slam the shift into first gear, pulling swiftly away from the kerb, the tyres screeching on the asphalt as I speed away far too fast.

Because of all the shouting, the baby is crying again. "Hush now, baby girl. We're just going to the shops," I try to sooth her with a sing-song voice. "Shhh, baby. There she is..." I meet her eyes in the rear-view mirror, desperately willing her to calm down. I can't stop and pull over, that would be a huge mistake. "Hush, sweetie, please, hey… sugar…it's okay."

Her eyes are riveted to mine, seeking out comfort – comfort only I can provide – I remain calm, as if everything's normal and gradually she begins to settle again. I know she's tired but she's battling wilfully against falling asleep. She must be exhausted with the effort of all the crying, poor little mite. She's rubbing her eyes now. "That's it, baby… go to sleep little one…" I breathe a sigh of relief. Finally, she's nodding off, the motion of the car, lulling her as it always does. Any minute now and she'll be fast asleep.

My relief is short lived as in the distance behind me, I catch a glimpse of his car pulling off our driveway. If he catches us, this will end in disaster. My stomach flips; I fight against the desire to slam my foot on the accelerator and hike my speed up to a dangerous level.

Keep cool Mary.

I'm willing myself to be sensible. I've a head start on him and he's in no fit state to drive.

Unbidden, my mind flits to the bargaining game.

'If he stops and goes back in the house to sleep it off, I'll wait it out for a couple of hours and go back.'

He doesn't.

'Okay then, if he catches me up and apologises, I'll turn the car round and go home so we can sort things out.'

He doesn't.

Instead, I hear a sickening crunch as he backs straight into the lamp post across the street.

In the rear-view mirror, I notice the neighbours are out now and trying to haul him from the wrecked car, checking him for injuries, attempting to calm him down.

Good luck with that!

He stumbles but already his movements and gestures are becoming a distant blur. Knowing he can't follow me, I relax my grip on the steering wheel. My knuckles and fingers are aching from the effort.

Glancing back at the baby, her eyes are closed in sleep. Innocent and pure, like an angel, she deserves so much better than this life.

I take a long, deep cleansing breath. I'm at the crossroads. Time to make a choice. Left, right or straight ahead?

With one last look at the distant carnage going on behind me, I smile in wonder at my beautiful, sleeping baby. Then, gritting my teeth with a new-found determination, I turn left.

Without indicating. Without hesitation. Without doubt. Without shoes on my feet and without any clue as to where I'm going.

Number seven: Get away – Tick.

Flicking on the radio, the irony of the track hits me... '*Two beds and a coffee machine*', by Savage Garden.

'Another bruise to try to hide,

another alibi to write;

another ditch in the road, you keep moving ...'

It could be the story of my life!

Chapter 1

Edi - Present day

The ever-evolving unwritten rules of student life are mind boggling. For example: - it's not cool to stay sober at a party. You don't admit that you like *Olly Murs* or *One Direction* - however *Little Mix* is acceptable - *go figure!* You must wait until the very last minute to start your dissertation... *Oh!* and you never, ever, ever call your parents.

In the last three years, on all of these counts I've failed spectacularly; well, except the last one. My parents are both long gone, so it was actually quite cool when I *'contacted'* them through the intermediary of a psychic reading one night. Our house-mate decided she wanted to try being Mystic Meg. It didn't work. Sam was rubbish and drunk but my credibility improved for a while, so it was all good.

The issue is, I'm a mature student. I'm thirty-six and half the pupils on my course are young enough to be my children. I'm deadly serious about this degree. I need, no, must achieve my goal. Failure is not an option at this juncture in my life. I don't want or need to be distracted by wild parties and drunken fumbles. Not that it's ever likely to happen.

Don't get me wrong - I've had the odd inebriated offer from the occasional, pale, skinny, hippie-type youth, who waits until he's either high or pissed, or both, before he has courage to quote that original line, *'Hey Edi, you are a hot, mature woman, you must know loads of things about, you know... how about we hook up and you can teach me, huh?'* Or *'When are we going to get it together, man?'* So funny and so 1960's! Hot, I'm not and don't want to be; been there, done that. It's time to be taken seriously and make something of myself, before it's too late.

It's ten-forty-five am. and I've been up for a couple of hours. I've purposely not turned on the radio out of courtesy to those still sleeping, but now I'm annoyed because I've missed Ken Bruce's Pop Master on Radio 2, and I'm creeping around like the politest burglar in the world, trying not to disturb the sleeping beasts lying around the place like African lions on the *Serengeti*.

Actually, I don't know why I'm being so considerate. The party animals didn't think of me last night as they raved until the early hours of the morning. Deciding they've had enough time to sleep it off, I resolve to boot them all into action and get them moving.

Flicking on the radio, Ken is playing the record of the week, which is the new one by Keith Urban – something about falling, crying and fighting. It's good so I turn it up – loud!

As the time hits 11:00 am. the news reader efficiently informs me a lorry has jack-knifed on the M6 near Birmingham, causing a ten-mile tailback. Some minor 'Z' list celebrity is suing the BBC for lack of privacy and a notorious gang leader and people trafficker has been found dead in the boot of his car; the police suspect his own people.

Threading my way through the living room, I can just about identify the different body parts belonging to both male and female specimens alike. I enter the kitchenette and find a pan and a large, burn-scorched wooden spoon.

That'll do.

Returning to the lounge, I stand in the one barren area devoid of bodies, bottles and sleeping bags, and start to bang my spoon on the pan, like a demented toddler playing in their grandma's kitchen. "Wakey, Wakey, Eggs 'n' Bakey! Rise and shine! ... Time to get up and go hunting. The early worm catches the bird and all that!" I holler as I clang and bash out a catchy rhythm.

Several of the male lion's jerk awake at once, roaring in protest at the invading poachers. *"Fucks sake Edi,"* groans a duvet.

19

"Whaah??...Who??" This time it's a disembodied head poking out the top of a sleeping bag.

"I'm up, I'm up," from someone who clearly isn't up and is, in fact, lying under the sofa.

"Get your skinny arses out of my flat. Its Graduation Day and I'm not going to be late. The party's over; the zebras' bolted, the antelopes are grazing on the grasslands and waiting to be caught. Come on, Out, OUT!!".

I watch in mystified awe as they all stretch and yawn with beautiful synchronicity. It's like attending a wonderfully choreographed *Matthew Bourne* ballet, only with the addition of farting and belching - so perhaps not really like a *Matthew Bourne* ballet then.

Lizzy and Sammy are the last to lift their heads. It's their flat too, so they've heard it all before and are under the impression my orders don't apply to them.

"Jeezus, give it a break, will you? You can be such a stiff, you know that?" Lizzy's a complete grouch this morning, but as she rises from the floor, stretching out her willowy limbs like a flower unfurling its petals to the sun, she looks like a Roman goddess. Tall, slim and blonde, with burning brown eyes that flash with flecks of copper - your basic nightmare - the combination is stunning. It's a shame she can be such a slob; although I have to concede, she has a heart of pure gold. Elegantly, she peels an empty crisp packet off her cheek and drops it on the floor.

By comparison, Sammy is the polar opposite; short and plump with a mass of unruly thick black curls, pale skin and cheeky, laughing bright blue eyes. There's Irish blood in there somewhere, but *God* knows where. She's a ball of fire, laden with an abundance of self-confidence, which mere mortals like me can only envy. Completely at ease with herself, she doesn't understand the concept of a negative body image or the so-called 'thigh gap'! She's her own woman, and, as such, totally adored by everyone, and never short of admirers. I love her dearly! She's Lizzy's BFF - whatever that means - they're completely inseparable and have the kind of genuine, supportive, girly-girl friendship to last a lifetime.

Scratching her curly head, she chirps, "give me ten seconds and I'll be a stunning masterpiece." Like Tigger on amphetamines, she bounces up from the couch she's been huddled on all night, then sits back down again just as quickly, clutching her obviously throbbing head. "Ouch!" she complains, "what's the time?"

"Just gone eleven. This lot need to be *vamoosed* and the place tidied and sorted before we leave. I'm not clearing up your mess again, so get moving!"

"Who died and made you God?" grumbles Lizzy with a very unattractive snort, pulling the now empty sleeping bag along the floor, and rolling it into a tight sausage.

"No one – my word is law." I bow and give them a Queenly wave. Turning to shoo out the remaining limp, farting, stretching, yawning lions I pause briefly, slamming the door dramatically behind them.

Chapter 2

The Graduation ceremony was amazing. I hung on every word Sir Sebastian Arthey KBE delivered in his address. It was inspirational, making all the hard work of the last three years worthwhile.

From my row at the back of the room I could see Sammy. She was at the front with the other 'A's'; it must have been killing her to try and stay awake and focused for the whole speech. It made me grin. Lizzy sat two rows in front of me with the 'P's' and I was with the other 'S's' on the penultimate row.

It took a good couple of hours for the parade of students to receive their rolled up blank pieces of paper and shake hands with an actual Knight of the British Empire. The real degrees are posted and delivered in padded envelopes later in the week.

Now we're enjoying a glass of warm, sweet, sparkling wine, hugging, kissing and congratulating each other, before we all leave for the very last time.

I'm stood quietly by the floor to ceiling window. I can't quite believe I've done it. I've achieved a first with honours and I'm now an official member of The Royal Aeronautical Society and Chartered Institute of Logistics and Transport. My degree in Airline, Airport and Aviation Management means I can work at any airport, in any country worldwide. After all this time, it feels surreal.

Lizzy comes cantering up to me like a young thoroughbred filly; all long legs and flying mane. "We did it!" Squealing, she envelops me in her arms and hugs me tightly, planting a kiss on the crown of my head. "I can't believe it. Us, we did it. You, me and her," she chirrups, jabbing her thumb over her shoulder in the general direction of Sam, who is slowly making her way over.

I can tell Lizzy's trying to hold back happy tears. This day has been a long time coming - for me at least.

"Well, well my ladies, what do we do now?" Sammy joins us, her mortarboard is at a jaunty angle and I'm guessing she's picked up a few spare glasses of wine sauntering across the room, greeting her minions along the way.

"We rule the world, of course... what else?" I say, with absolute conviction.

"I'd rather meet an ancient billionaire with a bad cough, marry him and rock his world. Then we'd live happily ever after – until he dies of sexual exhaustion!" Lizzy declares, a wistful look on her face. "Then I'd inherit all his money, excommunicate his ungrateful children from his previous wives, and live a life of luxury, spending my ill-gotten gains". I worry she might be serious!

"Wow, dream big!" Sammy quips, knocking back the last of her champagne, and dumping the empty glass on the windowsill.

"It's a plan, I suppose!" I laugh, passing my half full glass to Sam, so she can finish that too.

One of the farting lions from this morning's lay-in approaches us with a camera. He doesn't look much better than he did earlier, reclining in his grungy underpants and socks. But at least he's covered up with his cap and gown.

"Smile like you mean it, sexy ladies," he demands. "Say sexy."

"Sex-ee!" We chant as one, wrapping arms around each other and grinning like three utter nutters.

Three years of hard study. The Three Degrees I muse to myself. An Airport Manager, a Chartered Accountant and a Primary School Teacher. All ready to spread our wings and take on the world!... yeah, we did it... bring it on!

They say after every high there's a low. Well it's happened. My head is throbbing and I'm staring at the mess from this morning, still strewn all over the living room floor; only now it's spread to the kitchenette and the hallway. The girls have gone off with the lion pride to hunt, gather and party their way around the campus. Honestly, I couldn't face it - or rather, I didn't want to be the wicked *'old matriarchal lioness'* guarding the cubs, restraining them from their raiding, pillaging and debauchery. So, I've come home, under the pretence I've a headache, which ironically, I have. I think I talked myself into it.

I start to clear the mess like an automaton. Swiping a black bin liner from the cupboard under the sink, I fill it with the empty bottles, ready to take down to the recycle bin in the yard. Once that's done, I take all the glasses into the kitchenette and run the hot water, fill the bowl and squirt in some Fairy liquid, so I can wash the glasses. It's monotonous but calming work, and I'm happy when all the glasses are sparkly clean, lined up, upside down on the terry dish towel I've used as a makeshift drainer.

Next, I put the empty Pizza boxes and paper plates into the recycling then chuck the leftover food in the green food caddy. I methodically and meticulously work my way through the task of tidying, clearing, cleaning and putting away, until it's all done. Once I've hoovered and put the vacuum away, I take myself through to my bedroom and pick up the phone to call David.

"Hey Kiddo... how's it going over there in the big wide world?"

"Hiya, it's brilliant. All my friends are really nice and Nic has a teddy. I've been making bread and cakes today." David's really happy to hear from me but as usual has the attention span of a butterfly when the subject doesn't interest him.

"Wow, that's great, well done you; I have some news too – we all graduated today." He doesn't really understand what graduating means, but I explain that Lizzy, Sammy, and I've been given a special prize, for doing really well in our exams.

"Cool, you can bring it when you come to see me. Nic's teddy is too big so his dad got a smaller one to keep here." As usual, he's off on a tangent, far more intent on telling me his own news than hearing mine. I don't mind.

David tells me Nic is funny and very good looking. He has brown skin, big, curly black hair and he's very tall. David seems quite taken by his new friend. I'll have to meet him when I next visit, which will be on Sunday.

David says he misses me, but he loves his new apartment and doesn't want to live with me anymore. It makes me smile. It's not meant in a malicious way; he couldn't be mean if he tried. It's his way of asserting his independence.

The Beeches has been a fantastic place for him to do just that. He has responsibility and is receiving training, so hopefully he can get a job in the future. He has come on leaps and bounds, and is developing a real flair for catering and kitchen work.

David tells me that he loves cooking and making meals for the other residents. I'm so proud of him. At seventeen he's growing into a wonderful, caring young man. Of course, I'm completely biased, as is Lizzy, who adores him, whilst Sammy absolutely loves him, but makes fun of him all the time. It's hilarious to watch.

David is tall for someone with Downs' and he towers over Sam. He loves rubbing her curls with his knuckles and calling her 'Squirt'. She, of course, gives as good as she gets and calls him 'Carrots' in homage to his vivid red hair. Squirt and Carrots – they could be a double act.

I let him chatter on about Nic and his other friends for a while; noting vaguely he doesn't mention any girls' names. I hope I don't have to worry about him being gay too! I brush the stupid thought away and tell him I can't wait to visit on Sunday. He asks me to bring him a present.

"Like Nic's dad did. But not a teddy though, I want a model aeroplane, please," he asks, good manners persisting.

"Of course, no problem, kiddo," I tell him. "I'll pick up a Lego set tomorrow."

"We're having cottage pie for tea – I made it. I need to go now mum, because they'll mess it up if I'm not there to supervise." He makes me smile so much. He says good bye for now and we ring off. *God*, I love him. I can't wait to see my boy on Sunday.

I slept really well for me. I only woke up twice. Once for the loo and the second time, because I heard someone laughing in the lounge. After that it was a dreamless night as usual.

Stretching my arms above my head I turn onto my back. Swinging my legs out of bed, I count to ten while taking some deep breaths, in and out. It calms me. I get up and walk to the bedroom door.

The sight which assaults my eyes is horrific; absolute carnage. There are bodies everywhere. It's like a scene from a horror movie. Okay, that's a little dramatic because there's no blood – not yet anyway! After spending the best part of last night clearing away the mess, this morning it's as if I never bothered.

I'm incensed. Yelling and screeching my vehemence I turn into the proverbial banshee; flying in amongst the prostrate bodies which adorn every inch of free space. "You ungrateful, lazy, selfish, bunch of complete arseholes! It took me three hours to clear up yesterday and look at it! Look at the *fucking* mess. I can't believe this!" I pick up an empty pizza box and hurl it at the nearest head.

Storming back into my bedroom, I yank my wardrobe door open with so much force, it bangs against the wall. Fizzing in anger I make a wild grab for my running gear, knocking half a dozen jumpers off the shelf in the process. "Grrrr!" They can stay there, who cares?

Stripping off my pyjamas I fling them on my bed in temper, hopping about from leg to leg as I drag on my running gear, crashing and banging into my bedroom furniture as I go. 30 seconds later I'm dressed in leggings, vest, socks and trainers, I need to get outside. Storming through the lounge, the pride is slowly wakening, stretching, and not to mention the usual farting and yawning.

I hate them all!

My violent demonstration is hardly noticed as I barge out of the door, intending to slam it shut in temper... only the hydraulic hinge refuses to play ball, stalling the door in its tracks and slowing it down with a lazy hiss - the effect is totally wasted and just stokes my anger further.

Still chunnering, I run down the three flights of stairs, and straight out into the morning sunshine. I need to blow off some steam, before returning to the lion's den, or I might just do some physical harm.

At a steady pace, it takes me about forty minutes to complete two circuits of the campus. By the time I enter the quad, I'm focussed on my run and have almost forgotten the reason I was cross.

Entering the grassed park area, I make a couple of circuits of the track, before slowing to a walk. The lawn here is patchy and bald from the many impromptu games of football and cricket.

Locating a less sparse area, I flop down and lie on my back panting. Feeling calmer, I throw my arms above my head and stare up at the clear blue sky, catching my breath for a couple of minutes before rising to complete some stretches and check my watch.

Okay, I've been out for an hour and a half so I think it may be safe to go back now. I begin retracing my steps back to the halls of residence, waddling like a duck following breadcrumbs. My calves are tight; I need to get fitter.

By the time I start to climb the stairs my breathing has slowed to normal, and I've regained most of my composure.

Opening the door on half-open eyes, I'm not sure what vision will greet me. Feeling a bit guilty at my behaviour, I'm prepared to apologise for my earlier outburst. But I'm really pleasantly surprised when I enter the lounge to find it spotless, with two beautiful ladies perched on the sofa, drinking tea from china mugs. It looks like the W.I. has invaded and done a mad clean up. I shake my head laughing. They're absolutely priceless.

"Come and join us, oh wise Chieftess," says Sammy.

Lizzy, gives her a, *"what the F?"* look. "I thought you were a teacher? There's no such word as Chieftess," she scorns.

Sammy isn't fazed. "Well, Chief then, or Boss, or Lioness or Your Grace. It doesn't matter." Turning her big blues on me she gives me a huge, wry smile. "We're sorry Edi. It was a last blow out, before we've to be grownups forever."

Yeah – that's never gonna happen!

I can't stay mad at them, no matter how hard I try. "Okay, well I suppose I understand. But you're both coming with me on Sunday to visit David." I try to sound authoritative. They look at each other then back to me, incredulous.

"We wouldn't miss it for the world," says Lizzy, on a warm smile.

"No, and you should never underestimate the power of a *'hissy-fit!'*" Sammy raises her cup in reverence to my said 'hissy-fit', and the power there of.

I relent and take my seat on the sofa, picking up my mug of tea. My back is sweaty, but the tea is irresistible, I'll have this before I go for a shower. "Cheers, my dears, I need this!" I say blowing over the hot liquid and taking a healing sip. We clink and drink.

"Have you spoken to him at all?" Lizzy looks at me, it's a tentative question.

Sam keeps quiet, but flicks a look at Lizzy over the top of her steaming mug. Lizzy has only been to The Beeches a couple of times and was concerned David wouldn't settle down there. It is extremely thoughtful of her.

I tried to reassure her that, at the time, it was his idea. He was getting so frustrated at the day centre and wanted some independence. Also, while I continued my studies it was necessary for me to find him somewhere more permanent. It took me ages to find somewhere we were both happy with.

The Beeches is in Guildford, so it isn't too far away from me and once I start my new job, I'll still be within about ten miles, so regular visits will be a doddle.

"He was pretty full of it actually," I say, trying to make my voice sound reassuring. "He has a new friend, Nic, or Nicky or something - he's dying for you both to meet him." Just talking about David gives me a warm feeling.

"Whoa! So, the Carrot has a Parrott! Neat!" jokes Sammy, getting to her feet, obviously relieved. She picks up the empty mugs and heads for the kitchenette. "I, for one, am looking forward to that. It will give me some more ammunition for when he starts having a go at me," she shouts through the doorway, then lets out a creative string of curses, as the inch of tea I always leave in the bottom of my cup slops out, splattering all over the floor, showering her pink toe nails with lukewarm dregs and black ant-like tea leaves.

"*Fucks sake*! Edi, why don't you ever finish a brew?" I ignore the drama, and the systematic huffing and puffing as she mops up the deposit from the tiles.

I turn to Lizzy, giving her a watery smile. "I can't believe this time next week you'll be in America," I sigh. It will seem really strange without them around.

She grins back. "I know! We *will* be okay though. You know that, don't you? It's only for six weeks. We've got to be back before the end of August. For Sammy term begins on the 5th September. You won't have time to miss us, with your new job and all. I'll explain to David. He'll get it eventually."

I sigh again, pulling my feet up onto the sofa beside me - but my nose twitches as I get an unpleasant whiff of tangy cheese from my running shoes. Deciding it's a bad idea, I push them back down to the floor – these trainers are rank!

"It's not that and you know it. We've had three fantastic years in this flat. But honestly, I'm ready for the next step. I know you and Sam are going to have the best time, but please promise me that you'll stay safe; You know I worry about you." I'm fussing unnecessarily, I've drummed it into them often enough but it's instinctive, I can't help it.

"What do you think is going to happen?" Sammy wanders back in eating a biscuit; her cleaning duties, either forgotten or complete.

"Two sexy, single, British birds, straight out of University, travelling the vast plains of the U.S.A – *Nooo*, it's never been done before has it? *God*, Edi we'll be fine. We've a fully planned itinerary. All the accommodation is booked, and all the travel for that matter… were insured… stop with the wittering will you and enjoy your time alone. The brothel Madam will look after us… that's 'j' for joke by the way…" she quickly adds, spying my horrified expression.

"You *really* need to chill out," she continues. "Aren't you at least going to pay a visit to the hairdresser before you start your new job?" She ruffles my hair in a feeble attempt to distract me from worrying about their travel plans. Unfortunately, this only results in catapulting me into a state of high anxiety about my own near future and the concerns I've about my new job!

Choosing to ignore her I spring to my feet. "Right, I'm going for a shower," not wanting to contemplate my own insecurities.

Unrelenting, Sam continues calling after me. "Seriously, Edi, it's a bird's nest most of the time. At least have a trim." She's berating me, but her admonishments fade away to a distant squawk as I make my way to the bedroom.

Picking up my dressing gown and a clean towel, I enter the bathroom in a huff; My hair's not that bad. Bolting the door to keep out unwanted intruders I turn the shower on to maximum in an attempt to drown out her voice - which is still opining on my lack of any discernible hair management.

As the small bathroom fills with steam, I strip off my running kit, wrinkling my nose in distaste when I remove my trainers - *I must get some new ones; these really stink* - I drop my damp gear into the hamper then use the loo. When I'm done, I climb into the shower underneath the feeble spray. Dragging the ancient shower curtain across the tub I hum in gratified pleasure, cocooning myself in the stifling mist.

Mildew stains the stitching at the hem of the faded mint-green nylon. Gaudy images of Dory and Nemo swim gaily across the pleats of the shabby curtain. It's hardly an opulent bathroom with its chipped turquoise tiles and avocado suite, but it's still blissful.

Once I've washed my body and feet, I take my shampoo from the edge of the bath, squirt a blob into my palm, and rub my hands together before lathering up the bird's nest and quickly rinsing away the suds. I finish off by applying some conditioner and combing it through, allowing the water to rinse through my tangles.

My whole shower routine takes about six minutes and by the time I'm done, the water is tepid and getting cooler with every second - the hot water tank must be on the blink again.

I'm still smarting over Sam's comment about my hair as I try and fail to comb out the knots with my fingers. Perhaps the problem's the shampoo? It's a pound-shop special, which supposedly has the aroma of strawberry and cucumber, to make my hair shine with healthy vitality. It makes me feel like a golden retriever, but at least my hair's clean.

I towel dry my body, pull on my robe and drape the damp towel round my shoulders, preventing my hair from dripping on to my dressing gown. Leaning over the bath I clean the tub with bathroom spray; extracting some stray hairs from the plughole, I drop the them in the toilet and wipe the condensation from the cistern and mirror. After using the shower-rose to rinse the curtain, I finish by shaking off the droplets of water – not that it will make any discernible difference. Finally, I crack open the window an inch to allow the remnants of the steam to escape.

Back in my room, I can still hear the girls chatting and discussing their American adventure. I smile contentedly. I'm happy and excited for them; secretly jealous if I'm honest. I would have loved that kind of opportunity at their age. Closing the door on the girly chat, I unceremoniously plonk myself in front of my dressing table mirror. Flicking on the radio for some background music, '*Black Eyed Boy*' by '*Texas*' seeps into the room.

I stare at my reflection, scrutinising my thirty-six-year-old face. Biting my lower lip to stretch the skin, I jut out my chin and turn my head, checking my skin for any zits, black heads and stray hairs. Trailing my fingertips over my eyebrows, they could do with reshaping but I don't have the time or the inclination, or the money for that matter. My sprinkling of freckles is pale over my nose, my eyelashes are blonde, almost white and I've more than a few new crinkly lines around my eyes.

"Ugly mug," I say to myself, picking up my moisturiser. Squeezing out a generous amount I rub it into my face and neck. There's not much improvement but it makes me feel better.

Grabbing my hair dryer, I tip my head upside down, in favour of finger drying as usual. I can't be bothered with all the fancy grooming rituals they seem to have these days. Waving the dryer over my dark red hair, I flip my hair back so I can dry the front, twiddling the fringe and sides into some sort of shaggy, semi-style, eventually giving up and tucking it behind my ears. Before it's fully dry, I'm fed up with the whole beautification process so I switch off the dryer, and drop it in to the basket beneath the dressing table.

Another quick look in the mirror convinces me I'll do… no makeup needed. Well, it's needed but I persuade myself it isn't.

Pulling on my black underwear, my black jeans and an old Phil Collins tour t-shirt, I scoop up my black zip-up hoodie from the heap on the floor and zip it up. It's a bit Rock-chick come Goth, but who cares. I slip my feet into my red flip-flops, hang up my dressing gown, drop the damp towel into the washing basket with my other laundry and take it through to the kitchen to start a wash.

There's a note on the work top from the girls saying they're meeting the pride at the 'Solar and Dog' for a drink if I want to join them. Flicking on the kettle, I scrunch up the note and chuck it in the paper bin. I need to make a start on the packing really – it's an excuse but it's the truth.

After I've loaded the washing machine, I brew some tea and eat some cereal - even though the milk smells like it's on the turn - then I leave the washer humming away whilst I sort out my stuff, ready for packing.

By 6:00 pm. I'm starving and the girls still aren't back, but I've made excellent progress. My clothes are packed in my wheelie suitcase, my books and important stuff in an old blue holdall and my backpack is loaded with toiletries. My shoes are in Tesco carrier bags, and I even have a couple of bags for the charity shop. My stomach is growling. I broke off at 3:00 pm. and had another coffee with a banana sandwich, but now I'm hungry again. I fancy some pasta. I think we've a tin of tuna in the cupboard so I troll back to the kitchen to prepare my gourmet meal.

As if on cue, the second I'm ready to start serving up, I hear the jingle of keys in the door, and the peal tipsy laughter as the girls come rolling in. Thankfully, they're on their own this time. I tip the pasta into the colander to drain while retrieving three dishes from the top cupboard. The tuna was only a small tin, so to make it go further I've mixed it with some leftover sweetcorn, chopped tomatoes, diced red onion, a drizzle of olive oil and I've grated some parmesan cheese into another bowl. I'm dividing the pasta between the three dishes, spooning on the sauce just as the girls enter the kitchen.

"Mmm, that smells wonderful," Lizzy announces, wedging herself into one of the mis-matched kitchen chairs, pulling one foot up to rest on the seat so her knee is tucked under her chin. It doesn't look at all comfortable. Reaching over, she pulls a dish towards her while Sammy flops onto another chair, hooking her feet round the chair legs and does the same.

Taking three-pint glasses from the cupboard I fill them from the cold-water tap. "Corporation pop for the ladies," I quip as I join the girls at the table. "Did you have a good afternoon with the guys?".

Sammy doesn't remove her eyes from her dinner, chewing away at her pasta she nods her head, sneaking a sideways peek at Lizzy, who's picking at the penne with her fingers like an orphaned sparrow, dropping it into her mouth before chewing quickly and repeating the process.

Feeding time at the Zoo, I think to myself.

Lizzy picks up her pint of water and downs it in one without taking a breath. Placing the empty glass on the table she lets out an unladylike belch, then resumes picking out the sweetcorn and pasta from the dish, effectively eating round the onion and tomato; though she can't avoid the little bits of tuna that cling to the pasta. She's a fussy madam!

"Gotta love a party piece," says Sammy applauding, impressed at the huge burp and pointing her fork at Lizzy, before returning to her trough. I shake my head at them in dismay.

Lizzy pushes her bowl away and lowers her leg back to the floor. "Thank you, that was delicious," she's nothing if not polite. Obviously, she didn't find it delicious, because she's only eaten about ten pieces of pasta and the kernels of sweetcorn.

"Yeah, really wonderful." Sam agrees. Her bowl is empty, so that placates me.

"We need to pack. We've said our goodbyes to the boys so I don't think we will be having another teary farewell," says Lizzy.

Ah, so that's the issue, she hates goodbyes and is obviously putting a brave face on it. They're heading off to America on Monday morning. I've agreed to play taxi to the airport.

"Solomon can be such a girl sometimes," Sammy quips, scraping her chair back from the table and picking up the dishes.

"I'll do that. You two go and start packing. It's Sunday tomorrow and we need to get off early if we're going to spend the day with David." I let them off.

"Okie-Dokie, Smokie!... Come on then, *Deadly Nightshade*, let's do this thing." Feigning enthusiasm, Sam pulls Lizzy to her reluctant feet and drags her off to their room for a night of packing, and re-packing. Lizzy groans and grumbles her way out of the kitchen, like a small truck on-tow.

It is 9:30 pm. and I'm dead beat, so I decide to have an early night. Switching off the TV and rising to my feet, I stretch my arms above my head before bending and touching my toes. My back's stiff.

Standing back up, I switch off the table lamp and head off to bed. I can still hear the girls giggling and chatting as they decide what they need; what will go and what will stay. The music is muted, but I can still make out they're listening to *Green Day*. I thank my lucky stars I've already completed the task this afternoon while they were at the pub – a job well done. Stripping off, leaving my clothes where they fall, I climb wearily into my freshly made bed.

I'm asleep in about ten seconds. I don't dream.

Chapter 3

"Good Morning Sunshine!" Lizzy is up, dressed and, it would appear, full of the joys of spring. As I waken from my slumber like a bear coming out of hibernation, she brandishes a cup of tea under my nose. Bounding to the window she opens my curtains to... pouring rain!

"Look at that wonderful day!" She's a sarcastic madam!

"Up you get. Prince David is waiting," and with that she launches herself out of my bedroom like Wonder Woman. She has far too much energy this morning.

After a quick shower, I'm dressed in my customary black jeans, tour 'T' - this time it's 'Guns and Roses' - and oversized hoodie. I've eaten the soggy bran flakes, drank the warm orange juice and cold tea, made lovingly for me. The girls have washed the pots and are sat patiently waiting on the sofa like butter wouldn't melt, while I faff about in my bag, checking I have everything I need. I have everything... all I need is my bag and car keys, for goodness sake!

Thankfully my car starts first time. It's a twenty-year old, black, BMW 3 series, known affectionately as *Rusty-Bucket*. It's a bit corroded around the wheel arches and the doors, but the engine's sound. It's done over 120,000 miles on the clock and I'm about to add another fifty-odd. The wiper blades make a flip, flop, screech, sound on the windscreen as we set off. Sam's riding shot-gun and Lizzy's stretched out along the back seat. She starts snoring as soon as we drive off the campus. I knew the energy of this morning wouldn't last long.

As we approach the A25, I suddenly remember my promise to bring David a model aeroplane. "Bloody, bums and cock!" I swear, "we need to stop at the retail park and nip into Toys 'R' Us".

"Okie-Dokie, Smokie!" says Sam with a cheerful grin.

Brief detour complete, we're back on our way. Thankfully the rain has stopped. Lizzy's still comatose and didn't even notice the short sojourn. Sammy's examining the Lego Box, attempting to decipher the instructions. "Well, this will deffo' keep the Carrot busy," she announces gleefully. I'm sure it will, for about 5 minutes. David is a whiz with Lego.

After forty minutes - it should really have been thirty but I had to fill up - we arrive at The Beeches. Turning into the driveway, the main car park is full, so I drive round the back to where there's a couple of extra spaces alongside the conservatory.

Disembarking, Lizzy unfolds herself from the backseat, she reaches her arms towards the sky, stretching to release the kinks from her muscles. Her green vest rides up to reveal her toned midriff and the small bumblebee tattoo on her left hip. Gathering herself together, she performs a one-legged shimmy, tugging at the hem of her shorts between her thighs, dancing to releasing the wedgie from her bum-cheeks, while Sam and I watch patiently.

Completely oblivious to our scrutiny, she scratches her head, ruffles her blonde hair and she's once again the gorgeous supermodel. Ritual over, we all pivot on our heels, and start crunching our way over the damp gravel to the front entrance.

After we've signed in and said our hellos to Mrs Derbyshire, the matron, we make our way to the resident's lounge to seek out David.

I can't help the huge grin that breaks out when I see him. I take a private moment just to look at him; my heart is brimming, full with love and pride for my handsome young man. But as usual, my quiet time doesn't last long. Instinctively he knows we're there, spinning around and whooping with delighted glee before bounding over to scoop me up and twirl me off my feet.

"Hiya mummy, I mean mum!" he amends quickly. He has a lovely timbre to his voice.

My cuddle is short lived when he spies Lizzy over my shoulder. He drops me like a ton of bricks and making a dive for her, flings his arms around her neck and lands a huge sloppy one on her cheek. She's laughing hysterically.

"Davy-boy! Wow, you've grown again! I think that's tall enough now; I don't want you bigger than me kiddo." He swaggers proudly, enjoying the attention and swings his eyes over to Sammy.

"Don't even think about it, Carrot!" she says, pretending to back away holding the palms of her hands out in a keep back gesture.

He ignores her completely and makes quick work of throwing his arm round her neck in a mock Half-Nelson, then rubbing the 'bejesus' out of her head with his knuckles. "Squirt!!" he admonishes with a splutter of laughter.

"Gerroff, you little sod!" jokes Sammy, fighting free.

After all the greeting and rough and tumble, David grabs my hand and leads me over to where he was standing when we arrived. A group of young adults are sat playing a very competitive and lively game of Jenga. Mark, one of the team of support workers, who help with the residents' day to day needs, is trying to referee an argument breaking out about some supposed cheating.

David walks casually over to the tower of bricks and flicks it with his finger and thumb. We all jump out of the way as the wooden tower tumbles onto the table top, scattering the bricks everywhere, effectively ending any further argument!

"Game over!" he announces smugly.

"Well, that appears to be the end of that!" says Mark. "Come on guys, let's go outside and check what damage the rain's done to the veg garden. We can leave the *Dark Destroyer* here to clear up the mess." He gives David a pointed look. Gathering up the complaining group he herds them off through the conservatory to the boot room, to don wellies and cagoules.

"That wasn't very nice, David," I scold lightly.

"Well, they were making a mountain out of a mole hill. Martin always cheats, but it is only because his hands shake. It isn't his fault. I just helped them get over it." He's very matter of fact.

"Come on, I want you to meet Nic," he announces, drawing me towards the sofa. "Nic, this is my mum. Mum this is Nic."

He formally introduces me to a young man who's seated on one of the striped chairs off to the side. I didn't notice him with the Jenga players; he was sitting quietly, preferring to observe the game from a safe distance.

As he rises from his seat, I'm instantly struck by how incredibly handsome he is. He's extremely tall, at least six feet two or three. He has a smooth, dark olive complexion, like pale milk chocolate, and an impressive afro. But it's his eyes that are really striking. They're a stunning mix of pale green and amber. I've never seen eyes quite like them, they take my breath away. Nic is muscular and well-built. He could easily pass for a male model or movie star. It's clear he doesn't have Downs, and I wonder idly what his disability could possibly be.

"Hello Nic," I offer my hand. "I've heard a lot about you from David. It is lovely to finally meet you."

Nic looks blankly at David, who grins at him nodding encouragement. Eventually, after what seems like an eternity, Nic very slowly lifts his large hand, taking mine in his own and gives it one hefty shake. Then he drops it quickly, nods his head but doesn't speak. He looks in turn at Lizzy and Sam, then back to David.

"M...mmya...?" He mumbles the word, quietly, through gritted teeth.

"No, not Maya, that's Lizzy, and that's Squirt. You can rub her head but you can't kiss Lizzy," David states firmly.

"Err! I'm Sammy, not Squirt and no, you bloody can't." She holds her hand out anyway.

Nic avoids her eyes, looks at the top of her head, takes her hand and gives it one swift shake, as he did with me. Then he looks at Lizzy. He gets flustered and turns his head away as she holds out her hand. He seems distressed and starts to sway from foot to foot, bringing his hands up to his chest and holding them protectively away from her. Lizzy is completely unfazed. Nic is mumbling something, but I can't hear him. David quickly takes him by the shoulders placing himself in his line of sight.

"It's okay Nic. It's really okay ... she won't bite. She's just pretty, that's all." Very gently, David persuades Nic to turn back and face Lizzy.

Hesitantly, he lowers his hands from his chest and jabs his right hand towards her, fingers flexed, all the while not registering her eyes but keeping his head turned to the side. Lizzy gently takes his hand and gives it a single shake copying his own preferred action.

"Hello Nic. I'm Lizzy. It's nice to meet you." Everyone visibly relaxes when Nic seems to accept the greeting and calms down.

We spend a good hour with David. First, he shows us his apartment. It's a studio, as are all the units, but he's so proud of the fact that it's his own private space. There's a small fridge, a microwave and a toaster. He doesn't have a kettle as that isn't allowed outside of the communal kitchen, but he does have a small table and a couple of chairs. He has Perspex drinking glasses so he can offer his visitors soft drinks. The lounge area is furnished with a sofa and armchair so he can watch his own TV or listen to music on his player when he wants to get away from the hustle and bustle. The partitioned off bedroom is ensuite, the bathroom more of a wet room. Clothes are strewn on the bedroom floor along with several books and comics. It isn't very tidy, but it looks just like any bachelor pad should... I'm thrilled.

After we've admired his room, we're treated to a guided tour of the gardens and the vegetable patch. It's lovely to see the resident's enjoyment, caring for the plants and vegetables. They grow most of their own, and enjoy preparing and cooking them in the communal kitchen. David tells me he's the best chef and everyone loves it when it's his turn to make dinner. His best recipe is leek and chicken stew with mash potato, oh, and cottage pie.

As we stroll through the grounds, Nic follows behind like a silent shadow. He seems happy to tag along as David keeps up a steady commentary, including Nic in the conversation, not seeming to notice he doesn't respond or acknowledge anything. David's a brilliant tour guide.

It starts raining again as we're leaving the rose garden so we all troop back inside to the cosy communal kitchen, where the Jenga squad are brewing up and making sandwiches. They work as a team, methodically and cooperatively buttering bread, grating cheese and slicing tomatoes. This is all under the unassuming, gentle supervision of Mark, who himself is removing a tray of freshly baked scones from the oven. The smell is heavenly, reminding me I'm hungry. Everyone is busy, sharing the workload. Some are arranging plates, cups and saucers on the table, while others have a production line going, buttering, filling and finally cutting the bread into wonky triangle sandwiches, carefully positioning them onto a large plate. I take a peek at Lizzy. She doesn't like tomato and isn't fond of cheese either.

Before I can say anything, David pipes up, "can you make some ham as well please? Nic doesn't like cheese and tomato."

How does he know, the boy doesn't speak?

There are cheery approvals, everyone's willing to accommodate and happy to make more sandwiches.

Lunch is a lovely, lively affair. We all dig in and enjoy the wonky sandwiches and delicious warm scones, which are served with whipped cream and fresh strawberry jam. Apparently, David made the jam himself from fruit grown in the garden; with a little assistance from a local chef who visits twice a week, to give some support in the kitchen and provide skills training to those who are keen on catering.

David is proudly explaining the joys of jam making to an enthralled group. I have to admit it's scrumptious, and I notice for once that Lizzy's tucking in with enthusiasm. Sam's on her third scone, already! But still Nic sits quietly by himself on the periphery of everything; eating his sandwiches and silently observing the chatter and camaraderie of the rest of the group. It makes me feel a little sad.

After lunch, the girls are keeping David and Nic entertained with the Lego aeroplane so I take the opportunity to seek out Mark for a quick chat and catch up. I leave the four of them in the conservatory. David is ecstatic with his present and immediately sends Nic off to get his teddy to show the girls. Nic gets up and obediently heads off in the direction of the bedrooms, presumably to retrieve his toy.

I locate Mark in the kitchen. He's stacking away the pots while Wendy, one of the Jenga gang, is drying-up. He turns and gives me a big welcoming smile as I enter.

"That was a fantastic lunch. Thank you. We didn't expect to be fed," I'm really grateful as I forgot to pack any food.

Mark turns to Wendy. "Hear that Wend'? That's a satisfied customer if ever I heard one."

Wendy gives me a glowing smile. She's delighted with my praise and starts to hum a cheery ditty as she carefully folds her chequered tea towel, hanging it neatly and precisely over the radiator.

"Thank you for coming," she says joyfully as she passes me and exits the door to join her friends, who are watching a repeat of Countdown in the TV room.

Mark leans his shapely backside against the work top, folding his arms over his broad chest. He's about thirty with fair hair and a bit of stubble on his dimpled chin. Tall and well built, he looks strong, as if he could handle himself if needed. He's always smiling and has lovely straight white teeth. Quite a dish, but a little young for me, sadly.

"Well, what do you think of our Davey then?" he gets in first before I can strike up a conversation.

I always feel a little nervous talking about my son. I was only nineteen when he was born and it was a massive shock to discover he had Downs Syndrome. I was in a very small minority of mothers, especially because of my age, and at first, I found it tough to come to terms with. I still get a twinge of guilt, almost eighteen years later.

"I'm amazed at how quickly he's settled in. I really thought he'd want to come back home once the novelty wore off, but he seems so… happy, I suppose is the right word."

Mark continues to smile. If anything, it gets wider. "Yeah, I would say so. He's a brilliant kid, you know? It isn't easy with some of them, but he's obviously had a loving and caring upbringing so far. He really gets the concept of right and wrong, something that most of them don't always understand. He's caring and well grounded. The way he's with the other residents is really quite funny at times, you know. He doesn't stand for any messing about or diva behaviour, if you know what I mean. He's really very clever."

"Wow, thank you," I'm flattered. "To be honest, I didn't have much support when he was younger. It was just our little family unit." I don't want sympathy – that's just the way it was.

"We limped along, learning as we went. I just did what I thought was right at the time." I made sure he went to ordinary play group and mainstream schools. "It worked for us - I'm biased but I think he's wonderful - I'm so pleased he's happy, … what's the story with Nic?... they seem to be really close friends." I'm curious to understand a little more about this mysterious young man.

Mark makes a face, as if he's deciding whether to answer. "Well, you understand that I can't divulge any personal details because of privacy laws," he says cautiously, "but I can tell you he's in his early twenties and has a form of autism; although we don't have a complete diagnosis, he's definitely on the spectrum. You probably noticed, his communication isn't great, you know, he doesn't make much eye contact and can get easily agitated when he feels unsettled, but he's latched on to David, and well, David is just kindness personified, as you know. He takes it all in his stride."

Clearly, Mark's much more comfortable speaking to me about my own boy. "He's taken Nic under his wing and looks out for him. Nic's responding much better to his therapy and I think we've his friendship with our David to thank for that."

Our David! That's nice.

I raise my eyebrows and give my head a little shake as this sinks in. "That's good to hear. Clearly, David has the magic touch. I mean… well you know what I mean. I'm stunned. I was worried when he started speaking about Nic, you know…" I feel the blush heating my face. I'm ashamed of my thoughts, and it's awkward to say, so I blurt out, "I thought there might have been some attraction…other than friendship?"

Mark doesn't balk at my inappropriate comment. He just looks at me with a steady, unchanged expression. "No, we do have a gay couple here actually, but David and Nic are just great mates, not boyfriends. In fact, I shouldn't tell you this," he leans forward on a conspiratorial whisper, "as I'm sworn to secrecy, but David and Wendy have a bit of a thing going. Just holding hands and watching movies. Its early days - no sign of wedding bells yet so you don't need to buy a hat!"

He's smirking at me, making fun. He knows I'm uncomfortable with this line of conversation and I know he's trying to make me feel better by keeping it light, but I still feel strange talking about my son in this way.

I shake my head and silently admonish myself for being so ridiculous. Of course, they've normal relationships. Wendy - that was the lovely young lady who was washing up when I came in. I approve.

I decide to change the subject. "I need you to know I'm starting a new job next week so I don't think I'll be able to visit for a few days at least. I'll let David know, but I need you to be aware that I might not be easily contactable. If you need me, just leave a message on my mobile and I'll pick it up. Once I start, I'll let you have the office phone number."

"Oh, wow, that's brilliant. Not a problem, congratulations by the way. I believe you all graduated with flying colours."

Once again, I'm a bit shocked and surprised. "How do you know that?" I'm curious.

"Oh, Davey mentioned it a couple of days ago. He said you were all getting a special prize for passing your exams. I took it to mean you'd graduated. He does listen, you know, though he doesn't always acknowledge it at the time." He's teasing me again and I feel a stab of self-reproach as I, once again, underestimate my wonderful boy.

"Oh, I know. I just wondered. He was so preoccupied with telling me about Nic. Anyway, I'll leave you to it. I need to get the girls back. They fly to the States tomorrow, I'm starting work and moving to my new digs, and there's still loads to do."

I start swinging my arms, clasping my hands and releasing them, trying for a breezy approach while I back out of the kitchen.

"Don't worry about Davey, Edi. He's absolutely fine. Good luck with the new job and digs. Tell the girls I said to have a brilliant time... oh, to be young and foolish..." he sighs dramatically, brushing his hair from his forehead in an effected manner, pushing his backside off the counter. "Oh, Ms Sykes, if you could just let Mrs Derbyshire know on your way out, you know, what you said about contact for the next day or so... cheers."

I acknowledge him with a wave and make my way back to the conservatory. Countdown has obviously finished because Wendy has joined David, Lizzy, Sam and Nic. She's enthralled as David explains how the Lego aeroplane fits together.

I notice Nic is sat on the floor close to Lizzy and Lizzy is cuddling what looks like a fluffy puppy in her lap. Startled, I give it a second glance, thinking at first, it's real. Then, understanding registers, it must be Nic's teddy. It's actually very lifelike.

Lizzy, lifts her head as I approach. "All sorted?"

"Yeah, all sorted," noticing that it's pushing four o'clock. We need to leave soon if we're going to have some time left to finish the last bits of packing tonight. "Come on then you two. I hate to break up the party but we need to hit the road."

Groaning, Sammy picks herself up from the floor. "See you in a month or so, Carrots," she gives David a huge hug and rubs his head. I notice with a smile Wendy gives her a disapproving look. David is oblivious.

"Yeah, see you later D-B" says Lizzy, patting him on the shoulders and giving him a fist-bump. She hands the toy back to Nic, and he takes it from her without really looking at her. "It was lovely to meet you Nic. Thank you for letting me hold

Teddy." Nic swings his head in an arc a couple of times. I think he's acknowledging her in his own way.

"See you soon mum. Don't worry about me, it's all under control." David is so confident!

"Okay then," I laugh. "I love you lots." He allows me to give him a big kiss and a hug.

"More than Jelly Tots," he whispers in my ear so nobody but me can hear it. Over his shoulder, Wendy gives me the evil eye! I'm his mother for goodness sake!

"Bye everyone. Bye Nic, Bye Wendy. Come on you two. You still have a million jobs to do before tomorrow." With that we walk back to the front door and leave the happy bunch behind us.

Chapter 4

We finally arrived home at about ten-to-six. The roads were clear for once so we had a good run. Lizzy insisted we stop to pick up a takeaway to help us through the final bits of packing.

Now it's nine-thirty, and we've just about finished. The larger crates are stacked by the door ready to be transported to the storage depot. What's left of the pizza's just crust and bits of congealed cheese, sitting in the bottom of the grease stained box.

"Harry Potter marathon I think," Sam declares then starts rootling through the DVD's for the box set. Lizzy and I settle on the couch nursing our diet colas as Sammy loads the player. The credits start to roll and my mind inevitably begins to wander and reminisce.

We've had three great years in this flat. Despite parties, the damp and the time the boiler packed in and wasn't repaired for a week, we've been model tenants. The landlord's been great and because we didn't break anything, there's no additional fees due!

I vaguely register Hagrid saying *'You're a Wizard, Harry,'* on the periphery of my hearing, as my mind continues to wander. The only furniture I own is in storage ready for my new venture. The boxes of knick-knacks I've collected over the years will join them tomorrow; the landlord has kindly agreed to see to that for me.

An apartment comes with my new job - which really helps - although the jury's still out until I see it. I'm not holding my breath – it could be a dump!

Click, click. "Snap out of it!" Lizzy snaps her fingers in my face, breaking into my daydream. "Here, you look like you need this." She hands me a mug of coffee and sits back down, tucking her left leg underneath her, settling in to watch the movie.

"Thanks," I murmur gratefully as I take a welcome sip, resting my weary head against the sofa, submerging myself in the world of muggles and magic for a couple of hours.

It's late - in fact, far too late as we head off to bed. I try not to think about tomorrow, or the day after, or the day after that, when we will have gone our separate ways.

Sammy's adamantly trying to convince Lizzy that David could have played Ron Weasley. "Honestly, I mean, he wouldn't even need to dye his hair... I mean... real carrot-top and everything. Don't get me wrong, I think that Rupert bloke is red hot - ha-ha, ged-it? – well he is now, but David's David, ain't he?!"

Lizzy gives her an exasperated sigh. "Whatever... come on *Hermione,* I'm knackered and we're up really early tomorrow. We can continue this debate on the plane."

I'm smiling at Sammy's optimism as I enter my room. It looks empty and devoid of any character. Sighing, I tumble into bed and I'm asleep in about ten seconds.

We arose before the dawn; Monday morning is bright, it looks like it's going to be a fine day. We've greeted the sunrise and we're on our way to Heathrow, where I'm dropping the girls before I continue my journey.

Luck's on my side and I manage to find a space in the passenger drop off zone. Drivers can only stop for five minutes while they unload.

I can't help laughing at the girls. They're dressed in denim shorts, knee high socks and walking boots. Lizzy is wearing a cowboy hat and a red, white and blue checked shirt with hers. Sammy has on a yellow burnout oversized t-shirt and a flowered bandanna, with her unruly mass of curls spilling out over the top. She's a perfect cross between a 1980's John McEnroe and a palm tree. I'm relieved I can't wait for long, the good-bye hugs and cheery waves are giving me a lump in my throat, although I know I won't cry. I never do.

"Please, please take care of each other," I plead. "Ring me when you get there and don't do anything you shouldn't!"

"We will and we won't," they sing, far too excited to be emotional. Lizzy adds, "good luck with the new job, we love you."

Sammy steps back, dragging the bags and backpacks up the kerb and onto the pavement. She takes the opportunity to check her phone while waiting for Lizzy to catch up.

Using Sammy's distraction to her advantage, I'm surprised when Lizzy grasps both of my hands in hers and leans towards me, delivering one of her Paddington-hard-stares. "Remember... you *can* do this," she whispers so only I can hear her, "courage to fly, yeah? It's *your* time now." Squeezing my hand tightly, she gives my cheek a hurried kiss. "Courage to fly... we agreed... remember?" she repeats, close to my ear.

"Yeah... I remember... I won't let you down," I whisper back. "Now go and catch that plane before Droopy Draws over there explodes..." Sammy has put away her phone and is now visibly vibrating with impatience, waiting for Lizzy to join her. Shaking her head at our wayward friend, Lizzy wastes no more time, grabbing the handle of her backpack and slinging it over her shoulder. She gives me one last hard look - I get the message - then it's all systems go, as they giggle and shriek their goodbyes.

"See you in a month," they chorus together as if rehearsed, and holding hands, skip into departures dragging their luggage behind them.

Wistfully, I watch their backs disappear through the automatic doors as I reluctantly make my way back to my car. A waiting driver in a silver Mercedes honks impatiently wanting my space. "Okay, okay keep your hair on!" I hiss like a ventriloquist. Smiling through clenched teeth, I flick him a quick, acknowledging wave and climb behind the wheel. Pulling into the line of crawling traffic, I join the thong of cars queueing to leave the airport.

Chapter 5

Less than an hour later I'm completely lost. I've driven from Heathrow to Guildford on the M25 which was fine, then joined the A281 for Cranleigh. I found the exit which directed me to Cranleigh village, proclaiming it to be the largest village in England, but now I'm utterly confused, looking for the B road to take me to my final destination.

Needing to study the directions more thoroughly and desperate for both the loo and a coffee, I spot a blackboard easel at the side of the road for Babette's Café, a quaint English tea shop, and pull up in a convenient parking space just opposite.

The board bears a white chalk drawing; two wavy lines, depicting steam above a sketch of a cup and saucer beside an image of a slice of cake. The scrolled writing proclaims todays' special is homemade, honey and orange cake with a standard cappuccino for £3.95 - further options are available inside. It sounds good to me, and they must have a customer toilet, so I make my way over the road.

Opening the café door, a bell tinkles merrily. Finding an empty table for two in the window, I plonk my bum on one chair and drop my bag on the table in front of me. The café's old-fashioned, filled with an eclectic miss-mash of tables and chairs - the chairs are brightly painted with chintzy padded seat cushions, all the tables have floral cloths and the window is dressed in red and white gingham.

A pleasant mannered, grey-haired, middle-aged waitress with a glowing white apron and a not so white smile arrives to take my order. She has lipstick on her teeth; it draws my eyes and I'm instantly reminded of *Mrs Overall* from *Acorn Antiques*. Suppressing my amusement, I order the daily special and ask if they have a customer toilet. Pointing to the back of the café she wanders away to make my coffee.

After paying a much-needed visit, washing my hands and freshening up, I return to my table to find my cake and coffee have arrived. The cake looks delicious and the coffee is steaming hot.

Nibbling away at the cake and sipping the coffee I study the email and map containing what appeared at first glance to be fairly simple directions; I can't believe it's turned out so complicated I must be near, surely?

The cake and coffee have filled a hole, I'm replete, but still puzzling over the map as the waitress returns carrying a saucer containing my bill. "Was everything to your satisfaction madam?" she asks with a beaming smile. I notice the lipstick has gone, it's a vast improvement.

I return her smile, gratefully. "Yes, thank you. It was lovely." Rummaging through my purse I hand over a fiver, adding "keep the change." She thanks me and turns to take my empties back to the kitchen but I quickly call her back. "Err, excuse me, but do you think you could help me? I need to find this address."

"Of course, my lovely. Let's see." Returning, she places the cup and plate on the table and taking the email from me, places it flat and smooths out the crumpled paper.

"Ah, yes, you're not too far... you're looking for the air field then?"

"Yes, but I'm a bit lost."

"No problem... okay, you see that sign over there?" she points to the enormous brown tourist information sign – right in front of my parking space! "Turn left at the next junction then follow the road past the leisure centre. After a couple of miles, you'll cross to a bridge which goes over the canal." She's waving her hands like she's directing traffic. I bite my lip as she carries on with the mad routine. "There's a sharp turning on the left; follow the lane for another mile or so and you'll see the airfield - you can't miss it. You should be able to see the planes from the road."

Display over, thoroughly pleased with herself and delivering a final beaming smile, she picks up the used crockery and moves on to the next customer.

"Thank you, so much, I really appreciate it," I say to her retreating back. But she's already focusing on the next table.

Picking up my bag and paraphernalia I head out back to my car, feeling like a complete numpty. Climbing into my rust bucket, I feel even more of an idiot on reading the sign, large as life, looming above my head - I don't know how I missed the bloody thing - it declares:

Cranleigh: England's Largest Village.
Leisure Centre
Medieval Church
Arts Centre & Cinema

And last but not least… **Airport.**

Yep, I'm an idiot! And just to compound things, a small leisure plane hums overhead as it flies in a curved arc, clearly heading in the direction of the airfield. Driving off I make a left, trying to look like I know what I'm doing.

After a few minutes, I've passed all the attractions listed on the signpost and crossed the canal bridge. I can see the hangar buildings in the distance, a couple of beautiful jets and some smaller leisure aircraft are all lined up on the apron outside. I take the next left and drive the final mile or so along the lane, which runs adjacent to the canal. The view is stunning, and I'm beginning to get a nervous flutter of excitement in my stomach.

Abruptly, a set of tall iron railings appear, running left and right, along the length of the runway. They're so high they interrupt the pretty countryside view and the airfield beyond. In the centre of the security fence, an impressive pair of blue metal gates on runners are standing open. There's a sign attached to the railing about three feet square with painted black letters on a white background. It reads:

Royal Tudor Charters LTD.
Executive Air Travel and Logistics.

Underneath that sign, another smaller one in red says:

Private Property. No Trespassing.

Creeping along, I crawl through the gates at about three miles an hour, trying to work out where I should be going.

Everything looks pristine and new. The grass is closely trimmed and the runway markings are clearly defined. There's a modern white two-story building about a hundred yards away, which appears to be the main office. Outside there's about twenty parking spaces, some of which are reserved with name boards.

Choosing an unmarked space next to an ancient green Range Rover I park up. My nerves have kicked in big time now, my palms are sweating and I need another wee.

Why did I have that coffee?

Climbing out of my car, I smooth down my black trousers, rubbing my damp palms on my thighs; I'm feeling crumpled after my drive. Checking the back of my shirt is neatly tucked into my waistband, I look down and notice a white splodge on my crotch, near the zip, where a comma-shaped blob of cake frosting has dried into a beautifully, incriminating stain!

"Bloody marvellous!" I groan under my breath.

Licking a finger, I rub at the stain, scratching in vain at the dry flakes with my nail, but to no avail. The icing has soaked through the material and dried into a stiff, unyielding smear. Any hope of removing it with spit has long gone.

Abandoning the rescue attempt, I pull my white shirt from the waistband and tug it down in a pointless effort to cover the offending stain. The lightweight cotton is creased to Hell from the waist down where it's been stuffed into my pants.

"Crap!" I curse in annoyance. *Well it's either this or I look like I've just been ejaculated on by an elephant!*

Huffing in frustration, I know I look untidy and dishevelled but I can do little about it now. It's rather breezy, so tucking a wayward curl behind my ear, I make my way to the office feeling totally exasperated with myself. What a great first impression this is going to be!

Entering the revolving door, I give the brass handle a forceful push, but it's far lighter than it looks and I'm not met with the level of resistance I'm expecting. There's a distinctive *whoosh* as the door whirls away from my hand. The rear panel collides with my back, taking me completely by surprise; jolting me forwards into the small triangular cell. The deafening crash and resulting slam cause the door's safety function to engage, and the whole unit comes to an abrupt juddering halt; trapping me securely on one side of the glass, while my bag is left swinging on the other.

"Bugger!" Embarrassed by my complete lack of coordination, I push back against the panel. Reluctantly the door gives, reversing direction and creating just enough space to release my bag.

Careful not to make the same mistake twice, I gently apply pressure to the glass, inching it forward again before exiting into the cool foyer. *Could I look any more incompetent?* Thankfully, I don't think anybody noticed!

The office reception is bright, open and airy, reminiscent of an executive car showroom, only with aircraft rather than motor vehicles on display. White marble plinths are strategically positioned throughout the space, displaying beautiful scale-models of sleek jets, helicopters and old bi-planes. Framed blueprints and photographs of concept designs adorn the walls. David would be in seventh heaven.

I recognise all the renowned brands from my studies, the collection artfully depicting the progression of air travel throughout history. It's a fascinating and stunning exhibition.

Remembering why I'm here, I pull myself together long enough to drag my appreciative eyes away from the gallery and make my way over to where an efficient looking blonde receptionist is standing behind the desk. Her head is bowed in concentration, but as I approach, she looks up smiling.

Swallowing, I clear my throat. "Hi... I'm Edi Sykes. I'm here to meet Mrs Royal," I stutter feebly. I know I must look a fright with my stained pants, crumpled shirt and wild messy hair.

"Ah, yes, Edi... I'm Christina Royal." Flashing me a lovely sincere smile and holding out her hand, she strides from behind the reception desk to greet me.

Her voice doesn't match her appearance in any way. She's tall, easily five-ten, and is wearing an immaculate cream linen trouser suit, with a simple black silk camisole beneath the tailored jacket. The look is finished with a long gold chain draping from her elegant neck.

Her shoulder-length hair is beautifully styled, deliberately cut to look naturally effortless, swinging and swishing in gentle waves as she moves her head. My guess is she's about forty, but looks much younger.

With very pale light green eyes and minimal make-up, she's elegance personified, the illusion only broken when she opens her mouth, speaking with a lovely warm, broad, northern accent. She sounds like she might be from Manchester or Lancashire. It's a bizarre combination and I like her instantly, especially when she gives my hand a firm shake, resting the other on my shoulder, giving it a light reassuring squeeze.

"It's lovely to finally meet you," she says sincerely. "I hope you found us okay? We're a bit off the beaten track here, but I suppose that's normal for an airport." She's really welcoming. "I suppose, we'd better get started. I've received all of the necessary references, with a glowing letter of commendation from your Uni' professor, I must say. You were very highly thought of - they're extremely complementary. Everything seems to be in order." She's frighteningly efficient and fast talking.

Taking it all in, I blink and shake her hand, a little shell-shocked at all the glowing praise; considering this is the first time we've actually met face to face - all my interviews were conducted over the phone, which I found rather bizarre.

When I eventually find my voice, I manage to stutter a response. "Oh, thank you... err, thank you." I don't really know what else to say, I'm a bit taken aback.

Whilst thinking about how overwhelmed I am - I should at least try to behave in a professional manner - there's a gentle swooshing sound and I feel a ripple of cool air caress the back of my neck. My hair fans round my shoulders, and Christina's ruffles artistically as if a summer breeze has just blown across us.

Glancing over my shoulder, her attention's momentarily taken by something going on behind me. Instinctively I turn to look, following her gaze with my own. It's clear the draught is coming from outside - through the automatic door; *the* automatic door on the immediate right of the revolving door I made such a performance entering by!

I know this because, there, standing stock still on the rubber doormat, is the most beautiful German Shepherd I've ever laid eyes on. He's absolutely stunning. He must be a *he*, because he's huge; really tall. He has a noble, majestic head, silky tan ears, tipped with jet black points and intelligent, gentle, deep, brown eyes.

His top coat is well-groomed, long and glossy and shimmering a rich golden-blond. The silky fur lifts with the breeze revealing his dark chocolate-brown under-coat and as the air swirls about him, he just stands, statue-like observing us both. I know absolutely nothing about dogs but even I can tell he's a magnificent specimen.

"Well hello there!" Christina speaks directly to him, bending at the waist so as to come down to his level. Given her height, she doesn't have to stoop very far. My eyes follow him warily as he pads towards her on enormous leonine paws, his swaying tail giving me a firm whack, high up on my thigh as he passes.

Christina rubs him tenderly under the chin and all around his silky ears. Appreciatively, he closes his eyes on a leisurely blink and leans into her hand, soaking up the attention. I'm mesmerised and a bit apprehensive. I'm not used to dogs and this one looks like it deserves to be treated with great respect; he seems to love Christina though.

"BEAR!"

A clear command from a deep male voice immediately demands the dog's attention. Just the sheer power and resonance of it startles me - sending a shiver down my spine- causing me to straighten my back and hitch my breath. Daring to look I'm instantly floored by what I see.

Obediently, the dog whisks away from Christina and bounds towards the tall, well-built man standing in the doorway. He appears so large he's obliterating the sunlight. His frame is casting a giant shadow on the white marble floor, and the bright, mid-morning sun is forming a glittering halo around his huge form.

Dropping by his feet, the epitome of compliance and submission, the dog gazes up at the man with complicit reverence and adoration. It's all I can do not to join him.

The brooding giant inclines his head, nodding once at me, without any discernible facial expression; then he turns his stony gaze to Christina. I just stand staring, open-mouthed like a star struck teenager. *Jesus*, he's magnificent! The man and the dog make a formidable pairing, that's for sure.

My mouth is instantly cotton dry, and my pulse elevates to such a ridiculous rate I'm sure it can be heard externally. I'm finding it difficult to breathe - like all the air's been sucked out of the room - as if he's creating a vacuum, just by his sheer presence. An unexpected pull of attraction unfurls somewhere deep down in the pit of my belly; attraction unlike anything I've felt before. I'm totally transfixed and petrified at the same time.

His rough voice breaks into my daze, jolting me out of my sudden trance-like state. "Tina, the Cessna's ready. Tell Phillips, we can use it tomorrow." He also has a northern accent, though not as pronounced as Christina's. His voice is deep and rich, but he's so surly and abrupt in how he speaks to her, almost to the point of rudeness.

Dressed in greased-stained overalls, buttoned to the centre of his chest, he's wiping his large hands on an oily rag. He's extremely powerfully built and must be at least six-five.

He's black. His skin is light ebony and he has a smattering of rough stubble on his tight square jaw. His broad brow is damp, gleaming with light perspiration; evidence of the warm day and manual labour he's obviously been doing. The slight sheen emphasises how short his hair is cropped against his head, accentuating a few flecks of silver at his temples.

A clean white t-shirt is visible under his khaki overalls, and he has heavy brown work boots on his feet. Handsome, he most certainly is - but charming he most certainly isn't; and I feel as if I've been struck by lightning at the sheer sight of him.

Christina completely ignores his brusque manner. Keeping her warm smile fixed firmly in place, she introduces me as if he should know exactly who I am. "Silas, wouldn't you like to meet Edi?"

"Hmm, pleasure." Frowning disapprovingly in my direction, he nods again and tilts his head, giving me a quick up and down. An appraisal?

His eyes are a deep caramel colour and he has a straight Grecian nose with lush, full lips gracing his wide unsmiling mouth. I feel as if I'm being examined for any flaws - of which there are clearly many - his scrutiny makes me squirm with embarrassment. But internally I'm bubbling, and my tummy does a little flip at the thought of him looking at me.

Once his visual assessment is complete, he delivers a lazy blink to Christina conveying he finds me lacking in some way, and isn't impressed.

"Bear, come." This time his authority is in no doubt. The dog stands to heel and both he and his master leave as abruptly as they entered. The door swishes closed, the flow of the breeze disappearing along with them.

Letting out the breath I didn't realise I was holding, I turn my startled, wide eyes back to Christina, completely dumbfounded and blindsided by my involuntary reactions to Silas.

The goose bumps on my arms belie the fact that the day is warm and humid; my skin is prickling as if static electricity is fizzing all around me and the fine hairs on my arms and the back of my neck are standing up. *Who is that gorgeous, brooding and arrogant man?*

As if reading my thoughts, Christina informs me. "That, m'dear was my charming ex-husband and business partner, Mr. Silas Tudor." She's all matter-of-fact, turning and indicating I should follow her. The animated conversation continues as we walk. "The other half of the business, though he prefers to spend his time in the hangar and sheds with the planes and grease-monkeys," she says apologetically. "Google lies, love."

She's right there. He looks nothing like his pictures; not that I've paid a great deal of attention when I've looked, just a quick search to familiarise myself with their business really. She carries on talking as we march swiftly to the back of the gallery.

"Don't fret. I'm used to women looking at him like he's a God."

Oh shit, was it that obvious? I feel so embarrassed.

"He's a great looking guy and he really is a wonderful business partner." Walking on down a corridor, she adds "but sadly, he wasn't too great as a life-partner - if you get my drift."

I don't really but I nod anyway. She grins at me as she continues. "Great in bed - but absolutely crap at all the other domestic stuff."

I gasp in surprise at her candid openness. "We just clashed on everything. From decorating to taking out the rubbish; we just couldn't live together."

She's being mischievous and thoroughly enjoying my obvious discomfort. Her grin is quite infectious though - she's clearly picked up on my attraction but isn't the least bit perturbed by it – it must happen all the time!

"Err … um?" I still can't string a damn sentence together. She has no inhibitions and is oversharing; I'm a complete stranger for goodness sake.

"Yes, unfortunately we didn't agree on anything where home life was concerned." Oddly, she doesn't sound bitter in the slightest. "Thankfully we're in complete agreement about the business," she raises a neat eyebrow, "it works well and we're still really great mates. Business is booming, hence why we need you," she declares with another broad smile, halting at the back of the room.

"Excellent!" I just about manage to choke out a word. *Yay me!*

"Right, let me show you around." She leads me through some double fire-doors and into an internal vestibule, housing Gents and Ladies staff toilets. A no-frills staircase leads to the first floor and another fire-door separates the back area from the rest of the offices. The layout's impressive and well designed. There's the distinct smell of fresh paint and everything looks brand spanking new.

"The main office is upstairs, I'll show you that first. It's all mod-cons and provides state-of-the-art comfort for our employees. Part of your job will be working with HR to recruit the best, which, until we find the right HR Business Partner, will be yours truly!" she declares, tapping her chest and patting her hair in an affected manner.

Leading me through another fire-door and onto an open landing, the full open-plan office is spread out before me. It's bright and airy and has three glass walls, which effectively give a full view of the airfield, runway and hangars. The open countryside beyond and the silvery water of the canal in the distance add to the stunning vista. If I was one of their employees, this would be where I'd want to work... *Oh! wait a minute, I am!*

The backwall houses four teak wooden doors. Again, there are Ladies and Gents toilets. One door leads to the staff kitchen and break area, and another door is signed quiet room.

"Nice, huh?" Nice - that's an understatement. It's fabulous!

"Nice," I mumble in appreciation, all wide eyed and a little intimidated.

"C'mon, let's get to the exciting part. We need to go back down for that."

Leaving the open office behind us, we retrace our steps to the ground floor. Through the second set of fire doors, we're in a square inner hallway with four further teak doors; one on the left, two in the centre and one on the right.

Three of the doors have brass nameplates on them. The left one says *C. Royal M.D.* and the first middle one says *S. Tudor C.E.O.* The one next to that says *E. Sykes Ba. FFA.* A little shiver of glee runs through me at the sight of my name on my very own office door! The door on the right is blank.

"That will be HR, when we have it," Christina explains, "but I really want to show you this." Taking hold of the handle to *my* office, she swings open the door as if revealing a hidden secret...

And O.M.G and WOW! It is amazing!

Almost like an open-air room, it's designed to give the feel of being encased in a glass box, jutting out from the rest of the building and suspended in mid-air, several feet above the ground below. It's an illusion of course but an impressive one. The floor has white marble tiles, the ceiling dotted with subtle lighting, but the three plate glass walls give a panoramic view, just like the office upstairs. And for the second time today, I'm completely speechless. It's quite literally taken my breath away.

It's a revolutionary and daring piece of architectural design. Quite contemporary in fact, and I absolutely love it. Stepping inside and looking through the windows I can see the other office beside mine. But the architect has designed them so they're off-set. You can't fully see inside the next-door pod. They're open but private, it's very clever.

"Oh, wow!" I'm spellbound. "I mean, this is fabulous. Oh Christina, I love it!" Christina beams at me.

I turn slowly taking in my new office. Beautifully furnished, the sympathetic contrast of modern and traditional styles, creates a welcome juxtaposition, bringing an injection of warmth to the otherwise sterile appearance. There's a mahogany desk, a high-backed office chair and, an L-shaped sofa - upholstered in the same distressed brown leather as the chair - placed in the designated seating area by the huge picture window overlooking the runway.

In front of the sofa, there's a heavy glass-topped, mahogany coffee table standing on a pristine white rug. It's difficult to absorb it all. The only solid wall houses the door. It's constructed from traditional rustic bricks and supports a range of elegant book cases, which are stacked with books and an array of empty shelves, ready to be filled with ornaments and personal items. There are also two polished mahogany filing cabinets.

Christina snaps me out of my daydream. "This is me and this is Silas," she gestures vaguely at the two doors on either side of the water cooler. "Did you bring some ID? I need to have that as proof of eligibility to work and I'll also need to take a copy of your driving licence and passport, if you have one. It's just a formality, for HR you know." She glances at her huge gold aviator watch. "A car comes with the job. It's on order but will take a couple of weeks I'm afraid. You can use your own until it arrives. And you may need to travel abroad occasionally." She's suddenly all business.

Plunging my hand into my bag, I quickly riffle through all my junk for the envelope containing all my essentials. "Yes, I've all of those things with me." I manage my first full sentence since entering the building. Pulling the buff envelope out of my oversized bag, I hand it over. Christina tucks it under her arm, indicating her thanks.

I'm reluctant to leave my gorgeous office, but we wander back out and she continues the guided tour. I get to see the rest of the offices and the outer buildings. As she shows me around, I begin to relax and the conversation gets easier. When we get onto my specialist subject of Airport management and logistics I fall into my stride, speaking with confidence on all things aeronautical. I'm comfortable with my knowledge and Christina's obviously an expert in the field. We spend the rest of the morning in her office, discussing my role and her expectations.

Chapter 6

Soon mid-day rolls around, so we go and pick up some lunch from the nearby farm shop. It's typically countryfied and all the produce looks home-made, fresh and delicious. Christina picks out a mixed selection of salads and sandwiches, along with a couple of cans of pop, bottled water and some fresh fruit.

As we drive back into the car park, I notice some pine picnic benches on a patio area to the side of the office building. The patio is decked out with tubs of summer flowers, and a couple of older guys are sat, apparently waiting for the food.

They're dressed in similar overalls to the ones Silas was wearing earlier, only theirs are light grey. They seem to be perfectly relaxed, having a good old chin-wag about something.

Collecting the lunches, we climb out of the car and make our way over to the tables. Suddenly, Bear comes hurtling around the corner like a bat out of hell. He skirts the edge of the building, skidding sideways on two legs in his haste and darts straight towards me, like an arrow from a crossbow.

He resembles a police dog chasing down a criminal and I'm immediately catapulted into a state of complete terror. I freeze on the spot, raising my carrier bag over my head, revealing a couple of inches of bare midriff and the lovely icing stain on my trousers. Holding my breath, I stand perfectly still, hoping to God it's the right thing to do.

Within seconds, Silas strides into view, his stalking pantherlike walk is easy and masculine. Removing his aviators, he surveys the scene; clearly amused, but you wouldn't know it because he doesn't crack a smile.

The two old guys at the table have stopped talking and are now staring directly at me. I'm petrified. With my arms above my head, I'm flashing a good three inches of muffin-top and the dubious stain on my crotch stands out like a glowing beacon.

Christina is observing my reaction with a look of concern. And Bear is making a direct beeline for me!

"BEAR!"

The dog's reaction to his masters, deafening command is instantaneous. Immediately he halts and drops down, lying flat on the ground, in front of me; a demonstration of complete submission. I'm still frozen in place like some ridiculous statue, my ears are burning with embarrassment, and my arms still reaching above my head, like a parody of a wild west surrender. *Way to go Edi; could you look any more stupid?*

"Come on," sighing, Christina takes hold of my arm and coaxes me from my shock with a gentle persuasive laugh. "He's completely harmless when you get to know him. A great big softy. I'll introduce you." For a bizarre moment, I wonder who she means - the dog or the man!

Breathing out and feeling a little embarrassed once again for making a complete tit of myself, I lower my arms attempting not to draw attention to my dishevelled state. Bear stays exactly where he is, which means I've to tread a wide circle round him to get to the picnic table, while trying to get my racing heart back under control. Silas doesn't take his eyes off me. His expression is stony.

Setting the carrier bag onto the wooden table, I tug the hem of my shirt down, struggling desperately to straighten myself out.

"Gents, this is Edi…" Christina formally introduces me to the two old guys wedged side by side on the picnic bench.

One is called Charlie, affectionately known as Sparks; the other is Jim, known as Spanners. Like complete gentlemen, they stand in unison, but it's a struggle with their legs trapped between the bench table and the seat.

"Lovely to meet you," says Charlie, or Sparks as I've been told to call him. He leans forward, reaching out his gnarled hand, while Spanners offers a cheery salute.

"H… hi, nice to meet you both." Charlie's handshake is firm, his hand is rough, warm and dry. He's stocky, medium height with thinning grey hair that looks like it must have been blonde once-upon-a-time. He sports a neatly trimmed moustache.

Jim, or Jimmy Spanners, is the polar opposite; wiry in build and fairly tall, though not as tall as Silas. His jet-black hair might have had some help - it's almost navy-blue - but it's precisely combed and styled into a glossy D.A. with about half a tub of Brylcreem. Cleanly shaven he and smells strongly of Old Spice. He reminds me of a 1950's Teddy-boy and I find myself surreptitiously checking out his feet for brothel creepers or blue suede shoes. But not today - today he has the obligatory steel-toe-capped, black work boots - but I bet he has some for weekends!

Sparks and Spanners have worked for *Royal Tudor* since its inception eight years ago. They're old working buddies made redundant from Gatwick, when it made the controversial decision to subcontract the maintenance crew. They rub along very well for two people who are so different. But the distinction in their personalities and appearance makes the partnership endearing. I love the camaraderie they share. They've loads of old-fashioned cockney cheek and make me laugh. Christina and Silas were quick to recognise an opportunity and employed them both immediately.

The old boys joke and jape through lunch. it's a friendly gesture, a clear attempt to make me feel part of the team, and I appreciate their efforts. Their easy-going banter makes me relax and feel welcome.

Jimmy Spanners is desperately trying to educate me about music.

"Elvis was undoubtedly the King, but Little Richard, now there was a superstar." Rock 'n' Roll is clearly his great passion.

Charlie has me chuckling with some risqué anecdotes from the old Gatwick days.

Silas remains quiet throughout, just making the odd grunt or humming his acknowledgement to snippets of conversation. He devours his sandwich, keeping his eyes cast downwards as if in deep thought; flashing me the occasional disapproving glance while dropping the odd crust under the table for Dear, who seems content to lie placidly next to my feet.

As the boys are regaling Christina with yet another tall tale, I quietly take the opportunity to steal some furtive glances at my new boss. Silas's so unlike my idea of an entrepreneur.

Christina on the other hand has business woman written all over her, although she laughs like a drain when Charlie recalls a story about one of the Gatwick baggage handlers.

"Seriously, the old mukka, wanted to 'ave a go at drivin' the luggage trolley, 'e wasn't qualified so it was all a bit 'ow's-yer-farver," he says, tapping the side of his nose, "but never-the-less, 'e wanted to 'ave a go. So, we let 'im. It went fine 'till 'e got on to the apron, 'e stayed between the lines like 'e was supposed to. But then..." he paused for effect, "disaster!... some 'ow the Barmpot followed the wrong lines and ended up turning directly into the path of an Air France 737. Talk about everything goin' 'Pete Tong'. The whole airport nearly ground to an 'alt. You wouldn't Adam and Eve it!" Christina roars with laughter. Even Silas had the faint shadow of a smile at that anecdote. I'm beginning to understand why this business works so well. "I tell yer, I've seen some fings that'd make yer 'air curl!" Sparks shakes his head at the fond memories.

After lunch, I have a quick toilet break, where I try once again, unsuccessfully, to clean the incriminating stain off my pants. Then I go back to my office - I still can't believe it's mine - where I spend the rest of the afternoon being productive, unpacking my things and generally faffing about completing some basic tasks; resetting my passwords, stocking up on stationery, making a list of all the extra stationary I need to order tomorrow - yet another one of my jobs until I employ an admin assistant. Once that's done, I settle in my chair to review the small stack of C.V.'s that's been left for me.

After a couple of hours, I've whittled them down to a short list of the four most suitable candidates - two for office admin assistants and two finance/book keepers. It takes me about half an hour to share my thoughts with Christina, who's in total agreement with my choices, and gives me the go ahead to call them and arrange interviews for the following week. By four-o'clock I'm satisfied with my progress. Following a shaky start, it feels like it's all coming together at last.

With all the interviews arranged, I finish the afternoon by organising the books on the shelves into the correct order. Christina's already left for a business dinner in the City. Before going however, she gave me the keys for the apartment, along with the address and the code for the alarm written on a post-it.

She also gave me a box containing necessities - a lap-top, a pager, a mobile phone and a clicker type gadget to remotely open and close the metal gates. Last but not least, I've been entrusted with a full set of keys to the main offices and the aircraft hangars.

My new work mobile has been loaded with the numbers for Christina, Silas, Spanners and Sparks; pulling up the contacts screen, I add the details for Lizzy, Sammy, The Beeches and David. Eight contacts! I'm going up in the world.

Just as I'm placing the framed graduation photo on my desk, Bear walks in through the open door and stands staring at me with that way he has. Unsure of what to do or how to react, I keep my movements slow and try to remain calm; it's a challenge, just his presence is intimidating. *Surely, he can't be on his own?*

71

"Hi Bear," I try, tentatively. He gives his tail a slow wag in response to his name, and pads over to greet me.

Shakily, I hold out my hand out as Christina demonstrated earlier. He sniffs it, then licks it, then nuzzles my fingers. Gathering some courage, spurred on by his acquiescence, I take the opportunity to stroke his noble head and mumble some soothing noises at him, absently noticing he isn't wearing a collar.

His coat's unbelievably soft, and before I know it, I'm burying my hands in the warm golden fleece. "You're a good boy, aren't you?" I say as I caress the silky-soft fur around his thick neck. He leans his weight against my leg; he's as tall as my waist and I breathe a sigh of relief at his submissive gesture. This is some magnificent animal.

"Yes, he is," a deep velvety voice murmurs from the doorway. Bear turns his head towards his master, his tail sways in a slow wave but he doesn't leave me.

I jerk up with a nervous laugh. "You startled me. I should know where he goes, you aren't far behind," that strange heavy feeling invades my body again. It's distracting and disturbing, but thrilling at the same time. My limbs begin to tingle and there's goose-pimples on my arms. I'm mildly concerned this will happen every time I'm in his company.

"I didn't mean to. He thinks he owns the place. Bear, come. I'll take him out of your way."

Oh, please don't leave... "No, it's okay. If I'm working here, we need to get to know each other." Again, I'm not sure if I mean the dog or the man?

Silas stands with his hands in his pockets. It's a relaxed, casual pose; feet apart, planted solidly on the ground, back straight - he just looks at me steadily - his face giving nothing away. He's extremely serious and intense, but at least the frown of disapproval seems to have disappeared.

It's now I notice he's changed from his work clothes into dark blue jeans and a white button-down Oxford shirt. The cuffs of his shirtsleeves are folded back revealing corded, muscular forearms. He's wearing a chunky pilot watch with a brown leather strap. The dial looks like it's made of titanium and he's swapped his work boots for a pair of smart tan brogues. He looks a million dollars.

I on the other hand must, by comparison, resemble an unmade bed. My shirt is beyond creased, and the stain on my pants looks crusty and disgusting. It's been a warm afternoon and I forgot to ask how to operate the air conditioning, so my hair has frizzed. I feel crumpled and grubby, and must look an absolute fright.

"Bear, come!" he says again. With the second command, the dog trots back to Silas and out of the door. Turning full circle behind him, he comes to rest at perfect heel and sits by Silas's side, attentive to his master but keeping his caramel eyes tuned to me.

"Do you know where you're going?" Silas asks. "The apartment, I mean," he adds as an afterthought.

"Err, yes, thank you." I wave the post-it at him, like a girl-guide waving a flag at the Queen.

"Good; see you tomorrow then." Abruptly ending the conversation, he turns and strides out of the door. Bear stands and follows closely at his heels.

I watch through the window. A couple of minutes later he appears in the car park; swapping his keys into his right hand, I can only stare as his long muscular legs stride over to the battered old Range Rover, I noticed this morning. He opens the passenger door for Bear who bounds in, turning a couple circles before settling on the passenger seat, his tongue lolling out of his mouth as he pants in the warm evening sun.

Silas jogs around to the drivers' side, climbs in and reverses out of his space, pausing only momentarily to put on his seatbelt and aviators. Engaging forward gear the Range Rover roars out of the carpark, the big metal gates closing behind it with a resounding clang.

Chapter 7

Inhaling a deep cleansing breath, I exhale on an almighty sigh. *That's one brooding, sexy man!* The thought startles me - where the hell did that come from? I shake my head ridding myself of the inappropriate assessment of my new boss, and start packing up ready to leave. *You need to leave that well alone, Edi!*

I've double checked everything is locked and alarmed; in fact, I've triple checked. I jump into my trusty, old rusty, bucket; there's no air con, so I leave the door open for a few minutes, allowing the late afternoon breeze to circulate around me, cooling the stifling interior of my car, whilst studying the directions to the apartment block, which will be my new home.

I think I get it; back the way I came, through the centre of the village, and across the traffic lights to where I stopped this morning for a coffee. *Was it really only this morning? God, it feels like weeks ago.*

Recalling the events of the day, I think of the girls and smile. They'll be there by now.

Sticking the post-it to the dashboard I note the apartment block is on the righthand side of the road, so I shouldn't miss it. Reversing out of my space, I follow the same routine as Silas, sans the aviators; mine are a Boots special, which cost a fiver in the high-street sales, bargain!

However, I do miss it. Daydreaming, I manage to drive straight past it. I don't notice the beautiful gates, or rather I do, I just don't realise they're the gates to my apartment block.

"Hairy bums!" I curse, annoyed at myself.

Completing a very dubious U-turn, and upsetting several other road users, I ease my way back into the traffic, waving a thank you at the old man in a cap who let me in. It's easier this time, because I'm on the right side of the road to make a left into the driveway.

There's another clicker on the set of keys for the apartments so I press it and the gates begin to swing open. Driving through them I'm immediately struck by the regal appearance of these lovely apartments. The brass sign on the gate post says 'Steeple Mount'.

"Wow, welcome to your new home Edi!" I whisper to myself, leaning forward to gaze under the sun visor and up at the grand Palladian style façade.

The apartment block looks like a converted stately home. There's a manicured lawn at the front, bordered by the most beautiful flowers of every colour. A car park to the left has numbered spaces. My flat is number thirteen and that space is empty so I drive in and park up.

"Well, you're here, so you might as well take a look inside." I'm nervous but not sure why - I can't stop talking to myself.

Removing my suitcase, holdall and backpack from the car boot, I take in the majestic facia of the building.

"Jeez, Louise, it's a palace!" It's certainly not what I'm used to.

Locking the towing handle of my case in place, I decide to leave my boxes of bits and bobs until later. Slinging the backpack over one shoulder, I drape my lap-top bag across my body one way and my shoulder bag the other; feeling like a pack-mule as I grab the taped-up handles of my ancient holdall. Closing the car boot and balancing my holdall on top of my wheelie, I drag my suit case and knackered arse, huffing and puffing, up the path to the majestic teak panelled front doors.

Managing to find the right key first time, shoving the door with my shoulder so I can haul my belongings across the threshold with me, I stumble and trip into the marble foyer of my new home.

Fancy cream-coloured cards, with gold cursive lettering are slotted into the allotted places within a brass panelled frame beside the lift. Number thirteen has been updated with my name.

"Lucky for some!" I muse, letting the door swing shut slowly behind me.

Dropping my bags, I stare, open mouthed, totally in awe at the impressive marble and brass foyer. I hear a solid clunk as the door finally closes.

There's a fancy lift with brass effect doors, matching the brass balustrade curving up the white marble staircase. Reluctant to tackle the stairs with my collection of baggage, I press the call button. When it dings to a halt, I trundle inside, dragging my case and holdall with me, sweating with the effort. Checking the buttons, I select number four for my floor - the lift doesn't go any higher anyway - I expect the flats on the fourth floor must be the smaller ones - not that I'm complaining.

The lift glides silently and halts with a gentle bump, the chime of the bell signifying my arrival. The doors open and I bend to gather my stuff, dragging my case out backwards. It's only when the lift door closes and I turn around that I realise there's only one shiny black apartment door on this floor.

"Shit!" I'm on the wrong floor! The swish of the doors and the quiet 'ping' indicates the lift is already descending on another journey. "Damn it!" I shake out the post-it and check the details. It definitely says floor four, apartment thirteen and this *is* the fourth floor.

Peering at the black door, it does indeed have the number thirteen in brass numbers, loud and proud above a small spy hole. I look round me, as if expecting some other doors to magically materialise, but they don't. It's just one door and one flat. Perhaps maintenance is up here or something?

Leaving my luggage in the hallway I push the key into the lock and turn it. The door opens, so it must be the right place. On entering the apartment, the burglar alarm immediately starts to beep at me.

"Shit on a stick!" Panicking, I hurriedly enter the code in the panel and press unset; I don't want to cause an international incident and get arrested! The beeping ceases instantly, which is a relief. Turning to observe my surroundings, my bags are immediately forgotten.

"Holy *motherfucking* shit!" The curse slips from my lips before I realise it.

The place is vast; that's when the penny drops. This is the top floor and it's the only apartment. The floor space must be four times the size of those downstairs. It's the penthouse, and because it's on the top floor, it has an uninterrupted view of the hills in the distance.

A bit dazed, I drag my bags inside, and close the door. It makes a hollow resounding thunk. The place is huge, echoing and a bit clinical.

Leaving my case, holdall and backpack where they've landed, I untangle my shoulder bag and lap top from across my body, and drop them on top of my other luggage.

I don't know why but I creep on tiptoe into the main room. I'm behaving like an intruder. However, my hesitancy's instantly rectified when I enter the lounge. Standing up straight, all my unease and fear has been replaced with shock and awe. *"Whoa!"* The room is incredible.

The floor consists of pale cream marble tiles, lightly flecked with silver; the picture windows on the opposite wall are floor to ceiling, beautifully dressed; hung with a floaty pale cream voile and heavy cream damask curtains. There's built in wall cabinets in the alcoves - which must be custom made - the ceiling's really high with original period coving. A beautiful, modern, brushed steel chandelier hangs from the central ceiling rose.

The kitchen door stands ajar and I can just make out some smart modern units. Beneath a feature archway in the lounge, the marble floor incorporates two steps, effectively splitting the level to a majestic dining room. One wall has bi-folding doors, which I presume open onto a balcony, or veranda.

"Fucking Hell!" Pivoting on the spot I try and take it all in. The living room isn't furnished, which makes it appear even larger, but there's an oak dining table in the dining room surrounded by eight high-backed, cream leather chairs. I'll need to arrange for my things to be delivered so I've somewhere to sit, although I doubt my basic IKEA sofa will do much to enhance the appearance of this palatial apartment.

Walking into the kitchen, I examine the state-of-the-art appliances, pulling down the door of the stainless-steel double oven; it's spotless. The six-ring gas hob integrated into the central island looks unused and the surrounding array of high-spec kitchen units are finished with shiny black granite work surfaces, contrasting well with the warm cream of the cupboard doors. The floor tiles in here are black and white marble diamonds, also flecked with silver.

"Jeez!" In-between the base and wall units are partially tiled in plain cream, and the remaining walls are painted a muted olive green - a further subtle injection of colour's provided by the swirls of reds, golds and greens in the window blinds. I can hear the giant American-style fridge freezer humming, so it's plugged in and working. I can also see a wine cooler big enough to serve a modest sized bistro but sadly, it's empty - a chilled glass of Soave would've been appreciated right about now!

The spotless surfaces are free from any kitchen clutter, apart from a white tray sitting on the work-top next to the sink. There's a welcome note, and placed in the centre is a wooden container. It looks like a jewellery box until I notice the words Tea and Coffee engraved on the lid.

Inside, the box is split into two sections. One side is filled with different kinds of tea, including some exotic blends, and the other side has sachets of instant coffee, as well as some foil sealed coffee bags for individual cups. I drop the lid and give the box a stroke. There's also a bowl with lumps of crystallised sugar - white and brown - a white oval plate with individually wrapped biscuits, and a bowl of fresh fruit, I'm starving, so I grab a banana to munch as I continue to explore.

On the kitchen table is a heavy looking, cut crystal vase filled with a beautiful bouquet of pale pink peonies, stems of gypsophila and shoots of dark glossy green leaves. The heads of the peonies droop artistically; the arrangement is striking, the perfume, heady. A small white card rests on a little golden stand in front of the vase.

"Dear Edi,

Congratulations on your first day, lots of love from Lizzy, Sammy and David – Slay 'em!"

I'm beyond emotional. How thoughtful of them. Stuffing the rest of the banana in my mouth, I forget about my tour, and instead rush to find my phone. Checking the time, it's 6.32 pm. here, which means it is about 1.32 pm. in New York. I make a quick calculation out loud. "If they landed at about three, our time, they've had three hours to settle in."

Deciding to call, I find my old mobile, pull up Lizzy's number and press dial. The connection takes a few seconds, before it starts to ring. I'm pleasantly surprised when she answers almost immediately.

"We're here, we're here!!" she sings into the phone at about ninety decibels. Wincing, I pull the phone away from my ear. Gritting my teeth, I chance another listen. "Hello? Hello? Are you there?" thank goodness, she's speaking in a normal voice.

"Yes, I'm here," I reply, waiving the banana peel to indicate round the room. "Oh, thank you for the beautiful flowers, they're gorgeous. It's so lovely of you. How did you know where to send them?"

"Well, we couldn't let you start a new job and not send you a little token of our appreciation, could we? I spoke to that Christina bird, and she organized it for me. She sounds a bit scary. How's it going? What time is it there anyway? We're just off to explore Central Park, it's really scorching hot here." At last she pauses so I can get a word in - I can't believe she was so organized - I'll thank Christina in the morning.

"Yeah, it's been really good; brilliant, in fact. The whole set-up is amazing and the people seem lovely so far; it's only a small team at the moment. There's Silas," feeling my face heat as I say his name. "and Christina, who own the business, and Jimmy and Charlie, who work for them. There's me, of course, oh, and I mustn't forget Bear!"

"Who's Bear? He sounds fascinating."

"Ha, I knew that would get you. He's Silas's dog. A big beast of a German Shepherd; quite stunning actually. I need to make friends with him." *And his master!*

"Whoa! Sounds cool. Look, here's Sammy."

I hear some fumbling as she hands the phone over to Sam, who, distracted by the wonders of New York, isn't too enthused about speaking to me. "Hiya, hope the job's up to scratch. Bye … Oh, say hello to Carrots," she's adds as an afterthought.

"Sorry, she's too excited," Lizzy apologises for Sam's brevity.

I know her too well to be offended by it, "it's okay," I laugh. "Well, have a wonderful afternoon in the park. Once I get my iPad set up, I'll skype you so you can see this amazing apartment; it's huge. I can't believe it comes with the job." I'm actually smiling.

"Sounds fantastic… listen, I'd better go, Sammy's stamping her feet at me - alright *Dora the Explorer,* I'm coming - I'll speak to you soon, love to David. Bye!!" she hangs up.

Shaking my head, I stare at my phone for a few seconds, then reluctantly slip it back into my bag. At least we've made contact.

I gaze around the vast apartment, devoid of any furniture or personal effects, and a sudden fierce, loneliness descends upon me like an ominous grey thunder cloud. Hugging my arms round my body, I shamble through the rest of the apartment in a daze, barely noticing the lavishness of the spacious bedroom, or the majestic ensuite, with its stunning movie star, role-top bath and walk in shower.

I'm completely overwhelmed; everything is over-the-top and certainly not what I'm used to. It's sumptuous, magnificent and opulent, but I can't fully appreciate any of it. It makes me feel inadequate, unworthy and incredibly lonely.

Aware this mood won't do me any good, I force myself to imagine the girls' glee and child-like eagerness at the thrills and sights of New York. Willing the heavy cloud to lift, I search my mind for the courage and strength to force my worryingly, darkening mood into submission. Closing my eyes, and breathing deeply; very slowly, it starts to work.

But then I think of David. Rapidly, the sadness crashes back, like an avalanche of crushing fear. For the first time in seventeen years I'm completely alone. The realization hits me with devastating force, so tangible I start to hyperventilate, my body begins to tremble, and my mouth fills with saliva.

Recognising the symptoms, my heartrate ramps up to a dangerous level - I'm having a panic attack. Instantly nauseous, I make a crazy dash through to the lovely bathroom, drop to my knees before the beautiful toilet, and vomit my lunch and recent banana back up.

Dismayed, I remain still, desperate to gather myself, my nerves shattered at the extreme reaction.

This is stupid. I've had far worse things to deal with for god's sake! It's just an apartment, and a new job!

I really do need to pull myself together, this is ridiculous.

"Stop, stop, *STOP!*" I speak the words out loud, vehemently willing the negative thoughts away.

Sitting back on my heels and taking a deep pull of air, I try again.

"Just breathe," I sigh - *in and out, in and out* - it's a trusted technique for these moments, when overwhelming thoughts and sensations threaten to surface. *Think positive, be positive, just breathe… this is a good day.*

Calling upon my mindfulness technique, I close my eyes and picture the girls, running and skipping in slow motion through Central Park. In my mind's eye, they're holding hands; daisies in their hair, sandals on their feet and gossamer summer dresses swirling around them.

Gradually my heartbeat begins to regulate and my breathing slowly comes back to normal. *Breathe, breathe, breathe!*

After ten minutes of meditative thinking and keeping hold of the loo seat, I gingerly stand, rubbing some circulation back into my poor knees. Frowning at the mess I've made, I flush the toilet then give it a thorough scrub with the toilet brush. Annoyed at my stupidity, I rinse my mouth, spitting the water into the wash basin, then I walk through to the lounge, picking up my backpack and case.

Yes, I need boring routine tasks to get me out of this funk.

Hastily, I drag the case to the bedroom and dump it. Then I unpack my wash bag, returning to the bathroom to clean my teeth thoroughly, and wash my sweaty face. Stripping off my creased shirt, I wash my underarms. Finding there are no towels,

I groan, succumbing to drying myself on my crumpled shirt, then freshen up with some deodorant.

God, I've got to snap out of this ... It's not so bad... come on!

Recalling the road sign for the leisure centre, I decide I need a physical distraction. They must have a swimming pool or, at least, a gym. I'll pay them a visit, right now, tonight; I'll get myself good and exhausted so I'll sleep. Just the simple fact I've made a positive decision is working... I'm starting to feel better.

Yes, then I'll go to the supermarket on my way back

I spotted a Sainsbury's on my way through the village. I know from bitter experience, activity will help with my mood.

You're such an idiot sometimes, why'd you let yourself go there?

Emptying the suitcase, not bothering to hang my clothes - I can do that later - I find my gym gear and pull it on; my trainers are in the car boot so I'll grab them when I'm back downstairs.

Motoring with determination, there's finally a sliver of blue sky peeking through my mental fog. Rummaging for my swimsuit and a beach towel amongst the pile, I grab them both. The swimsuit is old, not very flattering, and the towel has a picture of Goofy on it; it's an old one of David's but it'll do for now.

Wrapping my swimsuit in the towel, I shake everything out of my back pack - dumping it all over the plush bedroom carpet - and stuff the towel in. Pausing only to grab my handbag, keys, phone, and re-setting the alarm, I'm jogging out of the door as quickly as I arrived. I'm like a scalded cat through a cat-flap, desperate to get out of the place.

Ignoring the lift, I hurtle down the stairs, hesitating only to press the door release and dash into the evening sunshine.

By the time I'm in my rusty heap of a car, I'm almost smiling again.

Still in need of a positive vibe, I dig out my *Claire Teal* CD and jam it in the player. Turning the volume up as loud as I can stand it - the uplifting rhythm of *Messin' with Fire,* invades my ears.

Rolling down my windows so the world can share the music, I pull into the traffic and head towards my intended destination.

Chapter 8

The Leisure Centre is easy to find. The main car park is full so I cruise around the back to the overspill, where I easily find a parking place.

Entering the doors, my nose is immediately attacked by the acrid, bleachy scent of chlorine, and my ears ring to the echoing sound of children, playing and splashing in the pool. Visible through the glass wall behind the reception area, it looks busy. I stand in the short queue, patiently waiting my turn.

The muscular young guy behind the desk is wearing a badge, which states his name's Alex, and he's a Personal Trainer. He looks about twenty-five, and has one of those scruffy designer beards that take a lot of grooming to look so untidy. The guy in front clears off towards the changing rooms, and I step up to the desk.

"Hi, err, can you tell me how much it is to join the gym please?" I ask.

"Yeah, sure no problem. Let's see…" Alex looks at me and gives me a *'paid to do it'* cheeky smile, as he fishes a leaflet out from under the counter.

Opening it on the desk, he turns it around for me to read. Pointing with a yellow highlighter, he explains the different packages.

"If you want a full membership, it's £26.60p a month. For that you get full access to the gym, swimming and sauna." He rambles on with his sales pitch, sensing an easy kill. "Full membership will give you use of all areas, including racquet sports and courts, as well all the classes and boot camp if you're interested." His smile is mischievously dazzling, but it takes more than a cheeky grin to impress me.

"Can I cancel at any time if I need to? I've only just moved here to a new job, so I've three months' probation to get through." I give him my best winning smile in return, to see if it helps.

"Sure, not a problem," he says again. "Do you want to give it a go? If you want a P.T. session you can book those through me, at £25 per hour." I sense he's getting a bit cheeky.

"Oh... err, not at the moment, I'm good thanks. I'll take the full membership please." Waiting for Alex to fill out my membership details, I pull my bank card out of my purse. "Would I be able to use the pool this evening?"

"No, not tonight, sorry. We've a swimming gala, hence the racket." He presents me with the forms, all ready for me to check and sign. "But tomorrow is open lane swimming until ten."

Borrowing his pen, I take a few minutes to complete the forms. Then he gives me directions to the gym and changing rooms, and reminds me again about the P.T. sessions.

"Have a good workout."

"Thanks," I reply wandering off in the direction of the gym.

I've a membership tag, which fits on my key ring, and he's taken my photo for their records. I still have my purse in my hand, so I push the boat out, spending a pound on a bottle of water from the vending machine.

Inside the gym, I'm met with the usual sounds and smells. These places always seem to use the same air freshener and detox spray. From what I can see the setup is familiar too.

The main room is split into four areas. There's the cardio section, with rows of treadmills and cross-trainers, and there's a stair climbing machine (I'll be giving that a miss), as well as a decent number of exercise bikes and rowing machines. Several serious-looking spinning bikes are set up behind a glass partition, ready for a class. Then there's the padded floor area which is flanked by mirrored walls on two sides.

There's a multitude of apparatus, from core balance balls to kettle bells. There's even a mini trampoline and something that looks like an enormous elastic band – I've no idea what that's used for.

The weight machines are in the middle of the room, and through an archway I can hear grunts and groans; the clanging of metal, confirms it to be the free weight area. Body-building central is not for me though, so I'll stay well away from there.

Three of the treadmills are occupied. A young skinny guy is going hell for leather, completely in the zone, listening to whatever is motivating him on his headphones. The other two appear to be a couple, and are both walking at such a steep incline they have to grip the frame to remain upright. Two attractive middle-aged women, swinging away on the cross-trainers and wearing expensive-looking fancy work out gear are holding what looks like a rather intense conversation.

Self-consciously I walk to the floor area to complete my stretching routine. I hate looking at myself in the full-length mirror. I don't have a bad figure, a bit dumpy perhaps, but my hair's a fright, all ginger and frizzy and my skin's far too pale. I look unkempt and dull in my washed-out black leggings and baggy T-shirt - no fancy gear for me – and my trainers still smell terrible; I was almost knocked unconscious by the noxious fumes when I removed them from the car boot.

With my stretches complete I decide to warm up on the cross trainer. Ten minutes later and suitably warm, I transfer to the treadmill and set the programme to random for thirty minutes. Settling into my run, I make a mental shopping list for on the way home.

The running is repetitive but soothing. The base rises and falls at intervals as I progress through the program and I'm well into my stride, my breathing has regulated and my heart beats at a steady rhythm. Checking the dials to keep an eye on my workout, I'm surprised to discover I've completed fifteen minutes already. It's flying by and I feel tons better.

As I hit twenty-five minutes the sweat starts running down my temples, and dripping off my chin onto the rolling road beneath my feet. Lifting the hem of my shirt, I use it to quickly wipe the perspiration from my face.

Nearly thirty minutes and 6K completed the program is coming to an end. The treadmill slows down to a light jog and then declines so I'm running level, rather than on an incline. Gradually, it slows to a walk and eventually comes to a stop, reporting the workout summary on the screen.

Picking up my bottle I climb down from the machine on wobbly legs and take a long drink. I'm not looking where I'm going so manage to trip over the end of the treadmill, catching my shin on the rubber belt. "Ouch…" The friction from the heated rubber burns my leg, leaving a livid welt, right in the middle of my shin. *Brilliant!*

Knocked off balance, I stumble backwards, flinging my arm out on reflex in an attempt to stop myself from falling on to my arse. Just in time, I grab hold of the side rail of the next treadmill along, which just happens to be that of the young guy - still running like a demon. He glares at me like, *'What the fuck?'*

"Oops… sorry," I mouth with an embarrassed smile. He turns away and continues to stare into space, back in the zone once more.

My little performance hasn't gone entirely unnoticed though; I try to look nonchalant as I straighten up, wondering whether to call it a night in an effort to stay alive, or try some weights.

"Enjoy your trip?" a deep voice asks, over the pounding music.

Someone thinks they're being funny. There's always one! I decide it isn't worth giving this guy a mouth full, so I just plaster a fixed grin on my face and turn to show I'm okay with looking stupid.

Instantly, I feel a complete fool, a sweaty, frizzy mess and a blushing, mute idiot. It's Silas! I didn't recognise his voice over the volume of the music, but there's no mistaking his stunning face. He must have been the one making all those obscene noises in the free weight room

"Oh... err, you're here!" Blushing profusely, I'm suddenly grateful for my hot workout face. I'm beyond embarrassed, this is awful. What a way to end my first day.

But there's a hint of a smile. He's either amused by my antics or possibly it's the look of me in my terrible gym attire he finds so funny.

"Yeah... I'm here." He looks like he's just competed in a Mr Universe competition and I look like – I don't know what.

His dark skin is gleaming with a light sheen of perspiration. His bulging muscles are tight and pumped, the result of his recent work-out. I on the other hand am flabby, scruffy and soaked with sweat.

He's wearing royal blue shorts and a marl grey vest. A black towel is draped around his shoulders catching the beads of sweat glistening on his thick neck.

Despite my recent glug of water my mouth is suddenly very dry. I fight an impulsive urge to trace a finger over the outline of his well-defined pectoral muscles, which are just visible above the deep neckline of his vest.

Abruptly aware I'm gawping like a goldfish, I pull myself together, standing up taller, flexing shoulders.

"Oh, err, Silas. Hi!" I can't think of anything to say. I just want to hide. I feel a complete and utter mess. I know I look like a bag of shite, but it's the unexpected pull of attraction that bothers me the most. He must see it in my face. Lord, this is wholly embarrassing!

"Did, you hurt yourself?" he asks, looking concerned. "These machines can be lethal when they want to be." He glances down at my bruised shin.

I immediately lift my leg and give it a vigorous rub, pulling the hem of my cropped leggings to hide the stinging red burn.

"Oh… no, no… I'm fine thanks. I wasn't paying attention." *As usual!* I sound huffy and abrupt, even to my own ears, so goodness knows what he must think.

He frowns at me. For some reason, I'm more comfortable with this facial expression - it feels normal for him to appear surly - he does though seem genuinely concerned, which is odd.

For the briefest moment, I think he's going to say something more, but he just nods at me then turns to walk away. That must've been the longest conversation we've had so far. I watch him go just as I did earlier this evening, but as he reaches the door, he turns to look at me. I'm still gawping at him like a moonstruck teenager. Again, he opens his mouth as if he's about to speak, but then another deep frown clouds his handsome face as once more, he has a change of heart. Shaking his head, he does an abrupt about-turn, pulls open the door and stalks out of the gym, the door gently swinging closed behind him.

Weird… what was that all about?

Curiosity wins, and before I can help myself, I've followed in his wake. Slamming my hand on the release button, I let myself out. In the corridor, I look around, wondering which way he's gone and spy the edge of a pair of blue shorts disappearing into the men's locker room.

Well, I can't follow him in there, so I give up the chase and head for the ladies' changing area, I'm ready for a shower. It's only now I remember I've nothing with me; no shower gel, shampoo or even a change of clothes - only the threadbare Goofy towel and my swimming costume... *Idiot!*

Removing my stuff from the locker I tell myself it's probably a good thing, as now I can make a clean, or rather, sweaty getaway, instead of having to face him again before tomorrow morning. Crossing the foyer, I wave a quick goodbye and mouth *"Thank you,"* to Alex, who's animatedly giving the gym spiel to a pretty young brunette. I jog out of the door to find my car - next stop, Sainsbury's.

Just as I'm leaving the car park, Silas emerges from the main doors. It doesn't look like he's bothered with a shower, either. His battered Range Rover is parked on the second row, and he doesn't notice me or ignores me as I drive past. Exiting the car park, I lift my hand in a vague wave and head for the supermarket.

Sainsburys is surprisingly busy for this time on a Monday evening. I negotiate my way around the aisles, ticking off my mental shopping list. First, I pick up the essentials, like bread and milk, then mooch around the fruit and veg section, where I stock up on my five-a-day.

"Fish, chicken, sparking water," I reel off the items as I shop.

Turning my trolley into the toiletries aisle, I automatically reach for the cheapest shampoo, but remembering the scolding I received from Sam about the condition of my hair, I trade-up to the next level. Before I can talk myself out of it, I add my choices to the trolley.

"You'd better be worth it," I grumble.

I'm crouching down to the lower shelf, picking up a box of tampons, when a pair of trainer-clad feet land in my peripheral vision. I close my eyes on a silent groan, pretending I haven't seen them. *Oh no!*

"This is becoming a habit. Are you stalking me?" Silas lands a lazy humourless gaze on me, clocking what I'm holding.

Hurriedly I chuck the boxes of Lil-lets into my trolley, then turn to speak.

"Yes, you must be frightened to death. One minute I'm the new girl at work, then at the gym - which is obviously unheard of - then I'm buying my groceries," I spit sarcastically. "Are you sure it isn't you who's stalking me?" somehow summoning the courage to glare straight into his intense eyes. It's easier to face him when I'm being defensive.

He raises his eyebrows in mock surprise and turns to the shelf before him. He picks up several boxes of condoms, giving me a sly grin as he makes a huge show selecting a bottle of Durex play, adding it to his basket. "You never know when you might need something … stimulating," he drawls over his shoulder as he ambles away.

Once again, I'm mortified and blushing in embarrassment. I huff my distain at his retreating back, humiliated, unable to conjure a suitable retort.

Without further comment and feeling totally insulted by his brashness I furiously spin my trolley around, and I'm almost running to the checkout and out of the shop, before he can find some other way to ruin my first day.

Chapter 9

I arrive back at the apartment just after nine. It's dark and I've no idea where the evening has gone but I'm glad of it. It means less time moping aimlessly about before I finally go to bed. I resolve to make a to-do list for tomorrow so I don't have another meltdown.

Unpacking the shopping, I try one of the fancy teas from the wooden box. There isn't a kettle, but the swanky tap in the kitchen has a boiling water function so I make a cup of posh tea before wrapping the salmon I bought in foil, and placing it on a baking tray in the oven. I can't be bothered prepping any veg so I'll have it with salad. I'm starving hungry.

Heading for a shower and reading the directions on the back of my new "luxury" shampoo, I can't help thinking cynically, even though it cost a bomb, it won't make any discernible difference to my messy mop, but I might as well give it a try. I'll have to use the Goofy towel, the only other things I've brought up from the car are my duvet and pillows. The rest of my stuff can wait until the morning.

Entering the bathroom, I cast aside what happened on my previous visit. Gathering the shower gel and loofah from my wash bag, I drop Goofy on the floor and switch the jets to high. There are several settings, but I settle on the all-over massage, which should help alleviate some of the muscle fatigue from my workout.

Standing under the beating stream of water I vigorously scrub the remains of the day away, until my skin is pink and tingling. The burn on my leg smarts with the heat, and has settled into a red raw teardrop shape in the middle of my shin.

As per the instructions, I wash, rinse and repeat, then leave the conditioner in for a full two minutes. This gives me time to shave the forest of stubble that's sprouted from my legs. Then I comb the conditioner through - something I normally never bother with - until the comb glides with ease, smoothing through my usually tangled tresses. Rinsing thoroughly and switching off the shower, I check the time on my watch to make sure the salmon isn't overcooking. Ten minutes from start to finish, which is longer than my average shower time – it must be the conditioner.

Swathing myself in *Goofy*, with my hair still dripping down my back I enter the perfect bedroom. Quickly I finish drying my body, then use *Goofy* to wrap a turban around my head. I spray under my arms, and pull on my fluffy purple dressing gown with the white hearts all over it – a Christmas present from David. I slap on some facial moisturiser, then traipse back to the kitchen for my dinner with my mouth watering and stomach growling.

"*Fucking, Jesus!*" I yelp aloud; my heart skips more than a few beats and lurches into over-drive.

Clamping my hand over my mouth to stifle any further outburst, I grip the edge of the worktop, steadying myself; my bare feet skidding to a halt on the slippery tiles, my back muscles jarring as I lurch to an abrupt emergency-stop.

Though it all happens in seconds, my thoughts are all over the place, my brain is whirling, my heart desperately trying to jump out of my chest. My blood pumps round my body at a hundred miles an hour… i*s this what a heart attack feels like?*

Silas is seated at the breakfast bar, cool as a cucumber, and totally unperturbed by my profane outburst. He ignores me as he sits there, bold as brass, still in his gym gear.

He's helped himself to a tiny cup of coffee and is apparently engrossed in something on his mobile phone. Apart from the intermittent flick of his thumb as he scrolls through the screen, he's as still as a statue, and doesn't appear to have noticed he's just scared the living daylights out of me. An aromatic swirl of thin vapour is rising from the coffee cup. I notice as well as the espresso, he has a hi-ball, filled with water – *my* sparkling water that *I've* just bought.

Closing my eyes, I count to ten in an attempt to recover my equilibrium, and take some calming breaths. Still rooted to the spot, I gently loosen my grip on the worktop, deliberately breathing slower in an aim to steady my beating heart. *I can't believe he's here. In fact, what the fuck is he doing here?*

Slowly, I open my eyes, trying my best not to start shouting or screaming at this arrogant prick, who thinks it's okay to just break in and make himself at home… *what an arse!*

I'm now on the defence; I've recovered from the initial scare and I'm angry - how dare he invade my privacy? Assembling my thoughts, I'm wondering how to deal with this, while he just sits, ignoring me, sipping his water - my temper is simmering.

What should I do?

Several options leap into my head; I'm currently in a state of undress under my robe, so leaving isn't viable, neither is screaming for help - I doubt I'd be heard - anyway I don't know what he's here for yet. I settle for playing it cool; although, unleashing my seething mass of fury upon him, is rather tempting.

Glaring through narrowed eyes, I will him to look up from his bloody phone and notice me, but still he refuses to acknowledge my presence. It's as if I don't exist… I'm invisible.

What an absolute, solid gold, arrogant prick!

Remembering I'm naked under my hideous, oversized, dressing gown, I pull the belt a little tighter, securing my modesty. I feel vulnerable but bloody annoyed at the same time, and I still don't know what to do. Clearly, I need to do something, so, taking a deep breath for courage, I stick my nose in the air, jut out my chin in indignation and deem to ignore him.

Yes, I'll just pretend he isn't here.

I've seen more of him since I left the office than I have all fucking day - I might have to rethink keeping this job - but decision made, I move to the oven to remove my salmon.

"That smells good," his husky voice breaks the silence, making me jump. He's very matter-of-fact, it's as if he hasn't entered my apartment uninvited and helped himself to *my* coffee and *my* water.

He's acknowledged I'm here, but he still won't look away from his damned phone. He continues casually scrolling through it, as if being sat there's the most normal thing in the world.

"I took the liberty of taking it out of the oven for you so it didn't burn."

Turning to the oven, I notice the baking tray has indeed been removed, and is sat on an insulated mat on the worktop.

"Err, Mr Tudor," I try formality, but the tremor in my voice gives me away. "C...can I ask why you're here? What do you want? It's quite late, and frankly... you could have spoken to me at the gym or Sainsburys. Is this about work? What's so important that it can't wait until tomorrow?"

Adopting an authoritative stance, consciously crossing my arms over my chest, and setting my face into a stern mask. I need to assert some control over the situation, demonstrate I'm not intimidated, even though I am, he's my boss but clearly, he has the upper hand!

"Normally a person would phone or ring the intercom - not just barge straight in!" I say tartly.

He obviously has a key. That thought is unnerving in itself, and I feel my temper beginning to surface again. It's not like me; normally I can keep my cool and assess a situation rationally, but I'm getting madder by the second.

"Is there enough for two? I've not had a chance to eat yet."

What? Of all the... I don't believe this!

He might be my boss, but I'm not going to be taken advantage of. That ship has long since sailed, and I'm a stronger person now. The bloody cheek of the man! He's still refusing to look at me - how rude is that? - I need a job, but not this bollocks. Unable to contain my contempt any longer, I don't care if I get the sack, I snap.

"No," picking up a plate, I load it with a large helping of salad before opening the foil surrounding the salmon.

A delicious aroma is released into the room as the steam escapes, and my stomach growls. I add the fish to my plate - it looks scrumptious – and yes, it's a huge portion, clearly large enough for two, but I'm not offering to share. Anyway, I've a good appetite and I intend to eat the lot.

Making a big deal of gathering my cutlery in one hand and the plate in the other, I perch on a barstool at the opposite end of the breakfast bar, as far away from Silas as possible. Taking a moment to rearrange my dressing gown, I start to eat my dinner.

"How did your first day go?"

He's asking me this now? I stuff my mouth then speak around my food, deliberately refusing to use any manners – he isn't, so why should I?

"Sorry, *Mr Tudor*, I'm confused. What exactly have you invaded my privacy for?" Dripping with sarcasm I garble round my fork, refusing to engage in either friendly conversation, or eye contact for that matter.

Childishly, I rest my elbow on the table - that alone would've earned a telling off from my grandmother - and continue to scoop up my dinner as slovenly as possible. I might as well enhance the image.

"It's my apartment," he answers, as if it absolves any misdemeanour. "I meant to ask how your day went when I saw you earlier, but I was... distracted." He sounds a bit cross. "I'm here now, because I want to make sure you have everything you need. It's been empty, for a while, so... just checking!"

Deeming to look at me, he puts his phone in his back pocket. He's still in gym gear, but has seen fit to don a pair of joggers and a hoodie. He drains his cup, then takes a deep draught of water before stepping down from the bar stool, and striding across the kitchen. His movement causes me to sit up and pay attention. Pausing my knife and fork, I glance up, unable to resist.

My appreciative eyes follow his moves; dropping open a cupboard door – it's the dishwasher – he places the cup and saucer in the wire basket.

Shaking my head to dispel the image, I try again to assert some authority. "It might be your apartment, but that doesn't mean you can just barge in like you own the place." I immediately realise the stupidity of that sentence – he does own the place. "It's very unnerving. I would prefer it if you didn't do it again - please."

God, I sound pissed off - probably because I am!

I should tone it down, he's my boss after all, and he seems to be genuinely interested in how my day went, although he has a very strange way of approaching things; a phone call would have served the same purpose, and been more appropriate, surely?

Assuming a politer attitude and sitting up straighter, I swallow my food, clear my mouth, and place my knife and fork on my plate, giving him my full attention. "I mean, thank you for the concern, *Sir*, but I'm fine."

I suddenly have a horrifying thought - maybe he still lives here, and I'm supposed to share! Then I remember he said it's been empty for a while and I relax a little. There's no furniture and he's got the dog to care for. This apartment is definitely not dog friendly.

"It's...look, I'm not very good with new people, I'm sorry if we got off on the wrong foot today," he offers; its conciliatory, but I'll take it.

I frown in confusion. I thought work was okay. I mean, we hardly spoke; I just got on with it. It was the gym and Sainsburys that unnerved me. Perhaps I misread things. Perhaps I screwed something up? Wracking my brains for what I might have done wrong, I can't come up with anything.

It must be showing in my expression, because he's staring at me intently again. I'm usually a good judge of character, but I really can't read him at all. He's definitely a conundrum.

Deciding it's not worth it and conceding defeat, I slide off my stool, and start to clear up.

"Silas, I've had a really long day and I'm very tired." It comes out as a sigh. "Do you need anything, or can it wait until tomorrow?" I've had enough of today.

He walks over and stands in front of me, looking down. I instinctively try to make myself taller by rising to my tiptoes, leaning my hand on the counter to force some more height. He still towers over me, but I'm not in the mood to be intimidated. I force myself not to back down, or look away from him.

The closer he stands, the more I notice the simmering tingle in my skin. It's like an electric field. His breathing is heavy, and it skims my face as he searches for the right words.

"I'm sorry," he says again. "Christina tells me I can be an arse sometimes. I like to push buttons. I know I can... intimidate people. But I didn't get that vibe from you so I needed to keep pushing. I think I went too far." He doesn't look sorry.

"Err, just a bit!" I snap. I know that my face is scarlet, and not just from the scorching shower. I've known him for about eight hours, I'm beginning to think Christina is right.

"Thank you for checking on me. I'll see you tomorrow. If you'll excuse me, I need to get some sleep."

I brush it off, wondering if I should just leave him there and go into the bedroom, or wait to see him out? Good manners prevail and I turn to show him to the door. I need to get him out of here quick, before I say something I'll regret.

Suddenly, he makes a grab for my left wrist; I freak out, snatching my hand away as if he's burned me. The sudden action causes the fastener on my watch to release, the loose band slips over my hand and before I know it, Silas is left holding my watch.

"What the hell do you think you're doing?" I shriek, seizing my wrist, drawing it protectively into my chest. I'm really pissed off now, scared, and on the way to hysteria. My heart has leapt into my throat again – I need him gone!

"I just wanted to say… I don't know…look, sorry." He's flummoxed, confused - he doesn't understand my reaction. I don't think he expected to touch me; maybe it was a reflex?

"You've already said that… twice!" I'm raising my voice in anger now. "Just put my watch on the counter, and leave… please!" I continue to shield my wrist from his eyes. Mine are wide and staring daggers. The towel has come loose from my head and dropped to the floor. I don't *want* to panic, but I can feel it rising in my chest as it did earlier.

Very slowly, and without removing his eyes from mine, he reaches for my right hand, gently taking hold and pulling it away, revealing my left wrist. Cautiously he raises it so he can look closer. My skin is on fire where he's touching me, and I can't summon the energy to pull my hand away. I'm anxious, I can't speak.

This is so unbelievably private - he's no right - but I can't find the strength to stop him. He just stares, rubbing his calloused thumb over my bracelet tattoo.

Very gently, and with awed reverence, he slowly caresses the string of tiny gold and black bumble bees encircling my wrist. They're delicate and appear to be in full flight; endlessly circling the white band of skin, devoid of any tan and for my eyes only. They're hidden beneath my watch for a reason.

His large hand completely encircles my wrist as he turns it palm side up. My breath stops as I study his face for any sign of acknowledgment. I've never revealed this to anyone, so why I'm allowing it now is beyond me. Still looking at the tattoo, he rubs his thumb along the raised ridge of scars that lie beneath the tiny flying insects.

I feel sick when the realization dawns on his face. Fleetingly, his deep caramel eyes fill with compassion, seeking out mine, before morphing back to his usual unreadable gaze. I see the silent question hovering beneath his stoic expression.

NO!

Very softly, I exhale, jutting my chin in indignation, yanking my hand back into my own protective grip. *It's private!*

"It was a long time ago," I grate categorically. No explanation given. I'm not talking about this. Not with him, or anybody else. Not ever… it's in the past and that's where it stays. "Please give me my watch," I whisper.

Without a sound or change of expression, he passes it to me. I struggle in vain to put it back on and cover my secret, but the fastener is sprained and it won't close. The clasp is broken. Annoyed, I toss the broken watch onto the granite work top.

Pushing my damp hair from my face in frustration, I look down at the floor. "I really need you to leave." My voice is barely audible.

"I'll see myself out. See you tomorrow," he says, his tone flat and emotionless.

Reaching the front door, he turns to face me, parting his lips to speak, his eyebrows knitting together, his thoughts causing him a serious dilemma. I know what's coming and I can't stand the empty feeling accompanying those two words. They mean absolutely nothing to me…

"Don't say it." Though I already know he will.

"Seriously, Edi… I'm sorry. Tomorrow will be a better day, I promise." And with that he leaves; the meaningless words ringing in the silent air.

Nodding helplessly at the empty void, I turn back to my half-eaten meal, feeling wretched and bereft. I scoop up the plate and tip the remains into the pedal bin. I purse my lips and swallow away the lump in my throat. I don't cry - I never cry.

I've no idea what to do. He's very strange. That whole episode was very strange. My feelings are very strange.

He's nothing like my stereotypical idea of a boss, but I realised that this afternoon. Tonight, has just confirmed it. He's stunningly handsome, way out of my league and far too intense.

I know it's stupid, ridiculous and embarrassing, but I'm attracted to him. I mean *really* attracted to him. And I haven't been attracted to anybody for more than eighteen years! Annoyed with myself for feeling like this, I tug on the belt of my dressing gown.

Shit, what do I do now? Bizarre doesn't cover this situation. I'm far too tired to give it any further thought tonight. It's past ten o'clock and I'm knackered. I'll see what tomorrow brings before making any snap decision whether to stay in my dream job or leave…

And then what? I really need this job. I worked my arse off for three damn years to get this job… God what do I do?

Scooping the *Goofy* towel off the floor, I gather my duvet from the living room and head for the bathroom. Looking in the mirror, I see a harridan. My eyes are wide, staring, and my hair is a wild damp mess. The unforgiving lights emphasize the stark paleness of my skin. The dark purple of the dressing gown reflects back at me, giving a sickly blue tinge to my face. My lips are white and pulled into a taught line. I look about a hundred and six, not thirty-six…!

"Jesus!" The word comes out in a rush of air, as I just stare at my ghostly reflection.

Grabbing my toothbrush, I load on the paste and go through the motions of brushing my teeth. Something normal. Something routine. I catch sight of my tattoo in the mirror. It's pretty, but it isn't there for decoration. I'll need to find something to cover it with tomorrow before I go to work.

After spitting and rinsing, I splash my face with cold water. The wild harpy in the mirror mocks me derisively. Unable to look at her anymore, I switch off the lights and go into the bedroom.

There's no bed so I just throw my duvet onto the carpet; stacking my pillow at one end, I fold the duvet over, so I'm enveloped in the soft downy cotton. The floor is hard and unyielding, but nothing I can't handle. I close my eyes and I'm asleep in ten seconds. I don't dream.

Chapter 10

I didn't close the curtains when I went to bed. After the craziness of yesterday, I just covered my head in the duvet and closed my eyes. Hence, this morning I've woken with the birds and brilliant, bright sunlight streaming in through the bedroom window. The light is intense, and I can feel the warmth. So much so, I'm sweating profusely beneath the duvet so I quickly kick my legs free, untangle my arms before sitting up and brush my matted hair from my face.

I'm still wrapped in my fluffy dressing gown, but now it's come undone so my breasts and belly are on display, and the cord belt is brushing my pubic hair. I look for my watch to check the time; realising I no longer have it - the events of last night filter into my waking brain. I'm not completely freaked by them anymore, but I do need to make some serious decisions today. I groan, I could do without this hassle.

"Okay, Edi girl, up you get." Drawing encouragement in my own tone, I rise stiffly from my makeshift bivouac. My muscles are aching both from the gym and the hardness of the floor, but, all-in-all, I slept quite well - though I wouldn't want to make a habit of it.

Without my trusty Sekonda, I've no idea what the time is but if I had to guess, I'd put it at about 6.00 a.m. I shower swiftly, wash and condition my hair - again, taking care to comb through the conditioner. Back in the bedroom I detangle my tresses with my fingers, then find a hairband, scoop my damp hair into a ponytail, and twist it into a knotted bun at the nape of my neck. It's a bit librarian, but it looks like it's going to be a warm day and I need my hair out of my face.

Searching through the piles of clothes on the floor for something moderately unwrinkled to wear for my second day, I locate some mismatched underwear and drag it on. After a mental debate about whether to wear a skirt or pants, remembering the embarrassment of yesterday's crotch-gate, I decide on a skirt.

Rummaging through a pile, I find a blue floral number that finishes an inch or two below my knee, just about covering the burn on my shin. Paired with a navy-blue vest and a lightweight pale blue cardigan, it looks a bit old maid and, yes, definitely librarian! My shoes are still in the carrier bags in my car, so I'll get them later. I've a nice pair of tan, cork wedge-heeled sandals; they'll do fine.

Finally arriving in the kitchen, I locate my broken watch and check the time. It's only just 6.30 a.m. so I scramble some eggs in the microwave.

While eating my breakfast, I scroll through my phone, noticing I've a couple of text messages from the girls. Lizzy and Sammy have sent some cheesy photos of their day in central park, sitting by the boating lake like *Carrie* in *Sex in the City,* and posing with the *Alice in Wonderland* sculpture, walking round the edge of the *Friends* fountain. There's even one of them beside a horse drawn carriage; the driver mugging it up along with them, the horse's soft nose's resting on Lizzy's shoulder. They appear to be having a great time. I send a quick text back and a selfie of my librarian outfit, proving I'm a working woman! That should give them a laugh.

Deciding to take a packed lunch to work I knock up a quick salad of chicken and ham. Then, I load the dishwasher and take a hasty scan through the apartment. The lounge still looks the same; beautiful but empty. The kitchen is tidy-ish with some evidence of use; as is the bathroom, but the bedroom looks like squatters moved in overnight, reminding me of my Uni apartment the morning after one of the girls' infamous parties. I huff a laugh at the memory. Making an executive decision, I close the door on it; something to do when I come back this evening.

Pushing my feet into my flip-flops I pick up my bag and attaché case with my new lap top, and check that I've my phone, keys, and all the other crap that I need. I leave the apartment by 7.15, remembering to punch in the alarm code before closing and locking the door.

Feeling energetic, I take the stairs again. Vaguely I note how easy it is going down, but coming up I might use the lift.

As I get to the second floor there's an old dear on the landing coming out of flat eleven. "Morning, lovie," she lets on, cheerfully. She reminds me of the waitress from the café, but she's a good ten years older. She's all posh looking in her floral dress, white bouffant hair and large patent leather handbag. She looks a bit like The Queen.

"Morning," I smile in answer, but don't stop for a chat.

Reaching the foyer, I press the button to release the lock and push the door, stepping outside into a glorious day. I'm immediately filled with a lovely, heady feeling of optimism.

Resolving to have a better day today I jump in my car, which doesn't even protest when I turn the ignition, willingly starting first time. Rolling down the window I switch on the radio. The D.J is squawking on about some new *Martine McCutcheon* record. Nope - not interested in that - sorry mate. I switch mode and locate my *Muse* CD…. yeah, *Dig Down* should do it! With the volume cranked up, I head off for my second day of legitimate employment.

Arriving at the airfield, the metal gates are open so I drive straight in. I spy Jimmy Spanners in the car park, fixing a sign to one of the parking spaces. As I roll up, he stands and turns to direct me in. The space has a white plaque which reads:

Ms E Sykes BSc (HONS)
Aeronautical Logistics Manager

In the right-hand corner of the name sign is an emblem of a red and white Tudor Rose, the gilded edges of the petals glimmering in the bright morning sun. I'm impressed, and a little thrill runs through me as I drive into my very own designated parking space.

Jimmy gives me a cheeky bow, with one hand behind his back and the other making a flourishing waving gesture, guiding me in. As I exit my banger - bags and baggage in tow - I can't help laughing as I reciprocate, bobbing a small curtsey, before I skip up the stairs and through the automatic doors. *He's a right one, that Jimmy!*

I'm still smiling as I enter the foyer, walking through the reception area to the back offices, taking the briefest of seconds to admire the display of aeronautical art.

Before I arrive at the corridor, I hear raised voices; I stop walking and stand still, wondering whether I should make my presence known. I can't help listening though.

"Honestly Silas, what the *fuck* were you thinking?" It's Christina, and she sounds exasperated. "You can't just barge in on people - it's rude. Have you no concept of personal space or boundaries? Sometimes I think you have shit for brains!" She sounds like she's talking about last night...how does she know?

"I was just checking she was okay. I didn't mean to freak her out." Silas isn't shouting, but he sounds frustrated - at whom I don't know. "If I was sure she'd come back today, I wouldn't even have told you, but as it is - her reaction was so extreme - you needed to know we might need a new Manager." Clearly, he's as pissed off as she is.

My reaction was extreme – what's he told her?

"Well, you'd better hope that your fucking little macho-man stunt hasn't scared her off. She's perfect for this job. If she doesn't come back, I'm holding you personally responsible. You can be such a fucking *dick* sometimes, Silas." She's really, *really* pissed.

I flinch in shock at her blunt assessment of Silas, but then remember they were married, so this is probably not the first time she's called him that. He doesn't seem at all bothered by the insults though, he must be used to it!

"It's *my* fucking apartment, I can go in anytime I like."

"*No*, you fucking can't! She's a tenant. You're the landlord. She's allowed *privacy.*" She's dripping contempt and he's completely unperturbed by it. "Have you arranged furniture?"

"Forgot to... She was fine." Now he sounds like a sullen schoolboy.

"Jesus! How the *Hell* we managed to stay married as long as we did is beyond me! You really have no idea, do you?" she sighed in exasperation.

I know I shouldn't be eavesdropping, but they aren't making any attempt to hide their row.

"Look, perhaps I should have phoned. I was just concerned, is all," he mutters. "Anyway, you'll be pleased to know, she gave as good as she got. She's a bit like you in that regard - no wonder you like her...

Eh?

"*Perhaps*?? There's no '*perhaps*' about it. It was a gross invasion of her privacy - you must've scared her to death!" She lets out an audible groan and I hear paper shuffling. "I do like her... very much. I'm glad she called you out on it. It took me too many long exhausting years to fathom you out and I still don't think I'll ever understand the way your mind works."

Really? She seems to have the upper hand now.

"You know I'm not good with people," he says gruffly.

"Women, you mean... you're not good with women... Oh, don't give me that shite, Silas - you can turn on the charm when it suits you." I think she's smiling. "Anyway, it sounds like she's got you pegged."

Have I?

"We've a ridiculously busy day today so you'd better be prepared to double up your workload, especially if she decides not to come back." She's calmed down slightly and, thankfully, stopped cursing.

Silas mutters something I don't hear; it sounds like the argument is over. I'm about to make my appearance, but I don't have time to think about it, because like a ghost, Bear wanders out of Christina's office and stands before me, with an expectant look on his face.

I take this opportunity to announce my arrival, a little louder than necessary. "Good morning Bear!"

He sits down directly in front of me, his pink tongue lolling out of the side of his mouth; then lifts a huge leonine paw. I smile and bend to give it a shake.

"That's new," Silas' tone is quiet but gruff.

Rising from my crouched position, I look up to see Silas pacing towards me from the direction of Christina's office. I nearly swallow my tongue, because today he's dressed in a navy-blue pilot's uniform. He's carrying his cap under one arm and a slim leather wallet in the other - he looks... magnificent. The overall effect is staggering and for a moment I'm struck dumb, just gaping in awed silence.

The tailored trousers emphasize his long muscular legs, and the monogrammed gold buttons and braided collar of the jacket do nothing to hide the breadth of solid chest beneath. His crisp white shirt makes a lovely contrast against his dark chocolate skin. I think I might be dribbling - looking like that, he's instantly forgiven for last night's misdemeanour!

My reaction must show on my face, because he looks relieved, if a little wary at seeing me back here today. He darts a fleeting, tell-tale glance at my left wrist, but I've covered the tattoo with a broad bracelet I found at the bottom of my wash bag. It's a white band of plaited leather David bought me for my birthday last year. It covers my tan line and secrets adequately enough.

After overhearing their brief argument, I reckon he'd meant well and I'll give him the benefit of the doubt.

"Umm, good morning Silas," I stutter, letting go of Bear's paw and straightening up.

"He learnt that last night. After I… I mean, he picks up new tricks really quickly." He sounds much more relaxed and friendlier than yesterday when he was so stiff and formal. But suddenly the switch flicks, and in an instant, the gruff, indifferent, stony persona reappears. *God, he's like two different people!*

"Bear, come." He carries on past me, all business-like. "It's good to have you on the team," and with that he's gone, before I can speak.

I stand with my mouth open, watching them leave. Then I spy Christina at her office door. She's languidly leaning on the jamb, arms loosely folded across her chest, silently observing our interaction. Today she's wearing a navy trouser suit with a red silk vest and again, the lovely, liquid-gold chain finishes the outfit. The ensemble is somehow reminiscent of Silas' pilot's uniform.

Twisting her lips in a cheeky, knowing grin she wrinkles her nose. She doesn't speak but raises one hand in a silent salute, then gracefully pushes herself off the door frame, sauntering back into her office, kicking the door closed with an elegant navy patent leather ballet pump; point made.

I look down at my own feet. The sight of her elegant shoes reminds me I'm still in my flip-flops, so I turn on my heels and retrace my steps back to my car.

I've got my head in the car boot, rummaging through carrier bags for my sandals, when I hear the sound of car wheels on gravel. Eventually, after emptying out every carrier bag, I locate my cork wedges and drop them to the ground. Holding on to the side of my car for balance, and without wobbling or falling over I hop out of my flip-flops and into the sandals. Gathering up my flip-flops, I drop them into the boot with the rest of my unbagged shoes, before thumping the lid closed and smoothing down my skirt. I'm curious to see who's arrived, so I turn and raise my hand, shielding my eyes from the sun.

The car's a Rolls-Royce. It could be a Silver Shadow, but I'm not as familiar with car models as I am with aircraft, so I'm guessing. It's a huge, navy blue beast of a thing, and there's a chauffeur in the driver's seat - I can just about make out his black uniform and peaked cap. The chauffeur pulls into a visitor space, and opening the door to its full extent, he steps out just as Silas strides over to greet the occupants; as always, Bear is trotting obediently at his heels.

Silas reaches the car as the chauffeur opens the rear passenger door, allowing me a brief glimpse of the man inside, before he too steps out onto the gravel. Silas's broad back is obscuring my view, but I can tell from his movements he's shaking hands and greeting the mystery gentleman - he must be tiny, because I still can't see him. The chauffeur closes the car door, quickly skirting around to the other side to attend to the other passenger.

I see the back of a head rise from the car; it's a woman - and she's incredibly tall. Her black hair flutters, a light breeze picking up the silky tresses swishing them around her face. Lifting a slim elegant hand, she removes a couple of wayward strands, which have become adhered to the bright red gloss of her full, painted lips; catching them with the hook of her perfectly manicured, and equally red-painted little finger nail, she smooths them down. I'm transfixed.

Turning her attention away from the chauffeur, she walks round the rear of the car. Every movement is grace personified and she's wearing designer everything; dark blue skinny-jeans, tucked into tan knee-high boots, with a white ruffled shirt, tailored tweed hacking-jacket and a colourful, Hermes silk scarf knotted elegantly round her slender neck. She has on black designer sunglasses, chunky gold jewellery and carries an enormous, tan, Birkin bag; the straps nestled snugly in the crook of her arm. As well as being tall she's as thin as a reed, taking the thigh-gap to the absolute extreme.

The woman makes her way to where Silas is standing. He sidesteps and half turns to greet her, which allows me a clearer view of the gentleman in front of him. He's tiny - by Silas's standard anyway - only about five feet nine, with a touch of *Tom Cruise* meets *Al Pacino* about him. My guess is he's smack-bang in-between them in age too - so I'd say he's round about sixty. He's handsome enough, with a head of thick dark hair; a bit over long, though it's neatly styled. The touch of grey at the temples gives him a distinguished Latin appearance. Clean shaven, his olive complexion is smooth, without any sign of major wrinkles, and it looks like he's no stranger to the gym.

Like the woman, he's expensively dressed, in a fashionable mid-blue suit, crisp white shirt, collar open and no tie. Tan loafers complete his outfit. He gestures to the woman, who flashes a huge smile at Silas, holding out that elegant hand - I frown when Silas takes it in his and kisses it - they're almost the same height! Childishly, I decide I don't like her!

The man dismisses his chauffeur with a flippant wave as Silas leads the couple towards office reception. Bear immediately takes the lead, but on spying me makes a bee-line in my direction.

I realise I'm gawping like a nosey cow, so jumping into action, I look for a quick escape into the office before I'm spotted. However, having stood there for the last few minutes staring, I'm far too late. Any furtive scuttling away would be noticed, so I remain rooted in place; a rigid smile on my face, while the three of them follow Bear, to where I'm standing, like the proverbial plumb.

Straightening up to my full five-feet-five and a bit inches (in heels) and smoothing down my skirt, I watch them approach. Bear reaches me first and sits by my side.

"Hello boy," I whisper conspiratorially, "you not too keen either then?"

He gives the floor a single thump with his tail, acknowledging my greeting. Silas and the couple arrive a few seconds later.

Silas halts when they're a few feet away. He's relaxed, smiling. Something I haven't seen before and the effect is... mesmerising. He turns side on and indicates to me.

"Please... let me introduce Ms Edi Sykes. Edi, for her sins, has recently joined us as Aeronautical and Logistics Manager."

For my sins?

"Edi, this is Montgomery Phillips and his lovely wife... Victoria."

"Good morning; it's very nice to meet you. Welcome to RTC." I offer my hand to each of them in turn. He has a firm, strong handshake, hers is flaccid and weak.

"Likewise, I'm sure," sniffs Mr Phillips, giving me a thorough look over, he's a bit leery and has a really posh accent, but seems genuine enough.

"Hi, Edi, is it?" Victoria's American and loud. I've no idea where from in America, but she screams trophy wife - perhaps she's an ex-supermodel or actress - it's more than likely she's Californian and she's easily thirty-five years her husband's junior. "Cute name, I love your outfit, it's so... British." She pronounces the 'T' in British as a 'D' and, clearly, she's clocked my librarian look and formed an opinion. *Yep, she's a bitch too.*

Silas's eyebrows form a quick 'V' as he takes in my skirt, vest, and cardigan combo. From the look on his face, I think he's formed the same opinion as Victoria. I ignore them both, self-consciously brushing the creases out of my skirt.

"Yes, well," Silas coughs. "Edi, Mr and Mrs Phillips have chartered the Cessna for today. I'll be piloting them to Paris. We're scheduled to leave at noon. I've left the flight plan and hire agreement on your desk." Silas speaks directly to me as if this information is nothing new.

Absently, I reach down and run my fingers lightly over Bears head, absorbing some Dutch courage. "Err, yes, I remember. Well, if you will come with me, we can complete the rest of the paperwork, then you can get underway." I animate myself, shaking off my nerves, motioning for them to lead the way through the automatic doors and into reception.

As they walk in front, Silas hangs back and gently takes my arm halting my progress. "Thank you for that," he whispers in my ear, sending a warm breath over the sensitive shell. The feeling is delicious and an involuntary, flush heats my face. "He can be a bit of a knob." I can tell he's grinning but I still gasp a laugh at his audacity.

He can be a knob? Seriously!

I bite back the desire to blurt 'it takes one to know one', as he drops my arm and follows them inside. I shake my head and trail behind him. "Bear, come," I say unconsciously.

Silas freezes in front of me and turns glaring eyes on Bear, who has decided to be *my* friend today.

"What?" I giggle as we both sashay past Silas, through the automatic door side by side. Oh, the power!

Reception is air-conditioned and contrasts well with the relentless breeze of outside. The florescent lights reflect off Victoria's glossy hair, making it look like she's wearing a halo.

I guide Mr and Mrs Phillips through the impressive lobby towards my office. Bear is still trotting along dutifully beside me. Silas has disappeared through the hangar door, presumably to complete some final protocol checks with Spanners and Sparks.

115

Stepping into my office, I notice some subtle changes and additions that weren't there yesterday. There's a cut lead crystal vase of blood red tea roses on my desk, the small flowers indicative of the Tudor Rose emblem on the plaque for my parking space. Their delicate fragrance is light and subtle. I spy the black box-like state-of-the-art Radar/Radio equipment on the side table, facing the large viewing window. The table adjoins my desk creating an L-shape so I can swivel my chair, and access it when required. There are also some headphones and a walkie-talkie, standing to attention in its cradle charger.

Standing on a new black-lacquered credenza, is a fancy beverages station. A stainless-steel pot of steaming fresh coffee is already made and some china beakers - also decorated with the Tudor Rose pattern - sit on a black glass tray. Without looking, I already know the wooden box contains a selection of fancy teas. Jugs of iced water and chilled orange juice are all ready to go, and an assortment of pastries and croissants sit invitingly on a white plate. I'm truly grateful. It all looks very professional and has to be Christina's doing.

"Please… what can I get you to drink?" I gesture for them to take the seats opposite me at the desk, then head to the credenza to pour coffee with two sugars and milk for him, peppermint tea for her. I place a couple of pastries on the side plates with a napkin as an afterthought, then pour myself a glass of water.

Once I've settled down at my workstation, Bear stretches out beneath the desk and positions himself on top of my feet. Hiding a smile, I wiggle my toes through his fur.

On the desk is a flat leather binder. Inside I find all the necessary paperwork Silas mentioned earlier. It's the inventory and a flight plan, along with a photocopy of the original hire agreement, identification documents for Mr and Mrs Phillips, some insurance forms and the final invoice, due to be paid today prior to the flight.

Meticulously, I run through the paperwork with Mr Phillips, as he sips his coffee and munches through a Danish, ensuring he understands all the fine print before I turn it to him for a signature. He dabs the crumbs from his lips and wipes his hand on the napkin, pulls out his black Montblanc fountain pen, removes the lid signing with a flourish, before passing them back.

"Oooh! thanks baby." Victoria claps her hands together in delight, oozing gratitude and charm at her husband. She has totally destroyed a croissant; breaking it into tiny bite sized pieces, but I haven't seen her put one of them in her mouth. Leaving the decimated pastry on the plate, she turns and looks directly at me, once again giving my outfit a critical eye. "Fashion week here we come!" she declares beaming, "it's amazing to arrive in style. We'll be the talk of the town." She's smug and I want to punch her in her over-made-up face.

Hiding my irritation behind a smile as fake as hers, I swivel towards the fancy equipment on my desk, thankful I know how to use it. Excusing myself from their OTT display of affection, I pick up the headphones and place them over my ears, effectively blocking out the sickly sound of sloppy kisses and cooing. I press the intercom and speak clearly into the mic.

"Could Flight Captain Tudor please return to the main office, where your passengers are waiting, thank you." It's weird to hear my own voice echo round the building.

I feel Bear stretch under the desk and rise to his feet. He wanders out and sits by my side as I place my earphones back on the desk. He's waiting patiently for his master but gazing impassively at the people opposite.

"He's so cute! Monty, isn't he cute?" There's that damn word again. *Cute? Bear? Is she blind? Majestic, yes, awesome, yes but cute! Come on lady… please?*

"Is he yours?"

"He's beautiful, yes," I agree, trying not to bristle. "But, no, he's not mine. He belongs to Mr Tudor," I say far more politely than I feel. "But he's really friendly and enjoys company. So, I guess he works here too." My smile is rigidly false.

"Aww, honey," she squeezes up to her husband. "Do you think we could have him?"

What?... He's not for sale Bitch!

"Oh, goodness me no! Bear most certainly isn't for sale." I'm appalled she could even suggest such a thing. The phrase *Spoiled brat* springs to mind.

"Oh, Honey, everything has a price. It's just a question of how much," she drawls slyly at me with a condescending look.

I can see that, I think ungenerously. She must be costing this poor schmuck a bloody fortune.

"Well, I don't think we could ask Mr Tudor to part with such a fine specimen my darling." *Specimen!!* "He might be breeding stock. Perhaps if there are pups in the future, we could have one of those, yes?" He looks towards me in askance. I'm gobsmacked, but relieved he seems to have grasped the issue.

"Of course," I say. I don't have the first clue, but I'll say anything to get off this topic of conversation. "I'm sure you'll get the pick of the litter." *Fat chance -if there ever is one, I'll make damn sure you don't even hear about it!*

Thankfully, Silas appears at the door. He enters quickly and doesn't seem to notice the queer atmosphere, or my alarmed expression – I must be hiding it well for once.

"Right then, all done?" he asks.

"Yes," I answer, pleased that this ordeal is almost over. "All signed, sealed and delivered." If this's an example of the kind of clients I'll be dealing with, I need to grow a much thicker skin.

"Good, good… the plane is prepared. There's champagne and nibbles on board all ready for you; if you would like to follow me."

The Phillips's rise as one. Mr Phillips shakes my hand in thanks. Victoria flicks her hair and blows me a fake kiss.

"Ciao, Edi, nice to meet you."

"You too." I fake a smile back as she heads out of my office, her husband trotting subserviently behind her.

Silas nods a brief thank you in my direction, then gives Bear a sharp look on raised eyebrows. Bear looks back at him with the same expression. *"Ooof,"* Bear announces lazily, laying his head on my lap. It's the first time I've heard him bark.

Silas glances toward me and gives me a grin, which I feel in the pit of my stomach. I curl my toes in my sandals, just to make sure I can still feel my feet. "That's a relief. I thought I was getting the silent treatment for a moment there. Bear hates it when I wear the uniform, he knows he can't come with me."

"Ah." I raise my chin in response. My mouth is going dry again. Does he know he looks a million dollars in that uniform?

"Would you mind keeping him with you for a few hours? Tina has to go into the City again so she can't take him. If I leave him with Spanners and Sparks, he'll just get under their feet and they'll spend all day playing catch."

"Err, yeah sure, he's no trouble," I say stroking Bears silky head. Yawning a whine, he ignores Silas completely on purpose – yeah, he's getting the silent treatment alright.

"Thanks. Bye, bye Bear. Bye Edi," he says as he leaves.

"Ooof!" Bear huffs again, showing his distain at the situation. Lying down, he rests his head on his huge paws – he's in a mood.

"Well boy, it looks like you're stuck with the amateur today." I give him a reassuring pat then turn to my equipment, and prepare to go through the departure procedures.

The office window is huge, affording me a magnificent view of the apron and runway beyond. Replacing my headphones, I commence the departure measures that will ensure a safe take off for the Phillips's.

I grin when I spot Sparks waving his paddles in the air. He's appropriately dressed in an orange boiler suit. Massive ear defenders protect his hearing from the roar of the jet engines. Competently and strategically, he's guiding the sleek Cessna Citation towards the runway. It's a 550 Bravo model, a few years old but still a beautiful craft. The tail number is RB – BNF.

"Romeo - Bravo ready for take-off." Silas's calm voice rings through the headphones.

"Roger that, Romeo - Bravo, airspace is yours, you are clear to go." My training kicks in as I check the equipment and charts, and for the next few minutes my attention is focused solely on the safe departure of flight RT001, my first as a professional air traffic controller. I'm buzzing with exhilaration.

Sparks ducks out of the way of the jet-stream as for a few seconds the Cessna remains stationery, an invisible film of vapour distorting the air creating a mirage, which shimmers from the engines in the mid-day sun. Then she moves, slowly at first, the roar of the engines kicking in; increasing her speed until she begins to rise, smoothly and gracefully, lifting from the runway, a graceful bird soaring into the clear blue sky.

It's truly a thing of beauty to behold. I watch as she reaches higher and higher, banking to the left, picking up the flight path. I can still hear the sound of her engines, growing softer as gradually she becomes a small speck on the horizon, finally disappearing behind the only cloud up there today. I return my eyes back to the apron, where Sparks is dragging the chocks back into the hangar; he lifts his hand in a salute to me - it's all in a day's work.

Yes, I'm staying. This job is worth it. All the years of study were definitely worth it... the thrill of today, my first official launch has more than made up for last night's shenanigans.

No question - I'm staying.

Chapter 11

I manage to leave the office by six pm. Silas returned at five as scheduled in the log, which I've meticulously updated, and despite what he said, Bear was ecstatic to see him. The flight was uneventful, which was entirely due to the commissioned stewards, who looked after Mr and Mrs Phillips with perfect professional courtesy.

After locking up my office and heading out to my car, I contemplate going to the gym. I think I'll just swim tonight. It's been a warm day and a long stretch in a cool pool will work the kinks out of my stiff muscles.

Reaching my car, I hear barking and look up to see Silas and Bear out on the field, reaffirming their bond. Silas is throwing a yellow tennis ball and Bear is bounding after it, leaping through the tall grass like a gazelle. Silas looks up and raises his hand goodbye. He's changed out of his uniform - to Bear's obvious delight - and back into his jeans, this time paired with a black T-shirt. I wave back and climb into my car. It's been a really good day.

As I drive into my parking space a white removal van is pulling out of the delivery bay. I have to wait until it's out of the way before I park up. Somebody must be moving.

I make the effort to pick up the remaining boxes from my car boot, stacking them on top of each other, peering over the top as I lift them. There are four carrier bags full of shoes and other crap to carry, but if I spread the weight of the boxes across my arms and hook the bags with my fingers, I should only need to make one trip. It isn't heavy, just awkward.

I balance the boxes precariously on my knee to open the door, placing the keys between my teeth as I enter the foyer. The lift is on the ground floor so I step in, pressing the button with my elbow. Exiting the lift on my floor, I drop the bags and boxes to the ground, and shake out my arms to release the stiffness. Unlocking the apartment door, I remember to punch the alarm code quickly before it goes off. Wedging the door open with one of the boxes I drag the rest of my stuff through into the living room. By the time I'm finally inside I'm knackered and sweating. "Jeeze," I huff while I lean on the wall - taking a moment to gather my senses - exhausted from the sheer effort of transferring my meagre belongings.

Straightening up, I stare open mouthed at the living room. There's furniture - and it isn't mine! A plush cream three, no, four-seater sofa has been placed in the middle of the room, facing the stone fire place. Adjacent to it is a smaller two-seater, in a contrasting rustic fabric. A tartan throw is draped over the back of the rustic sofa, and there are loads of assorted scatter cushions artfully arranged along the back of the cream settee. On the floor between the sofas, is a large vibrantly patterned rug, it's absolutely beautiful and looks like it might be Persian. Sitting on top is a stunning polished rose-wood coffee table.

"Wow!"

Continuing my observations, I notice a matching rose-wood entertainment centre, complete with large screen TV, and a rose-wood drinks cabinet sporting a silver tray, crystal decanter and glasses. The decanter is filled with a clear amber fluid, which I presume is whiskey. Though I'm surprised, I can't say I'm too shocked. This is obviously what the delivery van was doing here. The whole room is now warm and inviting.

I suddenly remember the shambolic state I left the bedroom in this morning, and let out a groan of dismay. In trepidation, I turn and jog to the bedroom door. Taking a deep breath, I take hold of the glass door handle and turn it, all the while squinting on half open eyes, anticipating the huge mess. But there's no mess; when I risk opening my eyes, I'm dumbstruck, staring open mouthed at the sheer luxury on show. There's a huge majestic bed, dominated by a stunning, silver-grey, crushed velvet headboard, perfectly matching the colour of the satin curtains. On closer inspection, the studs punctuating the padded diamonds are made of crystal, shimmering in the remnants of the subtle sunlight filtering through the window.

The bed itself is sumptuously dressed in a luxurious damask fabric. The bedcovers look hand finished, so delicate is the thread work. They're so beautifully embroidered in silver–grey silk thread I can't imagine sleeping in them. Intricately patterned with a light grey and silver fleur-de-lis design, the matching scatter cushions and pillows are arranged so neatly, it would be a shame to disturb them. Draped in artistic folds at the foot of the bed is a soft grey cashmere throw, fringed with shimmering strands of silver silk. The room looks absolutely perfect, like a photograph from an interior design magazine. The effect is both sensuous and relaxing... quite simply, it's stunning.

I'm in complete awe, I walk round the bed - stroking my palm over the silky covers as I pass - to the door of the en-suite; curious to see if there have been any changes in there too. Peeking through the door, I can tell it's much the same as it was when I left this morning, only now the heated towel rails are stacked with an assortment of fluffy white towels.

Another new addition is the three silver pillar candle holders, standing at varying heights on the tiled floor behind the bath. They look antique, having the same scroll-work and distressed appearance as the large mirror hanging on the wall, above the double vanity unit.

Three cream candles balance atop the pillars. I pick one up and give it a sniff. Mmm... a subtle floral perfume invades my nose and alights my senses. I can just about detect hints of rose and there's some violet in there too. It's lovely. I turn the candle upside down to read the label. *English Heritage Tudor Rose.* I might have guessed.

Returning to the bedroom, I wonder, with a tinge of embarrassment, what has become of all my stuff that I left strewn on the floor this morning.

Glancing at the built-in wardrobe, I check inside. On opening the door, I can't quite believe it... it's not a wardrobe but a huge walk in closet come dressing room. It obviously runs back to back to the bathroom, and is about the same size! It's deep and has enough hanging space on one side for a whole boutique full of clothes. The other side has several chests of drawers, and more shoe racks than I'll ever need.

Walking further in, my fingers absently trace a line along the bevelled edge of the dressing table. The rear wall is mirrored, well-lit by overhead sunken spotlights; the angles of which are perfect. I imagine they've been purposefully aligned in strategic order, ensuring the dresser sees them self in the most flattering light, guaranteeing they leave the apartment looking their best. The lights are motion sensitive, turning on and off as the door opens and closes.

Above the wardrobes are high cupboards and shelves. I spy my duvet neatly folded and placed in a clear PVC vacuum storage bag. My pillows are similarly packed on the next shelf. My meagre collection of clothes has been hung up neatly, but they don't take up much room. The wardrobe looks sparse - almost empty. All my work gear - what there is of it - is in one section; my casual stuff in the next, and the last holds my two posh dresses. There's the emerald green with the V-neck, which I wore for my graduation, and the red lacy Bardot style number bought in a rush of madness in the January sales, never yet having had the courage to wear. There's a ton of empty space - I'll never fill it in a million years. There're no shoes on the rails – they're still in carrier bags on the lounge floor. My underwear has been folded, *folded!* Properly, like in a lingerie store and placed in a drawer. Vaguely I wonder who got that privilege.

Still slightly shell-shocked at all the splendour, I head back to the main living room. Grabbing my stuff, I tote it through the bedroom and into the vast wardrobe. I think I could actually sleep in here. The closet is bigger than my University bedroom!

I spend some time stacking my shoes on the rails, and my other bits and bats in the appropriate allocated places. There's no way I'll allow my stinky trainers anywhere near this lovely wardrobe, and on a mission of mercy, I wrap them tightly in a carrier bag, leaving them by the front door to put back in my car, or even the dustbin! Now I've a swanky new shoe rack, my determination to replace them this weekend, come hell or high water, is a no brainer.

Satisfied that everything is finally in its rightful place and happy I've finished my unpacking, I traipse back to the kitchen to make myself some dinner - admiring all the beautiful new furniture on the way. I can only think this must have been Christina's doing. I must remember to thank her tomorrow.

I'm distracted from my thoughts when I hear the chime of a phone, indicating a text message. *Ah, speak of the Devil.*

It's my work phone so I fish it out of my bag to see who's calling. It can only be one of four people as I haven't given my work number to anybody else yet. Swiping the screen, I see the message is from Christina.

'Hi Edi, hope you like the new furniture. Thank you for holding the fort today. I think this business negotiation is going to take a while. BTW, I told Silas he owes you an apology! Let me know if he doesn't deliver! ☺ C'

I knew it was her doing. Clearly, she has impeccable taste. There's no way I could've created such a stunning look. I've absolutely no talent for interior design. Everything I own is mismatched; bought because I liked it, rather than statement pieces to go with anything else. I quickly text her a reply.

'Hi Christina, Thank you so much. It's beautiful. Please don't worry about Silas, there's no problem. C U tomorrow. Edi'

There... that should suffice... now what shall I have for dinner?

Instinctively I look at my watch, tutting when I remember it isn't there. Irritated, I check the time on the microwave clock. It's almost seven. With all the faffing and unpacking I've killed about three quarters of an hour since I left work. Now I'm ravenous, so I rummage through the contents of the fridge seeking inspiration, but I don't have any enthusiasm for the contents, even though there's plenty to choose from.

Uninspired, I'm weighing up the options between the vegetarian sausages, or the chicken fillets, when the phone chimes again. This will be Christina replying to my text. Picking up the phone from the work top I stare at the screen - It's Silas. I smile to myself as I open the message. Christina's obviously reminded him to apologise for his intrusion yesterday. She rocks!

'Good evening Edi, Bear would like to thank you for looking after him today. If you are free, he would like to invite you to the pub for a bite to eat and a beer. He understands if you have other plans. Kind regards. S'

Goodness! That's unexpected.

Looking at the squashed sausages and pre-packed chicken, I know, even if I cook it, I won't eat it, and decide it couldn't hurt to take Bear up on his kind offer. Even knowing Silas has been prompted to do this by Christina, I still appreciate the gesture - I really don't want sausages or chicken tonight. And anyway, the creative way he's offered, using Bear as an excuse, is quite charming. I text back before I can reconsider.

'Hi, please tell Bear thank you. I accept his offer of a pub dinner. He's very kind and was absolutely no trouble today. Where should I meet him and at what time? Regards Edi.'

He replies almost immediately;

'We'll pick you up at 7:30. Bear can't drive so I'll have to come too, I hope that's ok? Regards S.'

His response makes me smile. Apparently, he has a sense of humour after all; who knew? His hard, exterior shell seems to be softening.

Looking down at my outfit, I should change - I can't go to the pub looking like a librarian, so I skip to my new wardrobe to decide what to wear. Just entering the huge closet gives me a thrill.

Because of the warm evening I choose my trusted, crinkly sundress. The cream lightweight cotton is patterned with delicate pink flowers. An elasticated back and buttoned front ensure the bodice is nicely fitted; but more importantly, the floaty skirt's long enough to cover my pasty legs and hide the unsightly burn on my shin. Teaming it with my faded denim jacket I look a bit hippy-chick and as I can't be bothered with heels, I slip my feet into my flip-flops – there, that'll do.

Releasing my hair from its bun - it's started coming loose anyway - it was damp when I tied it back this morning, so now there's a distinct kink around the middle, just below my ears. My hair beneath the ridge is shaggy and wavy. Ruffling it with my fingers to fan it out, I'm pleased with the effect, it actually looks semi-respectable for once.

Checking my face in the mirror, I look, as usual, washed out, so I quickly apply a light dusting of blusher then sweep my pale lashes with mascara. Sadly, nothing can be done about the Dennis Healey eyebrows – they'll have to stay for now.

For some reason, on entering the lounge to collect my shoulder bag I start to feel butterflies in my stomach. The intercom buzzes; pressing the button, my voice sounds small and shaky when I speak into the microphone.

"H…hello?"

"Hi, it's Silas… Bear says please could you hurry up - he's hungry." There's a smile in his voice.

"On my way." Exiting the apartment, I catch myself grinning, a bit giddy and light headed. Never mind about Bear being hungry, I must be too…

Silas is waiting beside his old Range Rover. Still dressed in his jeans and shirt from earlier, he looks incredibly handsome. Immediately, I feel dowdy and dull, not to mention scruffy and untidy. Nervously I tuck a loose strand of hair behind my ear.

What am I thinking? This is a huge mistake. He's stunningly gorgeous, moody and… my boss! I'm not in his league at all. If ever there was a pity dinner, this is it. I should make an excuse and eat my sausages… on my own! Clearly, he's here under duress… orders from Christina aside, this isn't going to go well.

How embarrassing! Doubt invades my head as I walk towards the car. With his blank expression, it's impossible to tell what he's thinking. If he does find me wanting, at least he doesn't show it. His face is stoically impassive as he stands casually, waiting beside his car, one hand resting on the open door.

It's still warm and I suspect the Range Rover doesn't have air conditioning. Bear is sat up in the passenger seat. He lets out a muffled 'woof' in greeting when he sees me. His long tail swishes back and forth when he stands to look through the window.

"Hi," I mutter shyly as I reach the car. "Thank you for this. I was just deciding what to eat when you texted." I'm blushing, I can feel the colour creeping up my neck and onto my cheeks. *Why am I so nervous?*

"Well…" leaving his door open, he strides round to the passenger side. *Gosh, he's tall!* "we have to eat something and it's a pleasant evening. I was going to the White Hart anyway, then Bear reminded me of my manners." For some reason, I've forgotten how husk and rich his voice is - like warm chocolate. It just intensifies my fluster. "You look pretty," he adds on a cheeky grin. He's only saying that to be polite, but I can feel the tinge in my cheeks getting deeper. I must resemble a tomato.

For the first time, I notice he has a cleft in his chin. I stare at it for a beat, wanting to trace the groove with my finger. "Ummm, th... thank you," I stutter, surprised at the unexpected compliment and my wayward thoughts.

Now *he* looks embarrassed; as if he didn't mean to say that. Could this *be* any more excruciating? I risk a direct look into his eyes, then find I can't hold his gaze... it's far too intense. Instead, I look at Bear in the passenger seat.

"Really...Bear reminded you?" I try to sound confident and cheery, but it comes out sarcastic. Thankfully I don't think he notices.

Still flushed from my run down the stairs, I remove my jacket and fold it over my arm. Silas reaches his hand through the open passenger window, opening the door from the inside.

"The catch is stiff," he explains, as he opens the door for me. "C'mon, you, shift."

Bear snakes his lithe body between the front seats squirming his way into the back, leaving the passenger seat free for me. "Actually," Silas continues, "Christina gave me a right bollocking this morning." He frowns, and absently brushes some stray dog hairs from the worn green leather. "Something about not respecting boundaries and invading privacy...But I do owe you, for looking after this one all afternoon." He signals with his thumb over his shoulder at Bear, who whines with an elaborate yawn before lying on the tartan rug covering the back seat. It must be warm for him in there.

Stepping onto the sill I clamber in. Silas pushes the door closed, then leans his full weight against it, ensuring it's properly shut. Satisfied, he strides round the front of the car and gets in behind the wheel.

"I think I can forgive you," I offer. "After all, it's your flat. And to be honest, he was no trouble - I enjoyed the company..." I might as well be friendly; after all, he's trying to be nice. "So... The White Hart, Is that your local?"

"Sometimes," he shrugs, non-committal. "It's a nice pub and dog friendly. They do decent pub-grub, and there's usually a guest ale or two. Do you know it?" He's making small talk as he fastens his seatbelt so I take the time to admire his profile. He really is very handsome.

"No, never been," I reply, putting on my faithful Boots shades, hoping they'll hide my eyes so I can continue my inappropriate gawping. I might as well make the most of it while I can.

"Well, I think you'll like it. Bear does. I usually take him for a walk along the canal footpath after I've eaten. You can get to it from the pub car park." For the first time, he flashes me a full-on smile. It's dazzling and I'm dumbstruck by it. Jamming the car into gear, he puts on his aviators and we head out.

I still feel uncomfortable; unsure of the etiquette as far as going to dinner with one's boss is concerned. I'm enjoying the thrill of being in his company, but it still seems peculiar. However, Silas is behaving completely different to yesterday. It's weird; he's so relaxed. Until now he's been brusque and business-like. But this feels more like I'm on a first date; it'll be tricky negotiating the protocol.

I decide this is casual Silas, as opposed to boss-man Silas, or tacky-turn Silas... if they're all these men rolled into one, how the hell am I going to cope? I decide to give myself a break and stop all the analysing shit - just go with the flow for God's sake!

Christina must've really given him what for. Clearly, I only caught the tail end of their argument this morning. The thought makes me grin. She's really looking out for me.

131

"Christina told me she'd arranged for some furniture to be delivered, is it okay?" His abrupt tone jolts me from my daydream.

Is it okay? I want to say it's amazing, stunning, beautiful, but then I think perhaps she told him it's some second-hand stuff off eBay or something, so I just say, "yes, it's lovely, thank you. It makes life easier and it's better than sleeping on the floor."

He glances at me quizzically before turning his eyes back to the road.

Yep, mate, I slept on the floor last night!

I hear Bear yawn from the back seat.

Silas's manner becomes noticeably softer. "She has great taste. When we were married, the house was like a showpiece. I was afraid to sit down in case I rumpled a cushion. Her place now's just the same." I think he's as fond of her as she is of him.

"Does she live locally?" I ask. I'm on safer ground discussing work and Christina.

"Yeah, on the edge of the village actually. She likes the peace and quiet, believe it or not." He doesn't seem uncomfortable speaking about his ex-wife.

"Isn't it strange… working with your ex?" That question was a bit intrusive, but I suppose I can ask. I'm going to be working there too, so if there are any taboo subjects to steer clear of, I should know.

"Not really thought about it… it just happened. We were working together while we were married. She's a fantastic negotiator and what she doesn't understand about business strategy isn't worth knowing. I guess because it was an amicable separation we didn't even consider not carrying on. In truth, we get on far better now were just business partners."

It's much the same as Christina said, though thankfully, he doesn't mention the bed part. He turns a thoughtful gaze towards me. I think for a moment he's going to ask a question but he seems to reconsider, choosing instead to turn his eyes back to the road. Bear snores in the back seat.

We drive on for a few more minutes; the car, but for the rumble of the engine is quiet - no music - which seems odd to me. I'm sweltering, so I roll down my window allowing the air to circulate.

Following the bend, Silas swings left at the sign for the *Wey and Arun Canal*. "Do you have a partner?" he asks out of the blue. I suppose it's a reasonable question but it puts me on guard.

"Nooo… no, no! Just me I'm afraid." I give my stock answer; don't want to kick that hornets' nest.

"Playing the field eh?" He knows he's making me uncomfortable again. *Why does he do that?*

When I don't answer he seems to realise he's struck a nerve, and I'm pleased to see he looks a little contrite and embarrassed. Strangely, his discomfort emboldens me.

Okay then, two can play that game. "So… have you got a significant other? Or were the condoms just for show?" *Where the fuck did that come from? Jesus Edi!* My filter's broken! Perhaps that was just a little too bold!

"You've got me." He tilts his head completely blasé and totally unaffected by my inappropriate question. "There's nobody special at the moment - but you never know when an opportunity might come along… I'm a Boy Scout… I like to be prepared."

Woah!

I can't see his eyes behind his sunglasses; did he just wink at me?

His counter attack caught me by surprise and I'm still trying to come up with an appropriate response when we turn into the car park of a country pub. Bear immediately sits up and pays attention, clearly recognizing it.

Pulling into a space, Silas swiftly alights and opens the door so Bear can leap out, which he does; immediately cocking his leg and peeing on the car tyres.

"Gee, thanks boy!" Silas shakes his head in dismay.

Chuckling, I climb down, following Silas and Bear as they make their way to the beer garden.

Silas lifts his hand in greeting to a few patrons who are sitting around, eating, drinking and enjoying the last few hours of the balmy sunshine.

It's a lovely evening and this pub seems homely enough. There are random family groups scattered here and there, and even a bunch of biker types are huddled around a couple of benches, shoved together.

The canal runs alongside the beer garden, a few boats and barges are rocking gently on their moorings. A family of Mute swans have gathered on the canal bank. There's a cob, a pen and half a dozen little grey cygnets, preening and soaking up some late evening sun before bedtime. Bear spots them, but Silas does too and is quick to order him to "leave," which obediently, he does, albeit rather reluctantly.

We find a bench and Silas borrows a couple of menus from the people at the adjacent table. Their plates are empty, so that's a good sign.

"What would you like to drink?" he asks, handing over Bear's lead. "You'd better keep hold of this." He tilts his head towards the swans, knowingly.

Nodding my understanding, I take it from him. "Oh, err, just half of whatever's good please... the guest beer will be fine."

Silas strolls inside to get the drinks, leaving Bear to guard me; hanging tightly onto the lead I stroke his beautiful head wistfully. *I should bring David and the girls here for lunch one day soon.*

Silas returns with our drinks to catch me daydreaming, gazing at the shimmering reflections on the canal and enjoying the sunshine. "Penny for them?"

"Hmmm…" I respond quietly, shy at being caught.

Placing our glasses on the table, he removes a bottle of water from under his arm, opens the cap and pours the contents into a metal bowl situated beneath the table. He moves the bowl within Bear's reach and he gratefully takes a noisy drink. Once he's finished lapping up the cold liquid, he settles back on the grass, eyeing the swans with mild curiosity.

"Cheers," picking up my drink I take a welcome sip. It's lovely; a golden light beer with a frothy head, the flavour's smooth and malty but not overly bitter. "Mmm, what's this? It's really nice."

"Yeah, cheers… I think it's called Golden Lady. It's not too shabby," he says, taking a deep draft. I hand over Bear's lead and he threads it through the leg of the chair to secure him.

Focussing on his menu, he starts to peruse the daily specials. "What would you like to eat?"

That's easy. "The fish finger sandwich, please. With sweet potato fries if they've them." I don't hesitate. I can always judge the quality of any pub by their fish finger sandwiches. "Preferably on a white bloomer. If not… whatever they have is fine."

Looking a bit surprised at my choice, he shrugs his big shoulders. "Well, I'm having the steak and ale pie." Getting to his feet he takes note of the table number before going inside to place our order. Turning at the door hesitantly, tipping his hand to his mouth he makes the universal '*do you want another drink?*' motion.

"Yes please," I call but then add, "but I think it's my…." I don't get to say, 'round'. Shaking his head, he points to Bear,

135

who's still eyeing the family of Swans, now waddling around the beer garden searching for leftover scraps.

"His round!" he grins and enters the pub. There's that illusive smile again.

The evening's still very warm so I place my jacket on the chair beside me. The sun's rays are prickling the fair skin on my shoulders. Absently, I wish I'd remembered to bring sun screen – this place is a real sun-trap.

I'm sat, minding my own business, watching the swans mooch about under the vacant tables, and stroking Bear's head, when one of the biker group leaves his table and approaches me. Lurching on unsteady legs; his beer sloshing precariously up the inside of his glass. His mates are watching his progress with interest.

The guy looks sweaty and quite tipsy. I'm guessing he's been here most of the afternoon, enjoying the beer and sunny weather - his face is sunburned.

Uneasily, I watch him approach - my assessment continues as he strolls over. Scruffy, overlong dirty brown hair, straggly unkempt gingery beard, grubby ripped jeans and an ancient, heavy metal T-shirt that's definitely seen better days. He looks grimy and as he gets nearer, Bear removes his eyes from the swans and redirects them straight at him.

Glaring at the biker, Bear pushes up on his forelegs. He sits tall, ramrod straight, remaining still as a statue by my side. When the guy nears the table, he releases a low rumbling growl. It's a warning and its power reverberates through my palm, which still rests atop his soft head. Glancing down, I stroke my hand to his shoulder giving him a reassuring pat, but his focus is unwavering. Sensibly, the biker is cautious.

"Good-looking beast you've got there, love," He's stopped his approach and is now stood nursing his pint, a few feet from where I'm sitting. "He don't look very friendly though."

Keep your distance mate! "Yes, he's lovely, thank you," I manage to remain polite; there's no need to rattle his cage. But just in case, I add, "he's just being protective, that's all. Aren't you boy?"

Bear lifts his head at the sound of my voice, thumping the ground once with his tail, before returning his vigilant eyes back to the wary biker.

His glass is resting between his saggy pecs as he sways two and fro on his scuffed biker boots. Beer has slopped out, soaking his tee-shirt, leaving a nasty brown stain. He doesn't notice. His eyes are glazed as he takes another stumbling step forward, spilling more beer and gesturing towards Bear with his pint.

"Beast like that must be worth a few quid, I dare say - handsome, like." Slurring, his bravado gets the better of him and he takes a step. Bear gets to his feet.

"Sit down," I whisper. He obeys immediately; replacing his rump on the grass, glancing at me fleetingly before resuming guard duty. "I wouldn't know. He doesn't belong to me, he's my bosses." *Go away you, fat moron!*

"Oooh, out playing cosy with the boss, are we? Well darlin' I hope he's worth it. Does his Mrs know?"

He gives his mates a smug look over his shoulder, obviously feeling bolder, happy now that Bear's under control, he starts to laugh at his feeble attempt at humour. His mates join in, egging him on. I realise he's completely pissed, acting big in front of his gang. Little does he know, he's picked on the wrong woman...

"Actually, yes she does," I snipe, sarcastically - I detest cocky gits!

He squints at that, then rally's and scoffs at me. "Sleeping your way to the top?" Grabbing his crotch and giving it a tug, he starts eyeing me up and down. "I thought that was for dolly birds with big tits." He's obnoxious; his mates jeer in encouragement. "Though, you look like you might have a nice pair, hidden under that dress," thrusting his hips in a suggestive manner, he stares blatantly at my chest.

Knob! Hurry up Silas!

Temper simmering, which isn't a good thing, I decide I need to show my teeth, and retaliate.

Staring him directly in the eyes I flash my best sardonic smile, "You must be psychic," I spit vehemently, "we're going back to his place after for a threesome."

That stops him in his tracks. I can't stand arseholes, they bring out the worst in me. I refuse to be intimidated.

"Christ love, it sounds like you need a good seeing to! What's your boss got that I haven't? I bet he's sixty with a shrivelled-up pecker and false teeth." Laughing at his own joke, he wipes his mouth with the back of his hand. He's in his stride now and bent on humiliation. People are starting to pay attention.

"Good one Robbo, man!!" His mates are cracking up with mirth. They've all stood up for a better view, enjoying the show, spurring him on.

Nervously, beginning to get worried, I take a quick scan around the beer garden. I can't see Silas anywhere; the queue must be stupidly long. Some of the other customers have stopped eating and are blatantly listening to our uncomfortable exchange, muttering between themselves, wondering if they should intervene... they don't rise to the challenge.

Removing his hand from his crotch, he pumps a fist in the air towards his mates, acknowledging the *'good one'*. Then he makes an obscene gesture, indicating big tits and a wanking motion. His mates jeer even louder.

The aggressive action makes me see red; my temper flares and I lose all sense of reason. Bear stands once again, only this time I don't stop him.

"Well, I'll tell you one thing he has that you don't," I snarl through gritted teeth. I'm gonna go there, even though I know I shouldn't. The red mist has descended and there's no going back. It's the only way to shut this prick up, well and for good.

"And what's that then, Sweetness?" he's slurring and swaying, cockily. Bear has started to growl again.

Here goes, you twat! Mustering my courage and speaking softly, in my sexiest, sweetest most seductive voice I say. "A big, beautiful, hard, *BLACK* dick! You got one of those have you *mate*?" I make the wanking gesture back at him as I continue, changing my subtle husk for a louder tone, "Oh, and he *really* knows how to use it. So why don't you just *fuck off* before I let this beautiful '*beast*' loose and order him to rip your saggy balls off!!" I exhale.

That felt good!

As if affirming my outburst, Bear strains at his leash, and hurls a couple of loud barks.

Affronted, but not for long, the guy is about to respond when he looks above my head, his face blanches. Slowly he backs away, spilling his pint on his pants as he stumbles on the uneven grass. His mates have shut up too, and are murmuring to each other in low voices, turning back to their own conversations, sitting back down at their table.

"What did I miss?" Silas growls, jutting his chin, his eyes focussed on the retreating biker. I jump out of my skin.

Fuck!

He must have caught the atmosphere. I just hope he didn't hear me! He doesn't sound like he did.

"Oh n... nothing," I stutter, "just a drunken idiot trying to be clever. He was admiring Bear, but Bear didn't like the look of him." Tripping over my words I'm speaking too brightly; but I think I may have got away with it. The guy has made his way back to his gang who are consoling him and patting him on the back. What a hero!

"Hmm, well, he's a great looking dog. Aren't you Lad?" He speaks to Bear, whilst flashing daggers at the group of bikers; meanwhile, the guy, who's re-joined his mates, is staring at our table, affronted. Silas sits and hands me a pint of beer. *Another pint!?*

"They had no small glasses and the queue is horrendous. I'm sure you can manage." He sounds annoyed again. "If not, just drink what you can. Oh, and they've run out of sweet potato fries so you're on ordinary chips – hope that's okay?" he continues, still eyeing the scruffy mob at the opposite table.

"Yes, that's fine." I'm happy with the chips but it's the pint that concerns me. I don't normally drink beer; even as a student I left that sort of thing to Lizzy and Sam.

Settling, Silas looks more relaxed now the bikers have quietened down. We make small talk as we sip our ale and wait for our food. The sun is getting lower in the sky and there's the beginning of a fantastic sunset. The reflections on the water are dazzling. The sun is a glowing vermillion and orange ball on the horizon. As incredible and spectacular as the sunset is, I can't help staring at Silas. He really is a gorgeous man – it must be the beer goggles!

"Your hair's a nice colour," Silas declares suddenly. Seemingly, he's appraising me too; I hope he's not disappointed. "I don't mean to be rude, but is it natural?"

I get this question a lot. My dark auburn hair is both a blessing and a bane. It was murderous as a child; the constant basis of ridicule and bullying, making school a nightmare. Now I'm an adult, I appreciate the colour - I love that it's different. "Yep, all natural," I say smiling, delighted he approves. "I mean, I like it now, but when I was a kid, it was horrid to have red hair and freckles," I take a sip of beer – it's going down too well. "You can imagine… all the name-calling, I suppose it helped me grow a thicker skin; 'though I've dabbled with different colours, you can't seem to cover natural red properly - and none of them really suited me anyway so…this is me." God I'm rambling!

"It's lovely, very…unique. I like it a lot," he confirms quietly with an approving nod, leaning back so that the server can place his plate on the table.

"One Steak and ale and one fish finger sandwich with chips and salad." The young guy passes us some cutlery wrapped in a napkin and then asks if we want any sauces or condiments.

"Just vinegar for me please." I can't eat chips without it.

"Ketchup, and another pint of the guest ale and a Lime and Soda, when you have time mate, please." That's a good guess, lime and soda is my designated driver drink.

Silas didn't lie, the food's great. Chunky chips, beer battered cod goujons on a fresh, thick sliced white bloomer, slathered with homemade creamy tartar sauce, deliciously tangy, loaded with roughly chopped capers and served with a small side salad of lettuce, cucumber and tomato. I cut the sandwich into manageable pieces I can pick it up to eat.

Silas is tucking in to his pie. A wonderful savoury aroma rises with the steam as he breaks into the shortcrust. Bear pays attention by sitting up, licking his lips expectantly and letting out an appreciative whine. Silas scratches him behind the ear and drops him a piece of steak, which he gobbles greedily before lying back down. Good dog. I wonder if he's had his dinner yet? I look at Silas in askance..

"Don't worry about him. He's been fed already," he answers my silent question. "He's a dustbin!"

The server returns with our drinks, placing the pint in front of Silas and making to give me the lime and soda; however, Silas lifts his hand waving the beer in my direction.

"The lime and soda's mine," he says, "driving, mate."

Oh? That'll be two and a half pints I've had by the time we leave. I'll be on my back at this rate; funnily, I don't seem to care too much; I feel relaxed, not tipsy. As I carry on eating my way through my dinner, I notice as usual, I've managed to eat round the tomatoes in my salad; funny I always do that

"Well, how was it?" Silas has cleared his plate.

"Ten out of ten," I confirm with a nod. "I always choose it, if it's a new place. You can tell a good pub by the quality of their simplest food, I think. You can't go wrong really." Grinning at me, he seems pleased that I'm pleased.

By nine o'clock the biker boys have called it a night and roared off into the sunset. The evening has cooled considerably and the sky is darkening to a dim purply pink. I made sure I took it slowly with my drink. I couldn't manage another one; With the volume alone, I'd be up all night, peeing!

I hear a phone ringing. It's a couple of seconds before I recognise the familiar ring-tone of my personal mobile. Hastily, I rummage around in my bag but by the time I locate it, the call's rung off, the screen displays a missed call from The Beeches.

Bugger! "Erm…sorry Silas, but I think I need to get this," I say apologetically. Standing and walking a couple of paces away from the table I hit the redial button, Silas giving me a *go-ahead* gesture.

Mark answers on the second ring. "Hello?" I wait, impassively looking at the ducks on the water just for somewhere to aim my eyes. "Mark?"

"Hi, Edi, I don't like calling you this late but I need to ask if you could come in for a meeting sometime this week?" He sounds calm enough so I'm not on high alert.

"Err; well it might be a bit difficult. I've just started my new job. Is there a problem? Has something happened to David?" The flush of anxiety sobers me instantly and I start to panic. They wouldn't normally ring after nine o'clock.

"No, God, no nothing like that." The relief I feel is instantaneous but short lived, as Mark continues. "Well... nothing majorly serious," His tone is ponderous, like he's struggling with a decision. "There's been an incident this evening - with David and another resident... look, I can't really discuss it over the phone. Please don't worry."

That's easy for him to say! "David's absolutely fine, but if you could possibly find time tomorrow evening it would be really helpful." He sounds calm but insistent. Now I'm curious as well as anxious. *What's David been up to?*

"Would seven be too late?" I ask.

"No, that would be good actually. Everyone will have had dinner and be watching a movie. Seven's perfect." I detect relief in his tone.

"Err, okay then. I'll be there for seven." We say our goodbyes and I ring off. I'm niggling now. I hope it isn't a fight. It could be something to do with Nic. There's no point speculating, I'll have to wait until tomorrow.

As I sit down, Silas is giving me a funny look.

"What?" I say, immediately wiping my chin, checking for stray ketchup.

"Problem?" he asks on raised eyebrows. "You looked a little freaked there for a second." I can't tell if he's concerned or nosey.

"I'm not sure. That was my son's, err..." I don't finish, because I'm not sure how to. I just gesture with my hands hunting for what to say, without saying what I really should; but Silas gives me an out.

"Yeah, I got that. He's in a bit of trouble at school, is he?" I'm grateful for the misconception, and accept it willingly.

"Maybe… I'm not sure. They want me to go to a meeting tomorrow at seven o'clock. I can only assume there's been some sort of fight, or something." Strangely, I'm finding him comfortable to talk to when he's in casual Silas mode - and I haven't experienced this level of ease with a man in years; ever in fact!

"Boys, will be boys. How old is he?"

"Seventeen." I start to rub my arms, feeling the evening chill.

"Yeah, college rebel I'll bet. Mine's the same. He's away at the moment but it's always a worry, isn't it?"

I'm taken aback for a second. I didn't realise… "Oh, I didn't know you had children." Christina never mentioned it and I just presumed they didn't have any.

"Ah, don't get carried away. It's just the one boy."

"How old is he?" I ask, glad for the diversion from talking about David.

"He's twenty-two. Dominic's a great lad. The best thing to come out of our marriage, that's for sure." He looks at me with soft eyes.

He's removed his sunglasses and hooked them in the 'V' neck of his shirt. It's abundantly clear he loves his son very much. It's heart-warming to see this softer side. But no sooner has he spoken, he becomes guarded again. Glancing at the darkening evening he almost gives me whiplash as he swiftly changes the subject.

"It's going darker and I promised Bear a walk along the towpath before bed time. We'd better get a shift on if we want to be back before it's fully dark."

That suits me so I pick up my jacket and pull it on. I get my right arm in my sleeve and I'm about to put in my left, when I feel a sharp stabbing sensation in my right shoulder.

"Ouch!" I yell - it happens again, a red-hot needle of searing pain, then again... and again. "Ow! Shit, ow, ouch..." I shout each time, jumping about like an idiot. Alarmed, Bear dives under the table out of the way of my dancing feet. *"Shit, ouch, fuck, fuck!"* Shaking my jacket loose from my body, it lands in a crumpled heap on the ground. Silas is at my side like a shot.

"Edi... What is it?... Edi, for fuck's sake what?"

Alarm all over his beautiful face, he reaches for me, instinctively pulling me towards him, bending to look into my eyes for any indication of what has caused my sudden distress.

Searching out my discarded jacket, we both look, just in time to see a hideous, massive, ugly, great wasp crawl out from beneath the collar.

I've been stung!

Recoiling in revulsion at the sight of the enormous yellow and black insect, the realisation hits me like another vicious sting. My shoulder immediately begins to throb and burn; the explosion of agony intensifying the more I look at the horrible creature lazily crawling all over my jacket. I shudder in Silas's arms; my shoulder blades squeeze together just at the thought. Stretching up onto my tip toes I prance on the spot like a performing pony, as if it will help me get out of the way.

"Urgh ... Oh god, oh god it hurts, get rid of it. Please!!"

Closing my eyes, I'm squealing, pleading, burying my face into his chest, still shivering, I feel sick and my shoulder is on fire!

"Horrid thing..." he bends and I peek out from my hiding place to see him lift my jacket and give it a shake; the wasp drops to the floor. "Scram." Protectively, he draws me away and around to the other side of the table. I absently notice he doesn't kill it. I hate wasps, but for some reason this pleases me.

145

Bear is now taking notice of the commotion with interest, pacing beside us, trying to get a closer look at the wasp.

"Silas, don't let it get him!!" I wail, alarmed the revolting thing might decide to sting Bear too.

"Leave!" Silas gives Bear a stern look and the dog instantly backs off and lies flat on the grass beside the bench seat. It's a command that won't be ignored.

Gently, Silas removes me from his grasp. I'm clinging to him like a limpet. "Let's have a look. Wasp stings can be really nasty. Are you allergic?" He's concerned.

"No... no, just in pain. Damn, that fucking hurts." It's not easing, if anything, the pain is intensifying. I screw my eyes tight and try to count it out.

"Here, stings are alkaline so you need to apply acid." He picks up the vinegar bottle from the table and removes a spotless handkerchief from his jeans pocket. Folding it into a pad, he shakes on some vinegar; then turns me, so he can get up close and personal with the sting. "Hmmm, vicious little bugger... I would've thought one would be enough, but you've got four good'uns here." Very carefully he places the pad over the tender area and applies some pressure. It smarts like a bitch and I flinch at the contact, so he holds me still by placing his other hand on my left shoulder, while administering first aid to my right.

Just the touch of his warm hand stills me. Now I've a burning sensation in my left shoulder too, but it has nothing to do with the wasp! His hand is weighty and solid. It feels lovely and I realise it's the first time a man has touched me so gently for quite some time...

After about five minutes of him diligently applying the vinegar poultice, the fire in my right shoulder has subsided, and I'm left with a continuous dull throbbing. My left shoulder however, is aflame, albeit for a completely different reason, making me wonder how it would feel on other parts of my body.

Removing the hanky, he checks the injured area . "How does it feel now?" seemingly satisfied he's done what he can.

"Better, thank you," I whisper. He keeps his hand on my left shoulder, not releasing me.

Perhaps he thinks I might fall – I might just.

"That's good... good."

The beer garden is almost empty as he untangles the lead from the table leg and unhooks it from Bear's collar, allowing him to run free. He returns the hanky to his pocket and picks up my jacket, giving it another shake for good measure. Only then does he turn to look at me.

"Well, that was dramatic!" he states, on an exaggerated eye roll.

"Thank you for saving me." I smile, taking my jacket from his proffered hand, appreciative of his attention.

Warily, I too give it a shake; I doubt I'll put a coat on again without checking it for hidden dangers beforehand.

"Shall we walk this dog before there's any more drama tonight?" He nods towards Bear who's sniffing the spot where the family of swans was sunbathing earlier. They're long gone; probably roosting for the evening somewhere along the canal bank.

"Yes, let's," I whisper, my shyness has returned. With his hand on my shoulder, we stroll towards the gate that leads to the canal path. Bear is gambolling around behind us.

"Bear!" We both call in unison, our eyes focussed on each other, smiling at our synchronicity.

Bear careers past us, a dog on a mission. He runs about a hundred yards, turns, and hurtles back, wagging his tail and barking ferociously; skidding to a halt, he completes a full three-sixty before galloping off again. This pattern forms the progress of our walk. Bear, charging about and Silas and I, strolling along, stealing shy glances at each other every now and then. All the while, his hand remains on my shoulder. It's weighty and lovely, and somehow, it no longer feels strange to be out with my boss.

Chapter 12

By the time we arrive back at the apartment darkness has fallen. The walk back to the car was a bit precarious but we needn't have worried. Silas attached Bears lead, and the amazing dog deftly guided us to safety, completely sure-footed, keeping us firmly on the towpath and well away from the canal bank, ensuring there were no untimely dips!

We sit quietly in the car for a few minutes. The atmosphere has grown tense again. It was a quiet drive home, no small talk or music to fill the silence. Bear is really snoring now. He must be whacked. I know how he feels.

Switching off the ignition Silas turns to face me. It's deafeningly quiet, just the sound of the creaking leather car seats and the ticks and pops from the cooling engine. I can barely see his eyes in the dim light of the parking area. They're glittering and beautiful, God, I'm still buzzing from all the beer, or it could be the adrenalin from the wasp sting? I can't stop staring at him, or forget the searing heat of his hand on my shoulder as he held me still.

"How's the shoulder?"

Which one?

"It's good, just throbbing a little bit." I roll it and give a sharp shrug to demonstrate I'm okay.

"So, tomorrow evening, you're going to visit your son?" He poses the statement as a question.

"Yeah, at seven o'clock, I don't know how long I'll be." Why I added that, I don't know.

"Well, I really had a good time tonight," he lowers his eyes, so he's no longer looking directly at me before he continues.

Could he be nervous?

"If I'm not being too presumptuous, I'd like to do it again sometime." He lifts his eyes back to mine. "Perhaps without the wasp sting and the gooseberry." He jerks his thumb over his shoulder at the snoring dog.

Has he just asked me on a date?

"That would be lovely, but what about Christina? Won't she mind?" I'm troubled about her reaction if I went out with Silas again. I *really* want her to be okay with it though.

"Why does that bother you?" He looks puzzled.

"Well, she's your ex... you're my boss. Isn't it a bit... well... strange?" This is awkward.

I hear, rather than see him shrug his big shoulders on a sigh. The taciturn man is back... turning further towards me he lifts his hand and touches my cheek. I can't move. His hand is dry and warm, and once again I feel that burning flame heating my skin. I resist leaning into his touch, but I'm sure he feels me stiffen slightly, although he doesn't pull away.

"Did you enjoy my company?" he asks bluntly.

"Yes," I whisper.

"Did you enjoy your meal and the beer?" He's so close I can feel his breath on my face.

I nod and smile feeling the gentle friction of his fingers on my cheek as I do. "Yes."

"Do you like working at RTC?"

"Yes, so far, I love it!" immediately I'm on guard; where's he going with this?

"Well then, I don't see a problem. Christina, *certainly* won't see a problem. She has her own life and is always telling me to cut loose a little." He's getting closer. I can see his eyes clearly now. Bear ruffs in his sleep.

"I'm not very good at having male friends. I didn't have many in Uni' and they were all a lot younger than me - so I didn't go out that much." *I've* no idea what I mean, so he has no hope!

"Look, Edi, I'll be completely honest." His thumb brushes a line on my cheek. "I find you attractive. I think you're lovely... a bit unconventional, but lovely none-the-less."

"Oh!"

"I've not had a... real relationship for a while either, so I'm happy to keep this on a friendly basis. We can see where it goes - no pressure... but you need to know I'm attracted to you." He removes his hand and rests it on the steering wheel. I immediately want to grab it and put it back on my face. With a sigh, he swallows, his Adams apple bobs up and down, and I can't remove my eyes from his glorious throat; he stares ahead, out of the window. Mirroring his gesture, I also sigh and swallow, adding a lick of my lips for good measure.

"Okay... as long as it's okay with Christina. I would like to see where this goes too." I'm being honest but feel jumpy, like this could be the start of something. "I could do with a friend around here. I think I would like it to be you." I smile, letting him know I'm okay with it. I don't tell him I'm attracted to him too. That doesn't seem appropriate right now, but I do feel it, simmering away deep down. I'm still reeling from his admission that *he's* attracted to *me.* I find that very hard to believe.

Breathing out he stares through the window but I think I see a look of ... *what? Relief?* "So, tomorrow, after your meeting if it isn't too late, would you like to go out for dinner?" He's the embodiment of politeness - speaking to the windscreen!

"Yes, that would be lovely – thank you... if it isn't too late when I get back," I add smiling, but resist the desire to reach out and touch his hand, which is clutching the steering wheel.

He breathes what sounds like another sigh of relief then turns to face me. "Do you want me to walk you in?" He's relieved. "I can give you the full tour," now he's teasing.

"No, I think I can manage. Thank you for the dinner, and the first aid." My smile is getting bigger, he's really nice; I think I had him all wrong.

"Well, now you've a sting to match your burn," he says with a cheeky grin as I start to open the door.

Startled, I wonder how he knew about the effect of his hand on my shoulder, until I realise, he means the mark on my shin from the tumble at the gym.

"Ha-ha, yeah…!" I answer climbing out of the car, thankful he can't see my blushing face in the darkness.

"See you tomorrow then?" He starts to reverse slowly as I turn to see him off. Grinning at me, he leans out of the side window, all his courage has returned. "That's me and my big, beautiful, hard *black* dick!" He starts laughing at my stunned face as he raises a hand and drives out of the car park!

Okay… I didn't have him wrong… He's a twat!

Mortified, I stare after the car, my eyes wide, and mouth wider.

Oh my god, fuck, damn and bollocks! I'm in shock! *Jesus, he heard me!* Oh, that's so humiliating. I stomp towards the entrance of the flats, slapping my forehead with my palm, berating myself for being so stupid. *Of course, he heard you… half the bloody pub heard you, you idiot!*

Locating my key and on entering the foyer, adrenalin pumping, I run up the stairs, totally embarrassed and annoyed with myself. Slamming through the front door of the apartment, I'm horrified; of course, he heard me!

Lordy, what must he think?

Dropping my bag and heading straight for the bathroom, I ignore my work phone when it starts to ring; it can only be Silas at this hour. I'm not answering; he will only apologise again and apologies mean nothing to me, besides, he has just embarrassed the Hell out of me, so I won't be speaking to him tonight!

I strip off and turn my back to the mirror, performing some major contortions with my neck until the scattering of needle-like marks are visible in the reflection. Each one is encircled in white, giving the appearance of a tiny target with a red bulls-eye dead centre. *Bloody wasp!*

Shuddering at the memory, I notice a slight reddening of the skin around each white blob, where the vinegar has started to neutralise the poison. The throbbing is now a dull ache but the marks still look livid.

After a speedy shower, I go to the kitchen in hunt of more vinegar. Making it up as I go along, tipping the bottle carefully so I don't spill it, I shake a few drops onto a wad of cotton wool and secure it with a plaster to seal it in. Hopefully it will work its magic overnight. As an afterthought, I pop a couple of painkillers for good measure.

Unable to resist the urge any longer, I check my work phone, just in case it was someone else calling me, though I know that's hardly likely. Retrieving the shiny new mobile from my bag, I see it needs charging so as I rummage for the charger and pull up the missed calls. Yeah, it was Silas. He's left a voice message. Gritting my teeth, I press the key connecting me to voice mail. The recorded message kicks in, his voice is quiet. I can hear his gentle breathing. It's disturbing, but sexy as hell.

'Hi, it's me," he whispers, *soft and low.* *"Thank you for tonight. I'm not sorry about embarrassing you; it was brilliant the way you handled that idiot, did you really think I hadn't heard you? Your face was a picture."* He's still amused by my faux pas. I relax, feeling the trace of a smile tickle my lips. Thank goodness he found it funny. *'Oh, and just in case you were wondering... you got it completely right, Honeybee. Goodnight, sleep tight... I look forward to seeing you in the*

morning!' He hangs up, still chuckling. The sound is a rich and low bumble in his throat.

Oh my God!

Staring at the handset as if it holds all the answers to my curiosity, I analyse his message.

Honeybee? I roll my eyes.

Jesus! And he's bragging about the size of his manhood.

Good Lord… that voice! And now I'm more than just shocked, I'm aroused.

Feeling my face heat at the thought, I try to ignore the deluge of erotic images of Silas, which are suddenly flooding my imagination. I need to divert my attention away from all things large, hard and black, before I spontaneously combust. This isn't good. I can feel the beginnings of an unhealthy obsession taking hold. If I carry on like this, I'll be unable to function in my job and destroy everything I've worked so hard to achieve.

Resisting the temptation to *Google* him, just so I can see his picture, I desperately attempt to force myself to think about something else… anything else… steering my mind to more mundane tasks is the only way I'm going to quell my inappropriate thoughts. Breathing deeply to calm myself, I find the charger and plug in the phone. Then, as if on automatic pilot, even though it's taking a huge amount of concentration just to focus, I traipse through to the kitchen and fill a tall glass with cold tap water. I need to hydrate. All the beer has gone to my head and the sting on my shoulder is still throbbing wickedly.

Suddenly, the need for sleep is overwhelming. All the pent-up stress of the day has finally caught up with me and I'm about to crash and burn in a big way. So, I plod on heavy legs, into my bedroom. Even in my exhausted state I can appreciate the beautiful room, and the massive luxurious expanse of the king-sized bed. Placing the glass on the bedside table, it crosses my mind I've never slept in a bed this big… ever!

Carefully I remove all the sumptuous scatter cushions, stacking them neatly in the ottoman at the foot of the bed, followed by the precisely folded cashmere throw. With the cushions out of the way, the bed looks huge. Drawing back the duvet, I can tell the sheets are of the uppermost quality. Never have I experienced this level of luxury, it will take some getting used to.

Because the sun's been on the balcony for most of the afternoon, the room is far too warm. I open the patio windows, setting the catch on open-lock, so they're slightly ajar but not gaping. Then I climb into the enormous bed. Crawling naked across the huge mattress, which feels so extravagant and decadent, does nothing to alleviate the strange, unfamiliar, stirrings within me. All I can think about is how stunningly beautiful Silas' body would look, reclining against the crisp, white cotton pillows.

Christ! Groaning at the conjured image, the desire to hide my shame is overwhelming, so I pull the sheets over my head, swathing myself in the deliciously soft, cool cotton. Desperate for sleep to take me, I'm still analysing the strange events of the evening as I finally lay my head on the downy pillow.

What was it he said? 'I got it completely right.'

Oh, God! I need to stop thinking about him before I make a complete fool of myself.

Rolling onto my back, I place my left arm behind my head. My right hand, drifts beneath the sheet until it's resting lightly between my thighs. I can feel the gathering dampness on my fingers as I gently stroke and caress my delicate folds.

Unable to halt the visions, I imagine how it would feel to be touched this way by Silas. To be kissed and caressed by those luscious lips and large strong hands. It's no good; it's impossible to divert my wayward thoughts away from him, so I might as well indulge myself while I'm in my own private Idaho.

My breath becomes shallow and slow as I softly caress every curve and fold. I don't insert a finger or try to stimulate my clitoris, I just stroke and massage all around the moist sensitive area, gliding my damp fingers through my pubic hair, and all over my receptive flesh. It's a relaxation technique rather than masturbation to climax. Truthfully, I never really climax anyway; never have

The rhythmic touching and stroking calm's me. When I begin to feel the first ripples of a delicious tingling sensation, I remove my hand and turn onto my side. Folding my arm beneath the pillow and closing my eyes, Silas' face is branded onto the inside of my eyelids. It won't dissipate so I stop trying to make it go away and decide I may as well enjoy the intimate, if impossible, fantasy my imagination has created.

Having soothed and relaxed, finding comfort in my own body, accepting the fact I can't dismiss Silas's image from my mind; I slowly but surely, drift away into oblivion and, as usual, I'm asleep in about ten seconds.

I jerk awake with a violent start. Perspiration has matted my hair; the sheet beneath me is damp and crumpled from where I've been tossing and turning in my sleep. My breathing is erratic, my heart is galloping wildly in my chest, pounding so fiercely against my breastbone I can practically hear every resounding beat. My nipples are erect, alive and buzzing with sensitivity. Looking down, I see they've been teased into stiff points by the light friction of the cotton bedsheet as I thrashed restlessly on the bed.

I'm confused, dazed and there's a demanding, pulsing pressure in my groin, where a few hours earlier, I had soothed myself with my fingers. Supporting myself on my left arm and bending my left knee I press my foot firmly into the mattress, attempting to alleviate the heavy throbbing, sensation in my groin. It doesn't help. The change in position only increases the sensitivity. My body instantly reacts to the slight movement. The muscles of my lower belly tighten, every shift increases the heaviness further, intensifying the throb, making me pant and writhe.

I'm in desperate need of relief. Tentatively and with trembling fingers, I reach down and begin to explore. Ever so tenderly, unsure of the sensation coursing through me, I lightly brush the sopping wet area with my fore and middle fingers. Just one light touch causes my stomach to clench and the muscles in my vagina to contract almost to the point of pain.

I try again. My breath is coming in short, sharp, juddering gasps now, as once again, I apply the lightest of pressure to the swollen, hooded button of nerves between my thighs. As soon as my probing fingers settle on that sensitive nub, my body goes into an immediate, rigid spasm. Unable to control it, I throw back my head in sheer, unadulterated ecstasy.

"Aghhh," I scream loudly into the darkness.

The sudden release of air from my burning lungs comes out in a loud, incoherent cry, my body convulsing and exploding into an unrestrained and unexpectedly fierce orgasm.

Gulping in lungsful of air, I writhe and pant through the rippling explosion. Exhaling a moan of unadulterated pleasure, gasping and breathless, I continue to rub and massage myself through the wonderful lingering sensation.

My fingers are moving relentlessly now, increasing in both speed and pressure, flicking and skittering across my clitoris. My vagina walls are pulling and pulsing with a need I don't recognise. They throb and contract, clutching at nothing but desperate for something.

Once again, I feel the tension in my body building; rising to the pinnacle. Hovering on the edge, I inhale a deep breath, holding it for a few seconds before finally letting go. Tumbling into freefall, I groan loudly as I pant through my second release, my body shaking and trembling with pure exhilaration.

Minutes pass - or it could be hours; who knows? I'm in a complete trance. Opening my eyes to the darkened room, I can narrowly see the flutter of the curtains.

As my breathing calms, I slow the movement of my hand; easing the pressure to a gentle stroke and caress, gradually bringing myself back down to earth.

Jesus! My head is ringing as the blood pounds through my ears, blocking all sound but that of my own ecstasy. Still panting, I remove my hand and flop back onto the pillow, totally spent. Awestruck, I stare blindly at the bedroom ceiling. Completely exhausted but totally satisfied, I'm in total amazement at what my body has just involuntarily done. I know I was stimulated when I went to sleep, but that has *never* happened before; either accidentally, or on purpose. Any kind of sexual activity has been something to avoid. To my mind, orgasms were always a myth, perpetuated to sell a belief, women enjoyed sex too. I'm completely stunned. Of course, I know the concept of wet dreams. And I've even seen the results on occasion, when David was going through puberty and I changed his bedsheets, poor love. But I never for one instant, believed that it could happen to a woman, least of all me... I don't dream!

Finally calming down, I instinctively look at my wrist for my watch to check the time. My hair is sticking to the back of my neck and my cooling skin feels clammy. There's only the faintest smattering of moonlight filtering through the window from outside; I can just about see, now my eyes have adjusted to the darkness. Of course, my watch isn't there.

Wrapping a protective hand around my wrist, I feel the feint ridge of scars under my fingers. The outline of my tattoo is slightly raised, and I trace each one of the delicate bumblebees. My mind recalls my vicious encounter with the wasp earlier this evening. Shifting a little, I manoeuvre my shoulder to test it. There's still a dull ache, but it's been obliterated by what I've just experienced.

Then, another memory drifts in; a rich, soft voice in my head. *'Oh, and in case you were wondering, you got it completely right Honeybee!'*

Holy Hell!

Silas' voice message. I shake the errant thought away and rub my eyes with the heels of my hands. *Is that the cause of all this? Over stimulation and a wasp sting?* I feel like I'm on drugs.

My breathing has finally returned to normal. It's still dark outside; the voile drape curtain billows gently as the breeze wafts in through the open window.

Leaning over to pick up my glass, I notice my broken watch on the nightstand. The fluorescent, green glow of the illuminated dial tells me it's three in the morning. Downing a deep draft of water to quench my now bone-dry mouth, and replacing the glass back on the table, I lie back, staring into the dark.

Well, that was ...what ...interesting ...confusing ...wonderful ... sensual, or just plain embarrassing? I settle on surprising and enjoyable.

Finally, able to rest I close my heavy eyes and begin to drift into sleep. I'm gone in ten seconds. I don't dream.

Chapter 13

Wednesday morning, and I arrive at work early. I was wide awake at six am. and decided a quick visit to the gym would help jettison the feeling of restlessness I woke up with. After a gruelling thirty minutes on the treadmill, and a few sets of squats and weights I'm feeling much calmer and surprisingly refreshed from my disturbed night's sleep. The burn on my shin looks less angry today and it's grown a nice fresh scab overnight.

It's another lovely sunny day so I've secured my hair into a ponytail again. The only evidence of my nocturnal activities - the vinegar coated plaster - came off my shoulder during the night and somehow became entangled in my hair. The white, gunky adhesive was sticking to my tresses like chewing gum. I had to soak it in the shower and then use the scissors to chop out the really matted bits. Now I've some additional wispy strands, which are too short to tie back. Otherwise, all is well. Even the pain from the sting has receded. All I have to show for the wasp assault is a slightly red shoulder.

Due to the early hour, I'm completely alone, so I make myself a mug of coffee and settle down to the tasks of the day. I need to prepare the interview questions for the next week and I've a meeting with Christina about a possible new client, which will be really lucrative if the deal comes off.

By lunchtime, I've had a thoroughly productive morning. In fact, everyone's been really busy today. I've even been honoured with a welcome visit from my canine friend, who sat on my feet until I found it too hot and had to move him. I enjoyed a quick chat with Spanners, when he came to fetch the flight information for tomorrow's client. But disappointingly, there's been no sign of Silas.

I'm beginning to wonder whether he's regretting inviting me to dinner, when Christina wanders into my office. She looks lovely in a fitted cream and blue floral summer dress - the customary gold chain is her only jewellery today, apart from the beautiful stainless-steel Breitling pilot's watch she's never without - that reminds me, I must get mine replaced. It's driving me nuts being without it. On reflex, I twist the leather thong on my wrist - I miss my watch.

We have a great meeting. She's updated me on the proposals presented to a potential client - a Celebrity Sports Agency - It's an extremely lucrative company, managing numerous well-known footballers and prominent sports stars. Apparently, the owner has some other business dealings besides the agency, which is his main concern at the moment, and by all accounts he's an extremely wealthy, though private man.

Christina has worked tirelessly on landing this contract for several weeks, gaining his trust, while simultaneously keeping the requirements of Tudor Charters her top priority. In simple terms, *Royal Tudor Charters* will offer exclusivity and privacy to all his clients, providing executive air travel around Europe as well as the occasional long-haul flight.

The terms and conditions of the agreement are favourable; we can still retain all our existing customers, as well as bid for further business. However, the new client will take priority, hence the exclusivity. It's a major transaction and if Christina can lock in the desired agreement, this addition to our portfolio of customers will provide *Tudor Charters* the means and security to purchase two additional private jets, *and* guarantee business continuity, security and publicity for the next five years at least.

I'm impressed and ridiculously excited. As part of my role in this venture, Christina has requested I administer the purchase of the two new aircraft. Although I'm fully qualified to do this, I'm nervous about the possibility until Christina ensures me, I won't be left totally to my own devices – Silas will be overseeing the process and supporting me at every step.

161

The afternoon flashes by at a ridiculous speed and before I know it, the day is gone. However, Silas is still conspicuous by his absence. Ignoring the pang of disappointment at not seeing him, I start packing my things in readiness for my meeting at The Beeches.

I wonder what David has done?

It's knocking on for five-thirty pm. I've been here since seven, so I'm flagging. With the day being so mad-busy, I didn't have time to eat my lunch; my stomach rumbles as if on cue. Because I'm not eating dinner until much later, it might be a good idea to have something now. There'll be tea and biscuits at *The Beeches*, but if I don't dull these hunger pangs, I know I'll end up scoffing the whole plateful and ruining my appetite.

Screwing up my nose in distaste, I unwrap the clingfilm from the ham salad bagel I made this morning and take a huge bite. It's squidgy and warm, and the salad has gone limp and slimy, but I could eat a mangy horse, so it tastes divine to me. Reluctant to put it down, I clench the half-eaten bagel between my teeth, freeing both hands and continue packing my stuff into my bag.

My subconscious mind senses I'm being watched. Looking up to see who's there, a thrill of heat flushes my face when I find it's Silas. He's blatantly standing in my office doorway. He has his thumbs hooked into his jean's pockets and an amused look on his handsome face. He almost fills the damn doorway.

Casually, he observes me as I attempt, completely unsuccessfully, to look non-pulsed by his looming presence; while at the same time, continuing to load my lap top and the rest of my belongings into my work bag. It doesn't help that I've a soggy, half eaten bagel clenched between my teeth!

"Good day?" he asks, on a raised eyebrow.

Pausing mid chew, I place my now packed bag on the chair and remove the bagel, chewing quickly to rid my mouth of the last bite. Swallowing too hurriedly, it goes down the wrong way

162

and I start coughing and spluttering. "Hmmm, Ugh." Trying to clear the crumbs from my throat, my eyes are streaming and I'm unable to form any coherent words. Nodding my head, *yes,* but wafting my hand in front of my face to indicate I can't talk, I rush over to the credenza and quickly pour myself a glass of water. Coughing again, I just about manage to clear the obstruction in my throat. "*Ugh,* that's better," I mumble, taking a swig of water so hastily, I missed my mouth and most of it dribbles down my chin onto my white t-shirt. "Shit!" I curse bending forward, plucking my top between my thumb and forefinger, trying to shake off the excess water.

So far, I've managed to successfully conduct my working day without any mishaps or accidents; only to arrive at the last couple of minutes where I've succeeded in becoming miss wet t-shirt!

"Bollocks!"

"Erm, you missed a bit!" Silas strolls into my office and over to where I'm standing, wiping my chin with my palm. Grinning all over his lovely face, he hands me a napkin from the small pile sitting on top of the credenza. "Here, this might help."

Narrowing my eyes and pursing my lips, I snatch the napkin out of his hands. "Thanks!" I grumble ungratefully. I'm completely unamused, and a bit miffed he obviously finds my clumsiness so comical. Dabbing the napkin down the front of my t-shirt, I'm hoping it will soak up the worst of the water, allowing the shirt to dry by the time I get to *The Beeches*. I won't have time to go home and change.

As Silas watches me try and sort myself out, he slips his hands in his pockets and takes a breath to speak, bringing my attention back to him. "I know you have that meeting tonight, but would you still like to have dinner with me later?"

"I…err…yeah." I'm a bit surprised. "I really don't know what it's about so I don't know how long I'll be there. But if you don't mind having a late dinner, I'm fine with it." I give him a weak smile. I thought he'd forgotten or changed his mind.

Removing a hand from his pocket, he takes the empty water glass from me and places it back on the tray. He doesn't look at me when he starts to speak. "Look, if you think you might be late, I don't mind cooking. I could come to the apartment; I'll make dinner and then I can give you the proper guided tour." Keeping his head down, he raises his eyes to me, seemingly unsure. "I mean, there's a lot more to see than just the apartment - and I'll feel I've neglected my duties as landlord if I don't at least show you the communal facilities."

He smiles softly straightening up and replacing his hand in his pocket. Just that one action has the rush of heat returning to my body. My face is burning from the look he's giving me and my tongue feels like lead in my mouth. I get the impression he's forcing himself to appear relaxed.

He's just offered to make me dinner!

He continues, "I'm not Gordon Ramsey but I can knock up a decent stir-fry. What do you say?"

"What about Bear?" I feel a little uncomfortable, I'm not accustomed to male attention or company, and this will be the second day in a row we've had dinner together. I don't like to admit it, but I found Bear's presence comforting. If it's just me and Silas, it would feel more intimate somehow, and I don't know how I'll cope with that.

"Oh, don't worry about him; I'll take him on a long run while you're at your meeting. He'll be asleep on my bed by the time I leave the house."

"Erm…" That wasn't what I meant.

He's pushing me and I can't figure out why. Surely, he can't be short of a date? "Now… is that okay? If you'd rather I didn't coming to the apartment, we can go out. I don't mind. What do you say?"

It feels strange but where's the harm in two new friends having dinner - especially if one of them can cook a mean stir-fry?

"I've not got anything to drink other than tea and orange juice. I'll need to call at an off-licence." I've no idea about wine and I'm secretly hoping he offers to pick that up too.

"I can do that," he relaxes immediately. "You just concentrate on your meeting and I'll see you later." He's still smiling. He glances at the water stain on my t-shirt but it is only a quick glance. I will myself not to do my tomato impression.

Embarrassed, but pretending not to be, I raise my eyebrows and shake my head. "Well, if you're sure. It would be nice to have someone cook for me and good to see the rest of the resident's facilities at the apartment," I acquiesce, "and as long as Bear's happy, I don't see why not." I break into a full smile now.

"Cool, it's a date then." Suddenly realising his mistake, he quickly back pedals, raising his hands in submission. "I mean, it's not a date, date… it's a dinner date… oh you know what I mean." Flustered, he turns to leave, "see you later. I'll be there at about nine, so if the lights are on don't panic; it's me being a culinary genius, or the fire brigade has been called because I've burned the water or something." He's stuttering and stumbling over himself. It's funny so I laugh, shooing him away.

"See you later, '*Mr Ramsay*'!" I give him a cheery wave as he leaves. Indulging myself, I watch him through the window jogging to his Range Rover. Bear is waiting patiently in the driver's seat but soon moves to shot-gun, when he sees Silas approaching. Opening the door he climbs in, and I watch, fascinated, as he fastens his seatbelt, covers his eyes with his aviators and executes the perfect reverse turn before driving out of the gates.

Hmmm! I could watch him move all day long!

Hastily checking the time on my office clock, I need to get a shift on if I'm going to get to *The Beeches* for seven, so I perform my own departure routine; setting the alarms, locking the doors, before driving out of the compound and heading off towards my meeting about God knows what.

My stomach seems full of nervous knots; is it my pending meeting or the impromptu dinner that's causing it?

Chapter 14

Turning into the gravel driveway of *The Beeches*, bang on seven pm; there's still a few cars in the car park so I drive round to the overflow.

Taking a sneaky-peek through the conservatory window, I can see some of the residents engaged in various activities, but I don't immediately see David. Shaking my head and taking a breath for courage, I jog round to the entrance, my feet crunching on the gravel stones as I go.

There's no need for me to ring the bell; Mark's waiting in the porch holding the door open for me.

"Hiya, sorry if I'm a bit late," I wince breathlessly and duck inside.

"Oooh, that's you in detention. See me after class." He puts on a stern face and wags his finger at me in jest. "Take a seat in the waiting room and I'll be there in a jiff - I just need to let the staff know I'm in a meeting." Closing the door, he walks away to the communal lounge to speak to his colleagues.

After signing in, I traipse through to the waiting room where an elderly couple sit stiffly, side by side. The man is cross legged with one arm draped casually over the back of the woman's chair. A sliver of a red tartan sock is visible at his ankle. She's sat poker straight; feet planted firmly on the floor, her knuckles white where they're clutching tightly at the straps of the patent leather handbag resting on her lap.

They both glance up at me as I take a seat opposite them. The man smiles and nods a greeting, but the lady throws me a glare that could curdle milk.

What's her problem?

"Good evening… evening…hello," I say quietly nodding in their direction.

I wonder what they're here for?

Mark's quip about detention creeps into my mind and I bite my lip, so as not to laugh out loud. They really do look like they're waiting for the headmaster!

"Evening," the man says, in an upper-crust, home-counties accent. He's smartly dressed in burgundy cords, and a blue and red dogtooth checked shirt, topped off with a dapper mustard coloured tweed blazer. It crosses my mind the weather might be a tad warm for tweed but he must be pushing seventy; perhaps he feels the cold.

The woman purses her lips and gives him a disdainful look, then returns her glare back to me. She's similarly well-groomed, in a lilac floral dress and summer sandals. She's also wearing a jacket, in pale mint green, which complements beautifully the lilac flowers of her dress. She also looks around seventy. She doesn't speak to me, just returns her critical gaze back to the office door.

Definitely detention!

Feeling untidy and crumpled, I smooth my hair and sit straighter in my seat, waiting for Mark to return and rescue me. Thankfully I don't have to wait for long.

"Right then, thank you for waiting." Mark rubs his hands together as he hustles towards us. His smile is genuine enough, but I detect a hint of nervousness as he nods at the woman – who gives an audible sniff, still refusing to acknowledge me. "We should be okay for a while. If you would come with me, it'd be better to talk in my office." I look at the old dears, but they remain seated. Mark is addressing me, so I rise to my feet and meekly follow behind him.

He closes the door behind us and takes a seat behind his desk, gesturing for me to sit in one of the chairs opposite. This's uncharacteristically formal for Mark and I'm really curious now; who are those people and why are we here together.

Mark, quickly puts me out of my misery. "Edi, the couple outside are Frank and Jean Prestage. I've asked them here today because this concerns them as well." I look at him blankly. I've no idea who those people are. Their names mean nothing to me. I just shrug my shoulders and shake my head.

"Edi, Jean and Frank are Wendy's parents." I'm still none the wiser so I continue looking at him, waiting for him to elaborate further. "You met Wendy. Remember? Last time you were here; she was the young lady helping me wash up after lunch." He looks at me expectantly with raised eyebrows.

Finally, the penny drops; "*Ahh*, oh, yes I remember," I smile nodding. "She was lovely." But shaking my head hesitantly, "what does this have to do with me?" *Oh, my goodness - I hope I didn't do anything to upset her?* Casting my mind back to last weekend; I don't recall anything untoward.

"Well... it isn't really about you as such. It's to do with David." He looks at me, holding my eyes, searching for some sort of recognition. He seems calm enough, so I can't imagine this is a major issue. But I've absolutely no idea what he's on about. "Hmmm," he goes on. "When you were here last weekend, did David mention anything to you about Wendy at all?"

I'm suddenly on the defence, my protective instinct kicking in big-time. "No, why, what's happened. What did they say he's done?" I gesture to the door in the direction of the elderly couple waiting outside.

"No, no, don't be alarmed. He hasn't done anything. It's just, well," his body language remains relaxed and open - he's well trained - he takes a deep breath... "as you know, we've a policy when a resident has a visitor to their room, they've to leave the door open."

I nod, yes, I'm aware of this. It's a good rule, it's for their protection.

"Well…" Mark continues, "David had a visitor, but the door was closed."

"Oh?" I'm still puzzled. David would never deliberately break thr rules. Surely Mark knows this?

"Edi, the visitor was Wendy." He scratches his forehead before leaning forward in his chair and clasping his hands together on his desk, his fingers forming a bridge under his chin.

"Oh!" I say again, taken aback this time. David *has* broken the protocol rules. He's had a girl in his room - with the door closed. "Is he in trouble? I can speak to him if you like," I say relieved. It's a small matter I can sort out easily.

"Well… Edi, it isn't quite that simple." His gaze remains steady, taking another deep breath, he goes on. "When one of the support staff noticed the door closed, they knocked and entered the room but David and Wendy weren't there."

Weren't there? Now I'm confused.

"Look, there's really no easy way to say this… the care assistant caught David and Wendy in bed together."

Boom!!

Mark sighs and leans back in his chair; once again his body language is open and relaxed, but there's a ripple of concern in his expression.

"What!" I gasp, winded in shock. I can't think of what to say. Mark senses my rising panic and continues swiftly.

"It was completely consensual. There was nothing forced or sinister about it," he's quick to explain – trying to quell my alarm. "They're just two young people who are exploring their boundaries." He goes quiet, giving me some time to absorb; allowing it to sink in, then continues. "I know this must be a huge shock to you."

"Err…" I choke my response, "yeah, just a little bit!" Shocked is an understatement - I'm gobsmacked.

170

"It was a bit of a shock to us as well to be honest," he smiles at the thought. "They were very discreet... look... this isn't the first time a relationship has developed between residents, but it's the first time one's got... physical."

"I don't know what to say." My mind's reeling at the thought of David and Wendy having sex. Shaking my head, I try and dispel the worrying image, my alarm growing when I consider the elderly couple outside.

"Do Wendy's parents know?" remembering the frosty reception from Mrs Prestage, I fear the worst.

"Well, yes..." Mark says. "I spoke to them earlier, before you arrived." *I'm glad I wasn't here for that!* "They insisted, they wanted to stay and meet you."

I bet they did.

Lord knows how I'd feel if the shoe was on the other foot, and I was the girl's mother and some randy little git had taken advantage.

"I think it might be a good idea... you know, given the circumstances." He's guarded.

Suddenly I feel the urge to giggle... this is so unexpected.

"Yeah, circumstances." I shake my head and bite my lip. Desperately trying to push back the inappropriate laugh threatening to erupt at any moment. "Have you spoken to David? What did he say; does he know it's wrong? Is he in trouble? God, is he going to be thrown out?"

They can't throw him out! What would I do then? I'd have to quit my job... I'd lose the apartment... what about Silas?

Suddenly, it doesn't seem quite so funny. My mind is reeling with a million questions and reactions. *My little boy, he's only seventeen for God's sake!*

"*No,* no Edi...look, calm down." Mark raises his hands in an attempt to calm me. "Look... we're not about to tell them what

171

they did was wrong. On the contrary, there's nothing *wrong* in what they did," he's insistent. "No... absolutely nothing will happen. In the eyes of the law, they're consenting adults. It's a bit uncommon, but if you think about it, it's really natural behaviour." Mark is desperately trying to reassure me. "David doesn't see what all the fuss is about and Wendy, well, quite frankly... Wendy's over the moon."

"Hah! ... and under the bedclothes, apparently," I snipe uncharitably.

Mark ignores my sarcasm. "I'm telling you, they're deliriously happy, totally devoted - in love in fact." He relaxes back in his seat and watches me as I try to calm myself, absorbing it all in. I sense he really wants to show his delight in the situation and is waiting for my reaction.

"What will happen?" I look at him. *In love!...* I know my face is a picture of worry and concern. *God, what if she gets pregnant! What do I say to her parents?* I drop my head into my hands and groan. "God, this can't be happening!"

Unable to contain his glee any longer, I hear him give a slight chuckle.

Snapping my head up in disbelief, I hiss, "I'm pleased you find this funny!".

He just shakes his head mildly, "Edi, please look at this rationally. They're not hurt, or hurting anybody; in fact, they're *very, very* happy." *Happy!* "I wish *I* was that happy... the only difference between them and the next pair of randy teenagers is that they've Downs Syndrome. It really isn't a huge deal." I think he's frustrated with me. "I thought you, of all people, would be able to think logically and calmly about this - once you get over the initial shock that is." *Logically and calmly?* "I was banking on you helping Mr and Mrs Prestage through it."

Jeez, thanks Mark!

"Yes... David and Wendy have been caught red-handed, but to be honest, I'm really happy for them... If you think about it, it's rather wonderful." He's making complete sense of course. The only thing I've ever wanted for David is for him to be happy and content. How much happier could he be? He's in love apparently!

"Yeah, I'm...it's...I'm a bit shocked I suppose. But, yes, you're right. It *is* wonderful." The urge to giggle is back... *My boy's in love!* "What happens now though?" Wondering why David didn't confide in me, I pull on the sleeves of my t-shirt, gathering my resolve. I need to get practical in order to process this.

"Well, nothing really... we could supervise them more closely but that won't prevent them from having sex." He's in his stride, but I cringe at his casualness. "In fact, why should we stop them? My gut instinct would be to let this ride. They're both quite young. Wendy's only twenty-five and David is seventeen so it's still all new to them."

You're telling me... as of this morning, I was under the impression David still thought it was for peeing through!

"We'll educate them on being safe," he continues. "With your permission, we'll arrange for someone from family planning to meet with them. And as is our responsibility, we'll council them on the appropriate way to behave in company. But to be honest, as I said already, they're extremely discreet and respectful of the other residents. If they continue, then there's nothing to say they shouldn't eventually move into a shared apartment and live together. Or if it doesn't, and it all fizzles out, then they just stay where they are and it will all blow over naturally."

He really does sound like he's thought it all through. "My main concern at the moment is Wendy's parents," his face crumples. "They haven't taken it very well at all." He frowns; I can tell he's troubled more by their reaction than by the actual situation.

173

"They've very old-fashioned views where their daughter is concerned."

"Phew... Quite!"

We sit quietly for a few moments allowing me time for it to sink in. I give myself a mental pep talk. Yes, it's a lot to digest. Yes, this is a bit of a shock, but he's a healthy seventeen year old boy with all the urges of any other seventeen-year-old boy. He's in a safe environment. He's met and fallen in love with a lovely girl and while it might be unconventional, it certainly isn't unusual.

Suddenly, I feel very happy and proud of my son. A smile lights my face and I heave a sigh of relief; pleased at the way my thoughts have processed all this information. Straightening my shoulders, I make my decision. I look directly at Mark and grin. "Well, if this is what makes him happy, I will do everything in my power to help them. What do you need me to do?"

Mark's reciprocating smile is wide and genuine. Clearly he's both delighted and relieved at my reaction,. which makes me all the more determined to be a supportive mum.

"Okay," he sighs, "now for the impossible part. Mrs Prestage is understandably furious with us, with David and with you, for that matter." He points a finger at me, grinning in irony.

"We're all held responsible in her eyes. Wendy's totally innocent," rolling his eyes in exasperation. "She just refuses to accept that Wendy's a grown woman with a woman's urges and a mind of her own. She's convinced herself David has taken advantage." I can't say I'm surprised.

"Mr Prestage on the other hand has a different view. Whilst he's shocked at the shenanigans, he's not quite as appalled as his wife. In fact, I've a sneaky suspicion he might be secretly on our side - but he's terrified of his missus!" *Really! I'd never have guessed!*

"We've a job on our hands, Edi. Mrs P's threatening to remove Wendy from *The Beeches,* but I know that would be a disastrous move for all concerned. Together we need to try and convince her otherwise; she needs to know we can support this lovely young couple in their relationship, rather than punish them with separation. The burning question is, how?"

I see his dilemma and give it thought. "Has she actually met David?" It would be a good place to start.

"No, I didn't think that'd be wise at this time."

Maybe he's right... but... "Why not though? If she met him... you know... saw how lovely they are together and how happy Wendy is, it might help. Surely that would be a good thing?"

Mark purses his lips and raises his steepled fingers, tapping them against his lips, in thought. "Perhaps, but I don't think a formal introduction would be the best way forward just yet. I don't want handbags at dawn. But I'd support an *'accidental'* observation."

I sense a cunning plan forming. "What if..." Mark adds, miming quotation marks, "Mr and Mrs P. were to, '*accidentally,'* see David and Wendy together, engaged in some benign activity. You know... just having fun in each other's company. That might help." He wiggles his eyebrows conspiratorially.

I'm on board immediately. "Yes, yes...I know what you mean. If they just saw how happy and innocent this all is, it might bring them round a little." I'm enthused by his sneakiness! "We just have to make them understand... how hard can it be?"

Chapter 15

It took a bit of persuading, but eventually Mrs Prestage was calm enough to agree to meeting David - with Wendy - on supervised visits, so she could observe them together. Though how that's going to stop them going at it like rabbits as soon as our backs are turned, I've no idea. But if it provides her with some little comfort, then I'm all for it.

I smile to myself. My lovely boy has a lovely girl. Just the thought of them together, so happy, warms my heart.

It's dark and I'm not used to negotiating the drive back to the apartment in daylight, never mind at night-time. But I find the apartments without too much trouble and pull into my parking space. I notice Silas' Range Rover and a little shiver of anticipation runs through me.

Wait 'till I tell him what's happened. I'm sure he'll find it amusing... checking myself; I can't tell him everything, not yet anyway. It's a lot to take in. I'll give him the finer details – no need to elaborate.

Entering the apartment, I drop my keys onto the console table. Every time I come through the door it affects me the same as it did the first time. I'm still completely in awe with the stunning luxury of this place.

Now it's evening, the variable mood lighting has adjusted to reflect the time of day. It's subtle and ambient, immediately softening the shadows. The beautiful crystal wall lights are twinkling gently, bathing the stunning white furniture with a warm golden glow and inviting my weary body to sink into the deep sumptuous leather. The pillar candles on the mantle are lit, their flickering flames enhancing the relaxing mood.

Resisting the temptation to collapse onto the nearest sofa, I sigh on recognising the dulcet tones of Ella Fitzgerald's *Satin*

Doll filtering through the sound system. I love this song, it reminds me of when I was little and had dance lessons.

"Hello?"

"I'm in the kitchen," the music volume lowers, he must've turned it down.

"I'm just going to the loo." I inwardly cringe. *He really didn't need to know that.*

Darting through to the bathroom I lock the door. I'm desperate for a pee. I had three cups of coffee at *The Beeches* and I'm feeling uncomfortable now, after the drive home.

Suitably relieved, I have a quick cat-lick to freshen up then enter the walk-in closet. I need to change my top; this one's decidedly grubby and crumpled after wearing it all day. Choosing a yellow vest, which I don't think is actually mine… it's too small for Sammy and too yellow for Lizzy, so I'm presuming it's an unwanted impulse buy, donated to me… I pull it on. The neckline is indecent, leaving absolutely nothing to the imagination, so I contort myself, shortening the adjustable straps to a more respectable length. Once done, I drag the bobble from my hair and give it a violent brushing, tying it up again to hide the chopped off pieces. Checking myself in the mirror, I'm no Mona Lisa but I'll do.

"I thought you'd run out on me," he teases as I stroll into the kitchen. He has his back to me so I can admire his physique at my leisure.

"That smells great, I'm starving." My stomach growls in agreement as I mount one of the high-stools at the breakfast bar.

Looking around the spotless kitchen, I see the beautiful peonies are drooping a little, their heavy-headed blooms pulling at the flimsy stems; they'll need fresh water tomorrow. The flowers remind me I really need to check in with the girls. When I dropped them off at Heathrow, we promised we would keep in regular contact, but I've been so distracted over the past couple of days they've scarcely crossed my mind and I'm suddenly flooded with guilty selfishness.

On reflex, I go to check the time on my watch, before once again remembering it's broken. I touch the leather thong on my wrist, circling my fingers around the unfamiliar band, fidgeting with the stud that fastens the bracelet. It's a nervous habit. The girls — I hope they're okay. I'll call them after dinner.

"Red or white?" he asks, pulling me out of my daydream. Flashing a cheeky smile, he respectively holds up the two bottles, raising an eyebrow in turn to indicate which bottle.

"Hmm? Ooh, red please." I much prefer red to white though in truth I know very little about either.

"Good choice," he pours from the already open bottle and hands me a glass. "Salute!" He chinks my glass.

"Chin-chin," I say back, grinning.

I can do Italian too mister!

I take a sip of my wine. It's blood-warm on my tongue and immediately my mouth waters with the lushness of the bouquet, my taste buds instantly recognising ripe fruity blackberries.

"Mmm, that's delicious," I sigh in appreciation. "What type of wine is it?"

Ella is now crooning *'They can't take that away from me'*.

Stunning.

"Yes, it is nice isn't it... it's a Stemmari Sicilian Pinot Noir. Hope you like it - it's one of my favourites."

Expertly, he swirls the dark red liquid. Tilting the glass so the wine is almost horizontal, he positions his nose to the rim of the glass, then, closing his eyes, he deeply inhales the bouquet. Keeping his eyes closed, he moves the glass to his lush lips and takes a practiced sip; holding the wine in his mouth momentarily

178

to fully savour the rich flavour, before swallowing it down. "Mmm!" he hums in appreciation.

The whole performance is mesmerizing. I watch, enraptured as his Adams-apple bobs with the swallow; stretching the dark skin taught, and accentuating the fine stubble on his chin and neck, drawing my eye to his beautiful throat.

Mmm, yes very nice.

"Mmm," I mimic him, taking another welcome sip.

The wine *is* mouth-wateringly good, even to my uneducated palate. All I know about wine is it comes in three colours and is usually either sweet or dry. I feel under scrutiny. It's his turn to watch closely now as I take another taste. Unable to read his expression… perhaps he thinks I'm bluffing, I hold the wine in my mouth, just as he did, before swallowing. All the while, his dark eyes study me.

"I love it," I confirm, taking another too-large gulp.

Silas swallows, performs a small headshake, then lazily blinks his eyes before sighing. *What?… I mean it, the wine is lovely.*

"Dinner will be ready in five, I hope you like stir-fry chicken?"

Placing his glass on the granite worktop, he quickly turns to face the cooker, where several sizzling and steaming pans are omitting some delicious smells.

Perching on my bar-stool, I continue to sip my wine. His back is to me, so I admire his broad shoulders and narrow waist. He's dressed casually, in dark blue denim jeans, which emphasize the contour of his fine firm behind, and a black, fitted V-neck t-shirt, which does exactly the same for his well-defined biceps. Even the starched white pinny with the frilly edges can't detract from the view. Sneaking a look at his feet, he's wearing tan leather boat shoes with a dark blue trim and leather laces. No visible socks. He really knows how to dress.

As I hum along to the low dulcet tones of Ella, a thought strikes me. "I didn't know you liked music." *That sounds stupid!* "I mean, you never have music on in your car."

"Broken," is his simple one-word reply. He's adding to the wok and stirring and shaking, the sight is doing things for me... the sizzling of the food blends with the sound of the jazz perfectly. "Actually, I love music, especially jazz and blues. Ella is the queen of Jazz. I hope you don't mind?"

He adds some soy sauce, then picks up a packet of fresh egg noodles, opening them and adding them to the wok. The aroma is divine.

"No, I adore Ella." I really do. "But my absolute favourite's Claire Teal. She's amazing, a true Yorkshire lass. Swing and Jazz all rolled into one. I'm not too keen on all that 'Trad' stuff. It's beyond my understanding but I love a mellow sound."

"Yeah? Can't say I know her stuff... you'll have to educate me..."

Yes, Claire Teal, Steve Tyrell and Jamie Cullum, I really like. In fact, my musical taste is quite varied, usually driven by my mood. "I don't mind things like Muse and Bat for Lashes. I've even been known to listen to Coldplay occasionally." I don't miss his slight grimace at that last revelation. "I'm into lots of different stuff really. At Uni, I learned to tolerate most genres over the three years I was there."

I'm happy enough to talk about music. The fact he didn't have any in his car worried me, but now I know it's because the radio is broken, I'm relieved. I wonder why he hasn't got it fixed?

"Tea-up!" My plate lands on the counter in front of me. It smells amazing and looks even better. No pre-packed supermarket special here - everything looks fresh and crisp - all brightly coloured and home chopped. Noodles and stir-fry, what more can a girl ask for? "We'll eat this and then I'll show you around." Picking up his fork, he takes a mouthful, chewing lazily, and I do likewise.

"Yum, looks delicious," I take a fork full, it tastes delicious too.

We sit in companionable quiet for a couple of minutes while we eat; listening to the soothing sound of Ella and sipping the fabulous wine. Silas is the first to break the silence.

"So, what was the big emergency?"

Looking up at me through his long eyelashes (I hadn't noticed them before!) he carries on eating, waiting for my reply.

The big emergency? Oh, I'd almost forgotten…

Resting my fork on the side of my plate, I pick up my wine and take a sip; composing my answer trying not to give too much away. Here goes nothing…

"Hmm, well, yes… promise you won't judge."

With his mouth full, he completes a 'cross my heart gesture' with his free hand.

"Well, if you must know… my wonderful son has been caught shagging a girl in his room!" I blurt.

He chokes on his noodles. "Hah!" His laugh is a sudden, loud bark, booming rich and low. It bubbles up from the depth of his chest. The sudden loudness of it startles me.

"*You promised…*" I wail, desperately trying to suppress my own mirth. But it's pointless… continuing to chortle, he drops his fork and it clatters onto the worktop. He tries to swallow his mouthful of food but struggles against his laughter, causing him to choke and splutter. Grabbing his wineglass, he attempts to take a drink as he reins in his laughter, whilst eyeing me with a look of amused shock.

Swallowing his wine and coughing a bit more he thumps his chest with the side of his fist to help clear the obstruction from his throat. "God, Edi, I didn't expect that!" He starts laughing again, a low chuckle this time as I stare straight-faced at him. I don't know what to do so I pick my fork up in silence and continue eating, a distraction to hide my embarrassment.

Stabbing at a mange tout and biting it in half, I wait patiently for him to gather himself.

"I'm sorry…" he coughs, "sorry! That was just too funny!" I frown at him. He's calmer but I can tell he's still bubbling – the amusement clearly visible below the surface – just waiting to explode. "I was expecting fighting or maybe cheating on exams … not shagging!"

He starts to laugh again, deep and hearty. It makes me twist my fork in my noodles and bite down hard on my lower lip in an attempt to hide my own amusement. But it's no good; eventually, I succumb to my own laughter, joining him in his mirth and dropping my fork again so I can cover my red-hot face with my hands. It *is* funny, I suppose, but he doesn't understand the full reason why. Especially Mrs. Frosty-knickers-Prestage. Now *she* was a challenge.

Wiping my weeping eyes with the backs of my hands I explain a little more. "If you think that's funny, I had to meet the girl's parents tonight as well. That was a total joy… not!" I give a sardonic grin as I elaborate.

"Hah, hah, hah… no way…!" He's crying.

Silas laughs even harder when I tell him about Mr. and Mrs. P. and their not-so-warm reception towards me. It's such a relief to be able to share. And the more I share, the more he seems to enjoy my tale. The more he enjoys my tale, the more my confidence grows. I'm becoming quite animated, waving my hands in the air, trying to make the story seem more interesting and amusing than it actually was.

He's an appreciative audience, enjoying my performance, continuing to watch me intently as he finishes his food;

intermittently, interjecting short bursts of laughter at the occasional punchline, giving me my moment; alternating between bites of stir-fry and appreciative sips of the lovely wine - never once removing his dark eyes from my face.

He's got such a lovely infectious laugh, and he looks so relaxed when he smiles. A marked difference from the stern, gruff boss-man I met on Monday.

Engrossed in my embellished delivery of this vaguely interesting tale I almost forget myself and give it all away when he asks why the college was so concerned.

"Surely it goes on all the time with students?"

Unconvincingly, I manage to rescue the situation by making up some story about boys and girls not being allowed in each other's dorms. It seems to do the trick and in the grand scheme of things it wasn't a complete untruth.

Chapter 16

With the story over and food gone, we sip more wine and watch each other attentively. The warmth in his glittering eyes and the intensity of his gaze have me believing he's interested. But I'm so wary of getting close to anyone, it causes me to fidget.

The absurdity of an office romance, especially with my boss has me blushing again and those wayward thoughts filter back into my mind; the vivid memory of our brief conversation last night, and my body's nocturnal, involuntary reaction to the wasp sting and his teasing have me shifting uncomfortably on my barstool.

This is dangerous ground for me. Over the years I've worked so hard on my outer veneer, transforming myself, building walls and erecting barricades. Creating my new character, a façade of a hardworking, single mum. Perhaps a bit frumpy, not too concerned about her appearance. Not inviting, needing or wanting any form of male attention. Oh yes, the illusion is so perfect, so real, I almost believe it myself.

Ironically, I didn't intentionally go out of my way to make myself unattractive by ignoring all the things that would enhance my appearance. It just happened - make-up free days became weeks, then months then the norm. No flattering haircuts or highlights - I couldn't afford it for a start. No facials, manicures or pedicures and certainly no designer clothes, shoes or accessories - just a plain-Jane, every day, working mum.

But the way Silas is looking at me now, it's as if he can see right through my protective outer shell and into my soul. His elbows are resting on the counter. The rim of his wineglass is brushing against his full lover lip, which still bears the faint ghost of a smile; intent, intense, intrigued. Is there a hint of recognition perhaps?

"Who are you Edi?" he whispers against his glass; his candid curiosity startles me, it's a question that I've no answer to, not yet anyway. So, I just sit, staring back, a little bewildered, a little bewitched and more than a little bothered. My lack of reply causes him to shake himself out of his reverie.

"Never mind," sighing he tips his head to the side, pushing his stool back so he has room to stand and places his empty glass on the counter. He moves so gracefully for such a big man. My mind starts to wander. What would it feel like to be kissed by those luscious full lips? I can't seem to help it and my shameless thoughts have me blushing again. Desperately keeping a tight rein, I get to my feet and dither about, collecting the plates and cutlery, throwing myself into this mundane task, attempting to keep my mind from its inappropriate wonderings.

The subtle shift in the atmosphere has unnerved me a little. I need to change the mood, but gathering up the plates and cutlery and walking to the other side of the kitchen, deliberately keeping the central island between us as a barricade, won't help!

"That was delicious. I didn't realise I was so hungry. You're a great cook."

My voice sounds high pitched and wary. I stack the plates on the worktop next to the kitchen sink. Rinsing them under the hot tap, I waste some time arranging them inside the dishwasher. I do the same with the cutlery; all the while Silas stands, side-on, one hand leaning on the island, the other resting loosely in his jeans pocket. He's watching my every move, intently, as if he's searching for cracks in my armour. I'm nervous and feel under scrutiny, as if any minute he'll see who I really am.

As I'm closing the dishwasher Silas uses the opportunity to traverse the boundary of the kitchen island. Picking up the half-full bottle, he tops up our wine. He's already circumnavigated the island and is now stood in front of me, lazily leaning against the makeshift barrier. He hands me my glass, still scrutinizing my face closely. It's very unsettling.

"Are you ready for something sweet?" he asks me just as I take a sip of wine. Widening my eyes, I choke quietly as I swallow; does he mean dessert... or something else?

"Like what?" I return skeptically; where's he going with this?

"Well, I thought, as it's been such a warm day, we could have some ice cream. I promised you a tour of the communal areas so we can walk and eat at the same time."

Ice cream? That wasn't what I expected at all. His face has mischief written all over it as he pulls open the freezer and takes out two chocolate covered Magnums. Removing the wrappers from both and holding them up in front of me, "white or dark chocolate?" he asks. More inuendo?

"Oh, dark every time!" I purr, unable to resist the overtone. I smile demurely, taking the dark chocolate Magnum from his fingers and popping it into my mouth. The outer shell of the bitter chocolate makes a satisfying crack as I sink my teeth into it. Watching me with raised brows he grins, shakes his head, then chuckles again. He mirrors my actions with his white chocolate ice-cream, giving me a flash of his straight white teeth. The stark contrast of the milky white chocolate against his dark lips is distracting and so sexy I turn my back, hiding my heated stare!

This is stupid. One minute I'm nervous, timid and shy. The next I'm acting like a confident floosy – dropping unsubtle hints and batting my eyelashes. It's ridiculous. Even I'm confused at my conflicting behaviour. I'm grateful when my personal phone distracts me, the chime indicates I've a text message.

"Mmm, delicious; you going to get that? It might be the shagger!" he says, indicating to my phone with his ice-cream. I tut and give him a *'seriously'* look, removing myself from his overbearing presence for a couple of minutes. He really does take up a lot of room.

Picking up my phone I stroll into the lounge nibbling my Magnum, crunching through the bitter chocolate to get to the creamy, vanilla centre and call up the text messages. There's a text from Lizzy and a fuzzy photo of what appears to be Grand Central Station.

'Hiya, we're on our way to Washington. We're SOOO over N.Y.C.! ⬛ *I'm going to facetime you, so be prepared! Love ya,*

L & S. Xxx'

Just as I'm typing out my reply the phone chimes again. It's an invitation to FaceTime, so I click the icon and await the link to go live. As I'm waiting, Silas strolls into the lounge and peers over my shoulder. It's a perfectly timed manoeuvre, just as the phones make their connection. He's standing incredibly close to me, so close in fact that his chin's almost resting on my shoulder, and I feel his ice-cream-chilled breath breezing my ear. It makes my back straighten and the fine hairs on my arms stand up.

I'm just about to tell him off for invading my personal space and privacy, when the FaceTime window opens and Lizzy's pretty face pops up on the screen, grinning like a loon. With the screen this close, I can see the sun has encouraged her freckles to appear, peppering her smooth complexion - she looks stunning. Healthy, glowing sun-kissed skin, shiny blonde hair and gleaming white teeth, hair tied up in cute pigtails, she's wearing an off-the-shoulder blue and white gingham blouse, which enhances the turquoise blue of her sparkling eyes. She could be a cat-walk model on vacation.

"Hiya...," she yells loudly. "... Whoa, who the *fuck* is that?" Lizzy - ever the lady - blurts on the screen, just as Silas' face becomes visible over my shoulder in the small square at the bottom of the picture. Within half a second her facial expressions run a complete repertoire of emotions; from bursting with excitement then morphing into complete and utter shock at the dark and mysterious stranger standing behind me; finally, I see it shift fleetingly to curiosity, before eventually settling on child-like wonder.

187

"LIZZY!!" I'm mortified. "This is my boss… Silas… I mean… Mr. Tudor!" I can't think of anything to explain the late hour. She's so dizzy, she probably won't even notice the time difference.

"Oops, sorry!" She makes an apologetic face and raises her hand so we can see her wave at the screen. "Nice to meet you Sirius… I'm Lizzy and this is Sam… Sam, say hello to Sirius." She waves the phone in Sammy's face.

Sam, as ever, is distracted. It looks like she's a bit frustrated, puzzling over the train timetable in her hand, she absently lifts her eyes to the screen for the briefest of moments to greet me. "Hiya Edi! Hiya Sirius!" She mutters absently. Sam comes into view then her eyes widen in disbelief as she sees the screen, but she soon disappears as Lizzy swings the phone back to her own grinning face. As the phone arcs back around, I get a quick three-sixty view of what appears to be thousands of people jostling and bustling past them where they're stood in the middle of the station concourse, causing an obstruction to the flow.

Distantly, I hear Sammy's shrill voice, but can't make out a word she's saying. She's drowned out by the distorted echo of the platform announcer coming out of the public-address system. The brief glimpse I had of the station, as Lizzy swung the phone, confirms it's heaving with passengers. I'm not happy; this was obviously a rushed decision to call me and they've little or no regard for their personal safety in such a busy, crowded place.

Frowning at both the misunderstanding of Silas's name and the obvious commotion in the station I shout a bit too loudly back. "It's Silas, not Sirius! I'm sorry Silas… they can be really annoying sometimes…" I briefly turn my attention towards Silas, who is waving at the camera while sucking on his ice cream … he's as bad as they are. "They're in New York and a bit giddy," I explain. Turning my attention back to Lizzy, "it looks ridiculously busy there, are you being careful? Please take care. Don't get distracted!" I'm scolding and worried at the same time.

"Isn't it brilliant? Its rush hour." She's breathy with wonder, and far more excited than she should be at the prospect of being crushed to death by a marauding herd of stampeding commuters. "Look, they've just announced our train's due in ten minutes, so we need to get to the platform... but I'll call you tomorrow." She's not looking at me as she speaks; she's staring right at Silas, with a huge grin and wide blue eyes. In the background, Sammy's behaving like a demented kangaroo, hopping around trying to get a look in. She's being buffeted by a constant stream of passengers as they career through Grand Central. It's utter madness. The background noise is deafening and the hustle and bustle of the station is making it impossible to have any kind of meaningful conversation. We'll have to give it up as a bad job.

"Try to ring from somewhere a bit quieter next time," I yell. She's not paying me a blind bit of attention.

"Have a lovely evening... byeee!" I see Sammy wave her hand over Lizzy's shoulder as Lizzy tilts and waves the phone from side to side in an aminated goodbye.

The image freezes, mid wave, leaving them in a slanted, blurred image; but before the connection breaks and the screen goes completely black, I can still hear them shrieking and squealing - the voice disconnection has a delay. The station announcer has finally shut up but that only means Sammy's voice is loud and clear when she exclaims, *"Sirius, is she fucking kidding... Sirius Black... like in Harry fucking Potter! He's the real thin...."* Thankfully the line goes dead and I hear no more of her dulcet tones. I close my eyes in exasperation - I can't believe she said that. Mortified, I turn to face the music. I'm surprised at what I see.

Silas is grinning all over his lovely face. "Well, now that's done with, shall we take the tour?" Clearly, he's thoroughly amused at my embarrassment. Not in the least bit offended, he obviously heard everything and is not one bit bothered by it - thank God!

"I don't know who they were, and I'm sure it is worth knowing but the explanation can wait." Taking the phone from my hand he drops it onto the white sofa where it bounces once on the springy cushion before settling down. He holds out his free palm to me, "Shall we?"

I don't know if this is an indication to take his hand but I decide it would be a bad idea, so I treat it as an invitation for me to lead the way. He twists his lips in amusement as I do, bowing from the waist in mock gallantry as I waft past. Then, straightening to his full height, he places his warm palm in the small of my back as he guides me to the front door, opening it and waving me through.

Exiting the apartment, I stand waiting for him in the hallway as he pulls the door firmly shut and pockets his key; I notice he's set the alarm. Making the decision for me, he indicates towards stairs. "After you, madam!" We descend the stairs like two little kids eating ice cream on a school outing.

When we land in the foyer, it's gone dark outside and apart from Silas and me, there's no sign of life anywhere in the building. I've the urge to whisper but Silas seemingly doesn't. "We'll go this way first." His rich voice echo's off the walls as he guides me through what looks like a white fire door towards the back of the building. "This door's private, so you need to use this key." He indicates to the square brass key in his hand.

Unlocking the door, we pass into a narrow corridor. Our movement triggers the motion sensor lights. Blinking my eyes at the sudden, harsh brightness, the narrow space is now fully illuminated and ready for us to continue on our way to the rear of the property. There are several doors on either side of the corridor and another solid one across the end, which we head towards. Halting in front of the heavy door, Silas pulls it open and holds out his hand, indicating for me to go through.

I gasp in awe when I see what lies beyond. We've walked into a huge conservatory. There's a high, domed glass ceiling, giving the appearance of a Victorian pavilion. It must span the full width of the building, it's so vast. Vivid green vines of ivy and jasmine entwine their way up and around the marble pillars supporting the beams, which in-turn, support the domed glass roof. Grecian style planters decorate the otherwise open space. Stunning plants and palms are everywhere. And it's so lovely and warm - a hot-house almost. The daytime sun has carried out its job beautifully. The lingering heat of the day has been captured and retained by the insulated glass. Looking up, the heavens are clearly visible through the ceiling, revealing the stars in the black velvety sky above. And there's sound... I can hear the distant trickle of running water.

Pulling the door closed behind us, Silas sucks the last bits of ice-cream from his lolly-stick. Licking his lips, he drops his stick into a waste bin, which is discreetly placed beside the door and holds out his hand, palm up, to take mine from me. Quickly finishing the last bit of my own ice-cream, I pass him the small stumpy piece of wood. "Thanks," I mutter, then turn back to take in the fabulous surroundings. "Wow! I didn't know this was here!" My voice echo's as I step a little further into the room.

Stroking my hand over the cool marble of the pillar, I inhale the perfume of the jasmine flowers that bloom, grow and climb on the white diamond trellis. *Lovely!*

My eyes are drawn to the centre of the room. The pillars run in two parallel lines, forming double columns from the entrance door at the front, to the glass wall at the back. There are ten altogether, set at equal distances, five on the left and five on the right. Between the majestic marble columns is a sparkling, ginormous swimming pool.

The water looks crystal clear, cool and inviting. White marble steps lead down to the shallow end and between the first set of pillars to the right of the pool is a Jacuzzi. Opposite the Jacuzzi is a fountain, the jets of water spraying high into the air and raining down into the crystal blue water sending gentle ripples across the surface. Several white wooden sun loungers are strategically placed around the perimeter of the room, creating a spa-like effect. Low tables and plush, white wicker sofas form groups where people can sit and relax. It's beautiful.

While I've been taking all of this in, Silas hasn't said a single word. He's just quietly observed my reactions. I can't think of anything to say, it's taken my breath away. "Come on, this way, there's more to see." Leaving me with no option, he firmly takes my hand and leads me behind the Jacuzzi, past the sun loungers towards the back of the pool room.

My eyes are everywhere, like a child in a sweet shop twisting and turning her head, trying to absorb every bit of the space. Impatiently, Silas tugs my hand to get my attention, guiding me towards the back wall, breaking my daydream and bringing me back to the present.

"You can come in here anytime you like," he says. "It's residents only. But as there's a monthly fee, it only gets used by a few of the more discerning tenants. You'll mostly have it to yourself."

The cat's got my tongue. It's all I can do to nod in acknowledgement as we carry on towards the back of the room, where the pool ends with another set of marble steps. This time they're on the right. The water cascades over them, giving the appearance of a waterfall.

"Oh, my!" I'm gob smacked. This is unbelievable.

Silas is smiling as we come to a halt at the end of the swimming pool. Letting go of my hand, I watch as he reaches out and swings the bi-folding doors open - revealing the walled manicured garden. It's completely dark outside now but the garden is elegantly lit by twinkling fairy lights and low halogen spots. Strategically set at intervals within the decorative paving, the clever lighting creates intimate walkways and paths through the lawns and shrubs. Quite simply it's stunning.

"This is…I can't…it's just…I don't know what to say!" It's too much; I'm not used to this kind of luxury. I've had my moments in the past but the person I'm now, the invisible, plain, working mum, is a million miles away from the woman who would be comfortable here – I just can't take this in.

"Do you want to go out and have a look? There's a pond over there." Silas points to the bottom of the garden, where I can just about make out a high brick wall in the distance. "There are fish," he whispers, as if he's just let me in on a huge secret.

"No, I… it's a bit dark, perhaps tomorrow." I'm struggling but trying not to sound daunted by all this opulence. It's like I've fallen into the *'Secret Garden'*. I can vaguely hear the hum of distant traffic, but other than that, it's the perfect oasis of tranquility.

"Okay, well I've one last surprise but we need to go back upstairs for it." He pulls the doors to the garden closed and takes my hand again, leading me back through the pool room, pointing out the sauna and steam room as we go.

"Why did I bother to join the gym?" I muse to myself as we head back upstairs. Silas picks up on my question, turning to look at me.

"Well that's one thing we don't have here," he says, "it was either the pool or a work out room. The pool won the residents vote." I just look at him with incredulity.

When we get back to the entry door, he drops my hand again and ushers me through. I clasp my hands behind my back deterring him from any further hand holding. He notices but doesn't say anything. I detect a twitch of his eyebrows and he frowns, slightly affronted, but I'm not relenting. Back through the corridor we enter the stairwell and I follow him up the stairs.

Chapter 17

"I really am amazed. The pool and garden are fabulous. I think I may have a swim in the mornings now before I come to work," I say lightly.

Looking over his shoulder he smiles, but says nothing. As we reach the apartment door, he takes out his key to let us back inside. I hover behind him, all the while wondering what the next 'surprise' could possibly be. I can't for the life of me think what could top that conservatory, pool and garden.

Entering the apartment, he deactivates the alarm and waits patiently for me to follow him inside. Closing the door behind us, he turns and strides into the living room. He doesn't stop. "This way..." he indicates for me to follow him towards the balcony. I've not been out there yet, though I've taken a look at the magnificent view through the window.

There are Bi-folding doors again. Silas slides them open so they're folded back in a concertina, revealing the terrace in all its glory. The night sky is navy blue now and a sprinkling of stars are visible over the distant hills. There's not a cloud in the sky tonight, so the lights of the houses and buildings do nothing to diminish the brightness of the stars.

Silas steps out onto the terrace and I follow. The night is still warm, sultry even. The moon is a huge pearl globe, resembling an oil painting.

"This is the switch for the outside lights." Reaching to a raised, rubber block on the wall, he flips the cover open and reveals the switches. The terrace is instantly bathed in a dim, blueish glow, emanating from the globes standing atop the posts dotted around the edges of the decorative perimeter wall.

There's a sturdy marble dining table with six high backed chairs, which look like regal thrones. They cast long shadows onto the patio, highlighting the subtlety of the light. Off to the right-hand side, strategically placed to make the most of the magnificent view, two white tub chairs are grouped together with a two-seater sofa; a low glass-topped coffee table completes the job. It's outdoor living at its best and it's amazing.

I'm stunned. "Gosh Silas, this place is fabulous. I can totally understand why you've kept hold of it!" I trace the table top with my fingers and run my palm over the back of one of the chairs.

"I'll have to invite some people over to take advantage of all this!" Internally I laugh at myself – I've no idea who – I know nobody.

"Come with me, you've still not seen the best bit." I'm not quick enough, and before I know it, he's taken my hand again and is leading me across the terrace to the back corner of the patio, where there's a built-in curving staircase. I can't believe there's more to see.

The treads on the stairs are black marble, in stark contrast to all the white of the terrace, and they're spotlights at ankle height, illuminating each tread with an iridescent blue beam. A wrought iron bannister curves up the inside of the stairs and a white marble wall follows the outer perimeter; an iron handrail has been added, for additional safety. Climbing the steps, I can only assume we're heading up, onto the roof.

I'm right, but Holy-moly, what a roof! The floor is laid in large square black marble floor tiles; the boundary is bordered by a decorative four-foot-high wall, which marks the edge of the roof and the internal perimeter of the ornate roof garden. Large white planters brim with roses, shrubs, bushes and mini trees; all adding colour and texture, breaking up the stark black marble of the floor tiles.

The downstairs garden theme is repeated up here with the addition of globe and pillar lights; all of which are cleverly set at different heights, taking full advantage of the space and enhancing the view of the distant hills.

A raised decked area houses an outside wet-bar with more sofas and tub chairs. It's reminiscent of an exclusive nightclub. That's not all; the lower level is home to several wooden sun loungers and small tables. And just in case that isn't enough luxury, in the far corner, a six-foot section of the brick wall has been replaced with a panel of clear glass - offering an uninterrupted view of the countryside beyond – all of which is visible from the ultimate of decadence - a sunken infinity hot tub! I think I've died and gone to heaven!

"Oh my gosh, wow!" I'm breathless and virtually speechless. I sound like an uneducated dimwit. "Seriously Silas, this is just… amazing!" Amazing doesn't even cover it. It's the most stunning, opulent, expensive… not me… place I've ever seen in my life.

"I feel like I've won the lottery! Are you sure you don't want me to rent a room over a shop so you can let this out to someone who can pay you to live here?" It's not entirely a joke, he could earn a small fortune renting this place out to some junior entrepreneur with more money than sense.

Silas isn't amused. "*No,*" he counters sarcastically, turning to me and staring as if I've grown another head. "The apartment comes with the job. I expect you'll be working long and often unsociable hours. Believe me Edi, you'll be glad of having this place as a bolt hole once the business ramps up. Anyway, I don't want just any old Tom, Dick or Harry living here. I can tell by your reaction you'll look after it."

Feeling scolded, I look downward. Only then do I notice that he's still clutching my hand. It feels natural and comfortable but on instinct, I flex my fingers prompting him to releases his vice-like grip. Once free, I walk to the edge of the roof and take a tentative look over the top of the wall. Its high up, but I don't feel unsafe. The boundary wall is well constructed, wide enough to sit on and high enough to lean my elbows on the top and look out over the rooftops and street below. I feel like a queen on top of her castle, contemplating her realm. Turning so my back and elbows are resting on the wall, I sigh and smile at Silas in utter gratitude.

"Well, I'm truly grateful and thankful. I will look after it so well! I'll be scared to even sit on the white sofas," I joke.

"That sounded a bit like a prayer," he whispers. "For what we're about to receive... may the Lord make us truly thankful..." He doesn't say *Amen,* and I restrain myself from saying it too. I don't know what I want to receive, but I hope it's him doing the giving.

"I think that's Grace..." I whisper back, and for a moment, we just stand, silently gazing at each other across the terrace.

Silas is the first to break the mood. "Well," he declares, "the tour is over. No more surprises I'm afraid." Neither of us goes to move. He stares at me waiting for my response and I just stare back at him. I can't hide my attraction to him no matter how hard I try. I'm overwhelmed.

"I feel like I've been here for weeks, not just three days," I murmur "... in a good way, I mean." I catch myself before he thinks I'm being ungrateful. "It's such a lot to take in." I lift my hand to my head, looking around the luxurious rooftop again, "but I'll certainly give it a try." I'm feeling a little dizzy and I don't think it's from being this high up.

"Come on, we've a bottle of wine to finish downstairs. I might even stretch to something a little stronger." With that he reclaims my hand and leads me back down the black marble stairs, across the beautiful white terrace and into the living room. Releasing me only to close the glass doors on the patio, we leave the dark night behind us, locked outside.

Once indoors the living room seems very quiet. With the closing of the patio door the sounds of the night have disappeared and Ella finished singing long ago. For some reason, the sudden hush has me fidgeting.

"Some music is required, I think?" He read my mind. "Would you like a glass of wine or something else?"

"Wine would be lovely, thank you." Nerves have taken over again, I can hear it in my voice. I'm conscious we're alone and drinking. I've been here before and I'm well aware what could happen.

"Here, you sit down and I'll go and grab the glasses and play D.J. Is Jazz ok or do you want something different?" Silas seems as nervous as I feel; which weirdly, relaxes me a little.

"I'm happy with whatever's playing... you choose." I slump into the squashy sofa, but I'm soon twisting and reaching underneath me to remove my mobile phone, which I've sat on. Placing it on the coffee table, the sound of *Passenger 'Let her go'* drifts through the integrated speakers.

Looking around me, and absorbing the beauty of my surroundings, I can't believe my luck; there has to be a catch, surely? If this is for real, I can't help thinking I must have done something good in a previous life to deserve all this.

Silas carries two wine glasses in one hand and a bottle of wine in the other. I notice it's a new bottle, freshly opened. Bending awkwardly, he places the bottle on the table and the glasses on the coasters, before picking up the bottle again and filling the glasses just below half way, allowing the wine to breathe. He takes a seat beside me on the sofa - not too close for comfort, but close enough so there's no awkward gap.

Lifting both glasses, he hands one to me, then holds his own glass out to clink with mine. "Cheers. Here's to new jobs and new starts," he says.

"New starts and new jobs..." I mimic, touching my glass to his before taking a sip.

Resting his arm along the back of the sofa, he raises one knee and hooks his foot behind his other leg, making himself comfortable. Attempting to appear casual, I shift down in my seat, sinking further into the plush cushions, my head resting against the sofa back. Gazing up at the ceiling I nurse my wine to my chest and closing my eyes, I allow Passenger's childlike, wispy voice to sooth me.

"How long have you had the bumblebees?" The question stirs me from my daydream. I look over at Silas; he's staring at the white leather band on my left wrist hiding my tattoo.

"I got them after David was born," is my vague answer. He can ask all the questions he wants, but I won't be sharing very much anytime soon.

"When was that?" He's pushing again. I stare into my wine but I don't drink.

"Umm... about fifteen years ago now. David was about two at the time." *That's it, I'm not telling him anymore.*

"You were a young mum then?" *Ah, so this is where we're heading is it?*

"Yep, nineteen." *That's enough for now, please.*

"A gymslip mum... what happened with his dad? Is he still around?" *How rude!* He's still pushing and I need to shut this down... quickly.

"No, he's out of the picture," I offer, "...has been since before David was born. He probably doesn't even know he exists." *That's it, no more.*

"So, a single mum, it must've been hard for you." He's not giving up. *Close this down now, Edi!*

I don't hide my irritation. Placing my untouched wine on the table I turn slightly to face him so he knows I mean business.

"I'm not being funny Silas, but I really don't like to talk about it. If you don't mind, I'm tired. I've had a really long day and

199

I'm still reeling from all the surprises of this place. Can we call it a night?" *There, that should work.* Firm but fair.

He doesn't move, but just looks into my eyes. Then, he sighs and leans forward placing his wine on the table.

"Edi, I know we've only just met, but I feel like I want to know more about you, that's all. There's almost a ... I don't know... a familiarity about you, it's... odd." My face freezes and my shoulders lift as I wait for recognition to hit him; but thankfully, somehow, it doesn't. "You intrigue me and it's been a long time since I've met anybody that captures my interest like you do." Relieved, I let my breath go as my shoulders lower. "I didn't mean to cause offence."

In one fluid movement he rises from the sofa. My eyes rise with him but I remain seated, too tired and bewildered to stand. "I'll see myself out. It's been a lovely evening... thank you." He walks over to the kitchen and picks up his keys. "I'll see you tomorrow."

Looking thoughtful Silas, on reaching the door hesitates and as if it's an afterthought adds, "I'll be making the return flight to France on Friday to fetch the Phillips's back from Paris fashion week. You should come. It'll make a nice end to your first week." Decision made, he turns and leaves the apartment.

Remembering my manners, I call out to his disappearing back "Err... thank you for dinner, oh, and the guided tour. I'll see you tomorrow...." but he's already closed the door behind him. Passenger is singing about *Holes in his head.*

Staring into the empty fireplace I contemplate the abrupt end to the evening. Familiarity... that's disconcerting, I intrigue him... well that could mean the same as familiarity, couldn't it?

I run my fingers through my matted hair, then rub my forehead. I'm so confused, or am I just being over cautious? He's trying so hard to be friendly, a gentleman, and I keep making it difficult for him. A flight to Paris *would* make a nice end to my first week. I should be grateful for the opportunity to fly on a private jet. It will only be there and back and *anyway*, it's part of my role. *Don't read too much into it, Edi.*

Sighing, and before I can fall asleep where I'm sitting I lift my weary body from the comfort of the sofa and head off to my equally comfy new bed. I suddenly feel about a hundred years old. It's eleven o'clock - which is a late night for me - but I've really enjoyed his company.

Lazily, I complete my night time routine. After brushing my teeth and splashing my face I climb into the luxuriously soft cotton sheets. Resting back on the pillow and placing my arm behind my head, I gently stroke myself with my other hand. Closing my eyes against the semi-dark, I enter a trance-like state, rubbing light circles on my breasts, flicking my nipples into stiff peaks; tracing my fingertips up and down my breastbone, my feather light touch makes my skin tingle and goose pimples rise on my sensitive flesh, causing the fine, downy hairs on my arms to lift.

My hand moves gently, unhurriedly, exploring the familiar contours of my body, over my ribs, stroking the slight roundness of my belly, the dip near my hip bones and the squidgy flesh of my plump thighs. Running a line back up the centre of my body to my breasts I finally drift all the way back down to my groin, and the silky soft curls at the apex of my thighs. Once there I settle on a repetitive, rhythmic stroke.

Privately I'm imagining the hand belongs to someone else; a dark, handsome, beautiful, moody, someone else; someone with luscious lips and a deep husky voice and eyes as dark as chocolate caramel and as deep as the ocean; someone who finds me intriguing; someone who wants to know more about me…

I can feel his mouth on mine. He tastes of summer berries and his lips are soft and warm. The kiss is deep, strong, wanting and greedy, and I desperately want to kiss him back, but I'm afraid. I'm afraid of what comes next, of getting hurt, of the physical pain, of falling and being unable to stop. But the kiss is so tender and feels so right, so beautiful, I just want to surrender to it and not think about anything else…

It's dark and the stars are huge in the night sky but there's no visible moon. I'm outside, swimming in a deep pool. The water is jet black and except for the stars, there's no other source of light, so it's difficult to see anything around me. I can't feel the bottom and I'm treading water, trying to stay afloat. I can see the edge of the pool in the distance, so I start to swim towards it but it isn't getting any nearer…

The stars are now burning brighter, a blinding, searing white as they expand, growing larger and larger in the black of the night sky, reaching the size of tennis balls. They're spinning and spiralling all around me…

I'm no longer in the water, I'm swimming in the sky, defying gravity, grappling for stability, floating in the cosmos; I can see the Milky-Way, the edge of the Universe. The stars dazzle me, their too-bright light, orbiting around me like planets around the sun. Rotating faster and faster, they're creating a vortex; I flail and thrash, grasping at nothing, to slow down the dizzying whirl, but I'm unable to...

Suddenly, one of the stars bursts, exploding into a million golden fragments, shooting out jagged sparks of blazing tendrils. They reach for me; octopus-like tentacles alive with fiery orange and red fingers of scalding lava. The glittering sparks stretch towards me, singeing my skin, causing vicious blisters to appear.

Still spinning and flailing, I look at my scorched skin, it's burned and stinging. My naked body is covered in vicious welts, caused by the whip-like tendrils of the burning flames.

The orange sparks are paling to a vivid yellow, they're buzzing and spitting as more and more of the spinning stars explode all around me…

The scene has changed. The bursting stars are no longer releasing flames but a giant swarm of black and yellow flying insects, filling the empty space around me. Their enormous fiery stingers, like red hot pokers protruding from their engorged abdomens, are all aimed in my direction.

Panicking, I try to swim in mid-air. Arms flapping wildly, I'm kicking against the atmosphere with my legs, trying desperately to dive down. Down, out of the sky, out of the pitch-black cosmos of bursting stars and back into the deep cool black pool; desperate to escape the deadly swarm. The buzzing of the insects is growing increasingly louder and louder, an intermittent *Buzz, Buzz, Buzz…*

I jerk myself awake; yelling, thrashing my legs and waving my arms around my head, swatting away the invisible threat. My sheets are a knotted mess and tangled about me. I'm damp with clammy perspiration. Beads of sweat cling to my brow and my hair is soaked, clinging to the back of my neck where my head meets the wringing wet pillow. Sitting up with a jolt, I reach over and knock the alarm off the bedside table, silencing the buzzing.

I'm exhausted from the exertion… oh thank goodness… it was just a dream… a night terror… *but I never dream.* My first dream, since I was a teenager.

Flopping back on to my wet pillow I wait for my breathing to stabilize and my overstimulated senses to calm; desperately trying to rationalize the meaning of my nocturnal fantasy come nightmare, before giving up and crawling out of bed, ready to start the new day.

"Christ…" I mutter to myself. *This can't continue.* Three nights here and I've yet to have an undisturbed sleep. What's happening to me?

Chapter 18

Pulling into the Air Field, I park my rust bucket in my designated spot. Thursday has dawned dull and grey, finally there's been a break in the weather and there might be a thunder storm on the horizon. The air feels muggy, and though the temperature has cooled down, the atmosphere's now clammy and humid. By the time I climb out of my car, my thin cotton blouse is clinging to my back.

Christina's car's in her parking space but I can't see any sign of the Range Rover yet, which means Silas isn't here. Grabbing my bags from the boot, I'm just about to enter the building when I hear the growl of an old exhaust and the crunch of tyres on gravel. Silas has arrived. I decide to be polite and wait for him.

As usual, Bear's the first out of the car; bounding towards me in an enthusiastic greeting, tail wagging, tongue lolling, he's flying at about ninety miles an hour before skidding to a halt. Circling in front of me, he sits, ready for a morning fuss. Sweeping his tail back and forth his whole back end is wiggling from side to side.

Dropping to my knees, I lay my bags down before wrapping my arms round his neck and give his silky coat a rough rub all over his back. Patting his sides and scratching his ears, I kiss the top of his head. I've never really been fond of dogs, but there's something about Bear I can't resist.

"Good morning, beautiful boy. It's lovely to see you too!" I coo as I rub him all over. He's so affectionate.

"That's a better greeting than I get in the morning!" I look up, my arms still looped around Bear's shoulders as Silas strides over to the entrance. I smile, uncertain; does he mean the greeting I just got from Bear or the one Bear got from me?

Silas removes his aviator sunglasses so I can see his stunning eyes. "What do I have to do to deserve one of those?"

He looks at Bear, shakes his head then scratches him round the ears and says "Eh, boy?"

I still don't know if he means from me or Bear, but I know what I want it to be. "Bear, come," he commands gruffly and Bear dutifully lopes into the office beside his master, obedient as ever. Picking up my belongings I follow them through the automatic doors. Moody boss-man Silas is back.

Inside, Christina is pacing around reception, talking on her mobile phone. Bear bounds over to her in greeting and Silas groans under his breath. The rich sound makes me shiver. She looks over to us, raising a finger on her free hand, mouthing she will only be *'one minute'*. Raising a hand and mouthing 'Hi', I carry on through to my office, leaving them to it. I don't want to interrupt.

I unpack my laptop, fixing it to the docking station and while it comes to life, I pick up my post, sifting through the junk for the legitimate mail, then check my answerphone for any new messages. A candidate has left a voice message, requesting a change of day for next week's interview, and there's a quick message from Spanners asking me to review an email he's sent regarding an order for some parts for one of the microlights. There are no other messages. I make a note of both on my notepad.

Once my computer is logged on, I open my emails and start to filter through them. There's one from Mr. Phillips confirming they will indeed be returning to the UK on Saturday and thanking me for my assistance on Tuesday. I also have one from the other candidate accepting the date and time for her interview next week. I locate the mail from Spanners and highlight it for review. There are a couple from suppliers, one from the local weather bureau with an advanced weekly weather report, and the usual ten or so from companies and clients requesting information on services. Not too bad for overnight.

The final email is from Silas. He sent it at 3.05 am. from his personal email account. I open and start to read it.

'Dear Edi, Thank you for your company last night. I had a really good time. I didn't mean to make you feel uncomfortable with my inappropriate questions. It was inconsiderate expecting you to divulge your life story to someone you have only known for three days. I hope you can forgive me. However, I meant what I said. I really do want to get to know you better and I hope I've not screwed it up. You probably realise I'm not used to people holding back on me; as Christina says, I've an impatient nature. I completely understand if you never want to see me again socially but I will be disappointed. You can see from the time on this email I can't sleep. You should know you have been on my mind constantly since the first time I saw you. As I said last night, you intrigue me. If I promise to behave and not to pry or ask any stupid intrusive questions, do you think we could start over again, only this time I would like to take you on a proper date? I really hope you say yes but will completely understand if the answer is no. Yours in anticipation, Silas'

Oh my God! I sit back in my chair and exhale. My subconscious mind is screaming *yes!* But my sensible side is warning me to proceed with caution. What to do? *Oh, fuck it Edi, get a life for God's sake!*

I hit reply and start to type....

'Dear Silas, there's nothing to forgive. I know I can be over sensitive at times. But yes, you are intuitive. I don't trust people easily and I'm not yet ready to share my 'life story' as you so eloquently put it, but that doesn't mean I didn't enjoy last night, or your company. On the contrary, I enjoyed it very much and want to get to know more about you too. I would like to continue seeing you socially, if it's not inappropriate office etiquette or policy, you being the boss et al. I accept your kind invitation to a 'proper' date. Just tell me the time and place and I'll be there. Sincerely, Edi.'

Hastily, I speed-read through my reply and before I can change my mind I press send. I don't expect him to pick this up until he gets home tonight, so that will give me some time to digest what I've done. I vaguely contemplate whether I should speak to Christina, about this? Perhaps during lunch? I get up from my chair and make myself a much-needed cup of tea.

By lunch time I'm starving. I've cleared all my emails and approved the order for Spanners. My stomach rumbles as I glance at my invisible watch to check the time; I really must get a replacement. Looking at the wall clock, it's just gone one, so I stand up and stretch. My shoulder is a little bit stiff and I can only presume it is a combination of the healing wasp sting, my nocturnal exertions, and the fact I've been sat at my computer since nine o'clock without moving.

I stand in front of the huge picture window, staring at the distant rolling hills - it really is a stunning view. Reaching my arm over my shoulder I complete some stretches and neck rolls before shaking my arms out and completing some more; I finish by leaning over and touching the floor, resting my palms flat so I can feel the delicious pull in the backs of my thighs, calves and back. Slowly curling back up, and rolling out my spine so as not to cause a head-rush, I stand and reach my arms over my head. That feels so much better.

I'm about to leave my office for a bite to eat when the light through the window changes. The sky darkens to a deep purply grey, shrouding the hills that only a moment ago were clearly visible, and plunging my office into a brooding twilight. A rapid electrical flash of forked lightning splits the sky and hails the arrival of the imminent thunder storm. I count the seconds, one... two... three ...

BOOM!!!

The crash of thunder is so loud, the storm must be directly overhead. While I count the distance between the flashes and the thunder-clap, the heavens open and the rain starts hammering down in a violent torrent, pelting the windows and distorting my view of the airfield outside. I can see people scattering, the crew running for cover, most of them ducking into the hangars and taking shelter from the sudden deluge. Yeah, I won't be sitting outside with my sandwich today.

I love to watch thunder storms, the pent-up anticipation for the silver flashes as the clouds discharge their built-up static. The unpredictability, judging when the inevitable thunder clap will hit; is it going to be fork or sheet lightning? Is the storm moving towards me or away? Counting between the lightning flashes was something I did as a child, usually while hiding under my bedsheets, hoping that the storm would get closer and closer, then finally petering out to a squally shower, before desisting altogether. A wonderous aftermath follows. Puddles of shimmering water, where, just minutes ago, there was tinder-dry earth. The bubbling, gurgle of the fast-flowing current as the rapid deluge swiftly swells the woodland streams, bursting its banks, the heavy surging flow seeking the course of least resistance. Filling the ditches, overflowing from broken gutters; swamping the ground before being swallowed by the curb side grids. I love it all...

After the rain, the grass appears lusher; the leaves on the trees shimmer a brighter vivid green, delicately tipped with glittering diamond like spheres, tiny jewels of moisture, poised to drip on your head as you walk beneath them. But most of all, I love the smell; the cleansed earth, the musty tarmac of the pavements and the heady, zingy scent of ozone, transporting an indelible freshness as the sun breaks through the oppressive grey clouds. And if you're lucky, an arc of translucent splendour, a stunning, gleaming rainbow. All of this cumulating in a sense of renewal, a do-over, a fresh start... Yes, I love thunder storms!

Picking up my box of salad, I curl up on the office sofa and settle in to watch the show. The rain is teeming down now. I can barely see the perimeter fence. Large puddles have developed in a couple of uneven areas on the tarmac; they look quite deep. Sitting with my legs curled beneath me, contentedly I watch the storm, subconsciously counting seconds between the thunder and lightning.

At the last flash, I managed to get to six, before the thunder hit; *six miles*. It's travelling away from us, the gap between the flashes lengthening, the rumble of the thunder growing more distant with every growl. Even the rain seems to be easing.

A knock on my office door steals my attention from the window. Leaning forward, I place my empty box on the coffee table and unfold my legs so I'm in a more respectable seated position. "Yes, come in…" I call out. The door opens, and Christina pops her head in, scanning the office for me. "I'm here." She finally spots me on the sofa and gives me a smile. "I'm just finishing my lunch and watching the rain, come in…"

"It was quite something wasn't it?" Walking into my office she sits beside me. "It's a good job we don't have any flights scheduled this afternoon." Gazing at the rain, she seems distracted for a moment, "sorry about this morning. I can't seem to get this new client to accept final terms." She looks weary. The client must be a tricky customer. "Every time I think I have it nailed down, he moves the goal posts or throws in another stipulation. It's ridiculous." She leans back on the sofa, staring up at the ceiling.

"Oh no, I hope they're not going to change their mind." Part of the reason I have this job in the first place is due to the anticipated expansion of the client base.

Rubbing a well-manicured hand over her brow, she fluffs her perfect hair then flops her arms by her sides in submission. "I spent most of last night reviewing the bloody contract again. It's completely water tight, no room for further changes or compromise. I was certain he was ready to sign on the bottom line, then this morning he decides he wants complete exclusivity." It doesn't sound good. She slaps her hands on the

209

sofa in exasperation at his audacity. "No other client base for RTC, which, incidentally, is an impossible request. The man is bombastic beyond all the bounds of all *'bombasticity'* - if that's even a word!" Thankfully she grins at me - though she's obviously frustrated - she doesn't seem overly concerned, just annoyed. "I finished the call this morning by telling him he could take it or leave it. He won't get fairer terms anywhere else and he knows it!"

Oh? "So, did he sign then?" I really hope so, this deal means such a lot to Christina, she has worked like a trojan to close it.

She snorts derisively, "apparently, he wants one more day! I'll be sticking to my guns though; he's only getting twenty-four hours, that's it. If he doesn't sign, I'll rip the bloody thing up and send the pieces to him recorded delivery!" The confidence she has is inspiring. "Did you get your date with Silas?" *Woah, change of subject!*

"Err, well, actually he's just asked me. You don't mind, do you?" I hope she's okay with this.

"Hah! God, no! I think it's brilliant. He can be a bit difficult and stubborn, but I can tell, he really likes you. I told you before, we've had our time... it was good while it lasted, but it's better now. God, I don't even think we were ever romantically compatible." She shakes her head, seemingly bemused at the memory - *widening her eyes at me as if to say, 'I've no idea how we were ever a couple.*

"Trust me, we're much better at being friends; he looks out for me and I tell him what to do." That statement makes me laugh out loud. Slapping her thighs decisively, "right then, onward and upward," she pushes herself off the sofa. Leaning over me, she squeezes my shoulders, "just don't take any of his macho, moody, bull-shit and you should get along just fine and dandy." She laughs at the look of horror on my face and shakes her head. "He's getting better, honestly. It'll do him good to go on a date with a real woman."

"What, as opposed to an imaginary one?" feigning shock at her remark, but she's hit on something with that comment and it makes me feel a bit shitty. "What's the company policy on dating the boss, anyway?"

"In your case, I'll make an exception. Honestly, Edi... he wouldn't normally do this. The man is an island to himself." I've no idea what she means; I'm still a bit confused by her insistence that I date her ex. It's weird, if not a little bit kinky.

I decide to let it go. "Well, I'm not very good at relationships, imaginary or otherwise. But, if you are okay with it, I'm okay with it too."

"Oh, believe me love, I'm more than okay with it...you don't date much then?" she asks.

That's an understatement. "You have no idea!" I laugh back. I really do like her and I think I'm beginning to understand the relationship between these two. They love each other, but not in a romantic way. It's a cliché but they really are more like brother and sister. I can't imagine them ever being married. Not to each other anyway.

"Has he asked you to go with him tomorrow when he flies to pick up the Phillips's?"

I stand and slowly start tidying up my lunch debris. The rain's petered out to a faint drizzle. "Yeah, he did mention it, but he's got it wrong. Mr. Phillips has left a message to say they're returning on Saturday, not tomorrow." I need to sort that out.

"Oh, he knows ... where do you think you're going on your date?" She has a mischievous grin on her face. "As I said, he looks out for me and I tell him what to do. The last night of Paris fashion week isn't to be missed. I think you'll enjoy the sights." On that bombshell, she turns and stalks out of my office. There's a spring in her step; long, lithe arms swinging, clearly delighting in my surprise. Closing the door behind her, she leaves me, stunned... *What?*

"Christel!" muddled I stand staring after her for about five minutes. I can't go to Paris! For a start, I've nothing to wear and for seconds, and thirds, and fourths for that matter... I can't go to Paris, I've got nothing to wear! *"Fuck."* Startling myself into action, I quickly follow in her wake - I need to sort this out and quick! "Christina, hey, Christina...." I chase after her as she disappears into her office and closes the door. She knows I'm following so why did she do that? Knocking twice, I don't wait to be invited in. She's seated behind her desk, completely comfortable, the epitome of the composed business-woman. Her eyes are twinkling in mischief at my shocked face. "I can't go to Paris!" It's the only thing I can think of to say.

"Why the bloody hell not?" Her grin is infectious, but I still can't go and I can't tell her why.

"Who's going to look after Bear?" I need an excuse and it's the first thing I can think of.

"What's that got to do with the price of fish? Me... I always look after Bear when Silas is away. That's not a reason for *you* not to go. Next issue?" She blinks twice raising her groomed eyebrows, her eyes don't leave mine and the smile doesn't leave her face. She's smug, sat there all well-groomed, with her hands clasped on her desk like Margaret Thatcher!

"I've nothing to wear," counting on my fingers I blurt my feeble excuses one after the other... "My hair's a mess... where will I stay... I can't... it's just... oh God, Christina." I'm panicking and whining, finding stupid justifications not to go; and she knows it. She must think I'm such a loser. Flopping into the cream leather swivel chair opposite, I cover my face with my hands. I'm going to hyperventilate if I'm not careful.

"Okay, okay," rising from her chair she walks round and perches her pert behind on the desk beside me so I have no option but to look up at her. Suddenly, I feel very small. "Don't panic. You're only staying one night. It's a little boutique hotel off the Champs Elysees. No biggie! I thought it would be fun for

212

you, you know, to people watch." She sounds concerned. I wonder if she realises, she's over stepped the mark here. "Look, Edi, something like Paris fashion week is really special. An invitation to one of the end-of-season parties is like gold dust; they only come along once in a Preston guild and you'd regret it if you didn't go." I look at her, quizzically. She continues, "Rubbing shoulders with Kate Moss and the like... come on Sweetie... you'll love it. Not to mention you'll have a hot man on your arm..."

Hot man!... Christ!

"But..." I can't form a sentence. I've run out of excuses...

"No but's... I can give you the number for my hair salon. They'll fit you in this evening. It could do with a trim." Wrinkling her nose in distaste, she runs her fingers through my over-dry tangles - lifting the short bit where the plaster has been cut out and sighing. "Look, I'll give them a ring. You can have your eyebrows done and a manicure; my treat... pretty please?" She blinks at me with pleading eyes. She must think I look like an unmade bed. Moreover, she must think I'm desperate, or Silas is, or she's... desperate to palm him off on me...

I wonder suspiciously why she's so keen on the idea of us dating. *God!* she'll be begging next. I feel railroaded, but I'm starting to agree it could be fun. I decide to give myself a break. *What's the worst that could happen?*

"Alright, but I haven't anything to wear. It'll be jeans and jumpers!" I grumble, although there's a fizzing of excitement now I've calmed a little. I should be okay. I'll just keep a low profile. All those beautiful people will be too self-absorbed to notice little old me.

"What about that lovely green dress?" She's seen my clothes? Then it hits me, of course she has. I bet it was her who unpacked my stuff! "Jeans and jumpers will do for the day, but in the evening, you need a dress." I feel like Barbie.

I purse my lips and snort loudly down my nose, demonstrating my annoyance. "Yes, I suppose that will do."

"Good, that's sorted. Take an overnight bag." She pushes off the desk and claps her hands together gleefully. "I'm excited for you. It'll be wonderful. You'll see… honestly, Silas might be deep, but where you're concerned, I know he likes you." Returning to her seat, she picks up her phone and dials.

By the time I get back to my office, I've a hair appointment for tonight at a beauty salon called *Embrace,* which is centrally located in the village; I'm also having my eyebrows waxed and tinted and my nails done. It's been years since I had any beauty treatment. I'm not unfamiliar with the routine; on the contrary, there once was a time when it was a weekly event - but that was in another life - for now, I just need to gather my courage and enjoy the experience, while it lasts.

Chapter 19

As four o'clock rolled around, Christina all but bullied me out of the office; insisting I finish early so I've some time to pack and prepare for my mini spa.

I haven't seen Silas all day, but the last time I saw Christina she was still grinning like a Cheshire cat, and Bear was trotting at her heels like a shadow. He was obviously ready for his sleepover. She made sure I had my directions to the salon, as well as the name of the stylist; Angelica.

It's only quarter past four when I get home, the traffic was ridiculously light. After dumping my stuff, I head into the walk-in wardrobe to decide what to take with me. I've a couple of nice T-shirts. One is pale pink with a scene of galloping horses on the front; the other is light blue linen, more of a vest but it is biased cut, doesn't crease and looks fab with jeans. I don't wear either of them much. My skinny jeans are clean, so they will do fine.

Riffling through my drawers, I grab a couple of pairs of knickers and bras. They don't match and have seen better days, but I tell myself nobody's going to see them so it doesn't matter. Next is nightwear... I've none. I usually wear an old T-Shirt and shorts to bed. I find a pink vest with a bleach stain on the front, from cleaning the bathroom one time, and an old pair of marl-grey soft cotton gym shorts. The elastic has gone in the waist, but the lace cord still holds them up. Both items are creased to high heaven from being screwed up in my hold-all, but they will do for sleeping in. It's only one night after all.

My trusty hold-all is on the top shelf so I drag it down and dump it on the floor. Stuffing in my selected clothes for the weekend, and grabbing my toiletries, hairbrush, and a fancy scarf, I add a pair of flat navy-blue ballet pumps for walking – not that I expect to be doing much walking, but you never know.

Packing this quickly has prevented me from loading unnecessary stuff I won't need. That fizzle of excitement has grown a little and I start to hum, *'I'm so excited'* by the Pointer Sisters. Feeling a bit foolish at my sudden teenage reaction, I shake my head and shut up; focusing my energy on the remainder of my packing. Make-up - I only have a small selection - so I decant the few items I need into an even smaller travel-size makeup bag, remembering to include BB cream and my SPF 30 moisturizer. That should be enough.

The rain has left the streets clean and fragrant. The sky is blue once more and the sun is shining as I walk into the village to my appointment. I'm an hour early, giving me some time to window shop and mooch around, admiring all the small boutique-type shops lining the high street.

Strolling along, I pass a black and white Tudor style building, with a large display window and a shiny black door. I stop to admire the architecture and muse on the irony of the style. *Silas Tudor would fit right in here!* I blush and laugh to myself, realising the window is beautifully dressed with several collections of finely designed lingerie. All of its stunning and incredibly sexy. An exquisitely painted sign above the door says *Oreille Lingerie* in swirly gold lettering. Snap decision time; I've an hour to kill so why not have a quick look? What harm can it do? I could do with some new knickers anyway.

On entering the shop, the first thing I notice is the soft chime of a bell, announcing my arrival. The second is the lovely delicate perfume permeating the air and the third is the soft erotic music. It creates the perfect seductive ambiance. A very attractive woman of about fifty and a young sales girl are assisting a couple of middle aged, affluent looking women with some luxurious night wear. They all turn as I enter and I'm suddenly very self-conscious.

I feel exposed; I can only imagine what their usual clientele looks like. They must wonder what the hell I'm doing there...

I'm wondering what the hell I'm doing in there for that matter. About to turn and make a run for it I notice the younger assistant lightly touch the arm of the older one.

"Good evening madam." The older lady smiles widely, gliding over to greet me, leaving the other three to carry on with their own business.

"Hi," I whisper… why do I suddenly feel so shy? It's not as if I've never bought underwear before. "I hope you can help me."

"That's what I'm here for. I'm Oreille." She has a feint accent; perhaps Italian. "The lovely lady over there's my daughter, Sophia, and this is our empire." She waves her hand regally, indicating the interior of the plush boutique.

Up close she has the most perfect complexion. Her skin is smooth - not a single line or wrinkle in sight - it's clearly all due to good bone structure and genes; she's certainly not had any work done. Her hair's a thick, glossy chocolate brown, just a slight hint of grey at the temples, indicating that too, is natural. It's swept up in a French pleat at the back of her head - emphasizing her elegant neck. I want to be her when I grow up!

"Now, how can I assist you?" She looks at me expectantly. The intimidation I felt on entering the store is fading.

Looking around me, I see rails of stunning lingerie, in every colour under the sun. Satin, silk, lace, embellishments and frills; basically, every man's fantasy is here under this roof.

"I need some new underwear." *Stupid thing to say Edi, I'm sure she doesn't think you want to buy a bag of carrots!*

"Yes, of course. Are you looking for something special; perhaps to wear with a particular outfit? Or colour?" She's completely professional.

"Yes, actually I am." I try to calm my nerves, this feels weird. "I've a green dress I need some new underwear for. It's fitted and quite low at the front and back necklines." I'm wafting my hands around, indicating where the neckline finishes.

"Ah, that will be exquisite with your hair colour." I touch my hand to my mess of hair, conscious that it looks a fright. "And what shade of green is this gown? Perhaps we can start with that, then move on to the style afterwards? As you can see, we've a vast selection." She indicates the display around her. "I'm sure we will be able to fit you with some exquisite pieces today."

Unconsciously, I've followed her to the rails, standing at the rear of the shop. All of the underwear is displayed perfectly, hanging delicately from velvet hangers, arranged in a veritable rainbow of colour, starting with basic whites, all the way through the entire spectrum until it gets to the sheerest black.

I indicate to the shade of green that's the nearest match to my dress. "This is probably the closest." I reach out and touch the delicate fabric.

"Ah, *Bellissima*... I would call that an emerald green. We've some stunning items in that colour. You said that the gown has a plunge back and front, yes?"

"Yes, it comes down to about here." I place my finger between my boobs where the dress finishes. It's really quite low, but I've always worn it with a camisole underneath, so my cleavage is modestly hidden. It looks okay but spoils the effect a little.

"And for panties, do you need a support garment or something flimsier? How tight is the dress around your hips?" I like her practical approach.

"Well, it's fitted, but not too tight. A lighter garment would be best, I think. No *'Bridget Jones'* pants!" I laugh at my reference but she looks at me bemused, as if she's no idea what I'm babbling on about.

"I think I know just what you are looking for. I will take your measurements, and then we can try on a selection." For the first time I notice she has a tape measure draped round her swan-like neck.

I start to panic. I didn't expect that. "Oh… Err… no need". Hoping to stop the measuring I blurt out my size. "I'm 36C size 14 to 16 knickers." Well, I was the last time I bought underwear.

But Oreille won't be deterred, "Madame, this is my business, my vocation. If I don't measure you, I won't be able to provide the best fit. Please, it will only take a second." She indicates to a dressing room. "I assure you… you are in good hands."

Now I feel stupid. I've insulted this lovely lady. She's so professional, brushing off my rudeness with a flick of her hand.

"It is my job to help you enjoy this experience and relax." She hands me a glass flute of champagne from the silver tray sitting on the counter. This is some special customer service. A little Dutch courage will do me good so I take a sip, it's gorgeous.

"Now, if you wouldn't mind stepping into the cubicle, I will take your measurements, then we can have some fun with the lingerie."

Resigned to my fate, I walk into the large luxury cubicle. It's dressed to resemble an Italian boudoir. The lighting is subtle and there are mirrors on all sides. It's a long time since I saw this much of me.

Placing the delicious Champagne onto the fancy dressing table, I reluctantly remove my outer clothing and Oreille joins me in the cubicle. Oreille is very business-like, remaining detached from my embarrassment, just like a doctor would be. Clearly, she's seen it all before and probably worse, so I relax. There's no acknowledgement of my cellulite. No look of disgust at my stretch marks. She just loops the tape round my waist, hips and boobs, noting my measurements on a small white pad as she goes.

In no time at all she's done - notepad safely tucked into her pocket, and the tape measure back around her neck. To be honest, the whole procedure was pretty painless in a clinical sort of way. Standing in my knickers and bra, I'm waiting a little self-consciously for what comes next. Oreille gives me a demure smile.

Her lips are full and coated with a deep fuchsia-pink, lipstick. "Alright?" she asks and I nod quietly in response. "Well, Tojoro... you have lost a little weight recently I think, no?"

Her voice is so warm and soft. I expect it's a tried and tested approach; honed to give shy customers - like me - comfort and confidence. It's working. "You are a size 38inch hip and your bra size, 34D." I'm surprised... that's very different from the size I usually buy.

"A well-fitted bra is your best friend," she goes on. "I'm directly quoting Sophia Loren, and she should know... we're all aware of how beautiful she is." True, but I think she might be embellishing the truth a little.

"Even when hidden beneath your clothes, beautiful lingerie will make you look and feel like a Goddess." She's smiling now, so am I, my boobs have always been a bit larger than average but they've been balanced out by a small waist and my curvy hips. It would appear student life has helped slim me down a little ... who knew?

She passes me my glass of Champagne and I take a welcome sip. "Okay, I would suggest we try a plunge bra, considering the deep neckline you indicated; and satin for the material, yes? It is a smoother finish than lace, so it won't show if the dress is a bit snug." She leans towards me conspiratorially, whispering behind her hand. "But, a little lace on the trim won't hurt."

She exits the cubicle leaving me feeling exposed. Staring at my four reflections I drain my glass, thankful the lighting is subtle. I don't look too bad, these must be magic mirrors – my old underwear *is* shocking though.

Forty minutes later, I exit the shop feeling much better than when I first went in. I've purchased three new sets of underwear. They're all different and stunningly beautiful. The fit is fabulous; they didn't cost the earth either, but admittedly they were a bit more expensive than my usual M&S purchases. I refuse to feel guilty about it, I deserved a treat. Confidence restored, I walk down the high street to my next appointment.

At the salon, I'm warmly greeted by a bubbly, petite blonde. She's amazingly dressed in black leather shorts over black fishnet tights. A cropped polo neck jumper exposes her toned, pale, flesh at the midriff. There's not a hint of a muffin-top in sight and I'm instantly jealous. It looks like she's cut the jumper up herself as the hem is stylishly frayed. The look is finished off with bright red, classic, eight eye Dr Martens. She looks fabulous. Her hair's bleached, platinum blonde and shiny, cropped short over her ear on one side, graduating to a longer bob below her jawline on the other. Jet black eyeliner and a splash of vivid red lipstick completes the look.

"Hiya, I'm Angie … Angelica," she holds out her hand to me in greeting.

The salon is noisy with dryers blasting away and customers happily chitchatting over the noise. They're all draped in black capes to protect their clothing. A young boy of about sixteen is vigorously washing an older woman's hair at the back wash. To the rear are treatment rooms. It's a fancy set up.

"You must be Edi?" she carries on. "Christina rang and booked the appointment for you... she's brilliant. She has the most fantastic hair, I love styling her." She's chatty and bubbly. A typical stylist, filling the space in conversation with prattle and gossip.

Walking me in, she relieves me of my shopping bags and jacket, placing them in a secure area behind the receptionist's desk, before leading me towards the rear of the salon.

"The guy at the back, in the *'Brokeback Mountain'* shirt is Morgan. He's not gay – he just looks it." She rolls her heavily made up eyes for effect. "He's actually my boyfriend and a brilliant stylist. He'll be doing your hair today."

Morgan is busy with another customer at the moment, so I watch him as he works. He certainly looks as if he knows what he's doing; scissors flashing, his head bowed in concentration. His shirt's an absolute cracker... pink and blue checked with white mother-of-pearl buttons. He's even wearing the obligatory cowboy boots. Only the Stetson is missing... he looks ridiculously camp, but he wears it well.

"This is where the magic happens." Opening a treatment room door, Angie ushers me through. "Make yourself comfortable, I'll be back in a tick. Would you like something to drink? Champagne... water? Or we can run to tea or coffee if you prefer?" Wow, these fancy places really believe in pampering and pushing the boat out.

As much as I'm tempted, I don't think I could manage another glass of Champagne and remain sensible. "Water would be lovely – thank you." I remove my shoulder bag and place it over the chair while I wait.

A couple of minutes later Angie returns, wearing a white tunic and carrying a glass of sparking iced water, complete with fresh mint leaves and wedges of lime. Resting the water on the table, she asks me to take a seat so we can discuss which treatments I would like.

Agreeing to an eyebrow wax and tint, a manicure, pedicure, haircut and blow, I'm already regretting allowing Christina to plan my evening. Angie is obviously in her element so I try to relax and enjoy it. It's been a long time since I had any pampering.

By the time she's done, my nails look beautiful. Dark, almost black-red nail polish; it's dramatic but will look great with the green dress. I've not had acrylic nails, I don't like how they feel, so Angie has kept my own nails shorter and shaped them so they're neat and square. It's the perfect shape to compliment the dark colour. My eyebrows look great too. I've a naturally high arch, but she's left my brows a little fuller as is the modern look; then tinted them a deep auburn to match my hair. I'm impressed and can't stop looking at them. They really make my blue eyes stand out.

Next, it's time for my rats-tails… I'm wishing Morgan good luck with that challenge. Morgan settles me into the back-wash himself, running his fingers through my knotty tangles, assessing the damage, deciding on the appropriate shampoo and treatments needed.

"Your hair is a beautiful colour, but it's a little dry," he rubs the brittle strands between his fingers, then combs through from front to back a few times, looking in the mirror to find the natural fall of my hair line. Dry is an understatement, he's being kind. Fragile, straw-like, damaged, all of the above!

"Okay then, I think we need a deep conditioning treatment - then I've the perfect style for you. You don't need highlights; the colour is amazing and a good cut will bring out the natural red shades."

He seems to know what he's talking about. "Do you think you can trust me?" He's so camp – I can't believe he's straight. He continues running his fingers through my hair, smiling expectantly at me in the mirror. *Oh, what the hell.*

"I trust you," I say quietly. In for a penny and all that. It's the first time in years I've spoken those words to anyone.

Chapter 20

I stare in wonderous disbelief at my reflection in the salon mirror. I barely recognise the woman looking back at me. She's beautiful; with a lustrous mane of glossy dark, auburn hair, fair creamy complexion, guileless light blue eyes and full pink lips, all accentuating the light dusting of freckles scattering her nose.

I absolutely *love* my new hair. Morgan has washed, trimmed, styled and treated it as it's never been treated before. Any hint of the frizzy rat's nest has disappeared, along with about three inches of split dead ends, which are currently being swept up by the salon junior.

Morgan barely looked up from his task, working away silently. Concentrating on layering my hair, it falls softly in lush waves, framing my heart-shaped face; the length brushing my collar bone. It's shorter than I usually wear it, but it suits me and I could still tie it up if I wanted to. The sophisticated style is exactly what he said it would be, accentuating the different tones of red; ranging from a deep lustrous dark auburn to the lighter highlights of strawberry blonde, where the summer sun has lifted the colour. It shimmers and shines and I'm reminded of the once, young girl who hated this red hair so much she called it *'The curse'* and bleached it peroxide blonde to hide it. *What on earth was I thinking?*

"Ta dah!!" Morgan sings as he spins my chair round making my hair swish about my face. "A masterpiece if ever I saw one!"

"Oh Wow! Edi, it looks amazing. *You* look amazing!" Angie has just come back into the salon with fish and chips, a well-deserved supper for her and Morgan, a reward for a job well done.

"Thank you both so much! This is wonderful. I think I'll be able to manage this style without too much trouble." Turning my head from side to side, I try out my new look. I love it!

"It should be a piece of cake. Just remember to condition it after every wash. It shouldn't need much styling; the cut is appropriate to your hairline so it will fall naturally into place with very little persuading... Oooh, chips!" Distracted by the food, Morgan grabs the bag from Angie and flounces to the back of the salon and through the door to the flat upstairs.

I'm the last person to leave. After I've paid and made a follow up hair appointment for six weeks from now, I hug and again thank Angie. Seeing me out into the warm evening, I hear Morgan shouting Angie, her chips are getting cold. She rolls her eyes and grins at me, waving a cheery goodbye as she shuts the door and turns the sign to read closed.

I'm walking on air. My hair feels wonderful and I've three brand new sets of underwear, all wrapped in delicate pink tissue paper and folded neatly in the classy, shiny black bag with the gold cord handles, emblazoned with *'Oreille Lingerie'* in gold calligraphy. Swinging the bag as I walk, I allow myself to be optimistic about tomorrow.

Entering the apartments, I run up the stairs two at a time and through my front door. Taking my bags into the bedroom, I quickly rifle through my hold-all, pulling out my pre-packed old underwear and replacing it with the new improved versions, keeping one set back to wear in the morning.

It's seven fifteen, so I quickly send a text message to Lizzy and Sammy explaining I'll be away with work this weekend and ask them to face-time David. He'll be pleased to hear from them. The ping of my phone indicates a reply.

'That's soooo cool! Don't work too hard! Say hello to Sirius for us. Washington is FUCKING AMAZEBALLZ!!! We'll text the carrot tomorrow. Love you - L & S'

Well, that was easy. Strolling into the kitchen to make some supper, I can't help looking in the mirror at my hair and giving it a little flick. Baked beans on toast is quick and easy and one of my all-time favourites, so I make that. Opening a bottle of beer, I pour it into a tall glass and sit on a high stool at the breakfast bar, swinging my legs under the counter while eating my gourmet meal.

I think about the girls in Washington, then about David and Wendy. I've not told Lizzy and Sammy *that* corking bit of news I laugh to myself; they can hear that straight from the horse's mouth, they'll freak when they find out.

After dinner, I wash up and call David to let him know I'll be away this weekend. He's pleased to hear from me and while he seems keen to listen to me talk about my new job, he would much rather tell me his own gossip. He doesn't give a stuff I'm going away! What a blooming cheek! I sit and listen patiently making the appropriate 'Ooh and aha' noises when required. The call doesn't last long, they never do. It's wonderful he's so happy and contented.

The next job is to check my green dress. Taking it out of the clear polythene dry-cleaning bag, I check it for any stains that may have appeared since I wore it at graduation. It's clean and doesn't need ironing so I replace the polythene to keep it that way and lay it neatly across the handles of my hold-all. I only have one good pair of shoes, so they'll have to do. My black suede courts; they're pretty basic but look fine if I team them with my only going out handbag - not surprisingly, a black suede clutch. There, I'm packed.

I sit on the end of the bed and wonder what to do next. I've no idea what time I'm supposed to be at the airfield tomorrow as Silas hasn't contacted me since his email this morning. I'm beginning to think he's changed his mind when my work phone starts ringing. Diving for my handbag, before it can ring off, I fish it out and swipe to answer.

"Hello, Silas?" I don't even look at the name flashing on the screen.

"Hi, no it's me." *Christina!* "Hasn't he contacted you? God, that man is an absolute disaster sometimes." She's shaking her head, I can tell. "How did it go at the salon?" she asks.

"Oh, wonderful; thank you for the recommendation. Angie and Morgan are a pair of miracle workers for sure," I enthuse, with genuine appreciation.

"Marvellous, I knew they'd be great. Morgan is a bit of a **genius,** isn't he? Ha, ha… and Angie… well, I could eat her up!" She sounds tons better than this morning. "I just wanted to let you know that we've had an absolute decision from that new client and he will *finally* sign on the dotted line in the morning."

I knew it. That's why she sounds so different. "Oh, wow! That's fantastic news Christina, you must be hugely relieved."

"Yes… well… I'm not holding my breath. We've been here before. He'll be in the office from about nine'ish. And I expect to be locking horns, in battle with him for a couple of hours at least. *Sooo…"* she stretches the word out for effect, "if I don't see you before you leave, I just wanted to say have a great time and don't do anything I wouldn't do! … oops, too late, I already did!" She's so sassy. "I'm sure Silas will call you tonight. He said he would. Have a great weekend my lovely, bye!"

"Bye, and thanks again for the help with… well you know…" I love her.

"My pleasure hon!" and with that, she hangs up.

Hmmm, so Silas should have phoned me then? Oh well, I suppose he has the right to change his mind, but I can't help the huge stab of disappointment piercing through me at the thought.

Realizing he might have tried to call while I was being polished and preened and I could have missed it, I check my email. I left the office quite early at Christina's insistence. Perhaps he's emailed me with the details? I grab my lap top and fire it up - and there it is; the response from Silas, to my earlier mail. He sent it at three thirty, so he must be waiting for *me* to reply now. I'm such an idiot!

'Hi Edi, I was so relieved to receive your reply. I will have the jet ready and prepared for departure at 09:00 hrs. So please could you be at the office for 08:00? I'm really looking forward to this weekend. Fondest regards S.'

Wow, he's gone all formal boss-man on me again. It might be just business after all. I type a quick reply.

'Hi Silas, sorry for the delayed response. I finished early and have only just had time to check my email. I'll be at the office for 08:00 as per your request. I'm really looking forward to it too. It's a long time since I was last in Paris. Regards, Edi.'

There, that should suffice. I press send and shut down my laptop.

Checking the time, it's just gone eight. I'm restless and not ready for bed yet, and I don't want to watch TV so I decide to try out the hot tub on the roof terrace. That should kill an hour. I'll need to be careful about my hair so I find a large banana clip and twist it up out of the way. Dragging on my old black tankini and borrowing a towel from the heated rail in the bathroom, I pick up my beer and head outside. Slipping through the bi-fold doors, I'm soon out on the terrace and climbing up the fancy stairs to the roof garden patio.

The night sky is just turning a rosy pink. The sun is getting low and the earlier storm has left the air balmy and fresh. There's a slight breeze but it isn't chilly; in fact, it's quite warm. The view from the roof garden is just as stunning as it was last night. There's promise of a magnificent sunset in the pink and lilac sky. Once the sun has set, I imagine it'll be all twinkly street lights, sparkly stars and dark rolling distant hills. All around the roof garden the globe lights are coming on, softly sending out a shimmering, golden glow, illuminating the vivid green of the leaves and bright colours of the flowering plants. A moth is flickering around the numerous shrubs, which are swaying gently in the light evening breeze.

Leaning over, I switch on the hot tub lights and the jets immediately begin to bubble. The spar causes a light blanket of foam to spread over the top of the rippling water. A low rumbling hum from the pump breaks the peaceful silence. Dipping my hand in, I swish it around. It's lovely and warm, so I kick off my flip flops and drop my towel onto one of the wooden chairs. Grabbing the hand rail so I don't slip - that would be all I needed - I descend the steps and lower myself into the bubbles, taking care not to wet my hair, resting my neck on the edge of the tub.

Reclining back, I congratulate myself on my luck, wondering at the glorious sunset. Slowly, the burning orb descends to meet the earth. At first, it's a glowing red ball of fire, singeing the distant hills with fiery tendrils; then it becomes a half sun; then just the top arc is visible. Eventually, the sun disappears altogether, dropping out of sight behind a distant hill. There's a brief moment of total blackness as my eyes become accustomed to the dark. Then; as if on cue, the stars begin to make their appearance, emerging slowly at first, until the familiar constellations are all settled into position... bliss.

A few peaceful minutes pass and I'm completely entranced by my surroundings. Contemplating the events of the day, what little tension is left in my body ebbs away. The warm water is soothing. The popping and spluttering sound of the spa, contrasts with the low rhythmic hum of the pump propelling the jets of hot water; it's hypnotic. I could lie here all night watching the steam rising and disappearing into the night air.

Finishing my beer, I place the empty glass on the low table serving the hot tub. It's really dark now. The stars are so vivid, it's as if someone has broken a diamond necklace; scattering the diamonds onto an indigo, velvet cushion.

I start to hum... something... it's a tune, by *Rag and Bone Man*, '*Human*' I think. Closing my eyes and starting with my arms, I begin slowly stroking my limbs; up over my wrists, massaging my forearms in turn. Then my shoulders and collar bone, travelling round my neck, back down my arms before sweeping my hands softly over the rest of my submerged body. Oh, the feeling is heavenly.

There's a sudden moment of clarity and my heart leaps; I realise I'm not just hearing the song as it plays in my head. The music is *actually* filtering through the night air and I've been unconsciously humming along to the familiar tune because I can actually hear it! *Where's that coming from?* Perhaps it's one of the neighbours, they've excellent taste in music. Totally relaxed now, I carry on massaging my body, appreciating the impromptu musical accompaniment.

A flicker of movement in my peripheral vision startles me out of my reverie. Jerking up suddenly a tidal-wave of water splashes over the sides of the hot tub; soaking the tiled floor. All I can do is gasp and stare. There, stood bold as brass, at the edge of the decking, looking like a Roman God, is Silas! He's naked from the waist up and holding two glasses of red wine. He has a white towel draped loosely around his waist, and his dark, mocha skin is glistening in the glow of the subdued lighting. The sprinkling of hair on his broad chest, emphasizes his defined pecks and six-pack of tight muscles, rippling with every deep breath he takes.

The towel is slung low on his narrow hips, exposing the smooth dark skin of his taught flat stomach. He's seriously defined; every muscle is sharp. A couple of thick veins are standing out in stark relief on his under-belly, marking a trail from just below his waist to his hidden groin. He's obviously just been working out; his chest and arms are still coated with a light film of perspiration, his biceps bulging with tension.

Have I died and gone to heaven?

Chapter 21

It only takes a split second for the vision to sink in. "Silas!" I squeal, "you startled me!" Now I find my voice, I sound more than a little breathless. It's not surprising; the way he's just standing there really has taken my breath away,

"When I hadn't heard from you, I was worried you might've changed your mind about tomorrow." He takes a step towards the tub. "I thought I might see you at the gym. When you weren't there, I decided to come and check you were okay." He reaches the hot tub. "Here, I brought you this. It seems a shame to waste it." He hands me a glass of deep red wine. "It was still open from last night," he explains.

"Oh, err, thank you." I'm no longer shocked he's turned up unannounced. In fact, deep down I think I was half expecting it. If I've learned anything about Silas Tudor, from the last few days, he's not the kind of man who's afraid to make his presence felt.

Reaching out, I accept the proffered wineglass, silently praying it doesn't slip through my wet fingers. Briefly touching the glass to my lips, I take a small sip. The wine is at blood temperature and the slight taste helps to moisten my dry mouth. It's lovely. Twisting my body slightly, I rest the goblet on the side of the tub.

"Do you need a hand there?" A knowing smile curves his lips as he inclines his head; tilting his chin towards my lap. Looking down I realise my massaging touch has wandered between my upper thighs and I'm gently rubbing myself over my bikini bottoms

Embarrassed at being caught, I quickly remove my wayward hand, trailing it up my stomach until it's resting on my chest. Dropping my eyes in shame, I can't look him in the eye. The hem of my tankini is loose, it's ridden up, flapping in the bubbly water. The material lifts, exposing my belly and midriff. Uncomfortable with the slight exposure, I can't resist the urge to pull it down but the action is pointless. As soon as I release the hem, it floats back up again, driven by the vigour of the foam. I'm fidgeting and faffing like an idiot.

"You seem... jumpy." Silas observes my awkward performance, his eyes roaming all over my exposed torso. "You shouldn't be..." so sure of himself, it just increases my nerves. "There's no need to cover up on my behalf... you look good... really good." *God, that voice...*

"I'm not jumpy," I lie. "I just wasn't expecting company." Still fumbling with my floating top, my obvious embarrassment causes my voice to rise, sounding more annoyed than I really am. "I mean... I'm not nervous..." I repeat in a quieter tone, clutching the hem of my tankini so it stays put. Clearly, I'm nervous... and he knows it.

"Leave it alone..." he commands. "The water will just keep pushing it up. And anyway, there's nobody here to see you... except me, that is. And I'm not complaining."

The sound of his voice is enough for my body temperature to skyrocket. "No... I'm not complaining in the least," he whispers the last bit quietly, as if speaking to himself.

Focusing his eyes back on mine he says clearly now, "I asked you a question." *What Question?* "I said... do you need a hand?" I open my mouth, but no words come out. *A hand with what?...* Then I realise... he means with the massage... *Oh my Lord!*

Not waiting for my reply, he moves so he's standing directly behind me. Placing his glass next to mine, I feel him lowering. Slowly, he squats so he can kneel on the step. His thighs are spread wide apart, his knees either side of my tense body. Reaching forward, he rests his large calloused hands on my shoulders and draws me backwards, so I'm cradled snugly between his firm thighs. Then he begins a slow firm massage; his thumbs press deep circles at the base of my neck, between my shoulder blades, his fingertips alighting on my collar-bone. The intensity of his touch is quite unexpected.

My body stiffens at the intimate contact. As he applies more pressure, I feel my skin heating in response to his working hands; just as it did when he held me after the incident with the wasp. He must feel it too. I'm burning.

Skilfully, he continues with his expert ministrations, ignoring my obviously tense state - determined to make me relax and accept his attention. Within minutes of him massaging my tight muscles it begins to work, and unconsciously I roll my head to the side in full appreciation, jumping back when my ear connects with a very warm, very hard thigh. Unperturbed, his left hand ceases the massage and slowly, he strokes up my neck, until his palm is cupping my cheek. Tenderly he applies just enough pressure to force my head back to its resting place, leaning against his thigh. This time I stay put.

I murmured a sigh of pleasure; he responds with, "that's good, ha?" whispering softly in my ear. His breath tickles my neck. A delicious shiver ripples through me, belying the fact my skin is on fire. He *knows* it's good. More than just good, it's heavenly.

"I sent you an email." Lolling my head on his lap, I find my train of thought. He must have been waiting ages for my reply. "Earlier, when I got home from the hairdressers... I went to have my hair cut."

"I know you did; it came through as I was leaving the gym. I thought I would pay you a visit anyway. I didn't mean to startle you," his strong fingers continued kneading my knotted muscles. His touch grows firmer, his hands warmer. "You just looked so beautiful, lying there, wet and relaxed. I didn't want to disturb you." Stressing the 'T' in the word wet, he keeps on with his massage, whispering close to my ear. It feels divine.

I'm totally relaxed now. "If I'm being truthful, I half expected you to show up," I reply, boldly… "I'm pleased that you did… disturb me, I mean." *Where did that come from?* My brain appears to be so lax I'm unable to show any restraint. I should be telling him to leave but somehow, I can't.

"*Huh.*" He pants out a short laugh. "I can't seem to be able to stay away…" he whispers softly.

I go quiet. With a juddering breath, I savour the moment. I don't want him to stay away… and that scares the heck out of me. I've never craved company like I crave his… I've never wanted to be near a man, like I want to be near him and I've never *known* desire… not like I feel when he's near me. Not ever. It's incomprehensible to me. Alien.

I'm still pondering over these new revelations as his hands begin to move, circling my throat. Remaining behind me, he increases the pressure on my collar bones, the sheer weight of his hands has me squirming under his touch. So much so, I want him to move his hand lower and massage other areas of my body. My arms are floating limply at my sides. I'm so very relaxed. "Hmmm, that's nice," I breathe.

"It is… is there room for a little one? It's getting chilly out here." Once again, he doesn't wait for my reply. Removing his hands from my shoulders, he rises. Missing his tender touch immediately, my eyes open in response to the sudden loss. Instinctively, I lift my head. He's standing on the steps of the hot tub, watching me intently.

Removing his towel, he drops it on top of mine on the wooden chair. Then, raising one long, thickly muscled leg, he strides over the edge of the tub and onto the step beside me; all the while gazing intently into my eyes. Moving gracefully as a panther, without causing so much as a ripple, his other leg follows so he's towering above me; he's close enough I could easily wrap my arms round his bulging thighs and bury my nose in his groin. I'm sorely tempted.

He's wearing black swim shorts *and,* to my shock, sports a massive hard-on! I blink on a swallow. *Jesus!* Embarrassed but totally unable to look away, my delighted eyes follow his slow progress as he lowers his rock-hard body into the tub beside me; each sculptured muscle, each corded sinew, is taught and firm. He looks like Poseidon, commanding the oceans.

Once seated, he positions his upper body to face me and rests his sculptured arm along the rim of the tub behind my shoulders. His thumb begins to trace a lazy path, grazing the shallow groove between my shoulder blades. Up and down my back it travels, sending tingles down my spine with every stroke. His thigh brushes against mine under the water.

"So, where did you go?" he asks softly, his deep brown eyes bore into mine as if he can see my very soul, "when you left this afternoon, I mean. I was about to come and find you to discuss tomorrow."

"Christina insisted... I just went to pick up a few things," mumbling in reply, I sound a bit huffy. I'm still covering my chest with my arm, so I slide my hand back into the water. His eyes flick quickly to my cleavage, a split second later, they're back, drilling deeply into mine. I can't look away, nor can I read his mood.

Still unsure, I need to justify my early absence, so I babble on. "You know... just some essentials... for tomorrow." *Like, essential lingerie and essential beauty treatments... Well the hair really was essential, but the other stuff... maybe not so much.* Even though I had permission, or rather was bullied into it by Christina, I still feel like I've been caught playing hooky – he's my boss! Even if he's ridiculously hot, and I've consent from my other boss – who just happens to be his ex-wife!

He raises his eyebrows, breaking the intense eye contact for a fraction of a second, as he turns to pick up his wine. Taking a slow sip, he gazes at me over the rim of his glass. My acquisitive eyes are instinctively drawn to his full lips. Watching his slow-motion sipping causes my breath to hitch. A droplet of wine beads on his lower lip and I immediately want to lick it off. He dashes it away with a sweep of his tongue. I can't remove my eyes from his luscious mouth. It's stupidly embarrassing.

"So... my ex-wife had a hand in it?" he asks me. "She just can't help herself. I expect she's just pleased that I'm with a '*real woman*' for a change!" The reference to Christina's earlier comment isn't lost on me. It piques my interest and I just have to ask.

"What exactly *did* she mean by that?"

"Let's just say that Tina has not been very enamoured with my last few choices of... companion." He's being a bit cagy, but I think I understand the undertone. I wouldn't be surprised if Silas' previous choice of '*companion*' wears ridiculous platform shoes, tight mini-dresses and is possibly a good few years younger than him. Mid-life crisis following a divorce?

"Really?" Intrigue gets the better of me. I wonder who he's dated... I can only imagine.

"Well, let's just say I was playing the field. But it gets very old, very quickly... I was dating women I didn't like... too young, too shallow... too thin!" He says the last bit with a salacious grin on his face. "I like women who actually eat a meal, not just chase it round the plate. I'm too old for all that superficial shit."

"Ah, so you thought you'd try the older, fatter, brainier version? How does it feel, letting your ex-wife choose your dates for you?" I give him my best Paddington-hard-stare; jutting my chin in indignation. Thankfully I've developed a thick skin over the years and no longer care what people think of me. Clearly, he has no notion what he's just said, judging by the look on his face and is oblivious to my teasing.

237

"I'm thrilled with her choice so far... but I think I'm big enough and ugly enough to decide for myself," his voice has become low and seductive.

"And what have you decided?" I match my tone to his, narrowing my eyes beadily.

The bubbles are dying and the jets have ceased their powerful pulsing, the water of the spa turning from frothing bubbles to a gentle ripple. The tub lights and the lack of foam reveal the contours of our submerged bodies; visible but distorted beneath the shimmering water.

"Well, you're here now..." he whispers softly, flicking his thumb along my back. "My ex will be delighted to know I've found you all by myself." I shiver at that comment.

"I think you had a little encouragement." I know Christina has played her part.

Placing his glass back on the side, he edges closer so the full length of his thigh is pressed against mine. "She'd really like to think that. But contrary to popular belief, I like what I see; in fact, I liked it the first moment I laid eyes on it... even with the ridiculous shirt, the stained trousers and the wild hair... I liked all of it." He says all of this in a hushed whisper, passing his eyes over my breasts, they travel down my front coming to rest between my legs.

Subconsciously I press my thighs tightly together, but he widens his so his left leg is pressing against my right; forcing me to shift sideways, so I'm wedged into the corner of the tub. Invitingly all I want to do is spread my legs wantonly and open myself up fully in total abandonment.

Intoxicated by his closeness, I'm drunk on him. Raising his hand, he places a finger on my throat, slowly he glides it upwards, so it's under my chin, tilting it, forcing me to look into his eyes. "I *really* like what I see," he confirms, leaving no room for any misunderstanding. My breath stalls, as very slowly and deliberately he leans towards me.

"I like what I see too…" my voice is barely a whisper.

The world seems to stop spinning. For a few heartbeats we're suspended in time. Then, very gently and deliberately, he steals a kiss.

His lips are so soft, the fullness covering my whole mouth, so I naturally part my own lips, to accommodate his. It's dreamy. I've never felt lips so soft and firm at the same time. Slowly and deliberately he opens his mouth. His tongue skims my bottom lip, caressing, searching; purposefully, seeking my acceptance. I'm not going to deny him, this is heady, wonderful stuff; the heat of the hot tub and the night breeze only emphasizing the growing feeling of exhilaration surging through me.

Closing my eyes, I moan, opening my mouth further, which only encourages him to deepen his kiss. My legs are open now, my thigh wedged firmly against his. His big hand is still at my throat, stroking a slow line from my chin, to the hollow at my collarbone then back again.

Until now I've kept my hands still. They remain, one covering my breast, the other on my lap under the water. But it's becoming increasingly more difficult not to touch him. Tentatively I remove my hand from my breast and place it upon his chest; the flat of my palm feeling out the firm, solid muscles lying beneath the warm smooth skin. He groans his approval into my mouth.

Breaking the kiss and pulling back slightly, he watches my small hand, as I delicately trace my pink fingertips over his sensitive mocha skin. He's panting, and goose bumps are peppering his warm flesh in the wake of my searching touch.

Aware that he's still sporting a raging erection under his swim shorts, it's a challenge not to reach below the water and take him in hand.

Sliding my palm back up his throat, to the back of his neck, I lean towards him invitingly. I haven't had nearly enough of his mouth, so it's my turn to lead the kiss. I pull him toward me, feeling out the back of his head with my eager fingers. Raising my other hand, I cup his jaw, forcing the kiss to deepen.

Unable to resist the temptation, he nips and bites my bottom lip, an indication he wants to take over, so I allow it, submitting control, tilting my head so he can devour my mouth. We're both moaning now, the desire building, becoming urgent. He draws away again and stares deeply into my eyes, resting his forehead against mine.

"You're bad for my health," he whispers. "I can't think straight when I'm near you." The feeling is mutual, I just want to kiss him, over and over. "I can't remember feeling like this before. It's strange to me." He stares at me, his hand never leaving my throat, the other still resting on the back of the tub.

"Your, lips are so soft Silas, I could kiss you forever. I can't remember a time when a kiss has felt so wonderful." I can't actually remember the last real kiss I had, it's that long ago. I'm surprised I can still remember how to do it!

The intense feelings flooding through me at the joining of our mouths is incredible. I need to feel it again, just to make sure it was real, so I lean back in for more. He indulges my need, engulfing me in a firm embrace, wrapping his arm round my back and pulling me closer.

A juddering rumble indicates the hot tub is springing back to life. The jets begin to pulse and the water surges around us once again. The front of my tankini lifts with the force of the swirling foam, but this time I don't reach to pull it down. This time I allow it to rise, exposing my midriff and the underside of my breasts. We continue mindlessly, oblivious to the frothing water around us.

Silas's hand wanders down my front, stroking my breastbone, skimming over the wet material of my swimsuit until it's resting on the bare skin of my waist.

Our kissing has escalated to a new level. My mouth is hungry for his and our tongues are performing their own ballet as they roll and twirl together. The weight of his hand has me squirming against him, I'm mentally begging for him to caress my skin, to lift my top and graze my breasts. My nipples are rigid bullets, brushing against the wet Lycra; painfully erect with the desperate need to be touched, stroked and pinched.

As if he's read my thoughts, he starts to move his hand upwards; gently he cups the underside of my breast. At first, I jump at his delicate touch, but then I cling even tighter to his neck, my back arches and I unwittingly force my breast into his calloused palm.

Unable to maintain the intensity I break free tipping my head back, gasping. "*Ahh*!" I breath, opening my eyes and taking in the incredible beauty of the night sky. A trillion stars are twinkling like diamonds overhead. I'm intoxicated. Silas moves his lips to the hollow of my throat, licking, nipping, sucking.

"*Oh! Aghhh! Sssss!*" I hiss and pant through my teeth, relishing the sharp tingles on my skin and the searing heat of his mouth, as his tongue traces lazy circles on my neck and throat.

His hand begins massaging the exposed part of my breast, cupping and kneading, but not attempting to lift or remove my top to expose me further. The feeling is one of prolonged, intense, anticipation. I want him to touch my nipples, but he doesn't. I want him to thrust his hand under my swimsuit, but he doesn't. Instead, he chooses to squeeze, knead and gently caress the underside of my breast. It's the only part of my breast that's exposed and It's driving me crazy, with need and craving. I writhe, squirm and groan under his expert touch.

"Shh, hush now," he sooths me as he continues his delicious teasing. "Not tonight, Honey-bee. We've all the time in the world. And I want to take my time with you. Be patient my sweet, sweet girl."

"Oh, please, Silas, ahhh!" I'm shaking with anticipation. The heavy throbbing at my groin is almost too painful to stand. By now, I'm so turned on I'm sorely tempted to grab his cock and force him into submission, but I don't.

Drawing his head away but leaving his hand exactly where it is; The sudden absence of his mouth on my neck has me lowering my head. Bringing him back into focus, I feel drunk, my head is swimming, everything is amplified. The drubbing of the powerful jets, competing with the pounding of my heart and the rushing of blood through my veins, head and ears opposing, the swooshing water as it surges through the tub.

"We need to stop… before I do something, we both might regret," he whispers against my lips. "I don't want to rush this, it means too much."

"Yes, it does," I gasp, in agreement. I'm beginning to descend from my high. "I think we need to go inside before we end up staying out here all night." My senses are returning. "We're going to look like a pair of wrinkled prunes!" giggling, I lightly peck his full lips. He responds in kind, but slower, gently allowing us to recover from the intensity of our first intimate encounter.

"Come on, let's go and get dry." He nuzzles my nose and pulls my top down, so I'm decent once again. Leaning over the side he flicks the switch, instantly silencing the pumps and dimming the tub lights.

Gracefully he rises, the water streams down his body in rivulets. The dark shadows cast by the globe lights of the decked terrace emphasize the solid plains of his sculptured torso. The black swim shorts cling to his fine muscular legs, he looks like the centrepiece of a Roman fountain. His erection is still present, standing front and centre! My eyes rise along with him and I realise I'm gaping open mouthed, so I quickly pop it shut.

"Here," He offers, "let me help you. I don't want you slipping and hurting yourself before we even get to Paris!" Taking my hand firmly in his, he tugs me to my feet, steadying me before assisting me out of the tub onto the wooden decking. Dipping gracefully, giving me a fleeting view of his toned glutes, scooping up my towel from the chair and swinging it loose from its folds, like a matador unfurling his cape. Engulfing me in the soft white cotton, before grabbing his own and giving himself a swift wipe over.

"Come on, it's getting chilly." Clutching my hand, he leads me off the roof and down to the lower terrace. I'm starting to shiver. The temperature has dropped considerably with the night air; I'm desperate to get into the shower and warm up.

My new hairstyle is not as lovely as it was, despite my care with clipping it up. Some wispy tendrils are damp and now it needs to be redone.

"You're shivering." He wraps a huge arm round my shoulders, and pulls me into him, so I'm buried under his arm. He slides the door open and we step inside. The instant warmth of the lounge is a welcome contrast to the cool air outside.

"You go and have a shower. I'll finish tidying up and then we can put the kettle on and have a warm drink." He turns and walks back outside, presumably to collect the wine glasses and our flip flops, which were scattered on the decking. *Doesn't he feel the cold?* I shudder at the thought.

Hugging my towel around me, I jog through the apartment and into my en-suite bathroom and turn on the shower. Stepping in, still wearing my swim suit, I let the water heat my skin and run all over the Lycra, ensuring I rinse away all the chlorine before I pull off the wet costume, dropping it on the shower floor.

My hair's wet through now; I abandon the rescue in favour of a quick wash with my new shampoo, remembering to soak it in conditioner before rinsing. I sponge my body with exfoliating body wash and scrub my face. By the time I'm done, I feel squeaky clean and refreshed. One quick glance in the mirror reveals that my face is glowing and my lips are plump and swollen. Mmm kissing…

Now for the tricky part. Do I try to restyle my hair, or do I leave it to dry naturally? That's easy, quality time with Silas is more inviting than fighting with my hair for an hour. I perform a rough rub with the towel to remove most of the moisture, then scoop my hair and tie it in a ponytail; I'll mess about with it in the morning, trusting Morgan's word it'll behave.

I finish off by slapping on some body moisturiser. My skin is tingling and sensitive. Every time I relive the intensity of our kisses and his touch, I have to take a deep breath to calm down. Finally, I apply face cream, taking care to dab gently around my eyes with my ring finger.

Checking the mirror, my hair is damp but gleaming and I look radiant. It's amazing what a good snog does for your complexion! Pulling on my vest and shorts, I grab my dressing gown and head to the lounge in search of Silas.

He's in the kitchen. I stop dead on the spot. He's dressed in a pair of red, white and blue plaid flannel shorts - and nothing else! Holding a jar of coffee, he's about to put it back in the cupboard when he spots me at the door. "Good shower?" He reaches up to replace the jar and I almost faint at the sight of his back muscles stretching and flexing as he moves.

"Mmm, yeah, thanks." Remembering where I'm, I start to stroll into the kitchen and across to where he's stood with his back to me. Unable to resist his magnificent physical presence, I step behind him. Wrapping my arms round him and flattening my palms on his chest, I rest my soft cheek in the centre of his solid back, pressing my full bodyweight against him. He's warm, his skin smells wonderfully of white musk and sandalwood and it's silkily soft. He must have showered in the guest bathroom. I don't know why that surprises me; it's his place after all. I allow my lips to brush against his back, just once, then resume nuzzling. He shudders in my hold. The taught muscles of his back ripple under my cheek as he moves.

Distracted from his coffee making duties, he swivels in my arms so he's facing me. His arms lift, moving and engulfing me in a tight hug, drawing me close. His chin is sitting atop my head, my cheek is squashed against his stubbly pec. Burrowing closer I place a soft kiss in the channel between his muscles, right in the centre of his breastbone; the soft, trimmed hair tickles my sensitive lips. He in turn, kisses the top of my head.

"I'm thirsty," I mumble into his chest. "It's the spa, I think."

"Yes, you need to drink some water so you don't dehydrate."

Reluctantly, he releases his hold and pivots in my arms to resume coffee making duties. I continue to hug against his back. I know I'm hindering his progress, but I don't give a flying fig. I continue to caress and stroke his skin with my lips. He shudders again.

"Go and make yourself comfortable, I'll bring these through."

Grudgingly I release him and traipse into the lounge. *Rag and Bone Man* has finished and another soft voice is filling the silence. Instantly I recognise it, it's *Guy Garvey 'Angela's Eyes'*. I love *Elbow*.

Plonking myself unceremoniously onto the couch, I settle into the comfortable cushions and fold my legs beneath me. I've just closed my eyes, when I sense Silas's presence. When I open them, he has already placed two steaming cups on the coffee table along with two glasses of sparking water. The water is garnished with slices of cucumber and quarters of fresh lime.

"Here, drink this," he passes me a glass, then reclines back on the sofa, placing his arm around me protectively. This is heaven.

Slowly I sip the water, but soon my instincts take over and before I know it, I've guzzled the lot. Wow, I was thirsty. It was delicious too. The cucumber and lime really enhanced the flavour. I must remember that trick. He chuckles as he relieves me of my glass and places it back on the coaster. His own is empty too, I notice.

"Thank you, I was really thirsty." I smile up at him and he smiles back. "Why didn't you take it further?" I'm curious to know why he stopped when he did. I could tell he wanted more and for the first time ever I did too.

He sighs, "Edi, I know you would have let me and you would even have enjoyed yourself," he wiggles his eyebrows suggestively, but its temporary. Suddenly he's serious again. "I want to take it slowly with you. Savour the moment. When we make love… and it will be making love… I want you to experience ecstasy, not just a quick orgasm." *Oh Lord!*

I'm taken aback; *ecstasy, I've never experienced anything vaguely close to pleasure, let alone ecstasy.*

The open, natural way he speaks about sex makes me blush to my hair roots. "I think we could be amazing together. Didn't you feel it? Wasn't it profound for you too?" The sincerity in his stare heats my blood and my heart rate rises, recollecting our intense encounter.

"Yes Silas, it was wonderful." It was, I'm being truthful, "Amazing. I can't remember the last time a kiss made me feel like that," staring deep into his eyes. "If ever."

"Good." He's serious. "Me too." His brows knit together in a frown. A fleeting look of puzzlement crosses his face. "I guess…" he shakes his head and smiles as he searches for the right words. "…something just tells me that we need to take it slow. I want you to enjoy it. I want it to be… memorable." He kisses the top of my head again. "I never thought I would ever be the one to put the brakes on." He's back to matter of fact again.

"Usually, I'm all for sex on a first date. Hell, I'm usually all for sex without a date."

Christina's tart quip about a '*real woman*' springs to mind and I stiffen, wary of where he's going with this. Noticing I've become still, he hastens to put my mind at rest. "But you … you're so different." He strokes his fingers over my back soothingly. "There's something about you. Something… familiar yet mysterious at the same time. It's as if any sudden movement could spook you and send you running for the hills." He's not wrong. "And I don't want you to run from me. I want to know the real you. I want you to trust me."

His sincere words resonate within me, deeply. Right into my hidden soul. He knows instinctively I'm not revealing everything. He doesn't know the half of it, but for the first time in years I don't feel the need to run and hide, or resist the lure of a new relationship. Usually by now the desire to put up the shutters is irresistible. Usually by now I've sabotaged the chance of any further contact. I've raised the barriers; blocked any advances and shut myself off to my innermost wants. Usually by now I would be pushing him away; making excuses not to see him again, telling myself not to be so gullible. Men like him are not interested in women like me.

But for some reason, I'm going along with it. For some reason, I feel safe when I'm with him. I know I'm probably going to mess it all up and I'll end up losing my job as well as my self-respect. But I can't help it. This man is alluring. He's beautiful and strong. For the first time in years, I want to trust someone enough to let them into my inner sanctum, to find the courage to reveal my hidden true self, missing for nearly eighteen years. The self that could very well scare off the most ardent of suitors; the most valiant of knights in shining armour. It's time to trust someone other than me.

"Hey… anybody there?" he nudges me gently.

Grudgingly, I open my sleepy eyes. "Hmmm?" I've been drifting off, I'm suddenly so tired I can't keep my eyes open.

"I said, *I want you to trust me…* to take it slow." He untangles me from his hold and I immediately fall onto my side on the sofa.

"Okay!" I yawn… "I want to trust you… We'll take it slow."

Chapter 22

I kick my legs free of the duvet. I'm hot and sweaty and my mouth is parched dry. Squinting my eyes, I can tell it's still dark so it can't be morning yet.

Reaching out, I keep my eyes closed as I cautiously feel for my glass of water, which I always keep on my bedside table. Tentatively I make some exploratory pats with my fingers so I don't knock it over. There's a clink as my fingernail connects with the glass, but I can't quite locate it to take a firm hold. Giving up, I open my eyes in the semi-darkness and locate the glass. It's just out of my reach so I lean out a little further but I can't move.

Looking down I see a strong dark arm wrapped tightly around my ribcage, pinning me to the bed. For a brief moment, I'm filled with panic but only for a moment; now I'm wondering how I actually got to bed. The last thing I remember was snuggling on the sofa. Silas must have carried me. God, I'm hardly a lightweight, he must be really strong!

Gingerly, so as not to wake him, I inch forward. Stretching out my arm I manage to reach the glass. Slowly, desperately trying not to disturb his sleep, I pick up the glass and take a long glug. I still feel a bit dehydrated.

Silas murmurs something incoherently and pulls his arm so I'm squeezed and pulled back tightly against him, his cheek resting in the small of my back. Now I can't reach the table to put my glass back so I stretch down and place the empty glass on the floor by my bed, making sure to tuck it as far back as I can, so I don't forget it's there and tread on it in the morning. Relaxing back onto my pillow, I yawn, close my sleepy eyes and fall back into a deep slumber.

It feels like no time at all before I'm being coaxed awake. My shoulder is being gently rocked and a soft stream of air is blowing across my cheek.

"Edi, Honey, it's time to get up." My ear tickles with the warm breath of the whispered words "Edi, wake up sleepy head." My hair is being lightly brushed away from my face.

Rolling onto my back, I open my weary eyes to a vision of beauty. His handsome face hovers over me. He's sat on the side of the bed. One arm is leaning over me, effectively trapping me beneath the duvet. Stretching my arms over my head, I yawn loudly in his face and he doesn't even flinch; he must have a strong constitution to cope with my morning, dragon's breath! It makes me grin when he raises his eyebrows.

Growling, he drops his upper body weight on top of me, trapping me further and buries his head in my neck. My giggle turns into a full-on laugh as his growl becomes a snarl, he begins biting my neck. My arms fly down, my hands instinctively grip his shoulders, shoving, pushing against him. I start to kick my legs in vein as I heave and giggle beneath the weight of his solid chest. Reaching up, he grabs my wrists and pins them to the pillow at the side of my head. All the while continuing to growl, snarl and nibble at my sensitive neck. I'm trapped.

"Silas!" I'm breathless with the effort so I give up and stop fighting. "Please, I need to get up." Abruptly, he ceases the nibbling and growling, but stays where he is, inhaling deeply.

I just let him lie there for a few minutes. I'm also enjoying the intimate contact. He smells wonderful, so I'm guessing he's had a shower. I register that he's dressed, so he's been up for a while.

Finally, after what seems like an age, he moves, lifting his head from the crook of my neck to gaze into my eyes. The world shifts. It's as if the air in the room is suddenly thinner, making it difficult to breathe. We're both just staring at each other, taking in the planes of each other's faces. Absorbing. Learning. Remembering.

My own eyes drift all over his lovely face, eventually falling on to his full lips. I lean up in invitation and he takes the hint, dropping his lips to mine and sweeps a soft, gentle kiss over my mouth.   Moving his head from side to side, he licks the seam of my lips and I open to him like a flower seeking the sun. A deep moan leaves his throat and his tongue enters my mouth coaxing out mine. We relax into one another, the kiss building and deepening. Our tongues are swirling and probing. But before too long it is over and he pulls away, leaving me dazed and wanting.

He's gazing deeply into my eyes. I'm sure my look mirrors his own. Adoration, wonder, mystification, joy, fear; all of these emotions are visible in that one fleeting look. Pulling my arms back down he sits up, effectively releasing me from his man-trap. Levering me into a sitting position he keeps hold of my wrists and cradles them into his chest. Dropping his gaze, it draws my own eyes to his line of vision. He's brushing his thumb over the raised scars on my inner wrist, stroking the bracelet of tiny bumblebees covering the faded marks. He's thoughtful. I'm tense.

"Six," He announces, as he turns my hand over. Lifting his eyes to mine in question. "Six little buzzing bumblebees. Is that a significant number?" he asks. I turn my hand in his grasp, observing the bees for myself, refamiliarizing myself with the delicate tattoo.

"Yes… six," is all I say. He doesn't release my wrist but turns it again so he can see the other side, the upper side where there are no incriminating scars.

"There's a gap." He observes the small space, devoid of any colour or ink. A patch of pale, plain pink skin, where the circle of bees doesn't meet. The blank area is usually covered by the face of my watch. The void has some significance too.

"Yes... there's a gap." I'm not volunteering anything. He promised he wouldn't ask any uncomfortable questions. Yet here he is, desperate to ask uncomfortable questions. Unable to help himself.

"Come on then... up you get. You can't lie here all morning like a cabbage. We've a flight to catch." Dropping my hands like hot potatoes, he stands and indicates to the bedside clock. "Seven o'clock. I'd like to be at the airfield for eight thirty if that's possible." Bending at the waist, he gives me a quick peck on the lips then points to the bedside table. "There's a cup of tea for you there but it's probably gone cold. You go for a shower and I'll make you a fresh cup."

I'm stunned. He backed down, he didn't ask and seemed to understand I didn't want to talk about it. Is this a breakthrough? I'm amazed, he's actually listening to me. After he has left the room, I hop out of bed and head for a shower.

It doesn't take long before I'm done. I dress casually, choosing my jeans and a light blue silky jumper; it's another old hand-me-down from Lizzy, but the shade suits my colouring so it'll do fine. I dry my hair with the hairdryer this time, but I'm still not attempting to style it properly, opting once again to tie it up. Pulling on my baseball cap, I thread the ponytail through the loop at the back so it swings freely. I'm travelling today so that will do.

When at last I enter the kitchen, Silas is dividing a pile of freshly scrambled eggs between two plates. There are two glasses of fresh orange juice and the toast has just popped up in the toaster.

"Eggs... I hope that's okay?" My plate is placed in front of me as I sit at the counter. A slice of brown toast lands on the side and a fresh cup of tea is steaming in the mug.

"Wow, thank you." Picking up my knife, I butter my toast. I'm starving after my frugal evening meal of baked beans! "A girl

252

could get used to this. I like having a culinary genius around." I scoop a forkful of egg onto my toast and take a bite. I need ketchup. Leaving the table as Silas takes his seat I rummage through the cupboard. Quickly locating the ketchup and giving it a mock cocktail shake, I reclaim my stool. Squeezing a blob of ketchup on the side of my plate I'm happy, so I resume devouring my breakfast.

"Good?" He grins through clenched lips.

"Mmm, so, so, good," I confirm as I finish the last bit of toast and eggs. Downing the orange juice in one, it refreshes my mouth. It's icy cold and delicious. Silas has finished too, but before he can make a move, I scoop up our plates and drop them in the sink to wash up.

"Leave, those. Come and finish your tea," he complains, taking hold of my hips and steering me away from the sink. I land between his thighs, my wet hands dangling over his shoulders, the suds from the washing up water dripping onto the tiled floor behind him.

Playfully, I cup his cheeks in my hands, giving him a pair of white, sudsy sideburns. He grabs my wrists again and holds them out to the side, before planting a noisy raspberry on my lips. "Thanks, now I look like Santa." Letting me go, he snatches up the pot towel and dries his wet face. When he's done, I make a grab for the towel and dry my hands, then as he stands, I can't resist swatting his fine behind with the damp towel. It makes a loud cracking noise as it connects with his jeans. Smirking at me, he takes up the challenge and bends over, gripping the back of the chair and wiggling his arse at me, creating the perfect target and giving me a better shot. So, I do it again, laughing and swatting.

"Bring it on, Honey… is that all you've got." Wiggle, wiggle, shake, shake. I'm swatting and dancing around him as he waves, rotates and gyrates his lovely pert bottom at me.

"A-hem!" We freeze mid antic, as the sound of a disapproving cough permeates through our laughter. A tall dark-skinned beauty is standing in the kitchen doorway. Her slender arms are folded across her ample chest. Her stiletto-clad foot tapping on the black and white tiles.

"Tia! Hey... I didn't expect you this early." Straightening up, Silas is immediately in a serious mood.

"Evidently," Tia replies with a sneer. *Who the hell is this, now?*

"Edi, please let me introduce you to my sister, Tia, he says, "Mutia, this is Edi. She's the one I've been telling you about." He raises his eyebrows at her as if willing her to remember.

She tuts at him rudely and pushes herself away from the door frame. "Edi, hi, it's lovely to meet you." She holds out a very elegant hand and strides over, shaking her head as she passes her brother.

Her smile is warm and friendly, just like Silas's. There's definitely a family resemblance. Her teeth are gleaming white. She's one, beautiful, woman and I'm instantly grateful she's his sister. She's a stunner.

Gripping my hand in a firm shake, she takes me in. She's easily six inches taller than me. I feel like a shrimp in my flat dolly shoes. "Hi... err... Tia? it's nice to meet you too. Silas didn't tell me he had a sister." I glance in his direction. He's stood with his hands in his pockets looking completely unperturbed.

"Sisters!" She corrects. "No, I bet he didn't," she grumbles sarcastically. "I'm number one of three by the way; all sisters and all a nightmare, apparently!" She glares at him over her shoulder. Silas just shrugs in an '*it slipped my mind*' type of gesture. "I bet he didn't mention a cleaner either did he?"

"I was just about to, before you barged in." I think he's annoyed. "What are you doing here at this time anyway? You're a bit early." He walks over to me and puts a protective arm round my waist. If Tia notices, she's polite enough to not say anything.

Dropping her designer handbag on the worktop, she sighs wearily. "I need to get a head start today. I've got Christina's after here and then yours. The rest of the team will be at the airfield later, I've a date tonight so I want to get my nails done." Her nails are immaculate.

She speaks as if he should understand all of this. Rolling her eyes at me, she makes her way to the kitchen sink and starts opening the cupboard, rummaging around and bringing out a box of cleaning stuff. I'm confused.

"Erm?" Not really sure what to say. "You're the cleaner?"

"Yep, that's me. Silas runs the other business, I have a cleaning business. My brother is one of my best clients." I sense some sibling rivalry. "Our other two sisters work for me. Jasmine's full time but Chloe's only part time. For some strange reason she wants to be a pilot, so she's training." She smiles a sweet sickly insincere smile at her brother – as only a sister can!

"Tia, don't..." he warns. I suspect they've a typical brother sister relationship.

"I'm not being mean. He's soooo, sensitive. My big brother. Seriously, Edi, it's lovely to meet you but I haven't time for chit-chat. I need to get on. So, if you two wouldn't mind getting lost, I can crack on with the cleaning." She waves a marigold at us and sashays out of the kitchen toting her cleaning equipment.

"Sorry, about her," he says, exasperated.

"She seems lovely, but I don't really need a cleaner. I can manage." I've never had a cleaner. I'd have to clean before she came and that would stress me out!

He looks at me in horror, "it's what I pay her for. It's her job. You work at the airfield and believe me, as I said before, you will be putting in some seriously long days in the next few months. Seriously long; you'll be grateful of the help. Anyway, she's the absolute best in the business. Honestly, if you committed a murder, Tia could clean the crime scene better than *Winston Wolf*; so good, even *Gil Grissom* couldn't tell... come on, we need to hustle if we're going to make our departure slot."

"Three sisters eh?" I quip. But there's no mistaking the brotherly pride that simmers beneath his gruff exterior.

"Don't remind me..." He groans. I laugh. But how she cleans in stiletto's and a pencil skirt is beyond me.

I jump about a thousand feet in the air as *'Simply the best'* blares from the integral speakers; Tia's chosen music to clean by.

"See..." he yells over the deafening racket.

It's the only incentive I need and our cue to leave, so I grab my small shabby hold-all and my lap top bag. I've folded my dress and hopefully it won't crease.

In contrast to my scruffy love-worn luggage, Silas has a smart leather suit bag and a matching brown leather overnight bag with his initials engraved onto a brass name tag.

I sling my shoulder-bag across my body, leaving my hands free to carry all my other stuff. This time, we take the lift. As the door closes, I can still hear the sound of *Tina Turner* screaming loudly over the hoover.

Chapter 23

We drive to the airfield in Silas's Range Rover. The radio is still broken so we make small talk, mostly about Bear, the gym and the up and coming new contract that should be signed today.

He's being coy about his sisters though, so I drop the subject in favour of the weather! The day is bright and sunny. The storms of yesterday have blown over, making way for a clear and fresh morning.

We pull into the car park, just as Spanners is riding high on the pushback tractor used to tow the aircraft out of the hangars. He's hauling the Cessna onto the apron in preparation for our flight. His orange ear defenders are firmly in place, but currently a redundant fashion accessory as there are no engines running. Then I understand why he's wearing them as the dulcet tones of Sparks belt out *Love Me Tender,* at top note, while he's following behind the Cessna, waving his guide paddles in the air. They both give us a hearty wave as we clamber out of the car and grab our bags from the boot.

Leaving our bags beside the car for ease of transport, we make our way into the office. Christina's in mid flow on her mobile. *Doesn't this woman ever stop working?* Bear wanders to the back of the office and lies down in front of the fire door, head on paws. He's sulking. Now we're both getting the silent treatment!

"Yes, yes, wonderful; I'll see you in about fifteen minutes then. Yes, yes, not a problem, bye." Glancing our way briefly, before terminating the call, she acknowledges us with a nod and a smile.

"Problem?" asks Silas. I notice that Bear's sulk lasted all of about six seconds. He's loping his way towards us, tail swinging in greeting.

"What? No, no he's just being a bit of a wazzock." She seems a bit flustered, which is unusual. "Honestly, I'm beginning to

257

regret this bloody business deal before we've even started." She grumbles good naturedly, pulling herself back to the present. She doesn't mean it, but I know this deal has taken its toll on her and the strain of this final week of negotiations is beginning to take its toll. I'm pleased, for all of us, it should be finalised today - then, hopefully, she can get a well-deserved break.

I bend and give Bear a quick pat as he sits down next to Silas. Christina eyes me closely. "Well, look at you two… have a nice evening, did we?... hmm?" She folds her arms and dips her chin, grinning at us like a loon. Silas just ignores her, while I'm feeling shy and uncomfortable at her curiosity. "Come on then, spill the beans… *Oh shitting pigs in space!!*… sorry… it'll have to wait… he's here!" Tutting her frustration loudly at the interruption, she pats her perfect hair into place and picks up the black leather folder lying on the desk. Marching with purpose she strides outside into the carpark to await her VIP.

"Well, it looks like her meeting has arrived." Silas' eyes follow her. "Come on, we don't have a lot of time. We can't afford to get caught up in this contract meeting, but I suppose we should introduce ourselves." He isn't very enthusiastic at the prospect of meeting this new important client. I can't say I'm that keen either, but business before pleasure, I suppose.

"We'd better had. It won't take too long. Come on." Taking his arm, I give his sleeve a little tug and lead him reluctantly through the automatic doors. Bear follows on his heels, seemingly he's forgiven Silas for his absence. I secretly prey he'll get over the fact he's going to be left with the baby-sitter again very soon.

With Silas leading the way, we walk out to where Christina is patiently waiting for the new client to park his expensive silver Porsche.

"He even has a knob's car!" She performs a perfect ventriloquist whisper through a gritted smile as we arrive at her side.

"You don't mean that!" I'm shocked. The car is lovely. I'm sure he's a nice guy really, just a tough negotiator trying to get a fair deal for his business buck. Aren't most business men like that?

"No, I'm just jealous," she hisses, still clenching her teeth in a fake smile. "Here he comes ... hold on to your hat."

The car door swings open and a long lean, crisply-pressed trouser leg emerges. It's swiftly followed by the rest of him; unfolding gracefully from the drivers' seat his tall, trim frame emerges.

Raising a hand in our general direction, hailing a silent greeting, he reaches into the back seat and retrieves his designer briefcase. Even from this distance, it's transparent he radiates total confidence. Every fluid move is executed with an equal measure of power and elegance. He's very smartly dressed in a charcoal-grey suit and pink shirt, no tie.

The breeze picks up as he strolls over, ruffling his hair and blowing his neat blonde quiff onto his forehead. Instinctively, he lifts a tanned hand to brush it back into place.

It's an unremarkable action; a trait I've seen many times before. A common enough habit for a man who has a good head of hair and is keen to keep it in place. But in this instance, it is all too familiar... all too recognisable.

My mouth is immediately as dry as the desert. My blood turns to a freezing river in my veins. My heartrate accelerates to danger levels as I stare open-mouthed.

Fuck no!

Gasping in shock, I instinctively lower my head, hiding my face beneath the peak of my baseball cap. Frozen in place I'm beyond petrified; totally unable to move. This can't be happening. I just stare at the floor, my eyes not focusing; my mind in utter turmoil, my thoughts scrambled and disjointed.

Jesus!

Surely, I must be seeing things. Subconsciously, I sense something shift beside me. Christina has taken a step forward. She's walking out to greet him, leaving Silas and I standing side by side near the entryway to the foyer.

Everything has suddenly turned to slow motion. My heart is hammering so loudly I can't hear anything but the blood pounding through my ears. Needing to be certain, I risk another quick look. Perhaps my mind is playing tricks on me. Peering from underneath the rim of my baseball cap, I lift my eyes for the briefest of moments, hoping against hope I'm wrong. But one quick glimpse and I know I'm not mistaken. The sudden wash of overwhelming dread consuming my body confirms it. My world is beginning to crumble right in front of me.

Shit! no, please, it can't be! Please let it not be!

But no matter how hard I want it not to be him, I know categorically it *is* him. He's here and I'm trapped.

Panicking, I stare at the ground. Bear has stood up and is watching Christina intently. I don't know what to do. I'm starting to tremble. If I don't get out of here immediately, I'll either pass out, throw up or scream and run. So, I start to shuffle my feet, wrapping my arms around my waist, feigning discomfort. It isn't difficult, I feel dreadful. Breathing deeply and shifting from foot to foot, I retreat, backing slowly away before Christina can commence introductions. It seems to work. Keeping my head bowed I desperately try to calm my nerves long enough to make my escape.

Aware of my movements, Silas glances my way, frowning in concern. I mime urgently that I need the loo, making it look like an emergency; Turning quickly on my heels, I speed-walk for the revolving door and the sanctuary of the inner office, just as I hear Christina's clear voice ringing out a hearty greeting.

"Robert, good morning, I trust you had a pleasant journey?" Christina is as professional as ever.

"Yeah, I did, thanks, Chris." Voice recognition confirms my suspicions once and for all; it's most definitely him. My stomach lurches in fear at the familiar voice. Gripping myself tightly round the stomach, I fold at the waist and almost stumble.

Desperate to remove myself from his presence, I hasten escape; suddenly unable to get away quick enough, before my body collapses. I fly towards the revolving door, my palms slamming onto the glass partition so violently it whirls round, flinging me inside, to the safety of the office. Unstopping, I dive towards the toilets. Smashing open the door of the ladies, I stumble inside, panting and heaving. The sudden surge of adrenalin has me shaking and clammy with sweat. My hands tremble as I rest my forehead against the door, my heart's in my mouth and I'm nauseous.

Breathe, Edi! He, didn't see you.

But I still feel the need for confirmation; a small part of me doesn't believe it's truly him. Hesitantly, I tug very lightly on the door. I don't open it fully. Just a fraction; enough to reveal the narrowest sliver of the reception area. I wait, silently, peering through the tiny opening.

I watch in disbelief as they progress through reception, pausing momentarily to admire the fine examples of aeronautical engineering on display. He barely gives it the time of day. Typically, he hasn't the slightest interest in anything not relevant to *him*. Eventually they continue on towards the rear corridor leading to Christina's office.

Silas looks distracted as he glances in the direction of the ladies, worry etched all over his lovely face. I want to run to him, to hide in his arms, but I know I can't do that. Nervously, I close the door a little more so I'm looking through a thin gap, barely a centimetre wide. Squinting, I try to get a better look at my past.

From the security of my hiding place I observe him without being seen. His hair is lighter than it was. But it's still thick and wavy. He looks fit, a bit heavier, like he's been working out. But then again, he's eighteen years older, so I'd have expected him to have changed; I know I have.

His voice is unmistakable though; He still sounds cocky, arrogant and overly confident. Clearly, he's prospered quite well over the years. Seems he's made a success of himself; I sense 'Daddy's' money is at work somewhere.

My gut gives an almighty twist and I suddenly need to empty my bowels. I dash for the toilet, banging the door closed and dropping my jeans a split second before the inevitable deluge of diarrhoea hits the toilet pan. *Christ!* I'm sweating like a bastard. Another sickening wave of nausea washes over me and I rub my trembling hand over my mouth in an attempt to ward off the sickly feeling. *I will not throw up, I will not throw up!* Inhaling deeply, I swallow back the abundance of saliva gathered in my throat.

Steadily I assess the damage. I think I'm done, so leaning forward, I unravel some toilet tissue and clean myself up, thanking all that's holy there isn't much mess, considering. On wobbly legs, I stand and pull up my jeans, flush the toilet without looking and then wash my hands and face. I need to get out of here before he sees me.

The likelihood of him recognising me is slim, but I won't take that chance; I absolutely *can't* take that chance. I resolve to remain concealed until I'm sure they're safely out of view. I can still hear them as they walk through the back corridor but I can't fathom what they're discussing. Hopefully they're not talking about me.

Desperate to kill some more minutes, I use the loo again. Washing my hands again and splashing my sweaty face with cool water, biding my time. Pacing in circles. How long will they be?

After a few minutes, my breathing and heart rate have returned to some semblance of normal and I've stopped shaking. The nausea has abated so I check if the coast is clear. It is, so I take a tentative step into reception.

Perfectly timed it seems, as Silas is returning from Christina's office, looking rather like he's been given some really shitty news. His expression changes to one of instant relief when he sees me hovering near the toilets.

Wasting no time, he hurries over to where I stand, feeling very small, totally lost and utterly forlorn. I must look terrible. Making no attempt to hide his concern, reaching out to me, he draws me into him. Enveloping me in his strong arms, his body radiating the worry he's so obviously feeling at my sudden distress. I wrap my arms round his waist and bury my face in his firm chest. At last I feel safe and protected.

"What the hell was *that* all about?" he breaths, unsure, releasing his grip so he can study me better. He holds me at arm's length, scrutinizing closely for any further signs of sickness.

"My breakfast caught up with me," I shrug and grin, trying desperately to hide my fears and quash his concerns. "Sorry, I needed a *serious* toilet," rolling my eyes, attempting humour, I hope he gets the drift and drops the subject.

"Ah," thankfully, he does. He makes a face at me. "Phew, you had me really worried for a minute there. You looked terrified." My fear was obviously more apparent than I thought. I give a non-committal shrug. "Okay, well if the emergency is over, we'd better get rolling. There's no point in hanging around for Christina, Mr. Money-bags is dissecting the contract with a fine-tooth comb again… he'll be a while yet. Do you feel well enough to fly?"

"Oh, Silas, yes pleas,." relieved to get going at last. "I think some of it was just the excitement," I lie, desperate to leave.

He frowns, clearly suspicious but doesn't voice his concerns. I'm grateful. Taking my hand, he leads me outside and across the tarmac, onto the apron, where our transport awaits. I can't get there quick enough.

"After you, ma'am!" He bows and waves a palm at the steps of the plane.

"Why, thank you, kind sir," I reply in my best southern belle accent, then dart up the steps like an Olympic champion, eager to be out of sight in the secure luxury of the Cessna. I can hear Silas laughing at my apparent enthusiasm as I dive inside the fuselage. Little does he know…

"Just don't use the toilet while we're on the runway!" he calls at my retreating back. *Cheek!*

As expected, the small aircraft is beautiful inside. Plush cream leather seats are evenly spaced along the sides of the narrow cabin. Each row of seats has its own portal window and side table. A red carpet covers the floor, giving the aisle the impression of a catwalk, where the cabin crew can strut their stuff while waiting on the passengers, hand and foot.

Rich walnut panelling completes the luxurious effect. A heavy navy-blue curtain separates the stewards' area from the passenger seating and at the far end, is a door leading to a small, fully equipped bathroom, which I know from my studies will be complete with a full-size shower. The Cessna's an older model, but that doesn't take away any of the luxury. If anything, it all adds to the authenticity of the aircraft.

Silas has followed me into the cabin. Grinning broadly, he quickly shows me where the galley is and where I can get a drink once we're airborne. There's a mini-fridge full of wine, champagne and various bottled beers. There's also a small wardrobe containing several uniforms, which all appear to be fresh from the dry cleaners. On the return journey tomorrow, I will be playing air hostess so I appreciate the time today to familiarize myself with where everything is stowed.

Satisfied I'm feeling better, and not about to throw up or shit my pants any time soon, he kisses me chastely just once, then leaves me alone to belt up. The door to the cockpit is closed, but I'm not concerned. Once we're under way, I'll join Silas and spend the rest of the flight in the co-pilot chair. Choosing a seat, I settle down and strap myself into the comfortable soft leather.

My mind starts to review the events of the morning. Talk about emotional roller-coaster, I'm really giddy now, excited even. I can't believe that less than ten minutes ago I was freaking out, although I think I got away with it. I can't wait to be in Paris and put the English Channel between us. Sighing deeply, I mould myself deeper into the supple leather. Impatient to get going, I gaze out of the window waiting for the craft to move.

Finally, I'm beginning to relax, looking out of the window and completely lost in thought. I jump when Christina and Robert come strolling out of the office door and onto the apron. *Crap!* They must finally have come to an agreement. She's waving her arms animatedly, indicating the airfield and pointing at the Cessna. I duck my head and scooch down in my seat, hoping he can't see me through the tiny porthole windows!

Edi, don't be an idiot; Of course, he can't see you!

They've come to watch take off. It's all part of the elite customer experience I expect. Christina was right, he's a knob. Always was... Suddenly I'm angrier than I've ever been before in my life; *how dare he?* It's irrational but in this moment, I'm completely incensed; I've allowed him to once again to set my world into turmoil.

Staring at him through the tiny porthole window, I feel a surge of utter revulsion. My emotions are all over the place.

What the hell! This is ridiculous!

As quickly as it arrived, my anger dissipates and I'm suddenly seized by a feeling of calm. It hits me like a sledge hammer.

I'm an adult for Christ, sake!

I'm in control of my own destiny. I've options. I don't need to feel like this. I don't need to put myself through this.

I don't have a plan yet, but there are some things I know with complete, sudden clarity. I'm not going to be a victim anymore. I've worked too hard to achieve my goals, get a degree, to let it be destroyed by past circumstances.

Finally, I've restored faith in myself. The faith to get where I am. Faith in my self-worth and self-belief. I won't let him run me out of this job. I won't allow him to taint this opportunity. And more pertinently, I'll be dammed, if he'll ruin the fragile promise of true happiness, I think I could have with Silas. I grit my teeth and clench my fists. Narrowing my eyes at him through the tiny window, I'm determined.

Bring it on arse hole! I'm ready for this fight.

The sound of the engines change; revving up a notch, increasing the noise levels as the plane begins to taxi and I begin to relax. The further we travel along the runway, the stronger my determination. Whatever happens, I will not let him resume control. I escaped his clutches once and I won't be drawn back in.

The plane lifts gently off the ground. And as it ascends, so does my mood. What promises to be the best thing I've found in years, Silas, is sitting less than twenty feet away, through a thin walnut veneer door. I need to trust him. It's that simple.

The air pressure in the cabin changes and my ears pop. The engine sound fades to a light hum and we climb higher, breaking through the hazy morning mist, rising into the clear blue ether, soaring above the clouds.

Silas. Yes, I need to trust him. I need to be honest with him and share my past. To tell the truth for once. Let him in. If I'm going to get through this, I need him on my side; to understand. It will take some explaining but I need to grow a pair and man-up. At least I've a couple of days away now without the worry of a surprise reconciliation. I settle back in my seat. For now, I'm going to enjoy the flight and my quality time with Silas. Paris here we come!

Chapter 24

Paris Le Bourget Airport, is Europe's busiest business aviation airport, dedicated exclusively to private aircraft of all kinds. We landed approximately fifty minutes after we took off.

The flight was wonderful. Once we reached cruising altitude and the Cessna had levelled out, I unfastened my seat belt and joined Silas in the cockpit. He looked so handsome, dressed casually in black jeans and cream lightweight sweater, aviators, and head-set on, connecting him to the air traffic controllers. Wow, he could be a male model, posing for a photoshoot!

Completely relaxed, he gave me a huge smile as I squeezed into the co-pilot seat. The panoramic view from the cockpit was unbelievable. I'd been in flight simulators before and I was lucky enough to take a short internal, training flight while I was studying at Uni', but I'd never experienced anything quite like this. A completely cloudless sky stretched before us. And far away, into the distance, I could discern the curvature of the earth. What a magnificent sight. The expanse of the whole world, spread out beneath us, seemingly as endless as the eye could see.

We were totally alone, just the two of us with only the endless skyscape of clear blue ahead and the contrasting, darker hue of the English Channel below; the indigo and vermilion shades of the deep water, broken only by the occasional tip of white as the waves crested and broke on the surface. A feeling of sheer joy and exhilaration had me squealing like a child in wonder. Silas laughed at me as I bounced up and down in my seat in glee.

Now we're waiting for the airport security official to check our passports before we can continue our journey to the hotel.

"Bonjour, allo – *Tueur-noir! Alors; Bon-chance, Mon'amie!"* The French airport manager strides towards us waving his arm in the air and calling out a hearty welcome. I'm a little taken aback by his familiar greeting though; If my high school French serves me correctly – he's just called Silas '*Black Tudor*'. I know the French have a relaxed and informal approach to most things but that greeting doesn't sound too politically correct to me... Nevertheless, Silas doesn't seem to be in the least offended by it, so I'll swallow my indignation. He's obviously on good friendly terms with Silas, judging by the genuine demonstration of affection that passes between the two men.

As they come together, the airport Manager gives Silas a strong, sincere, hand shake followed by an exaggerated and very masculine continental embrace.

Gerard Moreau is in his late-twenties, I'd guess. And is - to quote Sammy - *'As fit as fuck!'* Lizzy would be performing a flirting demonstration worthy of an Oscar. Sammy would already be naming their children! I can't help smiling to myself as I imagine Lizzy flicking her hair, flashing her megawatt smile and feigning total disinterest. She'd be in seventh heaven. I vaguely wonder if he's attached. Then I wonder if Lizzy and Sammy are having a good time.

A fleeting twinge of guilt stabs at my conscience. It's only a token prickle... one which is soon replaced by a rush of anticipation when Silas places his hand on the small of my back as he introduces me to Gerard.

"Gerard, this lovely lady is Edi Sykes. She's just joined RTC as our Logistics Manager. She has foolishly agreed to accompany me on this... trip." Silas's smile is warm and genuine as he says this.

I don't miss the lift of surprise in Gerard's eyebrows at that snippet of information, but his curiosity soon passes, and his smile is typically seductive as he takes my hand. Though his grip is firm, his hand is warm and soft, and his nails expertly manicured. It's a complete contrast to Silas' large, calloused hands and immediately, I know which one I prefer.

Silas stiffens slightly when Gerard leans forward, grasping my shoulders and placing a kiss on each of my burning cheeks.

"Bonjour Edi," his voice is soft, rich and typically Gaelic. His accent is completely charming. He's the epitome of a French stereotype. I like him instantly. "Eet eez so nice to meet you. I would like to say, I've 'eadr all about you, but my friend 'ere has kept you a secret, no?" He furnishes Silas with another quizzical look, but Silas remains indifferent. "Silas eez a *very* good friend. I'm very 'appy that you can join wiz 'im zis weekend."

"Bonjour, Gerard. It's lovely to meet you too," I manage to break free of his hold and find my voice.

He's young but radiates with an enigmatic, confident maturity. It's really very attractive. His wavy black hair is well-groomed. Expertly styled and purposely over long, grazing the collar of his expensive leather jacket. He wears it brushed back from his tanned forehead; effortlessly casual.

He isn't particularly tall, but he makes up for it with his inscrutable, larger than life presence. He's immaculately turned out in dark blue designer jeans and a white, linen, *Ralph Lauren* shirt. The obligatory leather folio-case tucked neatly under his arm, completes the continental look.

All in all, he exudes the exotic sensuality I would expect from a Frenchman. Even with his diminutive stature, he's a man who would dominate any room, standing out from the crowd. I'd love to hear how he knows Silas. There's easily fifteen years age difference. I flick my eyes between them, trying to work it out. Silas picks up on my curiosity, putting me out of my misery.

"Gerard's father, Charles, is one of *my* father's oldest friends," Silas explains. "They go *way* back." This is the first time Silas's mentioned his own father. "Gerard's older brother Marc, was a close friend of mine. But he very sadly passed away about ten years ago; it was tragic, he was only thirty at the time." There's an edge to his voice... pain? Remorse? Even anger...

"Oh, that must have been difficult for you." I look at Gerard, unsure of what to say.

"Eet was terrible for my family. I was an unruly teenager. Marc, 'e was ze good son." I get the impression there's much more to that flippant comment. "Marc, 'e was my 'ero." Gerard has sadness in his eyes as he speaks about his late brother. "'E was an accomplished flyer. Everyzing zat I wanted to be... but on zat day ... well, let us just say eet was a terrible accident." He's suddenly very deep in thought. The memory is obviously still raw, vivid and painful. "Silas, 'e was a great support to my father. We will be eternally grateful to 'im for zat." The appreciation is truly genuine.

Reaching behind me, I grasp Silas's hand where it rests on my back, squeezing it tightly, indicating I understand. The affection for Silas in Gerard's voice is crystal clear.

Uncomfortable, Silas shrugs off the praise, "you would have done the same for me in similar circumstances; *Frère d'armes*, Oui?" He gives Gerard a consolatory squeeze on the arm and quickly changes the subject. "Where is the old man anyway?" His eyes scan the airfield, looking for any sign of Gerard's father. "Have you given him the day off?"

"Ha, ha! He's at the Chateaux with Maman!" Gerard's eyes are dark brown. His face lights up at the mention of his father and mother. "Zey have a, 'ow you say, a date day?" He's grinning widely; sombre mood forgotten for now.

"Well, we wouldn't want to disturb that!" Silas squeezes my hand and threads his fingers through mine; dropping his arm so our joined hands swing freely between us. I give him a shy smile. The thought of a 'date day' with Silas is very appealing. "Give him my regards... Katerina also. The *'vieux diable'* should be enjoying his retirement by now, just like Pops; Mum can't keep him off the golf course." That's the second time he's mentioned his father now. They really do know each other very well.

"Oui, oui, yes, I know." Gerard laughs. "But mine 'eez an old rogue, wiz a lust for life. Eez passion is my mozer; what can I say… eez French!" He laughs "and 'e is 'appy." Gerard opens his stance, leading us away from the apron and towards a waiting car. It's a silver Mercedes. "I 'ope you don't mind, but I thought you would need an auto. I 'ope zis will be okay?"

"Brilliant, thank you Gerard. When are you in the UK next?" They're so comfortable with each other. "If we can, it'd be good to get in a round of golf… I can ask Pops to join us." *Golf?*

"I 'ave business zere, in about six weeks, I think. I will let you know ze dates when I'm certain; I'll bring my clubs… I owe you a beating from last time." He opens the passenger door for me. "But for now, 'ave a wonderful time in my beautiful city." He lifts my hand and kisses it. "I 'ope to see you again soon, Edi." Releasing my hand, he raises his eyebrows at Silas; who chooses to remain silent, just shaking his head at the forward Frenchman.

"You too, Gerard. Thank you." I climb in and watch as they exchange a few words I can't hear; Probably in French anyway. Clasping Silas firmly by the shoulders, Gerard pulls him in and envelopes him tightly in a manly bear-hug. Then Gerard hands Silas the black leather folio, before slapping him firmly on the back. Another few words are exchanged, Silas encourages him to release his hold then slides gracefully into the driver's seat, tossing the folio case in the back as he does.

Rolling down the window, he leans his head out for a final goodbye. "Make sure you let me know the dates." He turns the ignition and the engine rumbles. "I'll be disappointed if you visit the UK and don't get in touch. Remember, I owe you a favour." Raising his hand, Silas revs the engine as the security staff load our cases into the boot. "We'll be back later on tomorrow afternoon. Can you make sure the Cessna is ready for departure?" He hands over a print-out containing the flight details. The folio must be something else then… "I'll review the contract and get back to you." *Ah, all becomes clear!*

Gerard swiftly takes the printout and offers an affirmative salute in return. "Mais bien sûr Monsieur, please pass on my regards to the beautiful Christina. Au revoir, mon'amie. Bon chance." The salute changes into a friendly wave as we leave him behind on the tarmac and head off into the city of love.

The traffic is horrendous! The short drive into the centre of Paris takes us well over an hour and it's almost noon by the time we arrive in the secured underground car park, down a small side road just off the Champs Elysees.

The hotel is on Rue de Bassano. *Hotel San Regal* is described as a small luxurious boutique hotel. If I was walking down the street, I would have passed it by, not even noticing it was there.

From the outside it looks nothing. Just a plain, ordinary red brick building, blending in with all the other plain, ordinary red brick buildings lining the many side streets, close to the Champs Elysees. I've no idea how Silas has managed to find two rooms at such short notice during Paris Fashion week, but he has. I suspect the ever efficient, Christina has had something to do with it.

We've adjoining rooms, with french doors opening out onto a shared double balcony, providing a partial view of The Arc de Triomphe. My room isn't large, which is typical of Paris, but it's stunningly decorated in a delicate palate of creams and golds. A pale blue satin canopy over the small double bed adds a splash of colour, as does the matching counterpane. There's a cream and gold dressing table and large ornate, free standing full-length mirror. A matching vintage style armoire and dressing table completes the set beautifully. It's indicative of Louis XIV. A miniature Versailles, if you will. The luxuriously deep pile carpet is pale gold in colour with a light fleur-de-lys pattern in a slightly deeper shade of gold adding a regal elegance. Ornate crystal table lamps, gold and blue scatter cushions and drapes complete the illusion. It is amazing.

Silas has left me alone to unpack my bits and bobs, saying he needs to review the contract Gerard has given him and he'll meet me in the foyer in half an hour, so we can go and grab some lunch.

After I've hung up my dress and hunted high and low, I'm exasperated to discover I only appear to have packed one black evening shoe! I'll be wearing my flats tonight! Flouncing in annoyance at my stupidity, I carefully unpack my new underwear and lay it in the draw. *At least you remembered that!* When I've unpacked the rest of my clothes and put my toiletries into the bathroom, I stow my bags, then sit on the bed gazing in awe, marvelling at my luck and the sumptuous surroundings. Who'd have thought I would be in Paris by the end of my first week in my new job? Moreover, who'd have thought I'd be in Paris with a hot man -Boss-man - by the end of my first week...? Certainly not me!

I'm more than ready for a cup of coffee, so I flick on the coffee maker. While I wait for it to brew, I check my personal phone for any messages from the girls or David. Of course, there aren't any, but when I check my work phone, there's an email from Christina.

'Hi Edi, hope you are feeling better. I just wanted to let you know that it's all systems go here! Finally, we've a signed contract. Am I wrong to feel smug ▢ Please let Silas know the good news, I've copied him in but he probably won't check his e-mail! Have a wonderful time and enjoy all the hype. Enjoy the party tonight!' Christina Royal.

Dropping my phone on the bed, I don't know how I feel. I'm suddenly reminded of my little meltdown this morning. I need to explain things to Silas, but when I try and compose my thoughts into sentences, my anxiety bubbles to the surface and the panic sets in. I've no idea how he'll react. I don't know him well enough to anticipate his response. For all I know, he could sack me on the spot and where would that leave me?

I suppose I could confide in Christina when we get back… yes… that sounds plausible. She's seems a level-headed person. I'm sure she'll understand. But then, what do I do about Bobby? I really don't want anything to do with him. He tainted my life once and I don't want all that hanging over me again. And he certainly mustn't find out about David. That would be disastrous.

I sit on the bed and drop my head in my hands. My thoughts are running riot. One minute, I'm full of resolve and determination, the next, I'm flying into a panic at past memories and what would happen if everything came out. *Christ!* It's not like I've murdered someone for God's sake! There are worse things in life…

And there I go again!!

All I ever wanted was a quiet life. Out of the limelight. Where I was unknown. After all these years protecting myself, hiding and running, I wouldn't know where to begin to explain.

And then there's Silas… not Silas, my boss, but Silas the man. The man who I'm beginning to trust; the man that makes me tremble when he looks at me. The man who makes me melt when he touches me; the man who has ignited a deep desire that, until now, I thought I had buried along with all the other things reminding me of my past self.

Everything has escalated so incredibly quickly. It's all happened far too fast. Less than a week ago, I was sat in my student digs; now I'm in a hotel room in Paris, waiting for my new boss to take me for lunch. A man I barely know but feel closer to than any man I've ever met in my entire life. It makes my head hurt thinking about it. This doesn't happen to normal people. What was I thinking? I've let myself get attached. My guard was down. My defences low. The truth is, I wasn't thinking. For the first time in years, I only have myself to be responsible for and at the first opportunity, I screw it all up.

This is typical, Edi!

I rub my hands over my face in frustration. "Grrrr." I'm annoying myself now! I've got to snap out of this mood and quickly. Silas will be knocking on my door any second; I need to shut down the negativity and enjoy today, because there might not be a tomorrow! My past is catching up with me at an alarming rate. One chance encounter and I'm falling apart.

Am I being stupid? I'm not even sure if I'll have any contact with him. I suppose it's possible, now all the official business is out of the way, one of his minions will take over and I'll never see him again. The thought cheers me up a little. It's a welcome scenario, so I hold on to it. For now.

A gentle knock draws me out of my slump. Swinging my legs off the bed, I bound over to the door and peep through the spy hole. It's Silas. His head looks huge through the magnified glass. My stomach does a little flip at the sight of him. He's standing on the other side of the door, gazing around him at the empty corridor.

I thought we were meeting in the lobby?

Wasting no more time than necessary, wrenching the door open, I'm suddenly grinning from ear to ear like the cat that got the cream. I give him a huge smile. No point in spoiling the day being sullen. I can sort out my problems later. At the moment, *he's* miles away, on the other side of the English Channel and I've a day in Paris ahead of me, with the most handsome man I've ever seen.

Chapter 25

"Someone looks a lot better." He pushes the door and enters my room without being invited. I don't mind. "How's your room? Wow! This is nice." Taking in the grandeur, he strolls over to the window. Pulling back the voile drape he takes in the view. "It's a bit of alright, isn't it?" Turning back to me he drops the curtain and stands, hands in his pockets, "Are you coming or going?" I realise I'm still stood poised, holding open the door, watching him. Letting go of the handle, I leave the door to close by itself, and wander over to Silas. I'm still grinning like a Cheshire cat.

"Well..." I whisper suggestively, "It could be both," I'm shocked at my forwardness. But after last night, I'm hoping there's another reason why he's brought me to Paris; other than playing air hostess on the return trip tomorrow. If I'm going to lose my job, I might as well make the most of it while I can.

He opens his mouth in mock horror. "Why Ms. Sykes, I really don't know what you mean." He seems very relaxed, more so than this morning. Wrapping his arm around my shoulder, he nods towards the door. "Are you ready for some lunch? I know I'm."

He kisses the top of my head and turns me so we're facing the exit. "Come on, there's a little Bistro at the end of this road serving the most delicious Bouillabaisse with homemade bread." I look at him in complete ignorance. "Fish soup," he explains. "It sounds awful, but believe me, it's delicious – you'll see." As we pass the bed, he grabs my bag and hands it to me. I drape it over my free shoulder, not wanting to let go of him. "Have you got your key?" he checks.

"Yep, all fine and dandy." I pat the pocket of my shoulder bag. "Come on, let's go for some fish soup." We leave the hotel room with our arms entwined. To the outsider, we look like any normal couple on a romantic break in this wonderful city.

La Bouche is the name of the tiny ten-table Bistro at the end of the road. It's quite dark inside, atmospheric. Old wine bottles are coated in cascading rivers of years and years' worth of candle wax. White paper table cloths cover an eclectic selection of irregular tables. They must help with the quick clear system; speeding up the turn round. All the chairs are mismatched, just like the tables. It's as if they've come from a flea market or house clearance.

Clearly, they've a regular clientele and an extremely efficient and speedy lunchtime service. It's quite noisy. The clatter of plates and shouts from the kitchen, ricocheting off the white tiled walls and the terracotta floor adds to the ambiance.

We're led to a small table for two near the bar. Silas pulls out my chair, waving the waiter away, insisting on doing it himself. Once we're seated, the waiter hands us each a menu card. It only has three items. A starter of tomato and cheese salad, the famous Bouillabaisse and a dessert of lemon posset. It's more of an information leaflet than a menu.

The wine list however, is another story. There are about six pages and I understand none of them. A connoisseur once told me when you dine in a small restaurant, you should always order the house wine; especially when in Europe, because the house often has connections with the best local producers. Silas does exactly that, ordering a half bottle of house red and a large bottle of sparkling mineral water. I must admit, I'm a bit dubious about the fish soup!

"Did you manage to get unpacked?" Silas ask as he pours some water into the chunky glasses. The waiter opens the wine and pours us half a glass each. Then he places the bottle on the table and walks away, without waiting for Silas to taste it. He's sullen to the point of rudeness, but that just makes me smile even more; How typically French. "Cheers," Silas lifts his wine, so I do too.

Taking a sip, I immediately decide that the connoisseur was right, the house wine is lovely.

"Yes, there wasn't much to unpack really. I managed to forget a shoe though. I don't know how!" Rolling my eyes, I try to turn my carelessness into a joke at my own expense. "But luckily, I've navy-blue shoes on, so these will go with my dress tonight." I stick my leg out and circle my ankle, showing off my basic ballet pumps. Silas, looks down as I tuck my foot back under the table. "Good job I didn't wear trainers, that would have been a fashion statement for sure!" I play with the stem of my wine glass.

Silas frowns. What's up with him now. I don't have time to worry about it because our starter has arrived; it looks delicious. Little gem lettuce has been used as boat-shaped cups, to serve the fresh chopped tomato, red onion salsa and cubes of white goats' cheese. I pick up a lettuce boat and take a bite. Mmm, the dressing is delicious, balsamic vinegar and olive oil; I can taste a hint of basil and lime in there too. I munch away merrily, noticing Silas is still looking at me a bit thoughtfully.

"What?" I garble, through my mouthful.

"Shoes!" he states, picking up his own lettuce cup. "You managed to forget your shoes?" He takes a bite. I watch his mouth as he chews slowly.

"Well, I didn't do it on purpose, and no, it was only one shoe. But I can hardly go out with just one shoe on, can I? It'll be okay. I told you, I can wear these." I kick my heels under the table like *Dorothy*.

"I suppose you can, but it's fashion week and we've been invited to a party tonight. Wouldn't you rather wear something a bit more… suitable?" He tucks into another piece of the lettuce.

Oh no! I'm going to embarrass him. "Well, I can't, can I? I've only got these with me." I'm a bit annoyed, he doesn't know me well enough to criticise me yet. Perhaps I shouldn't go.

"That came out wrong; Look, we're in one of the most fashionable cities in the world with the most amazing shops. Why don't we enjoy our lunch, then we can do a spot of window shopping; perhaps you might find the perfect pair of shoes for tonight. That's all I meant." *Oh!*

"Ahh, Ummm!" How typical of me to jump to a conclusion!

"Anyway, I owe you." He picks up the last lettuce boat and stuffs it in his mouth in one go.

"Silas!" I laugh at him as he munches away. Well at least I'll have room for my Bouillabaisse! "Anyway, what do you mean, you owe me?" I can't think what he possibly owes me for?

"A thank you – for coming with me. You didn't have to, but I'm pleased you did; I hate going to parties alone. I have to make small talk with all the 'beautiful people' and as Christina's probably told you, I'm not good at that kind of thing."

I'm a bit taken aback when he suddenly takes my hand across the table, reaching his arm around the candle. He stares into my eyes as he rubs a circle over the back of my hand with his thumb. The feeling is intense, my hand begins to tingle at his tender touch; it makes my breath hitch and I can feel a warm flush bloom in my cheeks.

He moves the candle so he can see me better. Leaning forward, he whispers so only I can hear him. "I mean it, Edi. I'm so pleased you gave me another chance. Last night was wonderful. It was a revelation. Like I know you, but I don't really know you... you know?" He tilts his head, "I need to know much, much more." *Well, that statement leaves nothing to the imagination.* "I understand you need some time. Time to trust me. To let me in." He's so sincere. "And I'm willing to wait and give you that time. Because, I've never met anybody who has had such an effect on me in such a short space... of well... *time*." He pulls back but keeps hold of my hand. Picking up his wine, he holds my stare as he takes a deep draught. "So, can we

280

go shopping?" The waiter arrives to remove our empty starter plates and places a ceramic tureen of delicious smelling soup in the centre of the table. Silas releases my hand and leans back in his chair. He gives the waiter a withering look. The sullen, moody Silas is never too far away, I notice.

"Yes, yes we can go shopping."

I'm going to buy the sexiest pair of shoes I can find, and wear the hell out of them. I'll try to look my sultry best tonight just for him. It's time to bring out the make-up! I'm out of practice with fancy parties, but It's about time I got back into the swing of it. What could go wrong anyway. We're hundreds of miles from home. I don't know anybody here except Silas, so I might as well enjoy myself.

The Bouillabaisse is fabulous, I don't know what I was worried about. Silas manages two helpings, but I'm full after one so I nibble away, picking at a piece of the homemade artisan bread while he finishes his second bowl of soup.

The café clientele is moving in and out so swiftly it's making my head spin. We've been here about an hour and I get the feeling we've overstayed our welcome when the waiter decides to bring our desserts, clearing the soup dishes before we've quite finished. He dumps our deserts in front of us with a gruff shrug, making me giggle and Silas scowl. The waiter backs down and visibly shrinks under his glare. It's amusing to witness. I wouldn't take Silas on either. He oozes menace, just in that one look.

Declining coffee, we pay the bill, and step out onto the shaded pavement. Crossing the road so we can walk in the sunshine, Silas places his arm protectively round my waist, moving me to the inside so he's closest to the traffic.

"You're such a gentleman," I coo.

"The traffic is dreadful, have you seen how these people drive?" he asks, just as a car zooms past at a ridiculous speed.

"tête de dick!!" he shouts the insult at the disappearing vehicle. "You're safer on that side." He's still scowling after the lunatic driver, even though he's a couple of streets away now. I wrap my arm round his waist and hook my thumb through his belt loop. This is all very cosmopolitan.

"It's very warm, isn't it?" I'm beginning to wish I'd changed into a tee-shirt instead of wasting time brooding over stupid shit!

"Hot," he whispers in my ear, then kisses my cheek. "Here, this place looks like they sell shoes." He opens the glass door before I've chance to notice the name of the shop. He ushers me inside. Oh, wow! Designer stuff is everywhere. *Intimidation city Arizona!*

The store is quite busy and everyone, including Silas, looks like a supermodel, except me. I need to get this over and done with quickly. Spying the shoe department, I unlink myself from Silas' protective embrace and head straight over. Black, I just need plain black, preferably stilettoes and perhaps suede.

"Edi!" he catches up with me, "There's no rush, look, those are nice." He points to a pair of black heels in a glass display case.

Wow They're certainly striking. "Err, yes… well, some of us aren't quite in the Manolo Blahnik, league!"

I couldn't afford them even if I wanted to. I'd be terrified of walking outside in them, though they are stunning. Black pointed toe, high stiletto heel, but with fine laces that criss-cross over the instep and tie at the ankle with little bows. Very elegant and sexy.

"Well, *I* like them, come on, just try them on… for me?" He pleads with me, giving me the wide eyed, little-boy-lost look. It makes me laugh. What harm can it do to humour him.

"Okay… just for you, but I won't be buying them." That's a given.

"Okay." His little-boy-lost look changes into a sexy wolfish grin, "now we're talking." He raises his hand and we're instantly joined by a handsome male shop assistant.

"Bonjour Monsieur, Madame, comment puis, - je vous aider?" he asks Silas.

"Pouvons nous essayer ces vous plait," Silas replies in perfect French. I stare at him in awe.

"Tu es Anglais?" asks the assistant.

"Oui, Anglais."

"Ah, not a problem, monsieur. Ze black yes?" He flips into English, like a linguistic magician.

"Yes, please." Silas takes my hand and leads me to a cream leather sofa, indicating that I sit, so I do.

"Zey are very beautiful, no?" the assistant says as he takes out a small gold key and unlocks the cabinet. "May I ask, what size Madame?" I'm a six in UK sizes, I think that is a thirty-nine in European.

"Err, thirty-nine I think." He looks at me, a little unsure then removes the shoe from the cabinet, turning it over to check the size.

"Zis is a forty, it will be too big I think." He replaces it in the cabinet re-locking the door. "If you will allow, I will check if we've your size in the stock." He gives us a little bow and wanders off to the rear of the store.

"Silas, I'm really not sure about this. Those shoes are locked in a cabinet for goodness sake!" I feel like leaving. I hope they don't have my size!

"Don't be silly, It's only for display. Look, here he is..."

"Ahh, Madame, you are in luck." *Am I?* "I 'ave found your size. Here, let me assist you." And, pulling out a small leather low-level stool, he sits in front of me and takes my calf in his hand, removing my ballet pumps. I don't miss the look of distaste on his face as he places them to the side. He turns up the hem of my jeans so a few inches of my leg is visible; thankfully, my feet are respectable following my pedicure! He picks up the elaborately decorated shoebox, removes the lid and unwraps the delicate tissue paper.

Taking his time, unveiling the shoes from their protective coverings. Then, he holds them up with reverence, as if they're a priceless artefact in a museum. Turning them this way and that for me to admire. They really are fabulous. I don't think I've ever seen anything so beautiful.

"Madame," he lifts my calf again and places the shoe on my foot. I feel like Cinderella. Silas observes him closely, making sure his hand doesn't drift too far up my leg.

Expertly, he criss-crosses the laces, and ties an elegant bow on the outside of my ankle, just above my ankle-bone. Then, he repeats the whole elaborate process with my other foot. All the while, Silas watches him like a hawk.

I'm still perched on the sofa. Jeans rolled up, with both feet off the ground. Too scared to put them down.

The assistant shuffles backwards and removes the low stool so I've some space, then offers me his hand, assisting me to stand.

Silas immediately blocks his way. "Here, allow me," he glares at the assistant, taking my hand in his, helping me to my beautifully dressed feet.

The first thing I notice is how comfortable they feel. The second thing I notice is Silas' face, and how he's staring at my feet. His nostrils are flaring, and he's breathing heavily. *Strange!*

"How do zey feel, Madame?" the assistant asks.

I hitch up the legs of my jeans a little higher so I get the full benefit of the shoes. Then I take a few tentative steps across the carpet to the mirror.

"They feel, lovely." I stop in front of the mirror and strike a few poses with my feet. Turning them out. Tipping my toe. Standing side on, so I get an all-round view, admiring the stunning design and the soft black suede. They really are something else. They make my feet look elegant, slimming my ankles and lengthening my leg; what bit of it is visible anyway. I'm gripping the material of my jeans, as if I'm swinging my pants, but the shoes still look amazing. It's a shame they'll be staying in the shop, but honestly, they're way beyond my simple budget.

I turn to walk back to Silas; he has the strangest expression on his face. I'm not sure what it is. Perhaps he doesn't like them after all.

"We'll take them!" he barks at the assistant, making me jump and the assistant beam.

What? "No... Silas... really... I was only trying them on. Remember?" I plead with him. There's no way I can afford these!

"We'll take them," he says again authoritatively, glaring at me, daring me to challenge his decision.

"Oui, Monsieur. Madame, please sit and I will assist you. Zey really do look magnifique! Stunning!" he gushes, obviously thinking of his commission.

I narrow my eyes at Silas as I sit down. He looks really rather cross. If he doesn't want to buy them, then why is he bothering.

"Honestly Silas I can manage with my navy pumps," I argue. The shop assistant looks at me in utter horror.

"We. Are. Taking. The. Shoes!" he states firmly, daring me to challenge him, indicating for me to shut up and do as I'm told.

"Looks like we're taking the shoes!" I mumble under my breath, resigned. There go my first months' wages; and I haven't even been paid yet!

285

The assistant packs the shoes back into the box and takes them over to the till. I follow, rummaging in my bag for my purse. This will no-doubt max out my credit card.

"What the hell are you doing?" Silas asks, frowning.

"Paying for the most expensive pair of shoes in the world!" I snarl through gritted teeth, "what does it look like I'm doing?" Pushing past him I step up to the counter, just as the assistant is packing the shoebox into a fancy store bag.

"Oh... I don't think so!" Silas physically removes me from the till-point. Taking both of my shoulders in his strong hands, he lifts me off my feet. I squeal in indignation as he swings me out of the way and moves me to the side as if I weigh nothing. "I'll get those," he says to the assistant, taking his credit card out of his wallet.

Irritated, I elbow my way back in front of him, "No... You can't." I try to muscle in, but I'm lifted off my feet *again*, and man-handled to the side.

"Edi... *I* will get these!" He glares at me, with that challenging look. I back off. Okay mister. Keep your hair on... I'm on to you though!

I huff in total ingratitude. I could have paid for them myself! I would have been skint... but I would have done it.

"Merci, Monsieur, Madame. Enjoy the shoes!" The assistant hands Silas the bag, which he snatches from him with one hand, while draping the other round my shoulder and trundles me away from the counter.

"I could have paid," I sulk.

He kisses my temple. "I Know... They looked *fucking* amazing. There was no way we were leaving the store without them!" he whispers in my ear. "I expect a private viewing again later."

286

His voice is so low and seductive. Now I know why he was keen for me to have the shoes! He found them sexy! The thought thrills me.

"Okay," I whisper back, "thank you, they're wonderful." I kiss him lightly on the cheek in gratitude.

"I know, I can't wait to see the full effect later!" turning me towards the door, he pauses, halting in his tracks.

"What?" Wheeling us both round, he heads back into the store. "Silas, what?" Has he changed his mind?

"I just remembered. There's something else I owe you." Purposefully, he strides forward, pausing in front of the huge white and gold floor plan. Looking for something. I've no clue what, it's all in French! Then, apparently finding what he's looking for, he swings us left and up the escalator. I've no idea what he's on about.

"Here we're," he says as we step off the escalator into the jewellery department. *Shit!* "I still owe you a watch," he states, matter of fact. "I destroyed your old one. Anyway, you can't wear that white leather thing with a cocktail dress and designer shoes, can you?" I just stare at him. Yes, he does owe me a watch, but from here? It will be far too expensive.

"Silas," I start, but he just ignores me, pulling me towards the watch counter. He's on a mission. Tugging on his arm, I attempt to halt our progress. But I might as well be trying to stop a freight train.

"Look, here they are," he points at the aviator watches in the glass cabinet. "You need one of these anyway. For work, you know. And these are much more feminine than the ones at home." He makes it sound so reasonable.

I must admit, they're stunning. Not as big as a man's watch, though quite substantial for a ladies' design. I really do like them.

The assistant sashays over and Silas doesn't bother with the pointless ritual of speaking French this time. He knows exactly what he wants and points to a beautiful Breitling, white chrome, ladies, aviator watch.

The crystal inset encircling the clear chronograph-style dial, suggest a certain appeal. The metal bracelet links are intricately woven enhancing the overall feminine design. It's stunning and I absolutely *can't* afford it!

The assistant removes it from the case, having first unlocked it with a small gold key; e*verything in this store must be worth a fortune!* Silas takes it from her hand, then faces me.

"May I?" he asks, politely.

Shyly, I offer arm. I'm not going to stop him, he owes me a watch! Gently, he removes the leather thong that covers my precious bumblebees, flicking his eyes to mine, checking that I'm okay. Then he picks up the beautiful watch and places it over my wrist. Discreetly he tests the fit, ensuring the strap is wide enough to cover my tattoo. It is. Gently flipping my hand over he fastens the delicate clasp before turning my hand back. It looks fantastic. It's the perfect size for my small wrist and considering its chunky style, it isn't too heavy either; but the bracelet is far too loose.

"Can you remove some of these links while we wait?" Silas asks the assistant.

"But of course, Monsieur." She's fluttering her false eyelashes at him, ignoring me completely. "It will only take me a minute. Can I check the size?"

Silas offers my wrist to the assistant so she can check my size. He's careful not to let go of the watch and holds it firmly in place as she fiddles about with the links and tries to take an accurate measurement. Even though his big hands are getting in the way, hindering her and restricting her movement, he's not going to let go of my hand; quite determined to keep my scars and tattoo hidden. Guarding my secrets.

Once she's satisfied her measurements are as accurate as they can be, she steps away, allowing Silas to take over. If she's at all puzzled or annoyed at his weird behaviour, she doesn't let it show. Turning his back to her, effectively shielding me before removing the watch, he hands it over so she can make the alterations. The assistant politely excuses herself and takes the watch into a small side-room, presumably the workshop.

Even though we're alone, Silas keeps a protective hand wrapped around my wrist, ensuring that my secret remains concealed from prying eyes. I'm moved.

"Once this is sorted, we're going back to the hotel, I need to go over the details for tonight. You can take your time getting ready. Is that okay with you?" he asks, drawing me against him. A solid ridge is pressing against my stomach through his jeans, immediately I'm turned on.

"Yes, that would be lovely," I whisper. "You didn't have to do this you know." He's working really hard to make me feel comfortable. He hasn't voiced it, but I'm sure he suspects my disappearance this morning wasn't just down to my hastily eaten breakfast.

"Oh, I know," he winks at me, then leans in and kisses my nose. "But this is fun, isn't it?" My lips receive the next kiss, then my forehead.

I'm just about to devour his lips when the assistant returns. I'm embarrassed but the assistant just ignores our public display of affection, as if she sees it every day. I suppose she must, this is Paris after all. Silas relieves her of the watch and places it over my wrist. It fits perfectly. Her sizing is spot-on.

Silas releases my hand so I can check the fit for myself, but there's really no need. It looks beautiful and feels fantastic. It's not too heavy, not too big, not too flashy... it's just perfect. I smile my thanks at him and he looks delighted with his choice.

"We'll take it, thank you," he says without looking at the glamorous shop assistant.

"Is Madame going to keep it on, or would you like me to pack it in a gift box?" she asks.

"I'll keep it on, please," I answer, looking deep into Silas' eyes. His nod of approval is so subtle it's almost imperceptible, but it is clear as day to me. His mouth twitches up at one corner and his eyes, oh, those deep dark eyes are smouldering.

"Certainly Madame. Sir, if you would come this way, I will take your payment." Reluctantly, Silas leaves me and walks over to the second counter of the day. I follow, feeling very special and extremely spoilt.

I can't resist lifting my hand and admiring my new favourite piece of jewellery. The fluorescent lighting captures the tiny crystals, causing a multitude of iridescent rainbows to glitter and dance around me. Reflecting off every surface they land on, they transform the immediate area into an enchanted grotto.

I don't notice Silas watching me, so mesmerized am I by the shimmering, specks of colour... I'm completely entranced. Like a fascinated child, turning my hand this way and that in order for the crystals to capture the light and chase the flickering shards across the walls, cabinets and ceiling.

Eventually I realise I'm under scrutiny. Self-conscious at being caught, I sheepishly turn my gaze back to Silas. He's smiling that rare, smouldering smile that has me blushing and tingling in all the right places. I drop my hand to my side out of the stream of light. The moment I do, the abundance of tiny rainbows and light-beams instantly drop away and disappear.

"It looks lovely on you." Holding both my elbows he steps so closely to me our bodies are almost touching – *almost but not quite*. "Now… enough of the laser show! Come on, we're going back."

He kisses my nose again then drapes his arm round my shoulder, my own arm naturally snakes round his firm waist. My thumb finds its way too, hooking into his belt loop. I can't wait to get back to the hotel.

As we re-join the hustle and bustle of the Champs Elysees, it's instantly noticeable there's a vast change in the atmosphere and the weather is taking a turn for the worst.

When we entered the store, the sky was clear. Although the air was warm, it was much fresher. Now, by contrast, the air is distinctly muggy and cloyingly humid. It feels charged with electricity; ionized, with that familiar zingy scent. The stormy weather of yesterday has followed us to Paris. The clear blue sky of earlier is clouded by murky grey thunderheads; it's growing more ominous by the second.

People are running, anticipating the worst. Crowds are scattering in every direction; desperate to reach shelter before the inevitable storm hits. The wind has got up. It snatches the loose tendrils of my ponytail, whipping them around my face. It's like a completely different day from when we entered the store barely an hour ago.

"This doesn't look good," Silas pulls me close. Neither of us has an umbrella, or a jacket. "If we get a shift on, we should be able to make it back to the hotel before it starts raining."

He pushes us quickly through the crowd back in the direction we came. It's difficult, there are too many people on the pavement going too fast. Dropping his arm from round my shoulder, he grabs my hand and leads me through the surging throng. Everyone else seems to be heading in the opposite direction, making our progress slower than it should be.

A sudden flash of lightning streaks across the sky. Automatically, I start to count. *One… two… three… four… five.*

A long low peal of thunder rumbles threateningly in the distance. *Five miles away!* Another flash, quite soon after the first, indicates that the storm is getting closer, *One... two... thr... BOOM!!* Not even three miles this time.

Suddenly a large woman slams straight into me, hard. She's not looking where she's going in her haste to get to her destination. The heavy collision wrenches my hand free of Silas's grip and knocks me backwards, clean off my feet. I land heavily with a resounding bump, straight onto my arse. My head snaps back as my shoulders hit the floor, only just missing the kerb.

Ooof! The fall knocks the wind right out of me and for a moment, I'm disorientated, lost in the sea of people.

An oblivious passer-by steps on my fingers. My pain is brief but the man who trod on me trips and loses his footing, causing him to stumble into the milling crowd. Glancing up, I see him scuttle away. Leaving me on the ground, he glowers at me over his shoulder– as if it was *my* fault!

With my head spinning, I snatch my hand out of the way so as not to be trampled by any more pounding feet; I'm struggling to get up, as the sea of people part and surge all around.

"Edi... *Christ...* Edi, are you okay?" Silas battles against the tide in his frantic attempt to reach me. "Hey, *fais attention!*" he yells, into the oblivious crowd. It's pointless, the horrible man has disappeared and the woman responsible is just a misshapen lump in a brown mac, trolling away in the distance. Crouching before me, he grabs my hand and pulls me to my feet. "Stupid cow!" he mumbles under his breath at the retreating woman. "Are you okay?" The whole episode has taken less than a minute.

"Yeah, just a bit winded, honestly," I pant, rubbing the dirt from the seat of my pants. My pride is smarting at the indignity but physically, I'm okay. "I'll live..." I try and make light of it.

He steadies me, checking I'm alright before he propels us forward and back into the scurrying bodies. "Seriously… I'm fine…"

Satisfied, he peers at the blackened sky. "We need to hurry. I think I misjudged this, Edi. We're gonna get soaked." And just like that, the heavens open and release a deluge of fat, splattering raindrops. We're instantly soaked to the skin.

The crowd of people turns into a seething mass. We're still reeling against the flow, heading in the opposite direction, fighting to get through to some clear space. It's like swimming in molasses only it's human, and it's frightening. Then as if Moses himself had parted the waves, we're jettisoned free of the crowd.

A patch of clear pavement stretches in front of us. Through the river of teeming rain, about hundred yards away, I can see a road junction. It's the street we've been looking for. We don't have far to go now, we're nearly there.

Silas breaks into a run, towing me along in his wake. In seconds he's reached the corner and turns into our street. It's empty, all signs of pedestrians are gone. Everyone appears to have found shelter, in the cafes and shops or the tiny bistros. We're the only people still out in the open.

Pulling up short, I halt. Tugging on his hand, I force him to do likewise. Bemused, he turns to look at me. His face is wet. Beads of water cling to his short, cropped hair and he's panting lightly with the exhilaration of our run and the heavy rain. He looks incredible. My own hair is plastered to my head. Rain is dripping off the ends of my ponytail and trickling down my back like a river. The deluge has thoroughly soaked through my sweater, and it's now clinging to my body like a second skin. The weight of the water renders the flimsy wool practically see-through, making it indistinguishable from my pale skin beneath. It's translucent. My bra is visible. I'm indecent, but I can't help the huge grin that feels like it's splitting my face into two.

Silas stops in his tracks and stands blatantly watching me. Tiny beads of rain are clinging to his eyelashes. He blinks and they wick away only to be replaced by a new crop of tiny droplets. He must think I've lost my mind.

Indulgently I lift my chin, tipping my head, squinting directly up at the moody sky and inviting the teeming rain to fall onto my face. Loving the feeling, I open my mouth like one of those baby birds you hear about when you were a kid - the type that would drink the rain until they drowned. It feels glorious, euphoric and liberating. Stretching my arms out to my sides, I spin in a wide circle like a child in the playground, my face upturned. The hard, persistent rain stings my eyes, slapping against my cheeks. A torrent of chilly water is running down my neck, finding the narrow cleavage between my breasts. Streaming between my shoulder blades at my back, it follows the column of my spine. Down, down it runs, fording a trickling path into the cleft of my bottom, soaking my knickers and jeans through to my skin beneath. Exhilarated by the relentless rainfall, I finish my childish game, bring my head back level. I'm breathless and flushed. Silas is looking at me in awe and wonder, his own bedraggled state of wetness completely forgotten.

Ignoring the rain, he reaches out his arms, taking me completely by surprise, he grabs my shoulders and hauls me forward so I'm slammed against his solid chest.

"Oh!" I blurt as he devours my lips with such hunger; it takes my breath away.

His hand fists around my wet ponytail and he pulls my head back so he can deepen the kiss. His other hand is still holding the carrier bag. He rests it against my lower back. I can feel his knuckles digging into my spine as he desperately tries to get me as close as he possibly can.

Stepping further into me, he drives me backwards with a force so strong that the momentum has me crashing against the wall. The sheer impact jolts our mouths apart, just for a second allowing us to take a well needed breath. Our eyes meet. He's scowling. He looks fierce, angry even. His chest is heaving as if he's just run the race of his life. I can feel the crashing beat of his heart beneath my soaked clothing, it matches mine in rhythm.

"You're turning me into a madman," he hisses, panting searing hot breath in my face he dives straight back in.

Taking my mouth, he's consuming me, it's frenzied, passionate, and I love it.

I moan loudly as I feel his strong hand massage the back of my head. It spurs him on. Pushing into me even further, he presses his solid body hard against mine.

The rain is pounding down now, a relentless torrent. But it doesn't stop him. I feel the shopping bag drop to the floor behind me. His hand, now free, immediately grabs my arse, kneading and pinching it with his strong fingers forcing me nearer.

Hoarsely, he speaks into my mouth. "Christ, I can't get close enough, Edi," pressing his hard groin into my lower stomach.

His mouth is hungry and demanding, seeking my submission. The knowledge it's me he craves is heady and empowering. Completely unable to resist, I kiss him back just as feverishly. My wet face is gliding over his. My hands are gripping the front of his drenched sweater so tightly my fingers are stiff from clutching the coarse damp material. But I *need* to get even closer.

Raising one leg I wrap it around his, hooking it behind his knee, allowing him access to grind his groin into me.

"*Jesus!* you're going to unman me woman! I've never been so hard!" His bold statement spurs me on. The button fly of his jeans is metal and it rubs firmly against me as he circles his hips. It's a little painful but I don't care. He growls, harshly into my mouth. "*Grr!*"

"Sssss! Yeah, *Silassss!*" I hiss out his name at the slight twinge of discomfort that soon dissolves into a pleasurable throb as he grinds his rigid cock against me. "Touch me." I plead into his mouth. *"Please Silas…"* I need him to touch me. Releasing his hand from my hair, he trails it down my side until it brushes against my hip. Gradually, the kiss eases and softens to a delicate skim over my swollen lips.

"I'm touching you…" gliding his hand across my stomach, he finds the hem of my sweater and without a thought for the pouring rain, or our position on the pavement he peels it up. "See…" Higher and higher it goes, exposing my midriff, my ribs, until my sodden sweater is resting on my chest above my bra. The delicate wisp of white lace is the only thing separating his hand from grazing my erect nipple. "I'm touching you here." Stroking my sensitive skin with the pad of his thumb, I can feel the force of his erection pinning me to the wall.

"Oh God!"

"And here…" His grip is almost painful where he squeezes my bottom, melding our heaving bodies together. The combination of the heat from his hand and the wet and cold from the rain sends tingling, shivers through my entire body. "And here…" His hips thrust forward, forcing the button on his fly to rub against my clitoris.

"Ahh," I breathe into his mouth.

"Shhh…" he replies, pulling back and gazing into my eyes. Unable to resist, my eyes drift down to my exposed chest, observing the contrast of my white lace and the pale pink skin of my breast, against the dark softness of his large hand. It is so erotic. "We should really go indoors before you catch your death." But he makes no attempt to move.

Leaning in for another kiss, his hand travels all over my body. Exploring, skimming the underside of my breast with his thumb, teasing my nipple through the damp lace. Surrendering to his touch, I'm desperate. My core is throbbing for release and I start to gyrate my hips seeking out that delicious friction I know is there somewhere. If I keep this up, I'll be coming in the street!

"Ahh... Silas, oh..." I'm falling, spiralling into oblivion. I release one of my hands and flex the stiff fingers, eager to feel him. We continue to kiss, hard, soft, slow, fast. All the possible variations of a kiss imaginable.

Swiftly moving my hand, I don't even trace his chest or feel his tight abdominals. I aim straight for his crotch, forcing my hand between our bodies and cupping him over his jeans.

The enforced separation causes the intense pressure on my clitoris to ease, and my building orgasm ebbs away slightly. It's a relief. I can feel his erection, hard and pulsing in my small hand.

"Jesus!" Silas whispers into my mouth as his hips jerk backwards at my unexpected touch. Then just as swiftly they slam back into mine, immediately resurrecting the delicious throb at my core.

Spurred on by his reaction, I fumble with his belt one handed. I need to feel inside his pants. Feel him... once his belt is loose, I start to undo the buttons of his fly. He doesn't stop me. With the top two buttons open, I lay my palm, fingers pointing downwards, against his hard stomach. Stroking the flat of my hand over his boxers, I slip it into the tight gap between his jeans and his underwear.

"Hard..." I whisper. It's an understatement. He's rock solid, filling my hand completely. I grind my palm against the material of his underwear, rubbing the cotton of his boxers and seeking out the slit in the material that hides the silky skin of his cock. The tips of my fingers are brushing the tufts of soft pubic hair that poke through the fly. He feels amazing.

At my touch, he cries out, "*fuck, yeah!*" and grips my breast so tightly that I whimper against his neck. The rain is still hammering down, we're jammed against a wall, out in the open, my chest exposed, my hand in his pants!

What the fuck am I thinking, I don't know, but at this moment I really don't care! "*So*, fucking hard!" I repeat, unable to say any more.

His heated touch is tantalising and teasing. I want him to squeeze my breast and tweak and bite my nipples. But he just continues to graze the underside of my breast with his thumb as I stroke the length of him inside his jeans.

The repetitive motion of his thumb over my sensitised skin causes a delicious friction and it starts to burn.

I moan again. "*Ahhh, Oooh, Silas!*" I'm so close, it's bordering on painful.

"Shhh, Honey-bee" he soothes me, whispering into my mouth, slowing his kiss but remaining pressed hard against me. "Soon." It's a promise. A confirmation of something.

Deepening the kiss once more, I pull my hand out of his pants so that I can wrap my arms round him. Grabbing onto his buttocks, pulling him closer, grinding myself against his hardness through our wet jeans.

"Mmm, Edi, slow down. Shhh." He tries to quiet me, but I'm burning with wanton desire. I'm so close now, I don't want it to stop. The cold rain is doing nothing to dampen the flames. "Edi... Hey... stop... hey." Eventually he captures my attention. I still my gyrating hips regaining some of my composure, but it's not easy when I'm this close to imminent detonation. Gradually, I come back down to earth... slowly as he holds me up. My brain filters through the feelings of pure ecstasy, seeking out the normal.

Eventually remembering where we are; in the middle of a busy street; in the middle of Paris; in the middle of a rain storm, I reluctantly retreat. Releasing his luscious backside, I trail my hands back up to his waist and unhook my leg from behind his knee.

Only then do I realise; the street isn't entirely empty. There are people running past us. Blindly scurrying, umbrellas open, ignoring the passionate display, right there on the crowded pavement. I dip my head to hide my burning face in his chest.

Oh god, one second more and I would have been ripping his clothes off.

Silas is oblivious to the people, to the rain. He just sees me. Kissing me on my damp eyelids, grazing my cheek with his stubble, caressing my breast with his thumb. He doesn't care who's watching.

"We need to go inside," I'm becoming increasingly aware of our audience, and growing more uncomfortably in my wet clothing.

"Let them watch," he whispers as he reluctantly pulls my sweater over my breasts, though the translucent material does little for my modesty. "It'll do them good," he teases. "Anyway, you're hidden. They can watch but they can't see anything."

But as he says this, he pulls away, stretching his own sweater over his still open belt and fly. Leaning down, he picks up the dropped carrier bag and taking my hand leads me towards the hotel entrance.

We fall into the lobby, breathless and dripping. Splatters of rain water hit the marble floor, running off us in a torrent. We're absolutely soaked to the skin; heated, panting and clearly in a dishevelled state from our illicit fumble outside. We make it to the concierge desk, but not without drawing attention to our tousled appearance.

"Number twenty and twenty-one s'il vous plait," Silas requests the keys from the concierge, who gives us a pointed, knowing look. *What's that all about?*

Then I notice the CCTV screen sitting on a low shelf behind his desk. One of the grainy images shows the street outside. There are several different views taken from several different camera angles. All cut into four separate black and white frames; one of which is the precise spot where Silas had me up against the wall! I'm mortified. I scan the lobby around me, looking anywhere rather than at the grinning Frenchman!

Silas clocks the look of horror on my face. He gives me a cheeky wink and a nudge with his elbow but says nothing. He's buttoning his fly and fastening his belt as if it's the most natural thing in the world. I don't know where to look as the concierge hands him the room keys. Silas mumbles a brief "merci." to the guy, who's obviously had the best cheap thrill of the day so far.

Grasping my hand, I'm led down the hallway where we run up the two flights of stairs to the second floor. Dashing into the plush corridor, I start to giggle at the thought of my uncharacteristic brashness. I've been on CCTV in the throes of a passionate embrace and I'm exhilarated at the thought. I should be feeling embarrassed, surely? Instead I'm buzzing, this feeling is alien, strange. But I like it.

Silas is completely unfased by the whole episode, joining me in my laughter as he leads me down the corridor in the direction of our rooms. Stopping outside mine, he opens my door for me, then leans in and kisses me lightly on the lips.

"Here… you go on in and get dry. Have a bath, or whatever and I'll see you in an hour." He ushers me in and hands over the damp carrier bag. "I'm looking forward to seeing you in those." He points to the bag containing my new shoes. I had almost forgotten them in the heat of the moment. I check the corridor for more cameras as I'm swiftly nudged into my room, spotting two, high on the wall in the corner. They're trained on the corridor. This place is definitely big on security. Silas catches my eye again, raising his eyebrows he nods, indicating I should go inside.

"Did you know?" I ask him. He just gives me a sexy smirk, confirming he knew alright!

"In you go. I'll see you later. About seven pm." He turns and walks to his own room, leaving me on the threshold of mine, breathless, wanting and dripping onto the expensive carpet.

Chapter 26

Once inside my room, I check my appearance in the huge mirror. What a mess… I'm completely bedraggled. My hair a straggly tangle. My soaking wet clothes are clinging to me like a second skin and I've black smudges of mascara under my eyes. But somehow, I look alive, radiant and happy.

Something new and exciting is stirring deep within me. It's like a hidden flame starting to lick the edge of dry kindling. It's as if I'm beginning to light up from within. An unknown, unexpected, hidden piece of me is starting to reveal itself; a rare butterfly emerging from my chrysalis.

Mindful of the precious contents I place the damp carrier bag on the bed. Reaching inside the bag with both hands, I carefully remove the box containing my new Manolo Blahnik shoes and lay it on the counterpane, beside the carrier bag.

Thankfully the bag has protected the box from the rain. Sighing, I reverently caress the box lid, "hmmm," I hum to myself quietly. "Hello, my beauties…" Nervously, I wipe my hands on the wet legs of my jeans, before lifting the lid to reveal the contents.

My hands tremble as they hover over the box lid. I'm perspiring at the thought of seeing the shoes again… how silly. *They're just shoes for goodness sake!* Although, they're the most expensive pair of shoes in the world. Well, perhaps not in the world, but certainly in *my* possession - and here am I - I'm a soaking wet mess!

Looking down at my shaking hands, I think better of it. Hesitating, before I ruin the whole day in my rush to reacquaint myself with my new babies, I change my mind about removing the box lid; I won't touch my shoes until I've thoroughly washed and dried my hands - properly.

Dashing quickly into the bathroom, I'm still shuddering and my hands tremble uncontrollably as my inept fingers fumble clumsily with my soaked jeans and sweater. I don't know if it is the sudden cold making me shiver, or the rush of adrenalin I feel every time my mind replays our searing kiss on the pavement. It's on a continual loop in my brain; a visual ear-worm.

My numb fingers continue to blunder and slip as I try to get a decent grip on the slippery fabric; it's a difficult process. The sodden material is clinging tightly to my body, reluctant to let go. After a short battle I manage to drag the wet wool of my sweater over my head, it instantly captures me, tangling in my hair and attaching itself to my face with a limpet-like suction; restricting my breathing. Fighting my way out of the drenched wool, I drag it down my arms. Tugging on the sleeves, I yank and pull on the cuffs until I'm finally released from its vice-like grip. Once free, I chuck the offending jumper in the bath, it lands with a dull thud. *God, that was like a frigging aerobic workout!*

Next, I peel my sodden jeans down my legs, I think they've shrunk! My knickers come down with them as I struggle and wiggle, contorting as I hop around in an effort to rid myself of the heavy, saturated denim. They get stuck just below my knees. If I don't sit down, I'll fall over!

Perching my bare bum on the edge of the tub, I yank on the hem of my jeans, pulling them inside-out in the effort. Eventually, the suction gives, releasing the material in a loud squelching sucking sound, finally allowing me to remove them. They must have doubled in weight with the amount of water they've soaked up. They join the sweater in the bath, as do my pants, socks and bra.

There's an old-fashioned iron radiator under the frosted window, so I place my water-logged ballet pumps face down on top, hoping they will dry by morning.

I'm standing naked, panting and shivering in the bathroom; exhausted from the effort of removing my wet clothing. I rub my arms. Goosebumps are pebbling my body and I'm starting to seriously tremble now. I can't seem to get warm. My teeth are chattering and my stomach is churning. Still, my brain won't let go of the vivid image of us cavorting on the street in the teeming rain. Each time I replay it, waves of desire surge like fire through my body, scorching my skin with chilled flames and elevating my heart rate even further, inducing even more shivers and shakes. It's a vicious circle; if I don't calm down immediately, I'll pass out from the sheer hypertension.

Swathing my wet hair in a towel, I grab the bathrobe from the hook on the back of the door. Enveloping myself in the thick fleecy cotton instantly feels better. "Bath," I say to the wall, then… "*Shit!*" cursing when I remember that the bath is currently occupied by my soaked clothing.

My brain is like scrambled egg. I'm reeling. Faffing around; rushing but getting nowhere fast. Totally disorganised, which isn't like me at all. I'm an affected mess. "Jesus, Edi, pull it together for Christ sakes!" I need to give myself a pep talk. I need to relax before I expire, I need a hot bath. That will definitely help.

Stepping back in the bedroom I search for the hotel information booklet. Housekeeping provides an overnight dry-cleaning service, so I locate the bag and drop my wet clothes into it. I dial the designated number, leaving the bag outside my door for collection as instructed. I can't help taking a swift glance in the direction of Silas' room, wondering whether he's soaking in the tub. *Don't get distracted!* Ducking back into my room I start rounding up my straying thoughts, I need to get ready. There goes that buzz of adrenalin again! *Jesus, am I sixteen?*

Now for that bath. I fill the deep antique tub, utilising some of the aromatic bath salts provided by the hotel. Steam fills the room and a sensuous scent of jasmine and vanilla permeates the humid air. I strip off my robe and step in. The water is scalding but because of my chilled state, I can't tell between hot and cold.

304

As my feet and legs defrost, the sting of the hot water starts to break through and I stand still for a few moments before lowering the rest of my chilled body into the steaming water. Griping the edges of the tub, counting slowly to ten, inch by inch until eventually, I'm accustom to the heat.

Once I'm comfortably seated, I lean back and stretch out. I can just about reach the end of the huge bath with my tip-toes, without going under. I lie still and close my eyes, concentrating my mind, listening to the intermittent drip of the tap and the popping of the occasional bubble. It's utter bliss. I can feel the heat permeating through my skin and warming my bones.

Unable to resist, I replay the kiss again in my mind. This time I imagine Silas' hands wandering all over me. A bead of perspiration dampens my upper lip. The water's gloriously hot and my skin is tingling as the expensive bath salts fizzle around me. It's easy to imagine that his hands are gently massaging me back to life.

Now I'm warmer and more relaxed I can begin my ablutions. I shave my legs, noticing that the bruise from my tumble at the gym on Monday is still visible. I'll need to cover that up. My under arms are next, then I scrub my face and body, and wash and condition my hair. I'm feeling human again. A quick check of my bikini area reveals that my pubic hair could do with a trim. Picking up my nail scissors from my washbag I carefully tidy myself up. I'm not shaving, that would certainly end in disaster, but a close, neat trim will do nicely.

The water is cooling so I step out of the bath and re-wrap myself in the robe and towel. There are some white towelling slippers in a clear plastic bag so I drop them on the floor and step into them. They're huge and make me waddle like a penguin.

Flip-flopping into the bedroom, I start to get ready for my night out with Silas. As I squirt myself with deodorant, I check the time; six-fifteen, that gives me three-quarters of an hour before we meet - plenty of time. I'm not entirely sure what to expect from tonight; once-upon-a-time, I did attend the odd celebrity party, but that was long ago - in another lifetime.

Laying my paltry selection of makeup on the dressing table, I try to remember how to apply it. These days I only wear blusher and mascara to mask my pastiness. I need to make more of an effort tonight, so I apply a light layer of tinted moisturiser as a foundation, dabbling it to a matt finish with a little translucent face powder. I apply some black kohl pencil, then a dusting of shimmering gold shadow on my eyelids. My brows looked neat and tidy after my trip to the beauty parlour, so I just brush them into shape. I flick my eyelashes with mascara and shade my cheeks with bronzer and blush, using a little more than usual because of the occasion. Finally, I highlight my temples with a bit of shimmer and dab on some lip balm. There, that looks okay. Better than okay... sultry in fact. I'm pretty happy with the results considering my lack of skill with the mascara wand and all things cosmetic.

Next, I dry my hair. The cut is so good, it just falls naturally into shape, glossy and shining for once. I run my fingers through the subtle layers, they tumble round my shoulders lying perfectly against my collar bone and emphasizing my natural, red and gold highlights. The lighting in this room is wonderful!

Time to get dressed... eagerly, I unwrap my new underwear. For a moment, I just stand and stare at the exquisite wisps of satin and lace. I'd forgotten how beautiful it is. Slipping my arms through the bra straps, I fasten the diamante catch at the front. Looking down, I can see how the emerald green satin, edged with the black lace trim contrasts against my creamy skin. The fit is amazing; my boobs are lifted and supported, my cleavage appears deep and sensual. The tops of my breasts are smooth, round mounds on my chest.

Then there's the knickers. Stepping into them, I shimmy them up my legs so they settle, neatly, in exactly the right place. Okay then. I take a deep breath for courage then turn tentatively to take a look in the mirror. *Wow*! The high legged Brazilian cut of the knickers emphasizes the gentle curve of my bottom, cupping my bum-cheeks. The delicate, black lace trim, grazing the line just above my groin; no VPL for me tonight! I just stand and stare at my reflection. Turning this way and that, looking for any imperfection or a bit of bulging flab or puckered skin – there aren't any; this is magic underwear!

In the mirror, I notice the dark penny-sized bruise on my shin from my tumble in the gym on Monday. It's clearly visible and needs hiding. Picking through my makeup bag, I find what I need and set about applying some concealer to my shin. Unfortunately, I'm an expert when it comes to covering bruises, though thankfully I've not needed to do it for a while. Once I'm done dabbing and shading, the bruise is completely invisible. I perform another couple of twirls in the mirror, swishing my glossy hair and admiring my new sexy underwear, mildly wondering what Silas would think if he could see me; but I reign in the thought quickly. I can't risk getting all hot and bothered again!

Happy with my appearance, I unwrap my dress from the polythene cleaning bag and step into it. I don't check the mirror again. I've worn it often enough to know how it looks. Then I walk over to the shoebox. I'm shaking again; I remove the lid carefully, as if I'm opening a treasure chest.

"Hello, my beautiful ladies," I whisper to them, unwrapping the tissue paper and lifting the glorious works of art to the light so I can admire the exquisite craftsmanship.

Perching on the edge of the bed I cross my legs. Reaching down, I place the stunning shoe on my foot, feeling like Cinderella again, tying the delicate laces into a bow at my ankle, just as the assistant had demonstrated earlier. When both shoes are securely fastened, I slowly stand up. Taking extra care not to trip or wobble, I walk steadily over to the mirror as if I'm balancing on a tightrope. A little trepidation fills my mind and

I'm suddenly concerned I might resemble mutton dressed as lamb.

Gulping down my fear, I open my eyes and reveal... me to me...

"Wow!" It comes out as a breathy sigh... it's all I can say. I look... *hot,* even though I say so myself. An awkward flush of embarrassment heats my face. I feel beautiful but at the same time shy and uncertain. I've hidden behind the security blanket of my frumpy, mumsy façade for so long I feel undeserving of the image reflected in the mirror. Shrugging off the unwelcome tension, I see a glimmer of the old me, peeking through my self-defence-shield. I need to embrace this, not hide from it.

The shoes really are the finishing touch. They're truly exquisite. Taking a few deep calming breaths, I smooth the satin of my green dress over my thighs, stomach and bottom, searching for any lumps and bumps; there are none. The illusion is complete. The magic underwear is doing its job beautifully, totally invisible beneath my non-designer cocktail dress. But I can't rip my eyes away from the shoes, they're amazing. I love them...

Drawing myself away from the mirror I find my suede clutch bag and fill it with the essentials I'll need tonight. Picking up my phone to drop it in my bag, I have a cheeky thought. Before I can talk myself out of it, I turn the camera on, point it at the mirror and take a posing selfie. I've never done it before and it feels ridiculously self-indulgent. Checking the photo, I'm happy with the result. Quickly, I take another one, just of my feet, so the shoes get top billing. Then I send a quick text to the girls:

"Well, here I'm in Paris, check me out! Hope Washington is amazing and you are having a great time. Love Edi ☺"

The reply comes instantly:

"Fucking hell! Is that really you???? You look really HOT Mamma!! Wow, I think you're having a better time than us!

Washington rocks. Going to see President Lincoln this afternoon! Can't believe you're in Paris!! Have a brilliant time tonight – hope you get a little somethin', somethin'! Hugs, S & L"

Somethin', somethin', indeed! That text contained far too many exclamation and question marks… not to mention spelling and grammatical mistakes. Sammy's a school teacher for goodness sake.

I start to smile, daring to hope they may get their wish, a sudden thrill makes me judder and blush. I chuckle at their cheek. At least they didn't laugh at my selfie. Perhaps they thought I was someone else. I certainly feel like someone else tonight.

Checking my new watch, I'm surprised to see it's just gone seven pm. Silas said he would be here by now. Nerves kick in big time and I suddenly need a wee. Hastily dropping my bag on the bed, I totter into the bathroom. Thankfully the steam has dissipated, but the room looks like a bomb's gone off. I don't have time to tidy it now, so I skirt round the pile of damp towels littering the floor, hitch up my dress, pull down my pants and have a last minute wee. Quickly I dry off and straighten myself out, I take a look in the bathroom mirror. Okay, the light is different in here, but I still look passable.

Teeth! I remember I haven't brushed them, so I make quick work of it, taking care not to get toothpaste on my dress. Then I go back into the bedroom, find my clutch and re-apply my lip balm, topping it off with a layer of red lipstick. *Phew!*... There, at last I'm ready. "Hurry up, Silas," I say to the door. The longer I have to wait, the worse the feeling of cold feet will be. As if he heard me, a light rat-a-tat-tat drums clearly on the glossily painted wood.

Gripping tightly to my clutch bag, I take a cleansing breath, puff it out and open the door… to a vision. His black suit looks sharp, his white shirt, clean and crisply pressed. He's devastating. He takes my breath away, standing there, his arms slightly bent at the elbows. Effortlessly suave, one elegant hand is straightening out the simple white-gold cufflink on the other. *Wow!* I hope I can do him justice in this old frock.

He stops his fiddling and stands stock still, staring at me. His eyes travel lazily down the length of my body. Appraising me. Is he appreciating what he sees?

My mouth goes bone dry. I'm not used to being scrutinised like that - not for a long time anyway - but I do recognise the look of hunger on his face.

Nervously, I wait for the familiar feeling of unease and humiliation to wash over me, but it doesn't. I don't feel grubby or objectified. I just feel... *admired*. It's quite a refreshing feeling. His gaze comes to an abrupt halt at my feet. I see his Adams-apple bob as he swallows. He breathes in slowly, then raises his eyes, they're smouldering with heat and promise.

"*My God*... Edi... Whoa! You ..." he clears his throat. "my ... I mean, wow! Edi. You're stunning." Although he manages to speak, his voice comes out gruff and quavering. Then he looks at my feet again. As though he's completely hypnotised by them. It's amusing. My lips give an involuntary twitch at the effect the shoes are having on him. His obvious nerves have a quelling effect on my own anxious state, and any sensation of awkwardness dissolves like an evening frost under the warmth of the morning sun. My fear is washed away by the sheer knowledge he's feeling just as nervous as me. And in its place, blooms a wonderous rush of empowerment.

Relieved, I resolve to enjoy my evening. Clearly, he approves, time to relax!

"Why, thank you, kind sir... you don't look too shabby yourself." It's a ridiculous understatement... he looks deadly!

Chapter 27

"Shall we?" he opens his arm in invitation, guiding me from the security of my room. Pulling the door closed behind me I step into the quiet hallway. *"Jeezus...* you'll be fighting them off tonight that's for sure." *I seriously doubt it!* He shakes his head, then offers me his arm. "I've ordered a cab. I don't think we'll trust the weather. Those shoes wouldn't stand up to another rainstorm." He gives me a cheeky wink then looks at my feet again. There's definitely a glint of danger in his eye this evening.

The cab is waiting at the kerb as we exit the hotel. Ever the true gentleman, Silas opens the door for me, guiding me into my seat before walking round to the other side and climbing in. Leaning forward, he speaks to the driver. "Four Seasons Hotel, s'il vous plait." Then, reclining beside me, he reaches over and rests his hand on mine, in my lap. He isn't seated too close, remaining on his side of the car, but I can still breathe him in, he smells divine. There's that hint of sandalwood and musk, it's like a pheromone to my senses.

The streets look fresh and clean as we drive to our destination. The light is reflecting off the drying puddles, which are still visible on the damp pavements. It's still quite warm following this afternoon's storm, but it's not as humid as it was. The driver keeps the speed slow as we join the main road and follow the cars along the Champs Elysees. The flow of traffic is busy but steady.

In the distance, The Eiffel Tower is lit up with millions of sparking, golden lights. Multicoloured laser beams blaze from the tip like an array of shooting stars, lighting up the evening sky.

The Arc de Triomphe stands majestic and proud at the centre of the Place Charles de Gaulle. My heart is in my mouth as we drive round the terrifying roundabout. I close my eyes and squeeze Silas' hand tightly.

"Nervous?" He asks me, squeezing back.

"Yeah, lil' bit…strange huh?" I really *am* nervous. My knees are knocking together as I clench and release my thigh muscles, causing my legs to jiggle. This is ridiculous. It's only a stupid party.

"Don't be, you look amazing." He looks at me with his sleepy dark eyes. His thumb caresses the top of my hand; I instantly feel a surge of adrenalin that has my heart thumping and my breath hitching.

"Thank you." I'm not used to this. I try not to hyperventilate as he stares at me.

"We're here." Abruptly he removes his hand from mine and within a split second, he's out of the cab and standing at my door helping me out. Taking my elbow, he guides me under the elaborate cream canopy and up the marble steps into the plush hotel lobby.

"Phew! This is something else." Gazing around me, I admire the stunning surroundings. There's a lot to take in. I'm standing on an actual red carpet. Beautiful people are everywhere.

That unworthy feeling of self-doubt is creeping up on me again and I get a sinking sensation in the pit of my stomach. Any minute now someone is going to point at me and ask what the hell I'm doing here. We creep along in line, queueing patiently as we progress through the lobby towards the entrance of the party. With every step closer to the doors, my nervousness grows a little greater. *Why am I here?*

I'm staring at the milling crowd as we queue with the other couples waiting patiently to enter the ballroom, and in my peripheral vision I catch a sudden fleeting glimpse of emerald.

Turning in the direction of the bright colour, I see the queue of people is reflected in the double mirrored doors on the opposite side of the lobby. And there, in the middle of the queue of people, looking straight at me, is a stunning woman. She's dressed in a vivid green dress, she has lustrous auburn hair. The tall, handsome man standing beside her has a protective hand in the small of her back as he checks his ticket. *Holy fuck!* The woman in the mirror is *me*, and I look... beautiful.

I'm the only woman wearing a bright colour. All the others have chosen to wear either elegant black, midnight-blue or silver-grey. My intense green dress stands out like a beacon beside the muted gowns and distinguished tuxedos.

The image is reminiscent of a '*Jack Vettriano*' painting – The title would be something like '*The Woman in Green*', or '*The Viper*' or maybe '*The Green Dragon*'! I'm mesmerised by my own reflection.

Silas still has his hand in the small of my back. His palm is warm and comforting as he guides me forwards, step by steady step. I notice we're the next but one couple in line. Not long now before we can enter the party, so I pull myself together and concentrate my attention on not falling over; although I can't help the odd self-indulgent look at my reflection. It feels weird, as if the woman in the mirror is looking back at me knowingly.

The smart liveried gentleman checks our tickets and waves us through, inviting us to enjoy our evening. The ballroom is packed with people; all milling around and chatting in small groups and clumps. Among them, there are several faces I recognise. Some from TV and some from magazine covers. Lots of them are models. And I think I recognise the odd designer, but I'm not that up- to-date with the fashion world so I would be guessing.

Silas interrupts my musings. "What would you like to drink?" Inclining his head, he nods towards the bar at the back of the huge room.

"Do you think I could have a whiskey? I think I need Dutch courage." Oh, I hope he doesn't think I'm a lush, whiskey is my preferred spirit. I can't drink vodka, although I don't mind an occasional G&T. Somehow tonight just feels like a whiskey night.

"Yes, sure. What do you want with it? Ice, soda, cola?"

"Just Ice and a splash of soda water please." I give him what I hope is an encouraging smile.

"Coming up. Why don't you wait over there," he points to a free elbow-high table off to the side. "I'll bring them over. It looks busy." He kisses my cheek fleetingly. "*God*! You look amazing," and leaving me on my own, he starts elbowing his way through the crowd to the bar. Turning on my expensive heels, I shimmy through the throng, keeping the free table in my line of sight.

There's a familiar tune threading the air. It's barely audible over the thrum of the crowd. *'Where Do You Go To (My Lovely)?'* by *Peter Sarstedt* – how appropriate. I hum along to the sad lyric as I stand by my table, people watching.

"*Edi*!" Startled, I hear my name called over the sound of mingled conversations and laughter. "Edi! *Salut*!" Turning, I see Silas' good friend Gerard from the airport earlier this morning, elbowing his way towards me through the crowd.

He looks rather devilishly handsome. Dressed in a mid-blue, three-piece suit and white shirt, his black hair is sleek and ruffled at the same time. *How does that work?* "Edi." He reaches me and clutching my elbows, plants a continental kiss on each cheek. He's carrying another black leather wallet under his arm. It's exactly the same as the one he gave Silas this morning, so I can only assume it's either a revised contract, or some other business he has to deal with this evening. I vaguely wonder how many black leather folio-cases he owns?

314

Stepping back so he can hold me at arm's length, he makes an admiring appraisal of my appearance, before letting out a low, appreciative whistle. "Phew, *sacre bleu*! Superb. You look beautiful." He releases one arm but keeps hold with the other. "Magnifique!"

"Thank you. Though I feel a little conspicuous. Everyone else is in black!" I grimace through clenched teeth.

"No, no, zis green is perfect for you." His eyes wander over my hair and face and he's still holding my arm. "Where is my friend?" he asks, gazing round the room. "I can't believe 'e's left you on your own to be eaten up by these 'ungry vultures." He gives the room a disdainful eye; clearly unimpressed by all the decadence on show.

"At the bar, look. Over there," I point at Silas's broad back. He stands a head taller than most of the men at the bar, but strangely, not all of the women. They must be those Amazonian models I've heard of.

"Ah, oui, I see 'im." He nods. "I'll guard you until 'e is back, I think," which is quicker than expected, because he suddenly releases my arm as Silas, drinks in hand, walks over to where we're standing.

"Gerard, I see as usual you found the most beautiful woman in the room." Silas hands me my drink and immediately wraps a territorial arm round my waist, staking his claim.

"Bien sur... 'ow could I not?" Gerard raises his eyebrows, again that quizzical look. "Did you manage to look at the details?" He raises his folio case, indicating the paperwork.

"Everything seems in order..." Silas replies a little curtly. He obviously doesn't want to talk business tonight.

The amber liquid swirls and sparkles in the cut-glass tumbler. I notice he has the same as me. I take a welcome sip, remembering to wet the rim of the glass with my tongue before I touch it to my lips; preventing my lipstick from staining the glass. Silas watches my little ritual, mesmerised; his head tilted to one side. I ignore him, turning my attention to the room at large, taking in the writhing throng of people. I swallow the rich whiskey. It's a smoky, peaty flavour and sends a scaring trail of heat down my throat to my stomach. Delicious. We sip our drinks. Silas and Gerard are having a muted discussion about some business, but I'm only half listening.

The room is absolutely buzzing. Everyone is mingling, calling out people's names, hugging and kissing each other. The atmosphere is electric with anticipation of the evening ahead.

Every single person here seems taller than me. Some of the women are well over six feet, probably models who have been working hard all week and are now ready to party. I recognise a few 'A' list celebrities amongst the crowd; at least one American actor and a couple of rock singers, although I can't recall their names.

I spot an actor from '*Game of Thrones*' and another guy from an American cop show, holding an intense conversation. They're stood close together, head to head, engaged in animated discussion. They're both quite short, but the two women draped all over them are at least eight inches taller. None of them seem to mind in the least about the height difference.

The *Game of Thrones* guy has his hand on the arse of a sultry dark-haired beauty. She leans on his shoulder, listening, seemingly engrossed in the four-way tête-à-tête. The other model has white-blonde cropped hair, a concave chest and looks totally bored. But she's still wrapped round the cop show guy like creeping ivy. It's bizarre.

"Edi?" I'm jolted from my people watching.

"Hmm?" I absently re-focus my attention on my own small group.

"Edi, Gerard needs my assistance with something, it shouldn't take too long. Will you be okay here for a couple of minutes?"

Silas looks a bit miffed at his friend, but it seems whatever the issue, it can't wait. Gerard is hovering off to one side, impatiently. He's keen to get whatever it is sorted out.

"I'm sure I'll be absolutely fine," I lie, feeling abandoned already. I wave my glass at him, then open my stance to indicate the scenes going on around the room. "I'm enjoying watching all this lot. It's fascinating. Go... I'm good... go... go!" I'm sure I'll be fine. I'll have to be!

"Okay, I'll be as quick as I can. Don't wander off!" Reassured, he kisses me chastely then moves away with Gerard towards some double doors on the left. I presume it's some kind of office or meeting room.

I watch them go with trepidation, suddenly feeling alone and vulnerable. Now they've gone, It's like I've lost my protection, leaving me exposed and conspicuous in my bright emerald green. Nervously, I run my hand over my dress, unconsciously ironing out any invisible wrinkles, making sure there are no creases or bumps. Forcing myself to stop fidgeting, I stand sipping my drink and allow the amber nectar to warm my insides.

Because I'm standing here alone, the tall table we occupied instantly becomes a target for others. Several people have spotted the valuable free space and, without asking start to stand close, resting their glasses on the table. Before I know it, I'm surrounded by half a dozen people. None of them know me and none of them care I had the table first. Skilfully they use their elbows to muscle me out; wedging themselves between me and the table so eventually I've no option but to step away, losing my place. The manners of these people are shocking.

I look around the room for somewhere else to escape to; somewhere unobtrusive to either sit or stand, where I'll be out of the way. I can't see any other unoccupied tables, so I've little option but to remain where I am in the middle of the room, watching the comings and goings of the beautiful ones.

My eyes drift back towards the *Game of Thrones* quartet, but they've moved on and in their place is a stunning black woman, I vaguely recognise, in a very tight, revealing black gown. The gown has no back, and hardly any front for that matter - just some narrow shoelace straps holding up the miniscule wisps of material. She might as well be naked. She's fawning all over a very tall, reed-thin Oriental guy. He's dressed in a pure white, silk three-piece suit and black satin shirt. Very Saturday night fever.

They're making a complete spectacle of themselves, kissing, fondling and stroking each other with no apparent concern that they've an audience. I'm suddenly feeling uncomfortable. Watching them, I'm reminded of my own little open-air encounter in the rain this afternoon. Gripped by overwhelming embarrassment, I'm unable to look at them anymore. They're consumed by each other and seemingly oblivious to the milling crowd around them, just as Silas and I were earlier. My stomach sinks at the thought.

I'm just turning away from the over-the-top scene when my attention is drawn to a short, stocky, silver-haired man dressed in a black tuxedo. He's flanked by four burly, bald, bodyguards. Each one must be nearly seven feet tall and probably six feet wide. They're huge; towering over everybody nearby. As the intimidating group approaches, the cavorting couple immediately spring apart from each other as if they've been tasered.

I watch them halt in front of the nervous pair, the bodyguards take a distinct step backwards in a curved line, creating a human shield and everyone in the near vicinity discreetly moves away. The created space allows the short man some privacy to speak to the two models. That's some well-trained security detail.

From my vantage point on the side-lines, I've a clear view, but I can't hear what is being said. The squat man's hair is pure white and very distinctive - I recognise him instantly. His name is Pierre Adrax, he's a very well-known, if not disreputable, French, fashion designer.

If you choose to believe everything you read in the tabloids, Pierre isn't his real name. And seeing him this close-up I can believe it. Though he claims French heritage, he doesn't look the least bit French. The story is he's of Pakistani origin but claims French residency because his Grandmother was born here.

Rumour has it he uses the fashion industry as a cover for funding, what are regularly described as *'controversial political activities'*. A fact that's well documented, if not proven. Although no newspaper editor has been stupid enough to call him a criminal, reading between the lines or every bulletin on the TV news programs, the connotation is clear.

Looking at him now, even with his diminutive stature, I can believe it. He exudes menace from every pore. I would not like to be one of those poor models right now. Just the sheer vehemence in his eyes has me trembling in my shoes.

Inaudibly, he utters something to the models, who both stand, head and shoulders above him, looking down at the floor in deference to his presence. With a flick of his hand, he gives a silent instruction to the bodyguards. The human wall breaks apart as two of the men-beasts step up to escort the models and the other two take up a new position either side of their boss. As quickly as they arrived, all seven of them march off towards the exit. There was no scene made and no objections raised. No attention was drawn or if it was, it was blindly ignored by everyone else in the vicinity but me.

God, that was intense!

I take a huge gulp of my drink, exhale the breath I didn't realise I was holding and turn my attention back to the room in general.

It's been fifteen minutes since Silas left me alone, I'm just checking the time on my new watch when I feel a large hand rest firmly in the small of my back and I'm instantly flooded with gratitude that he's returned to me. To be fair, he wasn't gone that long at all.

A smile teases my lips as I turn my attention back to Silas; however, it soon vanishes; I'm startled to see it isn't him who's now got his arm wrapped around me, but a handsome, young, blonde, Adonis. He must be a model. I recoil, a little shocked by his audacity; he's clearly mistaken me for someone else. Once he's realised his error, I expect he'll apologise and make an excuse to walk away.

But he doesn't. In fact, he doesn't seem in the least bit concerned. Instead of backing off he keeps his hand exactly where it is while his baby-blue eyes, start a blatant journey down the length of my body, only halting his wandering gaze briefly, when his eyes land on my Manolo clad feet, before they reverse and travel all the way back up again, ending on my stunned face. *What is it about these shoes?* Observations complete, he smiles and holds out his hand.

"I'm River... model," his southern drawl is exaggerated and somewhat pretentious. The half wink and crooked smile might work with some of these naïve girls, but it doesn't do anything for me...

"I'm not," I say, sarcastically as I shrug out of his grip.

"Not what?" He looks at me confused, as if he can't quite believe his southern charm has failed him. I think he's a bit thick. He certainly doesn't look like the brightest button in the box... nice, but dim.

"Not a model..." I say tartly. He can bog-off. I've no interest in barely post-pubescent pretty-boys!

"Oh, I can tell that. You're too old... Err... I mean, you're not tall enou'... err... slim... *shit!* Ma'am I'm sorry... I mean you're not thin and bony like them gals," he stumbles ineptly over his words. I just glare at him, arching one eyebrow in warning.

Careful sonny... but in all honestly, I'm not truly offended. Everything he's tried so hard *not* to say, is true. I'm not tall, or thin, or young. But it's amusing watching him squirm. "Jeeze-Louise, Ma'am, ah hope you don' mind me sayin' but... *damn lady! You. Are. Stacked!*" he blurts, obviously thinking he has hit on the right compliment to describe my short, curvy body! "Can I get you a drink... or would you like to get a room?" He comes close and whispers the last bit in my ear suggestively. *Is he pissed or what?*

"Seriously?" Leaning away and targeting him with my most condescending glare. I shake my head, slowly so he gets the message loud and clear. "*River*, is it?"

He gives me a hopeful nod. "Yessiree, Ma'am."

"Well, *River*... you need to take a dive. Go on... now... go and find someone your own age to play with." I flap my hand, shooing him away. "Bye, bye now." His eyebrows knit together in doubt. It looks like he's struggling with a difficult sum or equation. He just looks at me as if he doesn't understand how I could possibly not be in the least bit interested in his proposition. Poor Lamb!

I allow him time for the revelation to sink in, then bite my lip to supress my amusement when I see his expression do a complete 360-degree turn. In the blink of an eye and a flutter of his eyelashes, he reprograms his brain and his attention is immediately caught by something behind me. Presuming it's his next target, I take a glance over my shoulder, interested in what or who it could possibly be? As suspected, his radar has homed in on a very pretty young red-haired model. She looks about seventeen. I vaguely recognise her, so she must be well known. Possibly the flavour of the month for the top fashion magazines. Butterfly boy takes one last look at my smiling face, then moves off to pursue the poor creature. Breathing a sigh of relief at his disappearing back, I return to watching the crowd...

Come on Silas! What's keeping you this long?

Okay, so I've managed to get rid of one of them, but I can still feel lots of other curious eyes on me, making me uncomfortable. It's as if I'm suddenly easy prey just because I'm standing alone; or is it because I'm alone, I'm attracting attention?

Once again, I look for somewhere to either sit or stand inconspicuously and await Silas' return. There's absolutely nowhere free. The place is swimming with people so I shove my way to the bar and order another whiskey.

Drink in hand, I finally manage to find a small square of carpet that isn't occupied, somewhere between the bar and main door. I keep flitting my gaze to the office, where I know Silas is with Gerard... *come on guys!* Striving really hard to not look as out of place as I feel, I sip my drink, keeping a wary eye on the heaving crowd.

My second glass is empty and I'm beginning to feel the effects of the alcohol. Remembering I've only had some fish soup for my lunch, I'd better slow down the pace, or else find something to eat. I look around for a buffet table, finding nothing; just the free bar. It's stacked with scores of bottles of champagne and hundreds of champagne flutes. There's no food, not a single crisp, nut or twiglet to be had. Not even a server, walking round with miniscule canapés - literally - not a sausage!

Of course, fashion models don't actually eat, but you would think they might have provided something for us mere mortals, but alas, no. I resign myself to drinking scotch and remaining hungry. I order another drink – oh, make it a double...

The music has really got going now. Ramped up to a million decibels, it's ridiculously loud. It only makes the people around me talk even louder so they can be heard over the deafening thud, thud, thud of the heavy beat. I must be getting old! It's the Rolling Stones, I think. Yes... I recognise *Mick Jagger's* dulcet tones belting out *Sympathy for The Devil,* though it's hardly recognisable with all the additional din going on.

The lights in the ballroom have dimmed and with them it would seem, everyone's inhibitions …. Exhibitionists everywhere!

"Meredith?" I freeze. The sound of that name makes my ears twitch, like a rabbit's. I no longer hear Mick, the Stones or the drone of the masses; I'm on high alert. "Meredith, is that you. *O.M.F.G!"*

I'm floored. *Shit on a stick!* I don't know what to do, so I just stand still, staring. Careering towards me on six-inch platforms is Lynda Summers. I can't believe she's here - of all people!

"Meredith, it *is* you…*Fuck me sideways…* you look amazing!" I can't speak! "Where've you been hiding? It must be nearly twenty years!" She screeches over the loud music making a terrifying lunge for me. There's no use trying to lie or deny who I am. She's recognized me and I can't run. Flicking my eyes towards the door I know Silas is behind, a searing surge of panic has me moving towards Lynda with sudden focus.

Grabbing her roughly by the upper arm, I swing her round. Using more force than I really need, I start to propel her towards the edge of the room, away from the milling horde and out of sight of the office door.

"Hey!!... what are you doing?" She trots alongside of me, on her ridiculous shoes. The speed of my sudden movement has her spilling her champagne. "Stop fucking pulling… your hurting me." She snatches her arm away and staggers to a halt. "What the actual *fuck* Meredith?" Her glazed eyes cut through me unfocused and unblinking. She's clearly taken something.

"Lynda, you need to keep your voice down," I speak clearly. Dumping my half-empty glass on a nearby table, I turn and look up at her. She easily has five inches on me. And in those shoes, she's skimming six feet. But she looks unsteady, she's definitely high. It wouldn't be the first time.

Cautiously, I take her in. It must be close to nineteen years since I last saw her. Like me, she's aged, but unlike me, not too well. The years of excess have taken their toll on her looks. She's a bit jaded around the edges, a bit tired and dogged looking. There's the rigid evidence of Botox and definitely some lip fillers. Her long hair is still the same brassy platinum blonde, although now there are some badly applied extensions in there for added volume. Her figure is still exactly the same though. Ample breasts, tiny, wasp-like waist and long skinny legs that go on for ever. *'Sparrow legs'* Bobby used to call her…

While I'm making my assessment of her, it appears she's doing exactly the same of me…

"*Wow*, Meredith, you look… *fantastic*." It's completely insincere. "Are you back on the circuit? I've still got a few irons in the fire." She flips her hair over her shoulder, looking round to see if she's being watched. "I did a calendar this year and I'm doing 'Celebrity Big Brother' next year." Lynda was always the one who craved attention, it doesn't surprise me in the least; though she seems to have forgiven me for man-handling her.

She twiddles her hair and looks around, all the while checking for an audience. As usual, she's completely self-absorbed. In that regard, she hasn't changed. I'm hoping she's going to babble about herself, and forget all about me. "I'm on this brilliant diet, I just drink water during the day and champagne at night. It keeps the pounds off, but I'm half pissed all the time," she screeches with laughter as she looks me up and down. Obviously, I don't come up to scratch anymore. I need to get rid of her before Silas comes out of the office. "God Meredith," She sighs as she calms. Her glassy eyes are hardly focussing and she's swaying. "Where the *fuck,* have you been for the last twenty years?" she repeats. She's welling up. *Christ!*

"Oh, you know. Getting a degree, getting a proper job, keeping my head down." I'm anxious and babbling like an idiot. "All the boring stuff." She just stares down at me. It's freakish; she's a giant in those heels.

"A degree?" She looks shocked. "Like in a fucking University, degree... *you*?" She's shocked.

"Yep, working hard." *And now it's all about to be shot to shit because you've turned up at this stupid fucking party!*

"Bugger me!" she starts to laugh again. Uncontrollable, hysterical laughter. Yes, she's definitely taken something. "I can just see the graduation photo now! What a picture! Tits on display, degree in your hand, mortarboard on your head. That would make a brilliant page three image." She bends forward, her humongous breasts heaving as she tries to contain laughter. "Meredith, the model student!"

She wipes her eyes, her expression returning to some semblance of sincerity. "Seriously, Meredith, where've you been? You must know the sensation it caused when you disappeared? Bobby, was beside himself." *I bet he bloody was.* "All the papers said you had run away, but you never came back. Why?" Suddenly she grabs me and pulls me into her ample chest, knocking the breath out of me. "Oh, I've missed you. Bobby, will be *fucking* delighted when he knows you're back."

I wrench myself out of her hold, suddenly terrified. "NO!" I shout, "no, I mean no," trying to quieten my voice so I don't draw any unwanted attention. "I don't want *you* to say anything to anybody!" Making my voice as adamant as I can, I press the issue. "Lynda, you cannot say anything to anybody!" I jab my finger in her face forcing the point. "Do you hear me? I mean it. No one. Especially not Bobby."

Uncertainty fills her face. How can I get this through to her? "Listen to me... I've no intention of going back to that... life. Not now, not ever." My voice sounds severe, even to me. I'm gripping her by the arms again. Willing her to hear me, I give her a little shake. "I can't. Are you listening? I've grown up. I've changed. I wanted different things. New things. Better things and it's taken me this long to get them."

She looks a bit fearful so I ease up a little. "Lynda, please understand. I've worked *really* hard for what I have and I won't lose it; I'm not the same person anymore. *Meredith*... she's gone." She stares at me as if she doesn't understand what I mean.

"Okay. *Christ!...* stop pinching my fucking arms." She shakes loose of my iron grip, staggering backwards into the wall and bouncing off before steadying herself once more.

"I mean it Lynda. Not a word. I'm not Meredith anymore. My name is *Edi*, I've a good job... a great job... an amazing job, in fact and I can't afford to lose it. Do you understand me?" I'm hissing, threateningly through gritted teeth, glaring into her glazed eyes, getting in her face. I sound really angry, but I need to hammer my message home.

"Yeah, yeah, of course. I'm sorry." She rubs at her pinched arms as I close my eyes on those hollow words. "I was just so pumped to see you... you know? And you do look... amazing... really good." She backs off from me, subdued, quietening down. Staring at me in what, wonder, disbelief? I don't know!

One thing I do know is I need to get her out of the way before Silas returns, which should be any minute now.

Desperate for her to disappear, I try a calmer approach. "Look, I didn't mean to upset you... but honestly, I'm great... happier than I've been in years. Everything is good in my life. It's wonderful, in fact."

An image of Silas flashes through my mind. "I need to stay... *me...* Edi, not Meredith." I soften my tone, hoping she gets it. "Meredith's long gone, the glamour modelling and all that shit's gone with her. It's ancient history... Can you just give me that?" I'm pleading, I know, but I also know what she's like. She thrives on nasty gossip and feeds on drama. At the height of our careers, we were often pitted as rivals. It sold more covers that way – despite it being utter bollocks.

I didn't mind working with Lynda, but she played her part all too well and devoured all the ludicrous hype. She believed every word, relished the publicity, the bullshit and played along with it too; slating me at any given opportunity. It all added to the illusion created by the tabloids and the management companies. The punters lapped it up. It sold more papers, promoted the sale of posters, TV appearances and top-shelf magazine articles and centrefolds. It made us famous and earned a lot of cash for the industry. It made Bobby very rich, very quickly, and it's haunted me ever since.

"Yeah, Meredith. I mean Edi." She flits her eyes around, looking for an escape. Good! "Look, it was great to see you. I'm happy for you, you know?" She starts to back away from this crazy woman and I breathe a sigh of relief. She gets it – *finally*!

"There you are!" A deep voice from behind drags me back to the here and now. I straighten my back. "I've been looking all over for you."

Oh, perfect timing or what!

Chapter 28

Keeping my focus firmly on Lynda, not daring to turn my eyes towards Silas. She's just staring, open mouthed, dumbstruck. Before she can blurt out anything inappropriate, I hurl myself off the bridge, diving in quickly.

"Silas, this is an old acquaintance of mine. Lynda, this is Silas, my boss." Glaring at her in warning; Im hoping to God he doesn't recognise her.

"My pleasure Lynda," he offers his hand, which she takes. He shakes it once then releases it, as if it's burned him.

"Oh, ha-ha, nice to meet you," she simpers, unable to remove her greedy eyes from his fine form. I close my eyes and snort through my nose in exasperation. She's a nightmare!

Silas places his lips near my ear. "Honey-Bee, we need to speak to Mr Philips about tomorrow." Seemingly oblivious to the affect he has on Lynda, he places a protective arm round my shoulders. "They're in the VIP bar," pulling me to him. "Nice to meet you Lynda, he says dismissively over his shoulder as, gently, I'm removed from her space as he's guiding me away.

"Hey, call me Err ... Mer'...Err... Edi!" she shouts after us, stumbling over her tongue in her desire to call me Meredith. *Get me out of here!* I turn and wave. I'm never calling her!

"She was ... interesting!" Silas whispers in my ear, tightening his hold as we walk back through the crowd. "I can't imagine how you two know each other." He's curious, but he's going to have to stay that way. I'm keeping schtum on that one – for now at least.

"Well, you took a while... I had to make my own entertainment," I quip, a little too cheerily; cheery is not how I feel at this moment. "Where's Gerard?"

"He left. This kind of party isn't his thing."

Nor mine... I'm curious to know what his meeting with Gerard was all about, but I won't ask; it might be confidential. I'm relieved he's back though.

Attentively, he guides me through the people. "Hmmm... well next time I'm not leaving you. You attract far too much attention Ms Sykes!" he whispers, squeezing my waist and moving his hand down to caress my behind.

"Not as much as you..." I whisper back. He seriously does; all the models are looking at him, male and female! He's turning heads.

"They're looking at you, not me..."

"I doubt it..." but that one remark makes me worry about who else is looking and could recognise me? I eye the room suspiciously. My head is in a complete whirl, my mind, a cyclone of turmoil and doubt. I shouldn't have come. It was stupid to take a risk like this.

Reeling at all the unexpected events of today, I don't know how much more I can take. My old life has collided with my new life in a spectacular way and I don't know what to do about it. For nigh on twenty years, I've managed successfully to put that horrid part of my life firmly behind me. I've become someone new. It was difficult, but I've grown in confidence and striven to attain my goals.

I was always vigilant, careful - keeping my wits about me, trusting only a few and befriending even fewer. I've kept myself to myself, so how, in just one short week has my life taken such an unbelievable turn? One that I never, in a million years, would have predicted or expected.

Finally, I have my dream job. I've met someone I feel I can trust; someone I really like and I think really likes me. Someone I could only have fantasised about ever finding. Like a fool, I've taken my eye off the ball. I've let my guard down for a split second and believed in the fairy tale. And just like that - in the space of twelve short hours, it's crumbling before my eyes; falling apart. Burying my head in the sand isn't going to help this time.

"There they are," Silas ushers me over to a large group who look to be corralled in some sort of open pen.

The roped off VIP area is much closer to the main action, next to the stage and the D. J's booth. Running down the left-hand side, there's a makeshift runway, where half naked people appear to be prancing up and down, practicing their model walks just for fun. As we're so close to the speakers, the music is even louder over here, deafening in fact.

The VIP's have their own bar and several body-builder type waiters are milling around; dressed only in tiny boxers and bow-ties, 'The Buff-Butlers' strut about manfully, proffering trays of drinks and plates of minute canapes. Food at last but now strangely, I'm not hungry!

Silas nods to the bouncer, who unhooks the red silk rope and lets us in. Like a stunned child, I follow in his wake. I'm being hypnotised by the recognisable faces of the rich and famous. I've only ever seen many of them before on TV, in movies or magazines. I'm surrounded. It's like a living, breathing Tussauds exhibit, *The Chamber of Horrors!*

Everyone is partying hard. Drinking, chatting, laughing, kissing and fondling. They're completely uninhibited. Embarrassed by their hedonistic behaviour, I keep my eyes turned towards the floor and my mouth firmly shut. My brush with Lynda has completely unnerved me; I feel conspicuous and self-conscious in my vivid green dress.

An actor I recognise but can't place gives me a salacious wink as he walks by. He deliberately strokes the palm of his hand firmly over my behind as he passes; as if he's running his hand over the back of a chair, checking out the upholstery or plumping a plush cushion. I'm astounded and it makes me jump closer to

Silas. The guy just carries on his merry way, as if nothing out of the ordinary took place, a wicked leer twisting his mouth. Recognising I'm a little out of my depth, Silas pulls me closer to him protectively, as we continue to fight our way over to the Phillips's.

"Tudor! Good man, pleased you could make it to my little soiree." Mr Philips is bright red in the face, it's clear he's had a few. "Ah, and the lovely… err… um, yes,"

"Edi," Silas growls, clearly pissed that Phillips can't remember my name.

"Yes, of course. Looking very lovely tonight Edi," he says to my chest.

"Thank you," I respond politely. I've had enough of this party already and we've only been here about an hour. I really don't like the way people are looking at me. I'm convinced I'll be recognised and I'm shitting it.

"Monty," Silas shakes his hand. "You've had a good week I believe?" He keeps a tight hold of my waist, not letting go, preferring to have me welded to his side. I'm grateful and I lean closer.

"I'm broke dear boy!" Montgomery laughs at his own joke. "She's bought the shop. I hope there's plenty of cargo space in that plane of yours." His nose is glowing like a beacon and he has visible traces of white powder on his top lip.

Silas has noticed it too, rubbing his hand over his mouth indicating to Monty that he might like to do the same, before adding, "no need to worry on that score, Monty. We've got the room." Phillips gets the hint and gives his mouth and nose a discreet a rub. When he removes his hand, all trace of the powder has gone.

"Silassss!" A shrill, high pitched squeal pierces through the heavy booming rhythm of the *Kaiser Chiefs*. Victoria totters towards us wearing what looks like a silver lurex handkerchief.

331

"Oooh, you look delicious, darling." She leaps on him, wrapping her arms round his neck and smothering him in kisses.

Seething at her overfamiliar behaviour, I can only agree with the *'Kaiser Chiefs'*. As the music booms... if she's not careful... *'I Predict A Riot!'* She's totally ignoring me and is as pissed as a fart! Her minuscule, designer dress rides up her backside and hangs loosely on her skeletal frame. Her almost flat boobs are fully visible from the side, the loose material falling away under her arms as she links her claw like bony hands around Silas's neck.

In an act of sheer self-preservation, Silas removes his arm from around my waist and with both hands grabs her wrists in an attempt to prize free from her grasping talons. Meanwhile, Montgomery just observes the embarrassing spectacle with a huge shit-eating grin on his face. The dress hangs so freely her nipples are clearly visible, poking out from the side of her dress as she wrestles with Silas. Reluctantly, she concedes defeat and releases him, but not trusting her to keep her hands to herself, he holds onto her wrists until her arms are safely by her sides.

Eventually, with the wrestling match over, she notices me. "Oh... *you're* here!" she exclaims, looking down on me and flipping her glossy hair over her shoulder. *Is everyone here over five feet ten?*

"Yes, she is!" As if to warn her off, Silas draws me to his side and places his arm back round my waist. Victoria gives me a look that would curdle milk. I ignore it and put my hand flat on Silas chest, staking my claim. Her over made-up eyes follow the movement, narrowing in jealousy. I can almost hear her composing the next cutting remark.

"I see you've at least... *woops!*" She doesn't have time to finish whatever insult was on her tongue. Blindly reaching behind her, searching out the table for some well needed support, she misses it. Her hand flaps in mid-air as she starts to topple over. I supress the childish desire to yell *'Timber!'*

Like Bambi on ice, her skinny legs wobble and she staggers backwards on her skyscraper heels. I've no idea how she manages to remain upright, but somehow, she does. Her arms windmill as her bony arse collides with the table behind her, forcing her to sit down with a resounding thud. *Ouch… I felt that!*

Momentum causes her legs to fly up and apart, revealing no underwear! Laughing like a drain she finds the whole undignified episode totally hilarious. Cackling like a witch, she continues to flash her Hollywood-waxed fanny in the faces of every man in close proximity, Silas and Monty included. I don't know where to look and neither does Silas.

Monty however roars with appreciative hilarity at her antics, apparently enjoying the inappropriate spectacle as he helps her back onto her feet. Hauling her in front of him, he curls one arm tightly round her waist, drawing her back firmly against his front. "You're a naughty girl tonight, aren't you?" his other hand immediately travelling up between her twig-like thighs and under the hem of her miniscule dress, leaving absolutely no doubt as to which part of her body he's fingering. "Hmmm, slippery!" he sucks on her neck with slug-like, fleshy lips.

Even though I'm blushing to the roots of my hair, I can't draw my eyes away. Monty slobbers all over his wife's neck as he rubs between her legs under her dress. She, widens her stance, spreading her legs so he has easier access. She's revelling in my shocked expression as she rolls her neck in a blatant attempt to lure Silas attention. Groaning and licking her lips, she keeps her focus firmly on Silas, as she grinds against her husband's fumbling hand. It's all for show, a desperate attempt to draw a reaction to their inappropriate display.

Monty eventually removes his hand, satisfied that his audience has enjoyed the intimate view of his wife's most private parts. Sticking out his purple tongue, he makes a huge performance of licking his sticky fingers, sucking them clean of his wife's juices.

He watches my eyes intently as he tastes each one in turn. I'm both embarrassed and appalled, but annoyingly, part of me is hugely turned on. I can't believe what I've just witnessed.

Silas on the other hand has taken it all in his stride. He's acting bored, as if it's just another everyday occurrence, his acquaintances fondling and frigging their wives in full view of the VIP's and all their guests. Oozing contempt, he just eyes them both coolly and calmly. I'm impressed by his show of indifference. "Monty," He raises his voice over the blaring music, leaning in, yelling close to his ear. "I've a departure slot for two p.m. tomorrow. I've sent an email to your iPhone and I'll text a reminder in the morning in case you're too pissed to remember."

Beneath the cool façade, he's clearly irritated, impatient. His arm hasn't moved from its place round my waist and I feel safe and protected. I allow myself a smug smile, Victoria doesn't miss it; obviously affronted by Silas's lack of interest in her and his attentiveness towards me, her face hardens to the point of granite. There's loathing in her eyes when she looks at me and her mouth is a vicious slash where her lipstick has smeared. Refusing to be intimidated, I just stare levelly back, keeping my expression as blank as I can... *Fuck off!*

The music changes and *Snoop Dogg's 'Drop It Like It's Hot'* starts blasting out. There are whoops of delight from the models and celebs on the dance floor as they all start to cavort, bump and grind against each other.

"Come on darling, they're playing our song." Sensing a quick conquest, Victoria makes a sudden lunge for Silas, grabbing his bicep, desperate to separate us; a look of sheer delight flashes across her drunken glaze the moment she registers the hardness of tense muscle beneath his sleeve. "Oooh, baby... Sooo strong. Are you *hard* everywhere?"

Silas wants none of it. Unperturbed, and with almost imperceptible speed, he roughly seizes hold of her wrist. Without batting an eyelid or even glancing in her general direction he thrusts it at Monty. "I believe this is yours." He grinds, shoving her hand in Monty's chest, forcing him to grab hold.

Conceding defeat, she's tugging at the lapel of Montgomery's jacket, clearly desperate for him to follow her onto the small square dance floor in the centre of the VIP corral so they can finish what they started - in full view of everyone, no doubt. Monty relents, following in her scantily clad wake, shouting at Silas over his shoulder that he'll see him tomorrow. We're standing like two spare parts, staring after them; watching in disbelief as he blatantly thrusts his crotch into her twerking arse. This is beyond any kind of party I've been to before. I hate it.

Looking around me, I notice as well as mindless drinking and fondling, people are now openly snorting lines of cocaine. They're sprawled on the sofas, lying on top of one another. Some are prone on the floor - some even look like they may be fucking! It's getting out of hand and I'm completely out of my depth.

"Jesus, it's a *fucking* zoo!" Silas hisses through gritted teeth. "Let's go, I've had enough of this shitfest." I couldn't agree more.

Decision made and business dealt with, we manoeuvre our way to the corralled exit. I'm desperate to get out of here. The bouncer releases the red rope and we step into the main party.

Abruptly, the music stops and the sound of someone tapping a microphone draws the attention of the crowd. We stop walking, turning back towards the stage, wondering what's happening now?

I'm very soon wishing I was anywhere else but here. There, standing on the raised dais, swaying in the centre beneath a yellow spot light, is Lynda. *Oh, fucking hell. What's she doing?*

"Attention, everyone, everyone... attention! - is this thing switched on?" She barks into the microphone. Feedback whistles and lets out an ear-splitting whine as she gets too close to the mic. "You all know me," she slurs. People are looking at each other slightly bewildered. Clearly, not everyone knows her. "I've some fantastic news for you all."

Bollocks! "Silas!" I pull his arm, fearful that she's going to blurt something stupid. "Silas, let's go. I'm not interested in this." He nods in my direction. Seemingly he's not interested in this either. We start to head out, five more yards and we'll be in the lobby. I quicken my steps in my haste to escape.

"Today, my best friend was found." *Christ, shut the fuck up!* She's not making any sense and the M.C. decides she's off her tits and has enjoyed enough time in the spot light. "No, no, she's here tonight. Get OFF!" I hear her scream at the M.C.

Silas slows his stride and turns his head. That caught his attention. I trip, on purpose, wrenching his arm and falling on my knee in an attempt to realigning his attention back to me.

"Edi, honey, careful. Are you okay?" Bending quickly to assist me to my feet. I nod, indicating I'm just fine and once I'm up, I don't stop. I head straight for the double doors with determination.

"No, look, she's here... Leave off me! You, stupid fucking man," her voice is distant, they've managed to relieve her of the mic and it sounds like they're wrestling her from the stage. "Stop it, no, ... look ... gerroff me!!!"

"Thank you, ladies and gentlemen, normal service will soon be resumed..." The M.C. attempts to make light of the situation. I can hear bangs and crashes as he desperately grapples with a very drunk and uncoordinated Lynda.

"Meredith!"

Her muffled shout follows us as we exit the hotel. I close my eyes and ears in an attempt to block it out, hoping it didn't register with Silas. There's a scratching noise and some more stifled yells, but they're swallowed by the appreciative roar of the crowd, as the D.J cranks *'Mr Brightside's'* volume up to a deafening level. Thankfully, the party resumes. Lynda's outburst is contained.

Two more strides and I'll be outside. Everything is slowing down, I can't move quickly enough. It's like wading through treacle. I fly through the revolving door and jettison onto the red carpet, startling the doorman in the process. Silas stumbles out behind me. If he's at all flustered by my sudden desire to escape, I can't tell.

Once outside and back into the fresh evening air, I take a deep breath. Desperate to calm down, I pace the pavement in front of the hotel and as usual, in my befuddled state of mind, I start to bargain... *please don't let him register. If he doesn't say anything in the next two minutes, everything will be okay.*

But he's ominously silent as we wait for the driver to bring the car round. When it finally pulls up to the kerb, Silas opens my door and ushers me inside.

"Feels like it's going to rain again," he comments. I can't speak. I just nod, far too wound up to trust my voice to sound anything like normal...

If we get back to the hotel before it starts to rain, it means Lynda was so pissed she won't remember anything tomorrow.

The first drops of rain hit the car roof as we drive away from the Four Seasons and my heart sinks. I'm numb with fear and shock. My bargaining has never failed me before, mainly because I've always weighted it in my favour - but there's a first time for everything. This time is different.

Silas interprets my silence as tiredness and reaching out, takes my hand in his. My fingers are numb. "Good God, Edi, your freezing." Releasing his seatbelt, he slides over to my side of the car and wraps his arm tightly round my shoulders. Even in my shattered state, I warm to his touch and my heart rate rises. I'm still flustered, but now it's for a whole different reason. It's

337

incredible what he does to me when he's this close! It's beyond the realms of comprehension.

The further the distance from the horrid party grows, my level of anxiety decreases and I gradually begin to relax. We ride in comfortable silence back to the hotel, my head resting on Silas's shoulder.

That was an absolute shitstorm of an evening! Seeing Lynda was an unmitigated disaster. Who'd have thought it possible I'd cross paths with the two worst people imaginable; on the same day and in different countries? At least I managed to hide from Bobby! I laugh at the malicious irony.

"What?" Silas nudges me.

"Nothing... I'm just imagining what Christina would have said if she'd seen Victoria tonight," I bluff.

"Hah... Don't even go there." He laughs, but I suspect he's not convinced by my lie.

Leaning against Silas, I vaguely notice the lasers atop the Eiffel Tower have stopped. It must be later than I thought.

Chapter 29

The driver stops on the Champs Elysees, so we can jump out. Silas said it was easier than negotiating the narrow one-way street. The rain has stopped, it was only a light shower, so perhaps that won't count and Lynda will forget everything about tonight.

Touching my new shoes to the glistening pavement, cautiously avoiding any residual puddles, I walk with care towards the scene of our afternoon tryst and the doors of our hotel. Silas is holding me tightly, just as keen for me to not step anywhere it's too wet and ruin my new babies.

As we approach the recess where he so wantonly grabbed me this morning, I feel his arm flex. A thrill of anticipation shoots through me; he's going to do it again... He does! In a split second, my back is slammed up against the wall, his front is pressed against me on a growl and before I can even think, his parted, hungry lips are devouring mine like he's a condemned man tasting his last meal.

His hard body crushes against me with such force I can barely breathe; his tongue sweeps through my mouth. "You taste of whiskey," he whispers against my lips. "Give me your tongue." Without hesitation I comply. Willingly plunging my tongue into his mouth, surrendering to his demands. He sucks and pulls, biting and nipping with his teeth. "Mmm, I love the flavour, you taste wonderful," he mutters in a low tone, I can barely hear.

"Silas," I hiss, as his mouth leaves mine and finds my neck. His hands are on my ribcage, sweeping, stroking over the silky fabric. My breasts are pressed flat, bound to my chest by the weight of him. My nipples must be poking holes in his jacket they're so sharp and rigid.

On reflex, my hands move to his head. Keeping them flat, I smooth them lightly over the rough hair, the friction of the short stubble prickles the nerves in the centre of my palms. I dig my nails into his scalp, grazing the skin, scratching him.

He growls in appreciation and pushes his leg between my knees, causing me to open one leg to the side, tilting my knee outwards. His erection is rock hard against my stomach.

"Ahh, Silas," I cry out! I feel high! The back of my head hits the wall and I sense a sharp tug as my hair snags on the rough bricks, pulling a couple of strands out by the roots.

Greedily he moves back to my mouth. Re-entering, swirling his tongue with mine performing a dance of sensual pleasure. His lips are full and soft, a cushion against the pressure of his powerful kisses.

His hands start to drift, up to my breast and down to my waist; lightly, tracing the line of my zip with his finger nail, producing a zzzip-zzzup, sound as he scratches it up and down. Then, without warning, he takes hold of the tab. He continues the mind-blowing kiss as his hand travels down my body. The zip moves with it, slowly. Cool air tingles my skin as inch by inch the sensitive flesh is exposed.

With the zip fully open, he releases his hold of the fastener and slides his hand into my dress, caressing the soft skin on my side, spreading his fingers wide. Ever so slowly he begins to graze light circles with his thumbnail; it feels exquisite. Continuing to kiss the life out of me, he strokes a path between my breast and my hip.

It's divine. It's heavenly. It's sensual. It's on camera! *Fucking hell!* I suddenly remember the CCTV from this morning. Jesus, the concierge must think we're really something; twice in one day!

"Silas," speaking into his mouth, I push on his shoulders, but all he does is deepen his kiss and tighten his hold. The slow caress of his hand up and around my ribcage is driving me insane. "Silas, the cameras," I whisper against his lips. "They'll see." I'm not physically fighting him off, but I need him to know we're on show here!

"No, they won't," he mumbles back, reinforcing his certainty by grasping my breast with his other hand through the satin of my dress.

"You seem very sure?" I pant through my desire, keeping my lips against his. I'm not sure at all, but at the moment I don't care one iota!

"Oh, Honey-bee... they know we're here alright but they can't properly see what we're doing. I checked. The camera angle isn't quite right." He's grinning through his kiss. "But I think they could guess!" he breathes, biting my bottom lip and dragging it through his teeth.

His hand carries on drifting up and down my skin. I'm on fire now and I'm desperate for him to move his hand under my bra. But he doesn't. He just keeps up the passionate kiss and the rhythmic caressing of my flesh.

A middle-aged couple stroll past, arm in arm. They startle as they come upon us. Not really able to see properly, they stare openly as they pass, slowing down a little to enjoy the show. I don't give a flying fig! *This is what it's like when a man smothers you in attention, lady!* I propel my thought towards the woman who is now staring over her shoulder as her man hurries her away, clearly embarrassed. He probably thinks I'm on the game.

"Silas," I'm panting, I can't take much more of this exquisite agony. I need him to take it further so I let my hand trace down, from his head, along his ear, pinching his lobe with my nails, grazing the side of his face with my fingertips. Over his stubble, his neck, his strong, broad shoulder, his muscled biceps.

Reaching lower, I feel him clench the muscles in his abdomen as my hand lands on his taught waist. I flatten my palm and press it hard over his pants. I don't touch him, I just rest my hand on the defined 'V' at the side of the hard length beneath his zip.

He groans and shifts his hips, inviting me to touch his cock, but I don't. I just maintain the pressure, mere centimetres away from the promised land. *Now you know how it feels mister! So near, but oh so far!*

He pulls away, leaving my zip open, he grabs my hand and without a sound, tows me towards the revolving doors of the hotel. I lose a few more strands of hair to the grasping bricks of the wall as I lever myself away and follow him.

It's the same Concierge, from this morning. He just gives us a disgruntled look as we enter. Silas is right. He couldn't see, but he knew what we were doing and he's frustrated! Obviously, he was banking on us putting on a show.

Silently, I'm guided into the lift. As the doors close, Silas pulls me against him so I can feel his hardness against my back this time. He bends his knees, rubbing up and down against the crevice of my bum. *Dirty boy!*

"A bit of bump and grind in the elevator," he mumbles in my ear. "What was that song they were playing?"

"Drop it like it's hot," I reply pushing my arse firmly into his stiffness, whispering the song title seductively in his ear as I attempt a little twerk of my own.

Continuing to grind against me, he speaks the lyrics of the song *"When the pimp's in the crib ma, drop it like it's hot."*

I laugh and meld against him. But when he jerks his thumb to the corner, I stop moving. There's a camera in here too! It's trained directly on me, but I can only be seen from the front. Silas is behind me, grinding into me, his hand inside of my dress, feeling along my midriff under my breasts.

His hot mouth is at my neck. The concierge must be having a field day! He can't see anything, but if he has half an imagination, he'll be going home as horny as hell. His wife won't know what's hit her tonight!

Emboldened by Silas, I stare directly into the camera, pouting. Then I wantonly bounce my hips, gyrating into Silas as he sucks on my neck and feels me up. Finally, licking my lips for effect, I mouth *'Drop it like it's hot'* then blow a seductive kiss at the camera lens...

The lift dings to a halt and we stumble laughing, still entwined into the corridor. Silas immediately spins me round and takes my face in both hands, planting another long, hard kiss on my mouth.

"Here," he circles my slender bicep with his big hand and leads me to the wall, mid-way between our rooms and the lift. He presses me up against it, hard. I'm trying to remember where the camera is out here too. Deducing from this angle, we can be partially seen from the back and the side, but nothing more.

"They can watch, but they can't see!" he reassures me, breathing hard, then smashes his mouth back on mine. "They need to imagine what I'm doing to you!" He lifts the hem of my dress, and grinds his groin into mine, his knees slightly bent so he can feel the mound of my pubic bone, hard beneath my concaved stomach. "Fuucckk!" He snarls, gripping the back of my thigh and lifting it round his waist. I don't resist. I'm burning up. "They can see your leg, but that's all," he whispers. I don't care, I'll lie on the floor and let him fuck me here and now if he wants to!

"Ahh, oh yes, Silas, touch me, please!" I squirm relentlessly, desperate for friction.

Grumbling low in approval, he obliges willingly, moving his hand between my legs and cupping my damp underwear. Heated liquid immediately floods my pulsing centre, soaking the fine silk. Expertly, he applies some accurately placed pressure. Squeezing, massaging. His fingers deftly graze the seam of my knickers where it meets the crease of my groin, but he doesn't breech the barrier, choosing to tease me relentlessly instead.

The anticipation of his touch is driving me insane. The expectation that, any moment, he'll plunge his fingers into me is incredibly erotic. I hear myself moaning loudly as I writhe against his hand. I can feel all four fingers through the thin wisps of satin, and I know he can feel my entrance pulsing and opening for him as he rubs and caresses.

I'm squirming against the wall now, my moans growing louder, unable to quieten my desperate calling. My legs are going to give way soon.

"God, Silas, I need you to touch me, please." I beg.

"Soon... soon... Honey-bee; you are soooo sweet!" He swathes my mouth with his, rubbing me hard over my damp underwear, grinding against me with his rock-hard cock. "Taste me," he pushes his tongue into my mouth and I suck, hard. He tastes of whiskey and lemon. I trace round his teeth with my tongue. Exploring, learning, feeling him inside and out.

"I think it's time," his muffled words are like a spark to the flame and I heat up to about 110 degrees, I'm burning up.

He drops my leg but doesn't rearrange my dress. Stepping away so I'm exposed to him, but hidden from the peeping-tom concierge, he offers me his hand. I take it willingly.

One sly look at the beady-eye of the camera, he makes an open show of adjusting his bulging groin, before he removes his key from his back pocket. Tossing it into the air once, he catches it, then blows the camera a kiss. It's blatantly clear where we're going and what we're going to be doing once inside the room.

I giggle. "Are you always this incorrigible?"

"Why... don't you like it?" He waggles an eyebrow suggestively.

"Oh... I like it, fine enough Mr Tudor... Sir!"

He feigns shock at my cheek. "Let's get you inside then…"

Without further ado, he ushers me towards his door, taking his time unlocking it and with only the slightest touch, guides me inside.

Chapter 30

The room is warm and semi-dark, bathed in a subtle purply moonlight. The blood-red damask curtains are open, held back with a plaited gold velvet rope. The tie-back has heavy fringed tassels reaching down to the floor. There are no lights on in the room, the only source, coming from outside.

Golden moonbeams split the sultry darkness; chasing the shadows into the deepest recesses of the room. Shimmering fragmented light; the reflections from the full moon, intermingle with the dim, silvery glow of the streetlights outside. They filter through the cream viol, dressing the Georgian style French doors leading to the balcony; the decorative lace casts strange and intricate patterns on the walls and furniture. The effect is at once, both gothic and sensual.

One single shaft of pure evening light streams through the gap in the curtains. Perfectly centred, it angles downwards falling directly onto the large four-poster bed, which dominates the room, a vacant stage awaiting its players.

Through the window, the view is the same; a dull brick façade of the building opposite. Only when you step out onto the balcony will you appreciate the distant, view of the Eiffel Tower.

I absorb all of this in mere seconds, drinking in the subtle visual changes the dusk brings to the room, and with it the heady, sensual atmosphere of suspense. The external influence of the evening has transformed the genteel bedroom décor of the daytime into an intimate nigh-time boudoir. It's a setting that any Parisian, courtesan would be proud of.

The effect the scene has on me is visceral. Tense with expectation, I stand stock still, facing the window. I've only taken a few steps into the room but already I'm quaking in my expensive shoes. My back to the door, patiently I wait for an instruction. Just a touch or a sound will do, anything to let me know he's still here with me.

The air is alive with a sense of anticipation, fizzing around me, pulsing with a billion particles of static electricity. My flesh is stinging with it, I'm buzzing inside and out. All the foreplay and exhibitionism has made me desperate for more. Every one of my senses, primed and on high alert.

Fully aware of my laboured breathing, I can see my breasts heaving below the neckline of my gown. My ears are ringing; burning with a residual hum as if I've been to a rock concert.

I strain to listen, for something; anything, in in the hushed room. A creaking floorboard, a scuffed footstep, even some muffled noise from the hotel corridor or the street below - but no – there's nothing.

Focussing my senses for any sound or movement from Silas, there's just the faint panting of my skittered breath and the intermittent thump, thump, thump of my heart. The silence is all consuming, yet I know from the weight of the atmosphere, he's still here. But like a mystical spectre, he casts no visible shadow, and he doesn't make the faintest of sounds. Excepting my own resonances, the room is as silent as a church.

My skin is tingling now. So aroused, I'm beginning to tremble. Gripping tension in my muscles causes my legs to shake. Unable to control my nerves, I clench and unclench my fists, folding and unfolding my hands. This feeling is completely unfamiliar to me. This unfathomable feeling of need, desperation and desire terrifies me. It's unlike anything I've experienced before and I don't *ever* want it to stop.

After everything that's occurred today, I *need* for this to happen. I *need* to know it can be good. For once, I *need* to feel desired, wanted and worshiped. And more than anything... I *need* it to be with him. He's the only one who can break the spell and make me feel like a real woman.

But as I stand waiting, my self-doubt starts to niggle at my brain. It never fails me. And even with the desperate, uncontrollable want I'm feeling, I'm terrified I'll disappoint him and that will be it. He'll drop me like a stone and move on.

In the past sex has always held a certain amount of fear. Perhaps it's because I've never gleaned any satisfaction from the act. Even at thirty-six years of age, my experience is remarkably limited and the kind of sex I've had has never brought me any fulfilment or joy.

I've been told I'm unresponsive and totally frigid. So, deep down, I know I'm rubbish. Criticised for my lack of enthusiasm to certain acts and subjected to things I'd rather not partake in... humiliated in the worst way possible. Because of this, intimacy has never been something I've craved.

Sex was a chore, to get over and done with as quickly as possible. In previous encounters, I've never experienced physical pleasure; the earth has never moved. Sex was always a duty, a requirement, a demand. There was nothing in it for me. Not until now, that is. And I *need* to follow this through before I sabotage the whole thing with my pessimism.

Closing my eyes against the rising pessimism, I force myself to smother my negative thoughts. I can't let them in. I won't allow them to ruin this night and I won't allow my old fears to consume me.

All sense of nagging doubt is instantly doused when my ears twitch at the click of the door-latch sliding into place. I whip my head to the side listening for something, for any sign that Silas is moving. I still hear nothing, heightening my state of cognizance... Until...

"Turn around." His voice is thick with raw emotion. I comply, performing an elegant twirl, quite an achievement in these heels.

"Silas, I need to tell you something..." Although I'm wound like a clock spring, I'm so very nervous.

Stood just inside the door; he's shrouded in shadow and I can only see his silhouette. A monochrome outline against the dull white of the painted wood. Unmoving. He could be a statue. It only makes my breathing more erratic.

"Remove the dress," ignoring my stuttering, he delivers his order.

"Silas... I..."

"I said, remove the dress." His voice is stern. Gruff even.

"Silas... I'm not good at this..."

"I think I'll be the judge of that...now either you remove the dress, or I will." He sounds hoarse, husky, as if he's struggling for air.

Conflicting feelings pin-ball around my brain... he'll know how crap I'm soon enough. Submitting to his demand I reach down, seeking the hem of my dress, which is still bunched around my waist where he left it, and slowly peel it up and over my head, swinging my hair free so it swathes my shoulders. I drop the dress on the floor beside me. Stood before him, clothed only in my new emerald green and black underwear and designer shoes, I feel a heady rush of empowerment.

I hear him gasp. A sharp intake, a breath of surprise. Clearing his throat, when he speaks his voice is smooth, like rich dark chocolate.

"Come here."

Playing for time, I bend, with the intent to untie and remove my shoes.

"No!" he demands sharply. "The shoes stay."

"Oh... okay." Slowly, and as seductively as I can, I stand up. Then, swallowing deeply to quell my nerves, I take a couple of shaky steps towards the dark shadow that is Silas Tudor.

When we're about an inch apart, I stop. I can see him clearly now, his dark eyes are shimmering, staring at me with hunger and want; it intensifies my own desire.

Moving only his head, he leans down; angling towards me, slowly and with purpose. As our lips hover, barely millimetres apart, he pauses, inhaling deeply, breathing me in. Then… with almost unbearable tenderness, he touches his soft lips to mine so lightly, I hardly feel it; but the nerves in my lips ignite on fire.

The pure innocence of his kiss is intoxicating yet deceptive. Desperate to please him, I open my mouth, sliding my tongue along the seam of his full lips, tasting his masculine, musky flavour where the essence of whiskey still lingers. It's the only encouragement he needs. The pressure of his mouth increases, the pace of the kiss, at first easy and gentle, alters and becomes harder, more urgent and demanding. Our tongues dance and twirl together hungrily.

Far too soon he's breaking away, heaving heavy, uncontrolled, scorching breaths into my face. Lifting his hands, he firmly takes the tops of my arms and with conviction, propels me backwards, deeper into the moonlit room. When I feel the bed at the back of my calves I stop moving.

"Sit," he says.

Willingly, I drop onto the bed. His voice is laboured, loaded with the effort of restraint. His hungry eyes roam lazily over my body, lingering for a brief second on the small heart-shaped birthmark on my left breast, barely visible beneath the lace of my bra strap.

"You look stunning. Give me your hand." I offer my left arm, under no illusion about his intent. Deftly, he removes my new watch and places it on the bedside table. Gently, encircling my wrist with his fingers, he lifts my hand to his lips and tenderly kisses each and every one of the tiny buzzing bumble bees, hesitating only when he reaches the one, small patch devoid of any decoration. Purposefully, placing his lips into the space, he sucks at my delicate skin. Tilting my head, I watch, mesmerised. The delicious pull echoes in my groin as he sucks and nips at my tender flesh.

Finished, he removes his lips to reveal a circular bruise. It fills the void between the adjacent bees perfectly, completing the band and forming an infinite bracelet.

"That's for me," he concedes. "Now, lean back on your hands." My heart leaps wildly as I follow through on his request. I really want this, but I'm terrified I'll do something wrong and he'll be hugely disappointed.

Clearing the negative thoughts and keeping my feet flat on the floor, I recline on the bed, supporting my weight on my elbows.

From here, looking down the length of my body, I can understand what he means. I do look good. My stomach is a smooth gentle mound; a little sloping hillock between the bony nubs of my hip-bones. The two faint bumps are enhanced by the delicate stretch of satin and lace; the muted light emphasising every, hollow, curve and dip of my prone body. My breasts are perfectly supported, held firmly and securely by the amazing engineering of the soft, sheer fabric. The wisps of delicate black lace traces flattering patterns on my skin. It doesn't look like me. I'm transfixed.

"Stay like that," he says. Leaning back, he drinks me in. And I just lie there, watching him, watching me.

I still haven't found my voice, but I get the feeling that's okay. He doesn't need me to speak. He wants to lead this. His way. I remain motionless, admiring Silas as he stands, magnificent and brooding before me.

Reaching out, Silas places one trembling hand on my neck. Lightly caressing the length of my throat, circling his fingers round my neck and stroking his thumbs under my chin. It makes me swallow. Gradually he traces his hands back down my throat and neck to my chest; directing his fingers into the hollows of my collar bones, he circles the dip before continuing the line down my breast bone to my deep cleavage.

I see him swallow now. We're both breathing heavily. One of us will have a heart attack in a moment if this carries on. His hand is on the mound of my breast. "You have the most beautiful breasts," he whispers quietly "Perfect, soft, natural and I want to touch them."

He's not asking for permission. I feel his hand tremble at his tentative touch. The caress of his exploring fingers as soft as a butterfly's wing and not at all what I'd expect from a man with such large, strong hands.

The delicate, fluttering movement has me groaning uncontrollably; tipping my head and arching my back, forcing my breast upward into the cup of his palm. Closing my eyes, the sensation... the awareness of his closeness is unbelievable.

For the first time he has touched the top of my breast; I'm desperate for him to pay some attention to my rock-hard nipples. The waiting is driving me insane. I need to feel the sharp pinch of his fingers and the warmth of his lips, his teeth even. The silky satin has become as harsh as barbed wire and my sensitive nubs are screaming for release from the confines of my bra.

"Sit forward a little," he instructs. I lift myself up, supporting my weight on my palms; he reaches behind to unfasten my bra. It's a stumbling block.

"It's at the front," I whisper, thrusting my chest forward, leaning back on my elbows. His surprise is fleeting, causing a salacious grin to grace his face. His hands are shaking; he fumbles with the centre front fastening of my bra. His thick fingers are at conflict with the tiny gold fastener. Unhooking the clasp, he lifts the cups away as if he's unveiling a masterpiece; fully exposing my breasts to him for the very first time. He swallows and I sigh; rolling my head back so my hair falls over my shoulders. I'm now wearing a sort of bizarre, sexy waist-coat, open at the front, the satin bra-cups dangle freely by my sides, still framing my breasts.

My taught nipples sing at their blessed release, the tender, dark pink tips, pointing sharply in his direction, inviting attention. My birthmark is fully visible now. It is a small red heart on the side of my breast. I'm vaguely wondering if it resonates with him. Does he recognise it?

"Jesus, Edi," he whispers, he's hoarse again. "You're going to be *so* bad for my health. I feel light headed." He holds both his hands over my breasts, hovering so the centre of his palms grazes my rigid nipples. I cry out at the slight contact. "You're stunningly beautiful." His touch is so light I can barely feel it, but this is quickly followed by an electric shock, zapping straight to the junction of my thighs.

God, I want him. I don't care if I'm rubbish… I just want him so much!

"Aghhh, Silas, please." My legs part, falling opening of their own volition, my hips tilt involuntarily. He doesn't miss it. Bending over me he cups both of my breasts in his hands. Then, touches the very tip of one stiff nipple with his hot, wet tongue.

My head rocks back and an involuntary yelp leaves my lips. "Owww!" Deftly, he swirls a loop round the areola then takes the whole of the nipple into his mouth, sucking hard, swallowing and biting. "Ahh! Oh," I cry, arching my back.

Releasing my now engorged nipple, he steps back from me and kneels on the floor between my bent knees. Gripping my ankle tightly over the laces of my shoes, he raises one leg and rests his lips on the inside of my calf, keeping his eyes firmly on mine as the heat of his mouth sears my skin.

"Aaaaah!" I'm incoherent.

He moves his hand to the sole of my shoe, wrapping his fingers round my whole foot. Bearing his teeth, he slowly grazes my

353

ankle bone. Back and forth… back and forth he goes, nipping and caressing. With each pass of his teeth, my centre clenches in identical rhythm.

Closely, he observes my reaction; it's like a million volts of electricity surging through my system, travelling along my most receptive nerves; firing intermittent shockwaves up the inside of my legs and landing with a controlled, direct hit right at my pulsing core.

My clitoris throbs in response to his touch; engorged, buzzing and beating, the small nub swelling in anticipation. A raging fire attacks me, causing my inner walls and belly to contract violently; a dribble of hot liquid trickles unexpectedly from my vagina.

"Ahh! Sssss!" I hiss at the delicious torture. "Oh, yesss, Ahhhh!" My knickers are totally soaked, I can feel the bead of hot wetness running down my perineum to the puckered rose of my anus. *Jesus, this is intense!*

He drops my leg and watches as I writhe on the bed, my elbows are going to give way at any minute. My head rolls back on my shoulders, my soft tresses tickle my back between my shoulder blades. Closing my eyes to gather some coherence, it's impossible. I'm in seventh heaven, my eyes are rolling in delirium. My chest is heaving; uncontrollable heavy panting breaths and involuntary moans of ecstasy are falling from my lips. I can't take much more of this intensity, yet I don't want it to stop.

"Shhh…" His voice is soft, like crushed velvet "… quiet now… hush baby… remember… practice control in all things, Honey-bee." I'm whimpering softly, desperate to be quiet but it's a struggle. No matter how I try, tiny sounds keep escaping from my lips. "The more you control it… the more intense it'll be when you finally let go… *Shhh.*"

"Oh *God!*... I'm trying but... Silas... Aghhh!" It's no use, I can't prevent my voice from omitting these sounds of pleasure.

Smoothing his burning hands up the outside of my thighs, he reaches my knickers and starts to peel them down, pausing to look closer he exposes the first tufts of my trimmed pubic hair, blowing a gentle wisp of breath on my damp curls. The sudden cooling sensation sends me into orbit and I buck my hips, tipping my neck so the back of my head collides hard with the bed; my chin lifts and I groan loudly.

"Shhh... mmm... look how beautiful you are..." He sounds awestruck.

Lifting my heavy head so I can view the length of my body, I look down. What I see only enflames my passion even more... just the top of Silas's head is visible. He's fully suspended above my lower body supported by his forearms. His broad shoulders undulate as he moves; reminding me of a stalking panther. Beneath his shirt, his muscles ripple with strength and tension as they bear his upper-body weight with apparent ease. His large dark hands are a vivid contrast to my creamy white skin, as they stroke and move across my stomach. *My God*, it looks incredible – It doesn't look like me at all. I think I'm having an out of body experience.

Exploring, he examines the flimsy garments that barely cover me. The satin and lace are stretched tight across my pubis, strung in a delicate sexy band across my hips, half exposing my light golden curls. From this angle, it's reminiscent of a photograph from an erotic arts magazine. Narrow streams of muted moonlight only add to the eroticism of the image, gilding the sensual temptation of what lies beneath.

Unable to support my weight any longer, my elbows buckle and I drop my shoulders onto the bed. I retreat into a fantasy world; a world of unyielding, corporeal pleasure. Surrendering to the moment, I absorb the incredible sensations flooding through me.

Silas blows another stream of air over my exposed pubic hair then drops his chin onto my mound, so that his stubble and my soft curls mingle together; rubbing and chafing.

I squirm and cry out again. "Aghhh!"

"Shhh! Be still for me, Honey-bee... *still*.... I need to taste your nectar. Stay still for me. My God, you are *so* stunning like this, I can't stop looking at you."

Pressing my lips together to supress my cries, I try with all my might to remain still, as instructed. It's difficult. I'm soaking wet. The moisture is pooling in my groin. There's no way I can keep still for very long.

Hooking his finger into the lace band with care, he tugs at my damp knickers. I lift my hips off the bed, so he can peel them off without hindrance, revealing my lower half; finally, I'm fully exposed to him.

But I'm confused when he doesn't fully remove them. A few inches down my legs, he stops, leaving my panties so they form a tight restrictive band around my thighs just above my knees. The taught elastic makes me feel like I'm bound, trussed up in a silken banded rope. I can't spread my legs as far as I want to. My movement is limited so I've no option but to remain still.

I fist the silky counterpane tightly to prevent myself from moving. I need to hold myself down before I explode, I'm that wound-up. "Mmm..." Murmuring in pleasure, I force myself to stare at the ceiling... waiting...

Silas takes hold of both my ankles, raising my feet from the floor, he pushes upwards, causing me to bend my knees and rest the heels of my shoes on the bedspread. When I tilt my head to look, I can't see him. My green satin panties form a gossamer barrier.

Feeling the bed dip, I know he has knelt on it. But I still judder in shock at his touch - even though I know it's coming. Placing his hands on the insides of my thighs, beneath the tight band of my panties, he massages my sensitive skin. With each squeeze, he moves his hands a little higher until they're just centimetres away from my pulsing core. I can feel myself opening and closing for him, a willing oyster. I squeeze my eyes shut and wring the bed-cover tightly.

"Absolutely stunning," he whispers, his mouth so close to me I can feel his breath on my swollen lips.

"Huugh... *Ohmygod*!" He's *really* close.

"Your labia are so wet they're reflecting the light. I need to taste you, but I can't look away." He's admiring my vagina as if it is a work of art but I just want him to touch me! I try and twist my hips, encouraging him, inviting him. But he will do this in his own time, at his own pace... "Still now. Stay still for me Honey-bee. Shhh, hush sweet, sweet girl."

Then, at last, I feel his hands move, his thumbs rest on my labia making me jerk and cry out. "*Aghhh*!" Patiently, he waits for me to quieten before he proceeds.

Once I become still again, he very gently spreads my swollen lips, opening me further, exposing my tingling clitoris and my soaking entrance. "There, there now... Shhh, hush now. Oh my *God*, Edi, you are so *fucking* beautiful. Open for me," he demands softly, and like a willing marionette, I do.

At his command, my internal walls relax and my vagina opens like an unfurling rose - in readiness just for him. My body has developed a life of its own; tempting him in, beginning a steady pulse in time to my heartbeat. Unable to remain still and silent any longer, I thrash about in sweet, frustrated agony.

"Ahhhh! *Lord*, please! Aghhh!" I'm incoherent. Every sinew, muscle and nerve are pulled taught, like the strings on a violin. I need him to touch me ... NOW!...

Then I feel it... the sudden dash of his heated tongue licks up my swollen centre and lands with a quick flick on my clitoris. I scream, loudly! And I come... instantly... hard...immediately and without warning. The tight band round my thighs is holding me in place, biting into my flesh and restricting my desperate attempts to widen my legs.

All the built-up tension has exploded violently and uncontrollably with just one well-placed lick. My legs are trembling wildly, shuddering as the forceful spasms engulf me.

The combination of my sudden orgasm and my desperate struggle to open wide, has an unexpected gush of liquid to spurt from me. It shocks me into stillness.

Have I lost control and peed myself?

Then I feel Silas licking it up, lapping, sucking, growling. Once again, I start to moan and move, closing my legs against his head, trapping him between my thighs as he continues to indulge himself. He hums as he licks and sucks at my essence, tasting, as I writhe and flail on the bed in pure unadulterated ecstasy.

Tears of joy are flowing freely from my eyes, trickling along the tiny creases at my temples, wetting my face as they drip onto the bed covers. The emotion is overwhelming. But even in this moment of unbelievable divinity, there's an unwanted swirl of doubt, nudging at the back of my mind... *I hope I didn't disappoint him.*

Chapter 31

"Fucking hell, that *was* quick, Honey-bee..." he whispers against my quivering flesh. "It was amazing, but I think we can do better. You taste like sweet, sweet honey. I'll never get enough of your delicious flavour."

Thank God! He doesn't sound disappointed.

"Was... was it okay? I've... never... I mean... I hope... Oh... this is *soooo* embarrassing..." Why can't I just tell him? Covering my blushing face with my palms, I try to comprehend what just happened to me.

"More than okay." He looks at me quizzically, as if I'm nuts. Then realization dawns and his eyebrows raise. "Hold on... what do you mean, you've never?"

"No, no, I've... of course I have... I've just... not... Oh this is so embarrassing... I've never with a man... okay!" - *Never, with a man... I sound like I'm a virgin, or a prude... or a lesbian!* "I've never... come like that... with a man, or a woman..." I add just to be clear... "or at all... is what I mean." There, so now he knows... he's still kneeling between my legs. My juices coating his lips like lip-gloss and I'm spilling my mortifying secrets.

I see a glimmer of a smirk tweak the corner of his beautiful mouth and his eyes flash with wickedness as he digests this new tit-bit of information. "But if you've never..." he leers sexily, "then we *really* need to do something about that... don't we?"

Without further ado, very gently, he drops my feet. Then slides his hands up my thighs and grasps the material of my panties. One quick tug has them down by my ankles. Carefully he stretches the material so that he can pull them over my shoes before removing them completely and dropping them on the floor.

The blessed relief at being untethered is immediate and I spread my legs wide in gratitude. I'm panting in anticipation at what he's going to do next. My core is throbbing painfully but I do so *need* it again. To *feel* it again… feel him…

"Silas… I…"

"Edi, Honey-Bee; listen to me. You could *never* disappoint me. Whoever has told you, that you are no good, is lying." *How did he guess?* "Whoever he was, he was an idiot… he didn't deserve you. You are a beautiful, sensual woman. Just the sound of your voice, the way you talk, your gentleness. It's all part of who you are and it's intoxicating. Believe me…now, what do you want me to do?"

My heart explodes. All the crippling fear of inadequacy is quashed by his sincerity. It might be complete bullshit; a ploy to get him laid. But I can't be *that* bad or he would have been asleep by now! I tell him what I want.

"Silas, I want you to take me!" I whisper, my voice is breathy but clear. "I *need* you inside me. I *need* to feel you, here," cupping myself, the desperate need to be filled and feel that connection with him is taking over my conscious mind.

I trace my hand over my wet folds. "I need you to bury yourself in me so deeply that it hurts. I have to feel you *deep* inside… *hard*!" I'm begging him to claim me. "*Please…* wash away my fears and make me fly!"

His deep brown eyes are sparkling in delight. "All good things come *in* those who wait." He grins at his clever adaptation of the phrase, extolling the virtue of patience, which at this moment I don't have. I can only marvel at the strength of his self-control.

Stepping back with a cocky swagger, he starts to undress. I spread my legs as far as I can, exposing myself even further, but the main reason is to ensure I've a front row view for the best 'Magic Mike' show in the world.

"Touch yourself." He unbuttons his shirt and pulls it from his pants. Then he unfastens his belt, unbuttons his trousers and unzips his fly. "Edi, I said, touch yourself for me… NOW."

Softly, I reach between my legs and start to stroke. My fingers gliding easily over my wet flesh. I watch him undress as I slowly masturbate. My desire is building with every piece of clothing he removes.

Licking my lips, I'm impatient, but mesmerized. His body is beautiful. Dark mocha skin, gleaming like polished mahogany. A thin line of perspiration beads between his pecs and starts a slow steady trickle down the centre of his chest. Fascinated, I watch its journey, wanting nothing more than to lick it off.

Circling two fingers, I slide and flick them faster over my beating clit. Delicious pressure starts to build and noticing he's watching my skimming digits with intent, I move them in a figure of eight motion, so he can see exactly how I touch myself.

"Good, that's good… now, slow down, slowly baby, keep it slow, Honey…" I still my fingers, reverting to a more sedate pace. "That's it… wouldn't want you coming without me now…"

Rolling his broad shoulders, he shrugs off his shirt. *God, his chest!* He drops his trousers to the floor then kicks off his shoes and socks, his trousers go with them; flung into a distant corner in a heap. My fingers accelerate again as I stare hungrily.

Finally, there he is; standing before me, resplendent, in his black boxers. I try to subdue my hand, but it's difficult. I'm building nicely, ready for the next release, and the sight of him isn't making it any easier to calm down.

He looms before me, steeped in darkness, once again, an ominous, brooding shadow. But my eyes have become accustomed to the dark, and the dim light of the moon does nothing to hide the outline of his enormous erection beneath his boxers. He's a Greek God. A living, breathing, sculptured, masterpiece. The epitome of Michelangelo's David, honed out of the finest, smoothest, polished, ebony and he's about to fuck me!

Christ... I've died and gone to Adonis heaven!

Losing control, I scissor my fingers over my beating clit. Any second now, I'm going to come. I'm squirming again. I pull my legs up and spread my knees apart, wantonly opening myself even further.

"STOP!!" he demands.

Shocked, I instantly still my fingers. My impending orgasm retreats but my wayward hand continues to trace my body from my hips to my breasts. It's a blatant invitation. A deliberate come on. My legs fall wide, my vagina gapes open. Even in retreat, my impending orgasm has me pulsing in anticipation of imminent invasion. His eyes are hooded with intent as he watches my wanton display.

"Are you ready for me, Edi?" *Stupid question.*

"Yes, please. Let me see you. I need you inside me... *here.*" Licking my forefinger, I place it over my opening and push. Inserting the full length inside me. His eyes go wide and his nostrils flare with desire. It's my turn to smirk as I slowly pump my finger in and out against the wetness.

His jaw tenses in determination as, gripping the waistband of his boxers, he pushes them down his thick defined thighs, bending at the waist to step out of them before he's standing straight, legs planted firmly apart. He holds his arms out to the side in a mock unveil. *Ta-Dah!*

Oh my! ... with a choking gasp, I remover my probing finger from my tight passage, my legs closing on reflex when he reveals his sheer size. His penis is *fucking* enormous!

Black and shiny, and darker than the rest of his skin, it stands proudly erect, jutting from his body as hard as a rock, pulsing and throbbing in rhythm with his beating heart. I can't take my eyes off it and I certainly can't speak… I just gape in shock and awe at his incredible cock…

Reaching above his navel and with a girth as thick as a baby's arm, I've never in my life seen anything like it before! I cough in disbelief and incredulity.

Fucking Jesus! How the hell will that fit inside me?

As if he needs to prove a point, he places his hands on his narrow hips, emphasizing the enormity of his manhood. God, I'm gagging! I feel my insides clench and tighten. I need to relax if this is going to work so I open my legs and drop my knees as far apart as I can. My vagina responds in kind. Clenching and flexing, opening in anticipation. Another gush of hot liquid flows from inside me. I can feel it pooling on the bedspread beneath me. I said I want him inside me… and I do. I so need to feel the pain.

Silas steps forward and leans over me. "Are you ready Edi," he asks again. I nod, I'm so damn ready. Reaching out, I wrap my hand loosely around his thickness. My fingers don't meet. His girth is *so* impressive. I can feel every pulsing vein and every rippling ridge and I want it in me, now.

Tightening my grip, I start tugging him towards me by his dick, the pressure causes him to hiss through his teeth. Gripping hold, I draw him to me so he has no option but to lean down or risk a dislocated penis. Resting his knee on the bed, I feel it dip under his weight.

Oh Lord… this is it!

Supporting himself with his hands either side of my head, the other knee follows, so he's kneeling between my thighs. Lowering, he takes hold of himself, removing my hand and replacing it with his own. I adjust my legs, getting comfortable, or as comfortable as I'm able with a massive cock pointing at my tiny opening.

"Reach back and grip the pillow," he tells me. I stretch my arms over my head and fist the pillow tightly. "You may scream."

"I'll be heard!" But I know I won't be quiet with that inside me!

"Yes... they can hear but they can't see!" he says. "Ready?"

"Yes, God... yes." I'm so fucking ready!

I feel him stroke himself against my wetness. The touch of his hot, firm, flesh against mine makes me flinch. He doesn't pull away though, he just starts rolling against me, coating himself completely from root to tip, lubricating his length with my essence. Then I feel it. The head of his penis is wide, wider than my opening and he needs to apply a solid, firm pressure; it's very hard and totally rigid as it gradually breaches my opening. I feel myself stretching tightly around him as he slowly eases himself in.

"Mmm." I try not to cry out. It hurts, but the anticipation of the pleasure is spurring me on.

"Your, doing okay... relax baby..." he puffs, still holding himself in hand as he gradually guides himself deeper. It's painful, but I need it. "God, you're tight. You feel like satin on my skin... we're almost there, Honey." He removes his hand, allowing himself to balance on the bed to gain more leverage.

"Ahhhh...." I let out my breath, slowly as I feel him enter, inch by beautiful inch. Gradually my inner walls start to relax.

Steadily, he lowers towards me. Sweat is beading his forehead and he's panting. "Yesss... there it is. Open for me. Tell me it's okay."

"It's okay... I'm okay..." I pant. Instinctively I increase my vicelike grip on the pillow forcing my head to press back into the bed. I raise my knees so my inner thighs graze his ribs, the adjustment spreading me further and forcing him inside. "Oh..."

I can feel every solid, pulsing inch. He's huge and it hurts but the pain is morphing into an agonizing pleasure as he eases himself deeper and deeper. "Ahhhh!" I cry at the sweet combination of pleasure and pain. "Oh, God!"

"Feel me Edi," He gasps, leaning in and kissing my lips. That does it! Instantaneously, the heat of his mouth compels my vagina to unclench and he slides the last few inches inside. Deeply, fully.

The sudden deep penetration slams his pubic bone hard against my clitoris. The stretch of my skin and rapid thump as his tip rams against my cervix shocks my system. My vagina clenches around him so tightly, with incredible fullness and I immediately come again.

Fucking Hell!!!

"Agggghh, *FUCKKK*!!" I scream, incoherent, dropping into oblivion in total surrender. This has *never* happened to me.

I buck and flail, my legs quivering uncontrollably as the nerves judder and jump in conjuncture with my orgasm; wrapping themselves round Silas's waist in involuntary vice-like spasms as I writhe against him.

"That's it Honey... *Yesss!*" Unhurried in his own pleasure, he allows me my moment. He's a voyeur, observing my ecstasy with quite awe, holding himself still and deep within me, brimming with rapt concentration and determined self-control.

This pleasure is for me alone, and he's absorbing my every raging second. Lying beneath him, I gasp for breath. My internal walls contracting with tiny pulses as I come down from my incredible high.

Just as I'm beginning to calm, he feels my orgasm start to abate and my grip on him loosen slightly. His intervention is timed to utter perfection. Suddenly and with a mighty force, he begins to move. Urgently, pulling back and driving straight back in, hard. I scream and tighten my grip so fiercely on the pillow my fingers hurt and my legs around his waist contract so brutally I hear him huff out a grunt at the pressure.

"Ah… Oh shit!" I curse at the delicious invasion.

He pauses, taking a beat to check my state; using perfect judgement, he decides I'm ready and repeats the delicious move only this time it's harder and faster.

"*Fuck!*... again… do it again…" squeezing my eyes shut, I concentrate on the deep penetration… *Oh, it hurts so good!*

"*You like that?*" He does it again, then circles his hips for good measure.

"*Fuck yeah…*" I'm throbbing now, a deep dull ache in my belly, the like of which I've never felt before. I start to moan, unable to quiet my declaration of ecstasy. My orgasm has become a deep continuous pulsing; each pulse releases another shot of pleasure at my core.

"Ah baby…" *Thrust*… "It's good, but we can do better…" Placing a hand on my inner thigh, forcing my leg away from his side, he using the leverage to pound into me, yelling in effort as he forces his huge cock as deep as it will go. Slamming hard against me he repeats the move, only this time he doesn't pause, he just fucks me, relentlessly. Harder, harder, faster, deeper. "*Grrrr… take it all Honey… Sssss… Fuck yeah!*"

I don't think I'm breathing any more. I've never been so full, so open and so mindless. I am sensation. Nothing but feeling. An ethereal spectre on the edge of heaven. I've been transported to an astral plain of singular consciousness; a spirit in the ether, that's all I am. Every nerve, every pathway, every neurone is singing with glorious exultation.

But still I want more. I crave that delicious hit of pain. "*Oh… Yeah…Oh… Yeah… Oh… Yeah… Please! Silas, harder, fuck me harder… fill me!*" I'm building with every thrust now. Still, his hips piston back and forth, his hands grip my thighs firmly and before I know it, I'm soaring even higher. He raises to his knees and lifts me against him so he can drive deeper still.

"Gahh! Fuucckk. Aghhaag," His grunts are animalistic; punctuating each deep thrust. It only intensifies my own primal need to be fucked… hard.

"Oh, Jesus, Silas, fuck me! I'm gonna come again. Fuck me, fuck me, fill me up!" My mind is in turmoil as I cry out. I can hardly believe I'm partaking in this.

"Come on then, let it go, Edi, do it… *COME… NOW*!" he yells back.

And I let it go. This time the release is huge. Shuddering and shaking I scream, pulling the pillow over my face I yell my release.

My vagina is gripping and clutching, grabbing onto every bit of his length and width, sucking him deep as he continues his relentless pounding. I hear his own guttural bellow, an indication that he too has followed me over the edge of the precipice. He ejaculates deep inside me, the tip of his penis pumping scorching hot cum against my cervix at every drive. It doesn't stop, it just goes on and on and on.

My legs are cramping now. All the blood has left my feet and they're numb, starting to tingle with pins and needles. But still my orgasm doesn't subside.

I'm going to die!

But then, I feel him drop. Lowering his weight on to his forearms, he seeks out my mouth but only finds the pillow. Impatiently, he tugs it away so he can get to my lips. He stays buried inside me throbbing, while my insides relax and contract around him.

Capturing my lips, he kisses me deeply as if he's trying to climb inside me through my mouth; pouring all his intensity into me and I pour mine into him. My arms are round his neck, my legs wrapped round his waist. We continue to kiss as slowly, we free-fall back down to earth. Minutes or hours pass; I don't know. We just kiss and caress and slowly recover…

"Oh, my God, Silas. That was incredible…" I manage to wheeze, pecking his lush lips as we finally surface for air. Utterly spent, my mind is reeling in exhaustion.

"Yes, it was," he pants, staring at me with hooded eyes full of unfinished business. "But the first one's always easy!" he says, beads of perspiration running down his temples and dripping onto my chest.

"*What!*... What does that mean?" What *does* he mean? '*The first one*' - *I've had three!* Surely, he can tell. I'm still lying on my back, legs akimbo with a huge deflating cock inside me and my insides are thrumming like a beating drum.

"It means exactly what I said. The first one comes easy. Now we go again. It'll take longer and be more intense."

Go again! More intense! Fucking Hell! I'll end up in E.R. I look at him in amazement. He has some flipping stamina!

I don't have time to protest. He starts building up a steady rhythm, thrusting slow and deep.

"Can you feel that? I'm getting hard already." He grins down at me. "I want you on your front," he whispers against my lips. "But I don't want to come out of you."

Staying deep, he lifts my leg over his head with care, turning me onto my side, but keeping his growing cock inside me, maintaining our contact. It's a dexterous manoeuvre on both our parts but we manage it and suddenly I'm on my front with my left leg bent at the knee, my face planted in the pillow and Silas, buried balls deep inside me. His substantial weight is spread evenly across my back. He's heavy, but I'm not uncomfortable.

"Your back is so beautiful." He pulls my bra from my body then strokes a slow, firm line with his finger along my vertebra, stopping only to trace a light circle round each of the dimples at the base of my spine. Finally, his finger slows as it reaches the cleft of my buttocks. "Your very wet here." He keeps brushing his finger up and down my wet cleft while he thrusts lazily, circling his hips to increase his depth. "Sssss! Shit, Edi. This feels incredible. You're so wet. It's a tight fit, but I can slide in and out... do you feel that?"

"Mnnnn," I tell the pillow.

Demonstrating, he pulls back, so only the very tip of his cock is inside me, then slides back inside with ease. Hissing, he sinks his teeth into my ear. I'm groaning with wanton desire.

His weight is only half on me but the depth of his cock and the stroking of his fingers has me pushing back, I need him deeper.

"I think you're one of those amazing women who can ejaculate?" He forms it as a question. I've no idea, it's never happened before.

"I don't know. Is that a good thing?" I croak through my gasps. "Ahhhh!" My mind is turning to mush.

"It's a very good thing. Some might even call it a talent. Most women can't do it. You just seem to gush with every release. It's so fucking *hot*, it makes me as solid as a rock, see?"

He retreats and slams back in, *hard,* demonstrating just how *solid* he actually is.

"I'm going to fuck the living daylights out of you now."

He draws back again… and then out! I'm bracing myself for the onslaught, but it doesn't come so I raise my head, seeking his face.

"What are you doing?" I query. He can't possibly stop now, I'm wringing wet, wide open and completely gagging for it.

"Get up." He helps me to my feet.

The sudden pull of gravity causes a trickle of cum mixed with my own vaginal juices to run down the inside of my thigh; a thick globule lands on the expensive carpet between my new shoes with an audible *splat*!

Silas's sparkling eyes follow its journey. I see his cock twitch and a bead of pearly white semen appears on the tip. "Oh, fucking hell, that is so horny - I love it! Come over here dirty girl."

He takes my arm and leads me over to the window. Unlocking the French doors, he pushes me out onto the balcony.

No!

I'm naked. He can't possibly want to go outside, can he? It's started to rain again, and my sensitive skin is immediately assaulted by the few stinging drops that traverse the shelter of the canopy above us. The delicious chill makes me shiver but I'm not happy with the feeling of exposure.

Turning to face him, I start to protest. "Silas, *no,* I can't... not outside!"

I'm troubled by this. I'm not an exhibitionist but judging by our previous open-air encounters, Silas obviously is. It does though, feel highly decedent, standing here, naked in the rain.

"Yes, Edi... you can." I'm nudged further outside. "Feel the air, the rain on your skin, soak up the sensation," he growls as he moves me backwards towards the edge of the terrace. "Turn around and hold on to the railing." I don't argue. The rain is light, but Silas is right; the sensation of the cooler air and smarting needle-like raindrops is wonderfully heady.

Tentatively, I grip the slippery railing, gazing down at the wet Parisian street below. Up here on the second floor, we can't be fully seen from below or above. The only visible balcony is the adjacent one to my room. There are no windows evident in the building opposite, just the dull, red brick façade. We aren't overlooked - but yet I feel dangerously overexposed.

"Open your legs." Massaging my bottom with his big hand he starts kneading my skin, pulling and pummelling my buttocks. The sliding of his fingers against the crevice between my cheeks is made even easier now the rain has joined the lubrication party.

Reaching his hand under me, I feel his thumb enter me from behind, his fingers separating my enflamed folds. Dropping my chin to my chest, I close my eyes when his dexterous fingers

371

home in on my beating clitoris. Back and forth he flicks, while pressing his thumb against my front internal wall.

"Oh, Jesus, Silas." I grip the hand-rail tightly. My palms are slipping on the wet wrought iron. "Please, Silas, I'm going to come again." I can't help it, it's so intense I think I'm going to pee! "Fuck, Silas, yeah, ohm, Ahhhh!"

Knowing I'm close, he removes his thumb and fingers, fully aware that this delaying tactic will only intensify my release when it eventually happens. "Ask me... *woman!*" He growls in my ear "What do you want Edi, tell me what you need? *Ask* for it..." After a few seconds, he replaces his thumb and fingers; thrust, flick, squeeze... thrust, flick, squeeze, gradually building the speed and rhythm, applying just the right amount of pressure.

Unable to resist, I bend forward, tilting my pelvis back and opening my stance further in invitation. "Fuck me!" I demand, growling the word through gritted teeth.

Silas increases the pressure, twirling his thumb and flicking fingers in response. "I can't hear you..."

Giving him what he wants, I call into the rain. Throwing my head back and screaming my request up at the now teeming sky. "FUCK ME... FUCK ME, NOW!" I cry, my voice getting louder with each demand.

Removing his fingers, Silas shifts behind me, lining himself up, pending entry. "Hold on tight Honey, this is going to be *really* hard, so don't tense!" SLAM!! He enters me with a loud yell, topping out the volume of my own shouts as we roar and moan together. "Haa, Huugh, Haa, Huugh!" He heaves with each demanding plunge.

"Agggghh, yesss! Please, yeah, yeah, yeahhh!" My voice has now gone completely, I'm hoarse. He's so incredibly deep I can feel him pounding against my cervix. The sensation is unbelievable. There's a heavy pressure building in my bladder.

Oh crap! I'm going to pee! "Silas, I'm gonna wet myself," I shout at him, he needs to pull out so I can visit the loo.

"Hold on, just a couple more seconds, Sssss! Hold it Edi, hold your water until I say!"

Oh lord, I'm going to come and piss at the same time.

"Spread your legs so you don't ruin your shoes."

My shoes... scared that I'll cause them irreparable damage if they get soaked in urine and cum, I slide my feet sideways on the slippery tiles, widening my stance even more.

With my legs wider apart, I bend further forward to maintain my balance, giving him even more access, allowing him to increase his pace to an unholy level.

Unrelenting now, he hammers into my centre with unbelievable power. His lower stomach slaps my arse, his heavy balls colliding with my clit as I bend forward over the balcony railing. *Oh, this is too much...*

"Ahhhh, Silas, it hurts, I can't hold it anymore." Christ, it's impossible, I need to let go before I explode. *"SILAS!"* I'm crying now, my clitoris burning and my bladder fit to bursting.

Suddenly I feel his finger enter my anus. I jerk away, but I've nowhere to go other than into the railings and anyway, I don't want to go anywhere. The double penetration feels wrong, dirty, but at the same time, *fucking amazing*, and it makes me push against him even harder.

Then, everything happens at once... I feel him tense and stiffen as he rears back, the slight respite from his weight hits me, with an overwhelming, glorious, rush of euphoria. I inhale deeply and hold it. A heady weightlessness overtakes my body and I can't feel my feet on the floor. Now I *really* can't hold on any longer. *"Please, Silas!"* screaming in delicious agony, I *need* to release.

"Yesss! Do it Edi, go now, go, come on... dirty girl, let it go, do it!" He thrusts one last time with all his might and control.

"Now, Edi!" He yells in my ear on a huge drive. His cock slams against my cervix as his finger rams inside me and at last... I let it go!

A glorious orgasm hits me like a battering ram, my vagina squirts on ejaculation, and my bladder contracts, an involuntary spasm causing me to pee everywhere.

Silas is still buried to his root inside me, as my body reacts to the huge release of pressure; spurting, squirting, gushing hot urine and vaginal juices all over the balcony. Steaming, liquid is splashing on the Tuscan tiles, mixing with the rainwater beneath our feet.

Silas pulling his finger out of my arse and his cock out of my vagina, ejaculates all over the balcony floor.

Once again gravity plays its part, our combined bodily fluids mix together, forming a swirling, milky essence. Mingling with the rain, there's a frothing, flowing waterfall, tumbling over the edge of the balcony and down onto the street below.

"*Jesus,*" he heaves as he wraps his arms round my waist from behind. He must realise I'm on the point of collapse. "That was the *hottest fucking* thing I've ever experienced... You *amaze* me Edi... I'm..."

Yeah... I'm pretty speechless too.

Lost for words, he holds on to me ever so tightly, pressing his lips firmly into the centre of my back, preventing him from saying any more.

I too can't speak. Looking up to the sky, I listen to my own haggard breathing. A feeling of overwhelming shame overtakes me. I'm completely mortified at what I've just done. Embarrassed and appalled. But then, why do I feel so exhilarated and relieved all at the same time? I don't know what to think. I'm emotionally conflicted.

"Whoo-hoo, yeah, we hear ya up there!" A piercing male voice echoes from the street below. "Slam it man, shaft that fucking pussy!" The cat calls continue, reverberating in the night air. Americans! They must be walking on the street below, though thankfully I can't see them. Invisibly, they've borne witness to our tryst on the balcony and are making their appreciation known.

"*Nooo!*" I'm horrified. Turning into Silas's hard, wet chest, I bury my burning face in my hands. "*God*, No!" Swathing me in his arms, I feel his chest judder beneath me and look up to find a huge shit-eating grin. He's so beautiful. His stunning face is glistening with sweat and rain. Silver beads balance like tiny jewels on his eyelashes and on the short stubble on his head. He's also laughing! It isn't funny!

"Relax, baby… as I said before, they can look, but they can't see. They can listen but they can't hear." He *knows* I'm uncomfortable with this whole 'sex-in-the-open-air' thing he has going on, but obviously he isn't. "Let's go inside. We need to clean up." Gratefully, I let him lead me indoors, all the while ensuring I'm wrapped in his strong arms.

Once we're back inside the room, he closes the door, crouches down and very carefully remove's my shoes. I hold onto his naked shoulders as I balance before him, first on one foot, then the other.

His back is gleaming like polished mahogany; my own legs are so wet, I could have just walked out of the shower. Risking a look at my shoes as I lift my foot, I don't think I peed on them. I really hope they aren't ruined.

Silas inspects each one as he removes it. Unbelievably, they appear undamaged. I'm relieved. It's more luck than good management, considering we're both dripping wet, soaked through with all the cum, urine and rain.

His skin glistens as if he's been coated with baby oil. "Come on sweetness; a hot bath's in order for you Honey-bee." He leads me to the bathroom. "You'd better try another go," he points at the loo, indicating that I should have another wee.

"I can't go with you in here."

The moment I say it, I realise how stupid I sound. He's fucked me every which way and had his finger up my arse. I've also peed all-over the place while coming like a freight train! The incredulous look he gives me speaks volumes! Yeah, I'm being a girl.

"Edi, just pee, will you?" he laughs at my sudden shyness.

Huffing, I take a seat, I'm going to wee for England. Relaxing, a sudden rush releases the heavy pressure on my bladder. Once finished, I wipe myself with loo paper, but I'm so wet, the paper disintegrates like confetti, the little fragments of tissue just sticking to me. "Here, get in the bath, Honey-bee." In the time it's taken me to empty my bladder, Silas has filled the tub with hot, bubby water.

We change places. I climb into the tub and Silas stands proudly in front of the toilet; holding himself in hand, his broad back straight and solid, his feet evenly spread, he proudly begins to relieve himself, pissing like a champion racehorse!

We're so over our inhibitions!

Satiated, I recline against him in the tub, my weak arms resting on his bent knees. I'm aching all over. I've never had a sex marathon before, it was exhausting and exhilarating at the same time; now my libido has been ignited, if he wanted to do it again, I would jump at it. The sweet, stinging sensation between my legs is delicious.

"I'm all flollopy," I mumble, the silly word of my childhood accompanied with a sulky pout.

"Flollopy?" he whispers laughingly.

"Yes... *flollopy.*"

We've been sat like this for a good ten minutes. No sound, no words, just the occasional drip of the tap and the rippling, gentle splashes of the water as we stroke and explore each other's wet skin. Both rather pensive, lost in thought.

"No condom," he announces, reminding me of our recklessness.

"Sterilisation." It's a matter of fact, so I'm matter of fact about it. After David, I couldn't imagine having any more children; it was the sensible option.

"Vasectomy," he's as matter of fact as I'm. It's his business, so I don't pry.

"STD's?" Best check.

"I'm clean... you?"

Ha, very funny – I've had no sex for about fifteen years, so I guess I'm clean.

"Apart from a scorching case of Herpes and some genital warts, I'm S*ooo* clean..."

That ends that conversation. He laughs, but I can sense that he's not too sure if I'm having him on.

"'*J*' *for joke*! I'm clean… I'm clean." I put him out of his misery.

"I like your birth mark," he mutters, nipping my ear as he caresses my breasts absentmindedly. "It looks like a little pink heart."

"Hmmmm," is my only answer.

"It looks familiar somehow."

"Does it?" … *Please don't go there tonight!*

"Who's Meredith?" … *He went there!*

"What do you mean?" I try to act vague.

"Your '*friend*' Lynda was shouting something about Meredith and her 'being found'," He's fishing. "I thought for a minute that she was talking about you." *There, he's said it. Now what do I do?*

Pushing up, I rise and step out of the bath. Grabbing one of the white towelling robes, I wrap myself up before swathing my hair in a towel. "It was a long time ago Silas. Another lifetime. I was a different person."

I turn and look at him as he reclines in the tub. His face impassive, quietly contemplating me, in a non-judgemental way.

"Edi, I know it's in the past and if you want, it can stay there, but why do I get the feeling that you're avoiding the issue? What are you afraid of? If you keep running away, eventually you'll have nowhere to run to. Then where will you go?"

Point made, he slides and submerges himself beneath the water, his head below the surface, only his knees, thighs and cock visible through the dying bubbles. He's said his piece and has left the ball firmly in my court.

I hover in the bathroom doorway and watch him, as he lies submerged, beneath the bathwater. His insightful words have hit home. He's right, of course. I'm avoiding the issue.

378

Moodily, I traipse back into the bedroom and sit on the bed. I know I should trust him. I need to trust him. I can feel myself falling deeper and deeper. My control is slipping away and that scares the shit out of me.

He's perceptive… I'm afraid. But he's also misled on that score too; it's not the fear of being exposed that scares me now. It's the fear he wouldn't want me if he knew the full extent of my secrets. Having put myself in this position, I doubt I could deal with rejection on that level.

Coming to terms with the fact that I've let a man into my life, albeit just a bodily presence so far, is difficult - all those years, I'd convinced myself I didn't need any physical interaction; I was immune to carnal desires. I had no need for lust, no compulsion to feel. So, I repelled it.

I buried my personal wants and needs so deeply, it would take a blast of dynamite and a skilled archaeologist, to excavate them from their ceremonial burial ground in the dark pit of my soul. I told myself being alone was easier, better, I was happier that way. Without any physical contact; I didn't need anybody's arms around me, other than my immediate family. I certainly didn't need to be held, touched or caressed…

What a fool. What a misguided, delusional, self-indulgent idiot! Of course, I did; everyone needs to be touched, held. It's a basic anthropological requirement. And I didn't realise how much I missed it. Something as simple as the weight of another human body against mine. The pure intensity of how a single touch can light me up within… just to be alive. I didn't know how lonely and isolated I'd become, until I met Silas.

I must have been sat a while, because Silas has exited the bathroom, dry and wearing a pair of black, loose-fitting, flannel pyjama trousers. He walks over to me and squats before me, taking my hands in his. "Edi, please, talk to me. I'm not going anywhere. This is a good thing we have here. If someone had told me a week ago, that by the end of *this* week I would have met the most, beautiful, intelligent, selfless woman... I can't put it into words, but - a week ago I was... floundering, only I didn't know it. Now I feel alive again. Please, trust me. Speak to me, Honey-bee. Be brave." He's pleading. He could have stolen my words...

My handbag starts to ring... sighing, I drop his hands and manoeuvre round his crouching form to fetch my bag. By the time I've reached inside for my phone, it's rung off. Checking the call log, it's a missed call from Lizzy. I make a mental note to ring her tomorrow. I can't do it now. Then I notice another missed call. This one is from David. Neither one of them has left a voice message so they can't be urgent.

Bringing my phone with me I sit back down on the bed. Silas hasn't moved. "Urgent?" he asks on raised brows.

"No, just David and one missed call from the girls," I answer with a stifled yawn.

"The girls?" He's puzzled.

"Yeah, my Uni' house-mates are in the States back-packing. Remember? They're just checking in." Silas nods in recognition as I try to be as matter of fact as I can. "I don't know what David wants. I'll ring him tomorrow." I sound really sulky, though.

"Ah, David," he sighs sarcastically. He stands then sits beside me on the bed. I don't let him take my hand when he tries, I snatch it away.

"What does that mean?" I prickle. *What the hell does that mean?*

"Nothing, I... it's, well he seems to be a bit clingy for a teenage boy who lives away. Is he a bit of a mummy's boy?"

Oh, the utter cheek... I bristle, yanking the towel off my head in temper. *How dare he make assumptions?*

"David is ... well ... he's ..." *What Edi? What is David?*

Angrily I grab my phone and search my photo's. This is one secret that I can reveal right here and now! He'll either run a mile or make an excuse and that will be it. I might as well find out.

Here goes nothing…

Scrolling through my photo's, I find a lovely one of David and me, sat on the grass quad outside my Uni' digs. It was summer and we're both looking a bit sunburned, but I like it.

Jutting my chin in defiance, daring him to say something derogatory, I thrust the phone towards Silas. "There," I yell, "that's David… satisfied?" He takes the phone from my hand and gives the picture a long ponderous look. Then, he hands it back to me, his expression unreadable. "Well?" I ask, not really knowing what to expect.

"He has your colouring… Your hair is shorter on that picture. When was it taken?"

He's only noticed my hair? It takes the wind out of my sails. I wasn't prepared for that reaction… perhaps he hadn't looked very hard at David.

"Erm… A couple of years ago, when I was in my first year at Uni". He's derailed me with his change of direction. I look at the picture of my beautiful boy. As usual, he melts my heart. "He's very special to me. Not a mummy's boy, just a very special boy."

I run my finger over the precious photo. Somehow, just looking at David's smiling happy face calms me. I sit smiling at the photo of my handsome boy.

Silas is quiet, as if he's contemplating something. I thought this might happen. Not everyone appreciates how wonderful my boy is.

"I know he is," Silas whispers. Stunned by his comment, I look up to see his face. His eyes are shimmering with emotion.

Slowly, he reaches over to his bedside table and finds his own phone. Siding it open, he locates *his* photos and hands the phone to me. Holding his glittering gaze, I take it, looking down at the image; recognition dawns and I immediately return my eyes to his. My face must be registering my surprise.

"That's our Dominic," he points to his phone, "So, now you know, how I know, how wonderful David is," he says softly.

"Nic," I whisper, looking at the photo of the most handsome young man with green eyes and an impressive afro! "He has a teddy, a bear!" I echo David's words from last weekend. It registers. *"Bear!"* I can't believe it. Silas is Nic's dad! Which means Christina is his mum... I'm gobsmacked.

"Yeah, Bear loves Nic but some of the kids are a bit wary of him, so I don't take him to visit very often." He looks sad. "The toy Shepherd was a poor substitute, but thankfully a huge hit."

"Oh, Silas. We have the most wonderful boys!" Still reeling from this incredible revelation, I fling my arms round his neck, hugging him tightly.

"We do," he whispers into my neck. "Davey has been a marvel. Dominic was almost mute; would barely make a sound. Even the best therapy had very little effect. But amazingly, he will say the odd word now. And I think his friendship with Davey has a lot to do with that." The pride in his voice matches my own. "Davey just treats him like a mate. He doesn't see that he's different."

"I can't believe this... it's... bizarre." I chose my new job because of its proximity to The Beeches. This just seems really weird. "I... I just assumed that..."

"What? That I'd run. Make an excuse not to see you again... never assume anything Honey-bee." He strokes my damp hair softly. "Because, when you assume... you only make an *Ass* out of *U* and *Me.*" He's smiling but his deep brown eyes are soft. I can't get over the coincidence.

Suddenly I have an amusing thought, "Can you imagine what it would be like if we turned up to visit them together?"

Unexpectedly, I'm relieved *this* secret is out. Common ground, something we can share. It also means my other secrets can stay hidden for a while.

"Yeah. What a coincidence eh? Wait 'till I tell Christina. She'll be blown away. She loves Davey." He pulls back, his eyes are still brimming with emotion, but he too, looks relieved. "Is this the big secret you've been hiding or are there more?" He knows. There are so many more!

"This is it - for today," I whisper. "I'm shattered Silas. You wore me out. Can we just go to sleep?" I yawn again. I'm exhausted now and my muscles are aching big time. "I really can't believe that our boys are friends... it's incredible." I shake my head in wonder, trying to help it sink in.

"Come here, Honey-bee." He opens the covers. The bed looks soft, warm and inviting. Dropping my towel, I climb in and clamber over to the other side of the huge bed. My hair is still wet and my body is naked, but I don't care.

Once he's sure I'm settled, Silas removes his lounge pants and climbs in beside me. I turn my back to him and rest my head on the downy pillow.

Silas grumbles, wrapping his big arms around me , hauling me back so I'm cradled almost beneath him. Once he has me where he wants me, he wedges his penis between my thighs. He doesn't enter me, but I can feel him there, semi-hard and nestled. It feels so... comfortable. So good. I close my eyes and I'm asleep in ten seconds.

Chapter 33

I wake to the hum of the morning traffic drifting in from outside. At first, I think I'm back in my Uni' digs, then I remember my new flat. Eventually, I remember I'm in Paris.

I'm aching all over. Shivering and shaking. My stomach is churning with cramp and I feel like I have the flu.

Ugh!

Sitting up, the first thing I notice is I'm in my blue bedroom... alone. The second is I'm naked. My brow creases in confusion. I don't remember coming in here. The last thing I recall was being in Silas' room, snug and sated under his warm body. I search my brain for any memory of being moved but it doesn't come. What does come however, is an urgent need for the toilet!

Not again!

I leap out of bed and dash to the bathroom before I make a disgusting mess of the luxury 1,000 thread, Egyptian cotton sheets.

Perching on the toilet, I grip the side of the wash basin for balance as my body purges itself of everything I ate and drank yesterday. My stomach gripes and tightens in the attempt to rid my insides of the digested toxins. "Lord, help me!" I groan aloud.

Beads of perspiration dampen my forehead and my hair is soaked and clinging to the back of my neck. Grabbing some toilet tissue with a shaky hand, I use it to wipe my face, soaking up the cold sweat running down my temples. "God, in heaven!" I whimper.

Running over the events of last night, the intensity of our encounter weighs heavily and I can't shake the vivid imagery from my head. A dull throbbing starts behind my eyes.

I feel hungover, totally dehydrated and completely exhausted. Every muscle is screaming in agony and my legs feel like I've done a million squats. *Christ, I feel rough!*

Then there was that unbelievable revelation; complete shock that our boys are friends. A pleasant one, but a shock never-the-less. I'll need to explain things to David, really carefully. I snort a laugh through my nose. What am I thinking, he's probably too busy bonking himself sore with Wendy, to worry about my antics!

Ugh! Speaking of sore; my internal walls feel bruised and my labia are on fire. My clit feels like it's been rubbed raw. And what's with this hangover? My stomach gives one last spasm, but thankfully it seems I'm done... there can't possibly be anything left inside me. I clean myself up with toilet paper and take a trembling trip to the shower, determined to rid myself of this horrid inertia.

Remembering I've work to do today, I moan. My head is banging and I'm physically shaking. Yep, it definitely feels like flu.

Christ! Just what I need...

It must have been the soaking I got yesterday when we were caught in the rainstorm.

Leaning my forearm on the tiled wall I rest my forehead against the cool surface and allow the power shower to pound the back of my head and pummel my shoulders. My arms shake as I lean on them. It's all I can do to remain upright when all I really want to do is crawl back into bed. I force myself to wash my hair and body. It's a job and a half!

Feeling only slightly better once I'm showered, I head to the bedroom to get dressed. My jeans and jumper have been laundered and hung back in my wardrobe. That must have happened while we were out last night. I dress quickly, swapping the blue jumper for a green tee-shirt. It feels as though it might be a warm morning. Thankfully my ballet pumps have dried out, so I slip them on. The insoles feel gritty but I'll manage.

Perching at the dressing table, I flick on the television for background noise, and get on with rough drying my hair.

Whilst wafting the hairdryer around my head, something on the TV catches my eye. It looks like a live report from outside the Four Seasons Hotel; I recognise the front façade from last night. It must a report about the party.

Switching off the dryer, I give the item my full attention, spinning in my seat to face the TV the correct way around, flicking up the volume with the remote control as I do.

I don't really understand what the reporter is saying, but then a photograph of Pierre Adrax flashes on the screen. Straining my dehydrated brain to understand the language, I eventually catch a couple of words *'retrouvé mort'* ... *Retrouvé*? I think that means found and *Mort...? Found dead! Jesus!... Are they saying that Pierre Adrax has been found dead??* Oh my gosh, surely not? I only saw him last night and he looked fine to me.

I turn the volume up louder, as if that will somehow help with my understanding. The French reporter is babbling away, nineteen to the dozen and with my rudimentary smattering of GCSE French I can't grasp much of it.

Hurriedly, I flick through the channels, desperately trying to find an English-speaking one; eventually landing on BBC Breakfast News. The picture on the TV is the same, but the reporter is different. I recognise her as the BBC Foreign correspondent.

She's halfway through her piece to camera. "...in the early hours of this morning... Mr Adrax was apparently discovered by his ward, Mr Liam Zaio. Mr Adrax - a renowned fashion designer in his own right - was attending a celebrity party celebrating the end of Paris fashion week. Both Mr Zaio and his colleague Ms Django, were part of the team modelling the new up and coming Adrax brand 'Vanda'."

Oh my God! ... He is... he's dead...

The TV switches to a rerun of an earlier broadcast. The footage shows a gaunt looking Liam Zaio and Django, huddling together as they run the gauntlet of press reporters, photographers and paparazzi. They're leaving the hotel under police escort; presumably to give witness statements.

From what I can see of their pale faces, they look terrified and utterly distraught. As they struggle to force their way through the flashing cameras and jutting microphones, one of the huge bodyguards I recognise from last night, raises his palm in protection.

The TV bulletin switches to the reporter outside the hotel. "It's understood that both Mr. Zaio and Ms. Django were legal wards of Mr. Adrax, who 'adopted' them from their respective native countries when they were both young teenagers, living in poverty."

Oh, I didn't know that.

The reporter continues… "As of now, we've no further update on the circumstances of Mr. Adrax's death. However, we do know the police are treating it as suspicious and are undertaking a thorough investigation. Currently, both Mr. Zaio and Ms. Django remain in the protective custody of the French police. A spokesman for *The Gendarmerie Nationale,* insisted earlier that there's currently no evidence to link them to Mr. Adrax's death at this time."

Crap - they've been arrested. "We will continue to provide updates as they develop – Sophie Simpson for BBC News, Paris." The screen returns to the Studio, so I switch off the TV.

Wow! I can't believe it… he looked fine last night. He didn't look ill or anything. Suspicious death? Perhaps, they just don't know the cause yet. He probably had a heart attack. I wonder if Silas has seen this. It must have happened after we left.

Shaking my head in bewilderment, I swivel back in my seat and continue blowing my hair. Once it's dry, I scrape it into a ponytail; I'm still feeling like shit, but the shocking news has temporarily culled that sickly feeling. I don't bother with make up; I daren't look at myself that closely, I know I'll look horrendous.

With my hair dry and the TV off, my mind wanders back to everything that occurred last night. Analysing my thoughts, I slowly pack up my stuff. The sickly, headachy feeling is back and I'm moving like a snail. I don't know why I'm stalling. I don't know why I'm in my own room and I *really* don't know how I feel about last night.

A memory of Lynda drops into my head. Audibly groaning at the thought, I push it away. It needs to go back in the box with the lid shut down tight and sealed with gaffer tape!

There's a knock at my door. When I open it, Silas is standing on the threshold looking fresh, clean-shaven, bright and breezy. He's holding a Styrofoam coffee cup and a brown paper bag.

"Coffee and a croissant?" he offered waving them in front of my face.

My stomach lurches at the thought, and I fly into the bathroom without locking the door, dropping my jeans and sitting on the loo. I'm right back to where I was twenty minutes ago.

How delightful!

I'm shitting through the eye of a needle; what's wrong with me? I hope I haven't got gastroenteritis or something.

"Edi," his concerned voice drifts through the half-open door. "Are you okay, Honey?"

"Don't come in… I think I'm sick," I call back, groaning as I lean my sweaty head into my palms.

Jumping as the door opens further, I die a thousand deaths in embarrassment as Silas barges in, bold as brass.

Christ, the stench in here is killing me – God knows what he must think!

I feel far too crappy to protest. I just sit there, on the loo with my head in my hands as my bowels clench and squeeze and my stomach twists.

Fuck, surely, I must be empty by now?

"*Goddd*... I *told* you not to come in." I moan.

"Hey, it's okay." He kneels down in front of me and hands me a wedge of loo roll, not even flinching at the incredible stink I've made. "Do you need to use the bidet?"

"Yeah, I think I do," I whimper.

"I'll fill it for you then get out of your way. Hey, don't be embarrassed. We've all been there."

I doubt that very much. But the good part is, he's seeing me at my absolute worst and he's not running for the hills, so that can only be a positive thing. "Thank you, Silas," I mumble as I sort myself out.

"Did you see the news?" He calls from the other room. "That fashion gangster has been found dead... apparently we missed all the drama." Drama, I wouldn't call it that exactly, but I'm glad we weren't there.

"Yeah," I call back. "I saw that. I wonder what happened?"

"Who cares... one more scumbag terrorist is off the streets."

"Was he really?" I'd forgotten those rumours. Perhaps this is a good thing then?

"He certainly was – how are you feeling now?"

After I've cleaned myself up, yet again, I go back into my bedroom, where Silas has the coffee and croissant waiting. I still feel shaky and weak. "Like I've got the flu." Exhausted, I flop backwards onto the bed, flinging my arms over my head in a dramatic fashion.

"You know what this is don't you?" he asks as he lays out the pastries.

"Yes, food poisoning or something. It must have been the bloody fish soup!" I blow my nose noisily on a tissue and lob it into the bin. I'm being sulky and totally unfair. The fish soup was wonderful.

"Ha, no it's nothing to do with the soup. It is my educated belief that you are displaying all the typical symptoms of a '*bang-over*'!" he announces with a mischievous grin.

"What do you mean, '*bang-over*'?" Sitting up, I puzzle to understand what the hell he's on about. '*Bang-over*' I've never heard of it.

"Well, it's like a hangover, but from banging. A bang-over. Get it? Or you could call it a fuck-over or shag-over, but 'Bangover' rhyme's better with hangover." Oh, he's just *too* hilarious. He's making fun of me and making up words too!

"Well this 'Bangover' can fuck right off," I state categorically, reclaiming my prone position on the bed and hiding my head with my forearms.

He might be right though. All the muscles that hurt are the ones I used last night in our sexathon. It could be a '*Bangover*' or a '*fuck-over*' after all.

"Do bangover's give you a headache and diarrhoea?" I ask. "I feel like I've been run over by a double-decker bus." Forcing myself off the bed, I take a seat at the small round table. I doubt if I'll be able to eat anything.

"The good ones do," he laughs and wraps his arms round me from behind. I'm pulled up and dragged into his chest. I feel better immediately. I don't have time to enjoy it though. "You need to rehydrate. I'll go and get you some orange juice and Perrier."

Sitting me back down before I fall down, he makes to go out the door as I flop back into the chair.

"Silas, why am I back in my own room?" The question is out before I can stop myself.

He doesn't miss a beat. "I had some work to do, I didn't want to disturb you." On that note, he leaves and closes the door behind him.

When he returns - about ten minutes later - with a jug of fresh orange juice, a green bottle of sparkling water and two glasses, I'm back sitting on the end of the bed. No doubt he can sense something is wrong.

"What's up?" he pours the juice into the glasses and hands one to me.

"When I woke up this morning, I was back in my own room, in my bed, naked." I sip the ice-cold juice and look him directly in the eye, waiting for a response. When he says nothing, I continue. "I mean, there was no reason for you to move me. I can sleep through some tapping on a lap top. I've slept through worse you know. Why do I feel like you wanted to get rid of me?"

"I couldn't find your nightie. Believe me, I did not want to 'get rid' of you, as you so eloquently put it. I was working and I didn't want to wake you – that's it." He looks a bit put out I thought so little of him.

"That's not what I meant and you know it." I stare at him, waiting for him to catch up.

"I carried you," is his simple reply.

"Naked?"

His eyes flick round the room. "Yes," he confirms as they land on my face.

391

"Silas!" I can't believe he carried me out onto the landing while I slept, completely naked and in full view of the security cameras. *Thoughtless Bastard!*

"Edi, I've told you, they can look but they can't see." Standing, he starts to pace. He's getting agitated, but it's nothing to how I'm feeling.

"Don't give me that load of old bollocks," I shout, jumping up from the bed and getting in his face. "I was asleep. Unconscious, for Christ's sake. You can't just cart me from one room to another - *NAKED*!!!" I'm mad and feeling like shit. Not a good combination. I jam my hands on my hips to stop myself from lashing out.

"I… no… I… "

"You… WHAT?" I'm seething and he's bemused.

"You were hidden. I shielded you from the cameras." He doesn't see that this is wrong. "They couldn't see you, I would *never* do that."

"Silas, what if someone had come up the stairs, or exited the elevator? What if someone had been on the landing or in the corridor?" God, he's so dim, sometimes.

"No… I covered you up. In a sheet, see." He points to the bedroom chair. There's a cotton sheet I didn't notice before folded neatly on the cushion. "Edi," taking my shoulders, he bends his knees so we're eye to eye. "I would *never* do that to you… *never.*"

The feeling of relief is palpable. I breathe out a sigh. My head is still thumping and the shakes and aches are still there but the relief… "Oh." I slump forward, resting my damp forehead on his.

"Yes, Honey… I told you. They can look but they can't see… *ever!*" At last, he's getting through to me. How could I think he would be so crude to expose my naked body to all and sundry?

Because of all the exhibitionism last night, that's why…

"Now can we eat some breakfast? You look wrung out," He states dryly. He's right I'm so wrung out!

"Yes, thank you." I manage.

Chapter 34

After eating some breakfast, I begin to feel a little better. This *'bangover'* flu, or whatever it is, has really tipped me over the edge. My legs muscles are still a little stiff and my stomach is tender and aching.

There's a dull heaviness in my groin, like a really bad period pain and when I visit the loo for a wee, there's a light streak of blood on the tissue. I know it's nothing to be concerned about. It's due to the deep penetration from last night, my body's reaction to all the vigorous sexual activity after such a long time without. But the sight of it is disturbing and makes me shiver, another long past memory. Choosing not to think any more about it, I quickly flush the paper away and wash my hands.

On entering the bedroom Silas is on his lap top. He closes the lid as I approach him. He looks a bit distracted and his smile appears forced. "Just checking the schedule with Gerard," he informs me. "We're all still on time for this afternoon." On reflex, I check the clock. It's still only ten a.m. but it feels like I've been awake for hours. Without speaking, I walk past him and flop heavily onto the bed, issuing a loud theatrical groan as I land. Drawing my knees up to my chest to alleviate some of the griping pains and curling into a tight ball, I lie on my side and close my eyes.

"Edi," My shoulder is being gently shaken. "Edi, it's twelve-thirty." Peeling open my lids Silas is gazing at me from his seated position on the bed. "Here." Leaning across me, he hands me a glass of cranberry juice. I'm definitely getting my five-a-day today!

"Thanks." I sit up and take a long drink. He's diluted the cranberry with sparkling water. It's cold, sharp, fresh and delicious and I feel much brighter for my cat-nap.

"Feeling better?" he asks. I nod. I do feel better.

"I don't think I want another bangover for a while," I tell him. Then, realising what I've just said, I correct myself. "Perhaps next time, we forget the marathon and just go for the sprint finish?"

He laughs at me and kisses my nose. "Edi, it will never be a sprint finish with you. You'll get used to it. Trust me. You'll be an elite sex-athlete yet!"

"Yes, well, I'm not so sure about the contortions and gymnastics. Even my muscles, muscles are aching!" I smile.

"How's your head?" he asks.

"Better." I finish my drink and hand him the empty glass.

"And your stomach?"

"Well, I don't think I'll be running to the loo again if that's what you mean." The cramps are still there but they're more of a dull throb than the vicious aching of earlier.

"We'd better check out. I don't relish the drive to the airfield and I'm not hanging around for Phillips. If he's not there on time, I'm leaving without him. The guy's a solid gold prick."

"You can't do that." Incredulous, I climb off the bed and stretch. I feel tons better just for that small sleep. "He's a regular customer."

"I can and I will." He sulks as he tidies up his papers and puts his lap-top away. "We've got that new client, Hell, his business is worth ten times as much a Phillips'."

The thought hits me like a sledge hammer. My headaches returning with a vengeance. ...*Bobby*!... My stomach rolls at the thought. *Fuck,* I'll never get past this sick feeling whenever I think of him.

"Come on, Chuck!" He grabs our bags, he must have brought his through to my room while I was away with the fairies. "We need to get going." He walks over to the door, loaded down with luggage.

"Yeah, I'm coming… here, let me carry a couple of those." I follow him out of the room and remove my holdall from his grasp.

The return journey to the airfield is as difficult as the one into town yesterday. It's a good job we gave ourselves the extra hour. We arrive at one-thirty, only five miles yet it's taken an hour for us to get here from the hotel.

The concierge gave me such a salacious look when we checked out, I wondered if Silas had fed me a line about covering me in a sheet before carrying me to my room. Silas was clearly fuming at the way he was looking at me. There must be enough footage on that CCTV to keep him in wanking material for the next twelve months.

Gerard is looking as smooth as ever this afternoon as he hands over the now familiar leather folio to Silas. The jet, gleaming brightly in the sunshine, is ready and waiting for us on the apron. After saying our hurried goodbyes to Gerard and making him promise to visit very soon, we climb on board and begin preparations for our departure, whilst awaiting our clients.

Silas removes his uniform from the small closet, handing me a stewardess's uniform at the same time. It's a navy skirt and jacket with a white short-sleeved blouse. There's also a white silk scarf decorated with a beautiful Tudor Rose pattern. The skirt is a size twelve and the blouse is a size ten; so, there's absolutely no chance! I doubt they will be a comfortable fit, I've not been a size twelve since before David was born!

Silas of course has no inhibitions, he just strips off in the cabin, changing from his jeans and jumper to his uniform in double quick time. I choose modesty and move to the back to change in the small bathroom. There's hardly enough room to swing a cat and by the time I've managed to struggle into the uniform, I'm sweating profusely, with a nice bruise on my left elbow from colliding with the wall, whilst wrestling with the zip on my skirt. Thankfully, I've some deodorant handy, so I give my armpits a quick squirt, then retie my hair and apply some lipstick, blusher and mascara. Just that little bit of makeup makes a big difference – at least I don't look washed out anymore.

Surprisingly, the uniform fit's, but only just. The skirt is snug over my backside and the shirt buttons are puckered between my boobs but when I tie the scarf round my neck, the image reflected in the mirror looks both professional and smart. Smoothing back a stray hair, I run my hands over my hips and blow out a calming breath. "Okay Edi, you've got this… It's showtime," I tell my reflection.

Back in the cabin, I fanny about; polishing the champagne flutes so they gleam, filling the coffee machine, checking that the wine and beer are in the cooler. There are pastries and muffins, all sealed in cellophane wrappers, ready to be heated in the microwave at the passengers' request. I recall Victoria shredding the croissant in my office the other day and hope she doesn't want anything to eat – or destroy! Secretly, I hope she has her own hangover to match my *bangover* from Hell. She certainly deserves it after her performance last night.

As if on cue, a gleaming black Bentley glides to a halt on the tarmac. I watch through one of the porthole windows, curious, as a chauffeur climbs out and opens the rear door. *Yes!* I allow myself a smug grin as Victoria slowly emerges. She looks pasty, fragile and unsteady on her feet. Clutching her fur coat round her bony shoulders, she hugs it tight to her body; a clear indication she's feeling a tad delicate this morning. *Ha!* Her eyes are hidden by very large, very black, designer sun glasses and her dark hair is whipping around her pale face. She stands still, waiting for her husband to escort her up the steps.

"Edi?" Silas is waiting by the cabin door. I've been so wrapped up gawping, I've forgotten my duties.

"Oops," I scoot over to where he's standing. He discreetly caresses my bottom with the palm of his hand and gives it a little pinch, whilst keeping his professional eye on his approaching clients. At their arrival, he removes his hand from my arse, and extends it towards Mr Phillips. Victoria's looking really hungover. The merest trace of a self-satisfied smile tickles my lips.

Phillips doesn't look much better, but at least he can string a sentence together, while she just lurches into the cabin, waving a bony, manicured hand in front of her face. She weaves down the centre aisle, using the chairs as a support and swaying side to side, then flops unceremoniously into one of the cream leather seats.

"Tudor, the bags are in the car boot. My driver will fetch them." He turns his head to look for his wife. Spotting her slumped in her chosen row, he too moves down the centre of the cabin and takes the seat on the opposite side of the central walkway. It would appear they aren't speaking! This just amplifies my glee for some childish reason.

I raise my eyebrows at Silas and he winks at me. Entering the door of the cockpit, he speaks through his teeth, "Good luck, Honey-Bee!" then leaves me to it! Thanks a lot!

With some assistance from the ground crew the chauffeur loads the bags into the hold. With the door shut, the plane starts to taxi to the runway - I commence the safety procedures. Neither Victoria, nor Montgomery, pay a blind bit of attention. After checking Monty's seatbelt and wrestling with Victoria's limp body to ensure she's securely fastened in, I strap on my own seatbelt and we're off.

Ten minutes into the flight, I'm in the galley brewing coffee and heating pastries when Montgomery approaches me. His wife is out for the count. "Did you enjoy the party yesterday my dear?" He's far too close, invading my personal space and trapping me into the small area, behind the cockpit door. His breath stinks of stale tobacco and yesterday's alcohol.

"Yes, thank you Mr Phillips." Turning away from him, I try to continue with my duties.

"I must say, you looked stunning. That green dress… well, it was really lovely." He lifts his hand and picks up a tendril of my hair. "Really lovely, yes…" I turn and give him a withering look, trying my hardest not to gag at his reeking breath.

"Would you like some coffee?" I jerk my head so my hair slips out of his fingers. "Or would you prefer something stronger? Please, if you could take your seat - you're not supposed to be up here - safety reasons, you know," I say, trying to remain professional. "I'll bring your drink to you," I hear myself say. I'm pressing my back against the cabinets and sticking my elbows out attempting to put some distance between us.

"Really lovely…" He's looking at me very closely, scrutinising my face. Do I see a hint of recognition? Resisting the urge to hide I press myself further into the unit, wishing I could melt into the cupboard behind me.

"Mr Phillips?" I assert, "please… health and safety and all that!" I try for humour, hoping he'll take the hint. "You need to sit down."

Abruptly, snapping out of his contemplation, he shakes his head and steps away before saying, "Yes, I'll have a beer please. Peroni, if you have it." He starts to walk back to his seat and I heave a juddering sigh of relief. He's an old letch if ever I saw one.

After pouring his beer into a chilled glass, I place it on a tray and leave it on the side before knocking on the cockpit door to check if Silas would like a coffee. He nods his affirmation by giving me a cheery thumbs-up. Deciding that Phillips can wait for his Peroni while I serve my boss-man, I start preparing the coffee, pausing mid brew when I realise, I've no idea how he takes it. Instead of disturbing him again, I guess he takes it the same as me and add some cream and one sugar. If it's wrong, then Phillips will have to wait a bit longer, while I correct it.

Knocking once, I open the cockpit door and pass him his coffee. Taking an appreciative sip, he nods his approval and gives me a wink. I got that right then... I'm chuffed. Unable to stall any longer, I exit back into the galley and commence the arduous task of caring for my ungrateful passengers.

Carrying the tray over to Phillips, I notice he's left his seat belt undone. I place his beer on the table beside him, but as I turn towards the galley, he grabs hold of my left wrist, tightly, preventing me from walking away. I try and twist out of his grip, but my new watch pinches into my skin where he's holding on.

"Mr Phillips, is there something you need." I try not to panic, stepping a fraction closer to him to relieve the stress on my arm, his grip loosens slightly.

"You know, there were some interesting people at the party last night," he drawls. I don't miss the sideways glance at his wife to check she's still sleeping. "After you left, there was a bit of a commotion with one of the old washed out glamour models. Made a right spectacle of herself, she did."

"Mr Phillips, I'm sure I don't know what you are talking about. Please let go of my hand." I tug at my arm but he doesn't release me.

"Kept, shouting about her long-lost friend, she did. Making a scene, she was, bloody woman... said the girl was in the room; Meredith, or something." He stares at me intently; his eyes are a piercing blue, the yellowy-whites streaked through with red veins, bloodshot from last night. "Funny that... you'd left by then I think. What with all the kerfuffle, this morning about that old Gargoyle, Adrax, it almost slipped my mind..."

Kerfuffle! *Really? The man died.* He shrugs it off as an afterthought.

"Now... the only Meredith I can recall, is that little beauty from years ago. You must know the one? The Ice queen, they called her. Oooh, she was a stunner. Blonde hair, big titties," he doesn't even try to be discreet as his eyes travel fleetingly to my breasts. "Always a little sad-looking, never smiled. Remember?"

He's fishing, his inscrutable curiosity urging him to search my face for any sign of recognition.

My self-preservation nerve kicks in and I flash him my best cheery smile while at the same time, peeling my hand away from his, causing him to release his hold. "Yeah, I think I do now you mention it. It was a long time ago though wasn't it?" I'm babbling. "But I'm too young to have read those kinds of magazines."

Feigning ignorance, I back away as thankfully, Victoria starts to stir. Blinking, she removes her sunglasses and flips her suspicious eyes towards me, yawning loudly.

"Are we nearly home?" Whining and stretching her arms over her head, she looks at me, then at her husband. "I want a drink," she pouts demandingly. "Do you have any champagne?" She straightens up in her seat.

Grasping the opportunity to escape, I turn on my heels. "Yes, of course. I'll be right back."

Scurrying to the galley, I grab the small gold bottle from the wine cooler and a crystal flute. My hands tremble with adrenalin. That was a close call.

Taking them through to the seating area, I see that Mr Phillips has changed places and is now seated beside his wife, holding his beer. Handing over the champagne flute I open the small bottle for her. The cork makes an apologetic hiss as it pops out of the bottle and the champagne barely fizzes before it flattens to a few lazy bubbles rising in the narrow glass.

Victoria doesn't seem to mind as she takes a long quaff of the golden liquid before swallowing in exaggerated pleasure and settling contentedly back in her seat. Leaving them to it, I head back to the relevant safety of the tiny galley. I'm now wondering what else Lynda said after we left last night. To say the evening was eventful is an understatement...

Silas executes a perfect landing just after 3:30 p.m. The Phillip's chauffeur is waiting patiently in the carpark by their Rolls Royce, and Bear is waiting impatiently for Silas, just inside the automatic office doors. Both are pacing, to and fro, waiting for their masters to return, a parody of each other's lives. It's a satirical image and I immediately have a rush of sympathy for the poor chauffeur.

The Phillips' barely acknowledge us as they descend the aircraft steps and climb into their car. Their UK chauffeur has already loaded their bags and before you can say '*Jack Robinson*' they're driving out through the gate.

Silas and I watch them leave from our elevated position in the aircraft doorway. The relief, we're at last back on solid ground must be evident in my face, because glancing at Silas he gives me a watery smile in return. "C'mon, let's get inside... you did good Edi." Picking up his folio case he gently takes hold of my elbow as we descend the steps. The Chuckle Brothers are already carrying our bags and cases inside for us. Do they ever go home?

I know I must look shattered, but Silas looks as fresh as a daisy. I desperately need another shower and some comfy clothes; Silas needs to collect Bear, and make a huge fuss of him.

Christina stares at us knowingly through the glass. She's dressed casually in dark blue jeans and a lightweight ivory funnel-neck sweater. Her hair is tied up in a messy bun, yet she looks effortlessly casual, in that natural way classy women have.

Lifting her hand in a silent wave, she unlatches the door and releases the hound! He gallops towards us like a greyhound out of the traps. He leaps, launching himself at Silas - all four feet leaving the ground at once - but Silas isn't fazed; he just braces himself for the impact, before catching hold of him and cradling him like a huge furry babe in arms.

Laughing, we walk inside the building. On entering through the glass doors Silas releases Bear, who lands lightly on his feet.

Christina's greeting is a little more sedate; she takes the folio case from Silas with an incline of her head - "Done?" she asks.

"Done," he answers – before she welcomes us both with a warm hug. I've the distinct feeling that Silas has been in touch with her already this morning. She pulls me in tightly… yeah, she knows about David. Silently, we all three, stroll into the office, arm in arm. God, I need a coffee!

Chapter 35

Silas dropped me at the apartment around four-thirty, following a quick debrief with Christina. My eyes were heavy as I waved him goodbye and I couldn't quite understand why I've an ominous, sinking feeling in the pit of my stomach. It's an odd sensation, my body's reaction to my first physical encounter in, lord knows how many years, but I dismiss it, firmly filing it away to the back of my mind to be assessed and reviewed at a later date.

The main symptoms of my 'bangover' are nearly gone and apart from the dull ache that lingered in my belly and the sensitivity between my legs there isn't much to remind me of my illicit behaviour the previous evening. After emptying my bags and loading the washing machine, a bath and some food help restore my equilibrium; I feel much better from a good soak and something nourishing to eat.

That was a good couple of hours ago; now, I'm curled up on the sofa watching a repeat of 'The Great British Bake Off,' nursing a cup of milky coffee and ploughing through a stack of custard creams. I've already devoured a jacket potato with tuna and sweetcorn, two packets of cheese and onion crisps and a mint Aero. I've loaded up on the carbs and sugar, now for the first time since I got back to the apartment, I feel relaxed and content. But no matter how I try, I still can't prevent my mind from wandering.

Our intense encounter last night is playing on a continual loop in my head. Each time I try to dismiss it, it comes storming back, refusing to let me forget. And with each replay I relive another delicious moment. His kisses, his caress, his voice... the sheer look of him, his magnificent body; even his smell; it's all just so *real* and tangible.

Shifting on the sofa, I roll my head, my mind pulls at another strand of heaven from my brain; we're on the hotel balcony, I can still feel the sharp needles of rain on my sensitive skin. An involuntary shiver ripples through me; goose pimples rise on my arms as a physical reminder of the chilled night air.

I still can't get over how brazen I was. I've taken my clothes off for money once-upon-a-time, but I would never have imagined experiencing the unbelievably, elated thrill of last night.

In the past, being naked in front of people made me feel dirty, grubby and cheap. I was frigid. I'd always considered myself a total prude; even when I was posing nude, it was always conducted in the privacy of a secured studio with only two or three others present… and I hated every single second of it. It was just a way to earn money.

Last night was a complete revelation. Who knew I had hidden exhibitionist tendencies? Silas's risqué proclivities must be rubbing off on me. Sighing, another wave of contentment rushes through me.

I nibble away at my biscuits; splitting them down the middle and eating the creamy bit first, scraping the sugary sweetness off with my teeth before dunking the remaining naked halves into my brew. It's a disgusting ritual, but when I was a student, it was a way of making one biscuit seem as if I was eating two, and the habit's stuck.

The TV's murmuring away in the background. I watch blankly as Paul Hollywood scoffs a hand raised pork pie, declaring *'It's superb, that'* in his scouse accent, offering the gob-smacked contestant the much revered *'Hollywood'* hand shake.

Mmm, pork pie; I could just manage one of those.

405

I hear the jangle of keys in the door watching unsurprised, and unperturbed as Silas walks into the lounge. He helps himself to a custard cream and flops heavily onto the sofa beside me.

The credits roll as the programme ends. Silas picks up the remote and reduces the volume to a minimum.

"So," he says through his munching, "Meredith." Turning hurt eyes on me, he just stares, waiting for me to say something.

I turn cold... "You know?" I gape, horrified, my thoughts shifting instantly from our night of passion to my evening of horror. He just gives me a little shrug and turns his brooding stare to the television. The BBC news is just starting.

"I thought you seemed familiar when we first met. I thought I was imagining things." He keeps his eyes on the TV so I can't judge his mood. Leaning forward, I place my mug on the coffee table. I feel sick. "Then that awful woman at the party... then Philips mentioned something this morning. Eventually the penny dropped and I put it together. I looked you up... good old Google." He's smarting and angry and I can't blame him. He finishes his first biscuit and takes another.

"Silas?" I've no idea what I should say...

"Edi, or should I say Meredith." Eventually he turns his eyes to me. He looks down-hearted, wounded, betrayed even.

"Silas... I..." My past has caught up with me in the most dramatic way. All the hard work keeping out of the limelight, regularly moving location; changing my name. Uni', changing my career path; everything I've done, was for nothing. My determination to leave that horrible world behind, my self-preservation tactics have failed spectacularly, leaving me completely exposed. There's no way he'll understand.

"Meredith Snow!" he yells, throwing his arms in the air dramatically. "The Ice Queen. The famous glamour model. You must think I'm an idiot? The photos are spectacular, by the way... you should be proud."

"Don't..."

Disgusted, he stands and walks to the door. "You know, what's really sad, is I honestly thought we could have been good together. Really good. But this... you are *so* beautiful, but you are also a beautiful liar. I've no time for liars, Edi. This isn't going to work."

"No... Silas, please... I... I never lied to you." I stand, reaching out to him beseechingly.

He needs to understand what this is. My self-preservation, my sanctuary, my sanity is all on the line here. "Please try and understand. I had to let her go, she was poison. My life was poison. I was dying inside and I couldn't live like that anymore; ... I... I couldn't be Mary, - I mean Meredith, - anymore." I'm pleading with him, imploring him to listen to me. "I need to explain. Please, let me explain. It was all for David." I kneel on the sofa, reaching out for his hand.

As if on cue, the images on the TV change to the events of this morning. As one, we turn our heads to look at them. Alongside posed shots and archive material, there's new footage; a press real from last night, graces the screen.

Pierre Adrax is the picture of health as he marches towards the Hotel exit, with Liam Zaio and Django, breezing through the throng of milling people, leaving the ballroom. All three are flanked by the menacing body guards. Every single person in the picture is dressed in black and white - every single one of them that is, except for one woman. Her back is to the camera as she observes the scene. Resplendent in a vivid, emerald green, satin dress, she stands out like a beacon... me...

Shaking his head in resignation at the sheer irony of it all, Silas continues to put me firmly in my place. "It was a fucking sensation." He spits in fury... "the disappearance of *'The Ice Queen.'* All the papers ran with the story. One minute you were the overnight phenomenon; a mega star of the glamour modelling world was born. Your face and body were plastered across every newspaper and glamour magazine. You couldn't turn on the TV without hearing the latest story or seeing your image." He nods towards the screen as if to emphasize his point. "God, you were second only to Princess Diana in the fame stakes... then, within two years, you'd disappeared... gone into thin air. It was all over the tabloids. It was the best publicity stunt ever! One minute - at the top of the world - the next – '*poof*'... gone, never to be seen again." He flicks his fingers in a parody of a magician performing a cheap magic trick.

"I read that you left your *HUSBAND*! Your fucking *HUSBAND*! Oh, and he just happened to be your manager, they said." He's seething now, spitting the sarcasm in my face. It floors me, he's seriously angry. I need him to calm down and listen. I need him to understand. But he's right, I did do all of those things. But with good reason.

"Now you turn up at *MY* company... I need publicity, but not this kind. My business... my clients... I don't need this kind of publicity." Snatching up the remote, he switches off the TV before flinging the controller onto the sofa in disgust. "You..." he doesn't finish, he just drops his head and stands with his hands resting on his hips... waiting...

"You *have* been busy... doing your research, haven't you?" My voice is barely a whisper, I drop back to the sofa, dejected. I just take his wrath. "And of course, you believe everything you read in the papers."

He shakes his head, not understanding, "You have a husband? How did you stay under the radar for so long? Why this sudden change of career? Why me?" His brow is furrowed, he's really upset, but no longer yelling.

"Silas. Please come and sit with me," holding my breath, I say a silent prayer, hoping he takes the seat beside me. "I need to explain."

"What is there to explain? *Did* the papers get it wrong? Or is this *'new image'* all an illusion?" He looks really confused. I can't blame him.

"Please, just listen."

Warily, he returns to the lounge. He doesn't sit beside me, choosing instead to perch on the edge of the sofa opposite. Clasping his hands together, he drapes his elbows on his knees and leans towards me, despondent, waiting. "Well? You have my attention... and five minutes!"

Clearing my throat, I take a calming breath. Here goes nothing...

"You said I was a gym-slip mum." I start. "Earlier, when I said that I was nineteen when I had David... that's what you said... remember?"

"I remember," he whispers.

"Well, I was fifteen when I got pregnant for the first time." He gasps but doesn't move or speak.

"I didn't know I was pregnant. My mum was hardly mother of the year. She didn't tell me anything. When I started my period, I was thirteen, I thought I was dying. She just told me to be careful how I played with boys from then on – I had no idea what she meant."

I rub my face with my palms and shift on the sofa. This is so difficult...

"I'm listening..."

Honesty is my only option, so I continue. "I met Bobby when I was fourteen... at a party. He was the first boy to pay me any attention. I wasn't popular in school." I swallow, this is harder than I thought. Silas just sits, still, silent, staring, waiting.

"It was my friends fifteenth birthday party. She was allowed a sleep-over, but when I got there, the other girls were already drunk. She'd invited her boyfriend and he turned up with a whole bunch of his friends. Bobby was one of them. He was older than the rest of us so I didn't understand why he was there, but he seemed nice enough. He got me a drink and we started kissing; you know, like teenagers did back then." Nervously, I tuck my hair behind my ear. "After a while, the party was getting a bit raucous and loud. He suggested we go upstairs, where it was quiet, where we could talk; so, we went into my friend's bedroom."

I risk a glance at Silas. He's like a statue, without expression, so I plough on. "Things got a bit… heated, out of hand, you know… I didn't want to, but he ended up… anyway… well, you can work it out." I skip the sordid details, he doesn't need chapter and verse.

I hear him suck in air through his teeth. Humiliation consumes me. I can't look at him, but I have to keep going with my confession or I'll give up.

"Afterwards, he acted as if everything was completely normal. He told everyone I was his girlfriend. That felt good, because he was so popular and I was… well, I was just me. We started going out, like a real couple, you know. I didn't know it, but I got pregnant that night." I can hear his heavy breathing.

"When I finally found out, it was already too late. My mother disowned me. She drank herself to death over me." I drop my head into my hands at the shame of it. It's all coming out in a garbled rush as if I need to purge my mind of the memories.

Straightening my spine, I clasp my hands in my lap and stare at them. If I look at Silas, it will finish me.

"Bobby's family allowed me to move in. They were kind at first, though I'm sure Bobby's father had plenty to say when I wasn't around to hear it. They blamed me for everything." My voice has become hoarse.

"I had her by C-Section. You've seen the scar… after she was born, Bobby had some big plans for my future – *our* future."

The irony of that statement makes me spit out a derisory laugh.

"He was certain I had the potential to be a glamour model. He knew if I was successful, we could make a lot of money. It was in the days of page three, and all that hype." I'm on a roll now, I may as well finish it.

"He borrowed money from his father, and used some of it to get a photographer friend to take some promotional pictures of me. He sent those pictures to every magazine in the country. You probably looked at most of them when you googled me." I close my eyes, in disdain at the thought.

"Eventually they were bought by one of the tabloids. I couldn't believe it... I was nothing special, but apparently, I had what they were looking for... an innocence, they said. That was the start of it all; those first few photographs gave us our first break. We made enough money for a deposit on a flat and the kick start Bobby needed to get a foothold into promotions. We moved in, as a family, you know."

The memory of it is still as raw as if it was yesterday.

"I had no control over what I did... what *he* made me do." I'm hoarse with the effort of talking and shaking with emotion. "I hated taking my clothes off in public; but Bobby said I owed it to him to be successful, so I did it. I didn't know how to say no to him. So yes, I was an overnight success. One minute I was a young girl with a baby and no clue how to be a mum, the next I was all over the papers".

"Calendars and magazines came next, then the TV shows. Everything I did was scrutinised in the press. It was overwhelming and not what I wanted at all, but I was swept along with the hype."

If I didn't know he was there, I could be talking to myself, he's that quiet.

"What they didn't know, what nobody knew, was I was only sixteen; Bobby hid my true age. Made sure they always reported it as eighteen. Bobby controlled everything - he turned me into the Ice Queen - bleached my hair, watched what I ate, arranged my photoshoots. Before I knew it, I was posing for adult magazines as well as page three." I stop talking. My voice has become croaky. There's more, but I can't bring myself to say anymore. He's got the gist.

My hands are red and sore from wringing them together. I unclasp them and lay them flat on my lap. I'm still unable to look him in the eye. I'm a fool if I think he'll want anything to do with me now he's heard all the sordid details. I feel soiled and tainted, and I need him to either go, so I can pack my stuff and leave, or... I don't know what the alternative is, so I just sit and wait.

Finally, when he speaks, it isn't what I expect at all... "He raped you... at that party... he raped you." It's a statement not a question. "How old was he?"

"Eighteen." My voice is flat and cold.

"He raped you. He raped a child. He raped you, made you pregnant, then forced you to pose half naked for the world to see? I don't know what to say." He's boiling mad. I can see his shoulders shaking, he's wringing his hands together, mimicking my own actions of a moment ago.

"Yes," my voice is barely audible. I just sit quietly, letting him digest it all. He'll either go or stay. A fifty-fifty split. Black and white, no grey area.

"I'm confused; You said you were fifteen when *she* was born?" He asks.

"Yes."

"You said, *she*... if you were fifteen, that would make her..."

"Twenty-one... yes." Swallowing my damaged pride, I remain still... this is it. He'll tell me to leave and I will. He doesn't need this baggage. Risking a sideways glance, I can see he looks conflicted.

He shakes his head, trying to glean some understanding of what I'm telling him. "So, when you left... you took your daughter with you?"

"Yes, that was the main reason." This bit makes more sense so I explain further. "I had to protect her. I was receiving fan mail; most of it was trash, inappropriate content from sick minded men. But then, I started to receive hate mail. I couldn't get my head around the content; how those people could even think up some of the nasty things they wrote in those letters. They ranged from basic name calling, to people threatening physical harm... you know, *'watch your back, were gonna get you'* – I even had death threats. I was petrified but Bobby courted the publicity".

"One day, I returned to my car after a photoshoot to find someone had thrown acid all over it. Another time, I was walking in the park with the push-chair, minding my own business when some random guy thought it would be funny to follow me shouting sexist abuse. He eventually grabbed the handle of the buggy and spat in my face. I was terrified he'd do something to the baby so I ran all the way home. Another time, I was in the supermarket. When I got to the checkout, the woman refused to serve me because I was an 'inappropriate mother;' she caused such a scene I left without my shopping... I just picked up the baby and left. That was the last straw. I couldn't keep my daughter in that world a moment longer. I realised if I wanted her to have any semblance of a normal life, we had to get out... *I* had to get *her* out. But it was easier said than done. Bobby controlled my every move." Leaving had taken careful planning and a bag full of courage.

"So, you disappear, taking your child. Started a new life. Just like that?" he sounds disbelieving.

"Yes... sounds simple doesn't it?" Though it's not as simple as that.

"I remember the day it happened." His voice is calmer, so I risk looking at him. He hasn't moved from his stone like position, staring at the rug. "The papers tried to make out that there were *suspicious circumstances*. For a while, the disappearance of the '*Ice Queen*' gained as much publicity as the disappearance of *Lord Lucan*!"

"Huh, the papers… yes… they made a huge deal out of it. Bobby appeared on TV appealing for my return. He craved the publicity like he always did; turned it to his advantage. He tried to force the kidnap angle, although he knew I had left under my own volition."

"I tried to get it to stop. I wrote an open letter to one of the main newspapers at the time. I explained my reason for dropping out of public life, I felt hunted, and I just wanted my privacy back. They didn't print it, but they did report I was safe and well. They even offered money to people who sent in any photos of me – can you imagine what that feels like? It was like having a bounty on my head. All I wanted was to get away, disappear."

"The papers didn't mention anything about a child. How did they not know? Where is she now?" Our eyes meet for the first time since I started my confession. I think I see an element of sympathy, but I can't be sure.

"No, they didn't know about her. Bobby was very careful about that. Nobody is interested in a mumsy glamour model. She was a secret for a long, long time. As for where she's now; Washington, I think…" I let the information settle. "Her name's Elizabeth… Lizzy."

"Lizzy, as in, house mate, Lizzy? Lizzy from Uni'? That Lizzy." The penny has finally dropped. He's shocked.

I nod and smile as I always do when I think of her. "Yes, that Lizzy. So now you know. Now you can see why I had to get away. I couldn't expose my sweet, beautiful little girl to the ugliness of that world. She deserved better. So, I left." There's more, but I can't face it tonight.

Silas still looks puzzled. "And David?" he asks. "Where does David come into this story?"

"I didn't know at the time, but I was pregnant when I left." That was a dark day, I don't think I can go into the details quite yet.

"So, Bobby is his father too?"

"Yes."

"Does he know?"

"No." And if I have my way he never will.

We sit in silence for a few minutes, allowing the revelations to swirl and settle. I still have no idea what I'm going to do. A future of running and hiding is all I can see.

"Thank you for telling me." He stands. "I need to think about this. What effect it could have on the business if it comes out *The Ice Queen* is working for me..." It makes me wince the way he says it and I can't blame him for his trepidation. I'm a lot to take on, I know that.

At least he listened. I know this must be overwhelming to hear, to absorb, alone accept. I've only known him a week and I've offloaded all my horrible history onto him – well almost all. Walking to the door, he looks hopeless, dejected, conflicted. *Nice going Edi*!

I unclip the watch from my wrist and hold it out to him. He hesitates momentarily, his eyes falling on to the circle of bumble bees on my wrist and the small bruise that he put there, not even twenty-four hours ago.

There's a question brewing on his lips, but he shakes it away, unable to deal with any more.

Hesitating only momentarily, he takes the watch from my proffered hand, and places it in his jeans pocket. Resigned, he opens the door and walks through it, leaving me perched on the sofa in the middle of the lounge. The gentle click of the latch echoes round the silent room like a death knell.

Numbly, I walk into the bedroom and crawl into bed. Pulling the duvet over my buzzing head, I contemplate my options.

1. Find a new job.
2. Start again
3. ???????

That's it… there are no other options, no number three. I start again, simple as that…

Tomorrow, I'll collect my stuff from RTC. I'll ring Lizzy and explain, then I'll speak to David. Then I'll speak to Christina…

Chapter 36

On Sunday morning, I crawl out of bed. I feel surprisingly well considering everything that happened yesterday. All the physical aches and pains have gone but there's no ignoring the heavy ache in my chest. All things considered, my head is surprisingly clear.

I've gone into automatic pilot, I've dressed, eaten my breakfast and packed my bags without a second thought. There's no feeling of regret, no anger, no emotions of any kind. I've shut down that side of my brain. The only way I'll get through this is by remaining detached.

I drive to the office and pull into the car park. A twinge of remorse piques at me when I see my brass name plate on my parking space. No! I won't think about it. Climbing out of my car, I pick up my lap-top bag and using my keys for the last time to open the main office door, I walk with resolve, through the back and straight into my own office, which I had grown so accustomed to in such a short period of time.

Placing my lap-top bag on my blotter, I reach under my desk for the cardboard box, which ironically only five days ago, I was emptying; and commence packing up my small collection of personal items. It's mechanical. I'm going through the motions, methodically packing. Loading up my stuff, emptying my bookshelves. It all has to be sorted. Thankfully, there isn't much of it. I've only been here a week. But what a week!

Sensing I'm not alone, I look up to see Bear standing in my office doorway. I stop what I'm doing, choosing to remain still, waiting. And as I knew he would, Silas appears like a dark shadow behind him. He doesn't say anything, he doesn't need to. His pained expression speaks volumes.

Stepping into my office, he stalks purposefully towards me. Holding my gaze, his face remains a dark mask of hurt and pain.

I feel like a total loser. What made me even think he could want me. I'm damaged goods; sloppy seconds. Nobody in their right mind could want me, ever...

Coming to a halt in front of me, he continues to stare me down. Daring me to break eye contact. But I'm not submitting. He might not want me here, but I will leave with my head held high and on my own terms.

Reaching forward he takes my hand. I feel him slide his palm round my wrist, I hear the clasp of my watch click as he fastens it in place. He doesn't release my hand, but raises it up to his lips, all the while staring deeply into my eyes. I'm stunned into silent disbelief.

Uncurling my clenched fist so my hand is flat, he presses my palm against his lush lips. Kissing my lifeline, his eyes begin to close. His breathing accelerates as he slowly squeezes his eyelids together, blocking out my face. Inhaling deeply through his nose he pauses, holding his breath for a couple of beats before forcing my hand firmly against his mouth.

I can't move or speak. Dumbstruck, my heart is leaping, hammering, trying to jump out of my chest. I'm on tenterhooks waiting for him to say something, anything. Unable to hold my silence any longer, I let it go.

The noise coming out of my mouth is neither a cough nor a cry; it's a juddering exhale. Relief, amazement, gratitude, desire... all of the above.

The small sound grasps his attention. When he opens his eyes, they're glistening. His emotions have got the better of him too.

Lowering my trembling hand to his chest so that my palm is covering his beating heart, he presses it flat, firmly enveloping it with both of his. Every thrum resounds deeply within me, my own heart picks up the rhythm, matching his, beat for beat. My eyes are hot and stinging, glassy now, I can feel an unfamiliar prickle of tears.

"Please, don't go," he whispers. His voice is croaky, hoarse as if he's been shouting or talking for a long time. "Please," he repeats his plea. "Stay... we can work through this. *I* can find a way to work through this." The softness of his voice is hypnotising.

"Can you though? What about the business? What if just having me here causes problems? I know how much I've hurt you," I add, warily.

Placing his finger over my lips to silence me... "Edi, please, I was stupid. It isn't your fault. None of this is your fault. You're brave and kind and courageous. You built a new life for yourself and your children. Who am I to criticise what you did?" I open my mouth to say something, but he just presses more firmly. "I was upset, not at you, but *for* you. What he did... what he did to you... it was unforgivable... but you had courage... you had courage and you moved on. You were strong. Perhaps stronger than you will ever know. You found a way forward, out of that... Hell. A new path. I've no right to judge you or take that away. Please, stay. I'll find a way, find my path. Please stay."

Gently, he strokes the seam of my lips, a signal it's my turn to speak. "Silas... are you sure? I want to stay, more than anything, but you have to be sure." I don't think I was brave *or* courageous, just a desperate mother wanting the best for her children.

The look in his eyes tells me all I need to know. "Jesus... Edi, Honey-bee; do you ever think about yourself? *Christ*, yes, I couldn't *be* more, sure. Stay... please stay... stay for me, if not for you. You found the courage once... find it again. Find the courage to fly... like the bees... find the courage to fly. No more secrets?"

"Like the bees... yes, they need courage to fly." He gets it. Oh, the sheer relief - it's incredible. A huge weight has been lifted. I feel lighter somehow. "Yes, I'll stay, but there's still a lot more I need to explain." He needs to know everything to fully understand me.

Gratitude and calm flood through me all at once. Unable to resist I collapse into him and seek out his mouth. His tears are damp on his cheeks. Releasing my hands, he enfolds me in his arms, deepening the kiss. His own relief, is to me, so palpable and profound.

Pulling away, he wipes his eyes using the sleeve of his sweater. "Look at me, I'm a fucking mess." He tries to reassure me with a laugh. "Christ on a bike, I thought I'd lost you. I couldn't believe what a prick I was last night. As soon as I got outside, I wanted to come back, but I knew you wouldn't want me there. So, I went home. Bear gave me such a hard time all night. Even he knew I was being a jerk!" He's clinging on to me for dear life, rubbing his face in my hair. I can feel the strength of his heartbeat against my chest. It's comforting.

"Silas, it's okay. I understand. I'm a lot to deal with, my history, my baggage. I get it." He's the one who needs reassurance now. "We'll get through it. I've more to tell you, but you need to be able to cope with it, not have a meltdown every time I reveal a bit more about my sordid past." Clinging to his chest, I squeeze him tightly, as hard as I possibly can.

It's hard to believe after just one week this man has secured his place firmly under my skin and in my life. I can't resist him and I don't want to.

He rears away from me, puffing out his cheeks. "I want to hear it all… all of it, all of your story. I don't care how bad it is. I know there's more, I know I'll struggle with it, but I need to hear it, and you need someone to listen."

He's right. I need to expel the demons once and for all. I've bottled it up for far too long.

"I could tell you more if you really want to hear it, but what terrifies me is you might not understand, or even like me once you discover how incredibly weak and feeble, I was... *am, even.*"

"I want to hear what you have to say, but right now... I just want to put last night behind us. Can I take you home? I need to get closer, and I can't do that here."

I know what he means. He needs us to be physically intimate, it's his way of erasing all the crap from last night.

"Okay." There's no doubt, I need it too. I need warmth and safety; he can give that to me.

"Come on. I'm skriking like a big girl for fucks sake." He gives his face a rough brush with his palms and sniffs a couple of times. Pulling his t-shirt down he takes hold of my hand and leads me out of the office. "Bear, come," he commands and obediently Bear follows his master. I think I would follow him too in this moment. I would follow him to Timbuktu, if he'll just believe in me.

I do so want to tell him. For once I need to take a leap of faith, brave the choppy waters and treacherous rocks below. Have courage to fly, share my secrets....

Chapter 37

This time we don't go back to the apartment. Silas drives us out of the village and into the lush countryside. It doesn't take long, about fifteen minutes and before I know it, we're pulling off the road and into the shale driveway of an old converted barn.

"Wow! Is this yours too?" It's beautiful. There's a clear distinction between the old and new parts of the building. The new section has been sympathetically grafted onto the side of the old, effectively extending the place to almost double the size, giving the building an 'L' shaped appearance from the outside.

"Yep, all mine... and his of course." He jerks his thumb at Bear, who's desperate to be let out of the car. "There's about four acres of land with it, so most of what you see is mine. I built the extension and renovated the inside. It was a project after the divorce, it gave me a purpose. Come and have a look." I can hear the pride in his voice. I'm not surprised. I'd be proud too if I had the skill to create such a stunning home.

The property stands on an incline, while the house itself stands in a copse, the elevated position takes advantage of the panoramic view of the surrounding countryside. It's quiet and a bit isolated. There are no other properties visible, no close neighbours and the length of the driveway ensures the house is secluded from the main road, which isn't very busy either. Silas obviously values his solitude and privacy, and I can't blame him for that.

He leads me inside, through a tiled hallway, the cream painted walls are festooned with what appear to be family photographs, but I don't get a chance to look at them properly before I'm guided into the main living room.

Part of the old barn, apparent from the high vaulted, beamed ceiling, a mezzanine has been sympathetically added at one end; I can see from down here, it's been set up as a library.

Below, the lounge is warmly furnished in an array of autumn shades. There's a selection of worn rustic furniture and a couple of large antique rugs protect the original oak parquet flooring. Oak and glass double doors separate the lounge from a large country kitchen. A reclaimed railway sleeper has been used to create the mantle over the inglenook fireplace - which is also holds an array of framed photographs - The brick hearth is scorched from years of burning logs. It's stunning, and such a contrast to the apartment; this is much more a home.

Bear bounds in and quickly finds his bed in the kitchen. He's snuggled down and snoring before I even know it. This dog loves his comfort!

"Come with me." Without hesitating, he takes hold of my hand. Silas leads me through the kitchen and out into the back garden.

Nestled in amongst a the copse of trees and shrubs are three wooden out-buildings. There's a workshop or garage, an office and what appears to be a large wooden shed.

"In here…" He leads me into the one that looks like a shed. It's not a shed…

The instant we're inside, Silas is removing his clothes. Peeling off his shirt he hangs it on a peg on the wall. He points at me, waiving his finger up and down my body, indicating I should get naked too. I don't hesitate, dragging off my tee-shirt and hanging it on the nearest peg. Then I sit on the wooden bench and take off my shoes, socks and wrestle with my skinny jeans.

Silas is already down to his boxers. I can't help but admire all the tight, rippling muscles in his back as he fiddles with the switches on the wall. I'm unable to draw my appreciative eyes away from that magnificent, physical work of art.

He turns to face me; I'm stood as naked as the day I was born, without a hint of shyness. His beholden glare is intoxicating. I'm totally exposed but for some reason, it feels completely natural.

I can tell he approves; likes it even, but I'm completely transfixed by his physicality. The man is a perfect specimen if ever I saw one. His lips twitch into a knowing smile, as he peels his boxers down his bulging thighs. This guy must have played rugby in the past. Nobody gets thighs like that without a few encounters with the oval ball!

Silas takes a large stride and his solid body is just inches from mine. Teasingly, the tip of his standing erection brushes against my midsection. He towers over me. Without heels, I must be at least fourteen inches shorter than him, I feel really tiny in comparison.

"Let's relax and take in some heat." Leaning down, he kisses me tenderly before removing a couple of fluffy white towels from a hamper. Unlatching the pinewood door, he ushers me into the sauna.

Heightened by the sudden confines of this small, claustrophobic room, my senses - smell, taste, touch, sight and sound are all intensified. The ambient lighting glows a dim red and my nasal passages are immediately invaded by the pungent aroma of hot damp pinewood, intermingled with the fresh, minty, slightly medicinal vapour of eucalyptus. Overpowering both of these scents though, is the dry almost acrid smell of burning charcoal. My skin becomes sensitive and my eyes begin to prick as they grow accustomed to the intense heat.

Silas shakes the folds from the towels and spreads them out so they cover the benches. There are two levels and Silas climbs onto the higher one, taking a seat on the towel and resting his back against the wooden wall. Aware that the higher up I go, the hotter it will become, I'm not quite as brave. So, plumping for the cooler option, I plonk myself gingerly on the bench below, sitting between his lovely feet and resting my head on the inside of his thigh.

I'm still struggling with watery eyes and not yet acclimatised to the dry heat, when Silas, picks up the ladle and spills a bowlful of cold water over the glowing embers. The coals begin to pop, sizzle and hiss in protest, sending a cloud of steaming vapour surging from the grate.

Bracing myself for the inevitable blast, I vie to relax as the steam creeps around my shoulders like some unholy, invisible demon from Hell, singeing my skin with fiery fingers. Over my neck it goes, gliding down my arms, skimming my back before finally swathing me completely from head to foot in a blanket of intense, stifling heat. I close my eyes and concentrate hard on adjusting to the cloying atmosphere.

Gradually, the oppressiveness subsides and I become accustom to the increase in temperature. My heaving lungs grow less desperate and I can breathe easier. They no longer burn with the overpowering scent of eucalyptus, and with that relief comes a feeling of utter relaxation and calm. Steadily, any tension melts away and my bones begin to heat, warming me from the inside. It's utter bliss.

Sensing my relaxation, Silas lowers his hands and firmly massages my shoulders. His strong fingers glide over my damp skin with ease; I roll my neck, hearing the small bones crackle as the tension releases. Circling my throat with his hands, he squeezes and kneads, and slowly his touch travels down my chest until he's unashamedly massaging my breasts. I rest my head between his thighs and give him full access to my sweaty body.

"Hmmm, that feels amazing." My voice has a strange echoing sound in the confines of the small wooden room.

"Yeah, your breasts feel amazing," he hisses, reinforcing his words with a firm squeeze and a pinch of my nipples for good measure. The sharp twinge resonates in my groin.

Wrapping my arms round his calves I start to reciprocate the massage; tracing long soft strokes, up and down his lean lower legs, stroking his feet, pushing my fingers between his toes before retracing my fingers back up his shins. Deliberately I feel every sinew and taught muscle in his calves until my hands are resting on his knees. I can feel the muscles in his legs tensing and relaxing at my touch.

Unable to resist any longer, I twist my torso so I'm sat sideways on my bench. Here I can reach up and gently caress his thighs. His legs are hard, solid muscle. The definition of his quads is fascinating. The perfect outline of each individual muscle clearly defined. I trace round each one with the tips of my eager fingers.

I'm level with his abdomen and sitting between his spread legs there's no avoiding his massive erection. It stands high and proud, revealing his heavy balls resting on the bench beneath.

He's stopped massaging my breasts now; submitting to my ministrations he slowly exhales and reclines, resting his hands over the top of his thighs and spreading his fingers. His head is tipped back, leaning against the wooden wall, his hooded eyes closed in anticipation, he's soaking up my tender touch. His breathing is deep and steady, and his smooth dark skin is gleaming with a light layer of perspiration.

Pooling at the hollow of his throat, a wayward trickle of sweat breaks free and trickles down the centre of his chest. I watch its journey, following the plains of his muscles, between his pecs, a bumpy course as it surfs the waves of his rippling abs; down, down, until it stops just above his navel, trying to decide which path to take, left or right?

Seeing this my eager tongue involuntarily licks the salt from my lips and before I know what I'm doing, I'm kneeling up on my bench, lapping eagerly at the glistening stream of warm sweat. I hear him groan, low in his throat. I feel his stomach muscles tense at the lash of my tongue on his taught skin.

Encouraged by his reaction, I teasingly trail my tongue up the centre of his body, tracing a path until I'm at his throat. He lets

426

out a strangled moan as I flick my tongue into the crevice of his collarbone and lick at the puddle of perspiration which has gathered in the hollow. Then I reverse direction, licking and kissing all the way, sparing a moment to suck hard on each of his dark hard nipples, pulling them between my teeth and flicking them with my tongue, before continuing on my pleasant expedition southward. Back down I go, between the mounds of his bulging pecks, over his slab-like abs, until I reach his navel. I swirl my tongue round the outer rim a few times, just teasing before plunging my tongue into the shallow divot of his belly button. The noise he makes is sensual and animalistic.

The light smattering of hair tickles my lips as I trace them back and forth over his taught skin. Then, satisfied that I've licked his torso clean of every drop of sweat, I continue on downwards, following the line of fine stubble that creates a guiding pathway directly to his trimmed pubic hair.

Resting my lips lightly on his flat abdominals, I nip at the firm, tight flesh of his stomach; the sensitive under-belly where the nerves are most receptive to my butterfly kisses. My hands are resting over his, atop his thighs, our fingers gently entwined. My hair is brushing across the ultra-sensitive skin, causing the muscles of his belly to undulate and ripple, I can tell he wants to delve his hands into my hair, but I restrain him from doing so, keeping my own hands firmly over his. It only increases his desperation to turn the tables and take control. As much as I would like him to, my determination to follow this through on my terms wins and reluctantly, he concedes.

I pull my mouth away and look at the magnificent sight in front of me. His erection is pulsing; resting on his stomach, a tower of throbbing, engorged, silken, flesh, desperate to be touched.

"Edi," his voice is husky, no doubt due to the dryness of the air surrounding us. "Take it." He doesn't move his head, but his eyes are challenging me to defy him. I won't, he knows I need to

427

taste him as much as he needed to taste me yesterday. "Take it deep," he demands. "Now!

Encircling his base with my right hand, I cup the fingers of my left round his balls and squeeze. I'm not gentle. He gasps and winces but doesn't stop me. Flashing him a cheeky smile, I stick out my tongue and claim my first delicious taste. Taking my time, licking a long, firm line from base to tip, I flick my tongue over the glans and push my tongue against the slit.

He jumps. "Aghhh, *fuck!*"

His fist instinctively grabs my hair. His grip is tight and harsh, but along with his vocal responses, it only serves to spur me on.

Increasing the pressure with my tongue and striking a few firm flicks across his glossy head I begin my exquisite torture. A glistening white pearl of pre-cum seeps out of the opening and I paint it over my lips, as if applying a layer of lipstick, coating them with his glossy essence.

Hesitating for the merest of seconds to catch my breath, I part my lips and take him firmly in my mouth, forcing him in, relaxing my jaw, I lower my head, taking him deep into my throat. Tendrils of my damp hair still stick to the tight skin of his lower belly and groin.

The effect on him is instantaneous. "Fucking hell, yeah!" he yells, unrestrained, calling out. His hard body jack-knifes into an involuntary spasm, knocking me backwards and off balance.

Steadying myself, I pull back slightly. My mouth has filled with saliva and it's dribbling down my chin. I wipe it away with my hand, gathering up the sticky liquid, slathering it up and down his shaft, jerking him off, squeezing him tightly, daring him to come.

"Agggghh." He's thrashing about on the bench, desperate not to shoot his load too soon.

Taking pity on him, I slow my jacking fist to allow him some respite from my sensual torment, then take him in my mouth again. This time, I pump my mouth up and down, causing his cock to collide with the back of my throat over and over. Now I have my rhythm, I relax my jaw and take him as deep as I can.

Unable to hold back any longer, his other hand leaves his thigh and rests on the back of my head. His fingers bunch tightly in my hair, tangling in the damp tresses. I pump harder.

"Aaaaah. Yeah, take it, deeper!" He thrusts his hips, forcing himself into my mouth.

My jaw is aching at the sheer girth of him. Jacking my fist, I increase the tempo, taking him deeper every time. And just as I feel him tense, just at the point of his ejaculation, I stop; pausing mid thrust. Stilling my movement, holding him deep in my throat, applying more pressure, tightening the suction, swirling my tongue along his shaft. The effect it produces is profound and exactly what I want.

"Fuck, no, what the Hell!" He's on the brink of explosion, hovering, desperate for release, but my sudden emergency stop has prevented him from tipping the edge. "What, are you doing?... go! Jesus, Edi, I'm about to come... move, finish it, go!"

He's cursing and frantic; I have him just where I want him. His muscles are bulging, his tendons flexed to snapping point but I hold still; prolonging his agony and his eventual pleasure, delaying his release.

Breathing through my nose, I loosen my suction ever so slightly, allowing him to slide back out of my mouth. Saliva coats his cock.

"Oooomyfuckinggoddd." He's struggling, but I keep every movement slow and precise.

"Shhh, Boss-man… My game, my rules… You. Will. Wait." I punctuate each word with a pump of my fist and a lick of my wicked tongue.

"Jeezus…!" Sensing that he's beginning to calm, I decide he's ready for phase two.

Clamping my lips tighter and shielding my teeth, I push down, keeping the pressure firm. A delectable, delicious, slow descent; in he goes, deep into my throat, until his tip is only just grazing the back; then I swallow… the action sends him into shuddering trembling seizure, but still, I don't let him come, pinching the base of his dick to control it.

"Pahhh, aggh, grrr!"

He's wildly incoherent. Watching him fall apart is incredible. It empowers me. This giant of a man, is turning into a primal, Neanderthal being. His movements are involuntary, his head is rolling against the wall, his hands are tight fists of iron, tugging and yanking at my hair in an effort to get as deep as he can. His legs are thrashing, jerking pistons. Every single muscle and nerve, seems alive, like a hundred writhing, living creatures squirming beneath his ebony skin.

Slowly, and deliberately, I draw back again, releasing him from my mouth with a slurping, resounding pop. A ribbon of saliva strings from my lips to the tip of his penis. Gathering it up and coating my palm, I slide my hand around him, pumping my fist hard, down his shaft, colliding with my other hand as it squeezes and pulls at his turgid sack.

"Hell, I'm coming, Jesus, Edi, fuck, I'm gonna come so hard."

Brilliant; he's exactly where I want him. Releasing his ball sack, I extend my pinkie finger. In his thrashing movement, he's shifted down the bench so the rose of his anus is exposed to me. As I place my mouth once more over his pulsing head, I stab my pinkie-finger into his arse, knuckle deep. His yell of surprise is replaced by a primal scream of utter ecstasy as he slides further down the bench giving me better access to his tight ring.

Taking this as affirmation he's okay with what I'm doing to him, I firmly massage his prostate, while at the same time, I suck hard on his dick. Then, in a triumphant finale, I slam him so deep into my mouth that he collides with the back of my throat. It's the last straw, he can't take any more and the dam breaks.

"Aghhh," he screams as he ejaculates.

It's a spectacular explosion. An eruption. A violent, spurting volcano of red, hot lava into my mouth. With every pump of cum, I prod with my finger again and again, causing more of his salty semen to release, massaging him through his climax, completely emptying his sack of his seed, milking him dry.

"Aghhh, Yesses! Fuucckk! Yeah!" he yells as I remove my finger, and slowly but gently slide him from my mouth and lift my head.

His essence is dribbling from my lips, I lick it away and swallow, hungrily, wiping the last drips away with the back of my hand.

Take that Mr Tudor!

"Christ all mighty, that was the best head I've ever had," he pants hauling me up so I'm sat between his legs on his bench. "Fucking hell, I'm shaking." He holds out his hand, demonstrating the effect my epic B.J. has had on him. He's panting and sweating, not just from the sauna. I can feel the tremors still pulsing through his body. Wrapping me tightly in his arms, he says, "fuck, I'm wiped out. I owe you some serious attention, but I don't think I can move."

"That'll teach you… now you know how I felt on Saturday night!"

Smug and wholly satisfied with my performance, I know that was one of my best.

431

What can I say? Of all the times I've had sex, giving head was preferable to having *him* inside me It meant I had a modicum of control. I perfected my technique and used it as a defence mechanism. If *he* wanted sex, I gave him head instead and I was careful to make it good. I never, ever enjoyed it – not until now at least. It was a complete revelation to me that I would ever enjoy it, but watching Silas, as he fell apart, knowing I was the reason... well, that was just awesome.

"I don't even want to know how you got that good," Silas pants in my ear. "Just promise me that you won't *ever* do that to anyone else." It's a demand I'm happy to comply with, but it reminds me of my own discovery yesterday.

"Only if you don't," I whisper back. The thought of him pleasuring other women is sickening.

"You want exclusivity, you can have it. We only have sex with each other from now on." That wasn't what I meant... I haven't had sex with anyone else in years and have no intention of doing so in the foreseeable future. I can't imagine I'd want to be with anyone else anyway, but if he needs to commit to me in that way, I'll accept it for however long it lasts.

"Can we just be as we're? I'm new to this. I know I'm a grown up and everything, but I feel like I'm only just learning to enjoy it. Physical intimacy wasn't... *pleasant*. I developed a talent for head, but only ever as self-preservation. Would you be surprised to know that you gave me my first ever orgasm?" I correct myself quickly, adding "I mean, with another person. I've had one before, but I was alone..." I'm embarrassed revealing this but at the same time, I'm coming alive. My inhibitions are melting away. I've never felt this kind of chemistry. Perhaps I'm hormonal! Who am I kidding? Making light of these burgeoning feelings isn't going to wash.

"Seriously? I would never have known." He's shocked and he looks sceptical. "You seemed to enjoy yourself well enough on Saturday." I'm not sure he believes me.

Planting a kiss on the top of my head, his hand travels up and down my spine in a tender caress. "I'm not opposed to experimenting… are you?"

"No, I want to. And I want to do it with you." I really do want to explore this new and wonderful sensuality he's awakened in me. With him, its different. It's like I never knew what my body was capable of.

"Christ on a bike…" He says again. "I can't move. One last ladle of water and we will call it quits for the sauna tonight. Okay?"

"Okay," I say tentatively.

Reaching over, he ladles another bowl of water over the dying embers. I brace myself for the fiery finger demon, but this time I'm ready for the creeping heat and embrace it. Reclining, so my back is against his chest, I allow the invisible dragon to envelop me in his sizzling embrace.

Chapter 38

After we shower and dress, Silas brews a pot of tea. I feel refreshed and cleansed. My face is glowing, red and shiny, but I don't care. We've settled our differences, relaxed and comfortable in each-others company, snuggled together on the over-stuffed sofa in the lounge. Bear has woken up and is chewing on a squeaky toy. Every chew delivers a painful squawk from the abused rubber chicken.

"What would you like to do for the rest of the afternoon?" he asks out of the blue. I know what I'd like to do, but I may have scuppered that when I drained him dry earlier!

"Err…" I don't get to finish.

"Let's go to the pub," he announces. "It's only…" pausing, he looks at his watch "*Christ*… it's two o'clock. Let's forget I was a prize Pillock yesterday and go and get pissed. What do you say?" He's still smarting from his diva behaviour… interesting.

"Okay. But only if I can have a fish-finger sandwich." Yawning, I agree. And anyway, I could do with some food.

"And then, can I request a sleepover? My place?" He raises his eyebrows in askance. *Ah, promising!*

"My place is your place," I remind him.

"It is, but *this* place is also *my* place, and *this* place has… possibilities." *Possibilities?* "Come on, let's go. We'll leave the cars and walk. If you're going to spill the beans, I need some fresh air and a couple of pints first."

I'm not going to argue with that. Any bean spilling will require Dutch courage; for me to tell it and for him to hear it.

"Bear, come." Bear instantly drops his toy and my ears are instantly relieved. He bounds to the back door where his lead is hanging from a hook. Silas grabs it as we pass, leading us both out into the mellow summer afternoon.

Holding his hand seems natural and right. I love how his fingers entwine with mine. Strolling along the leafy lane beside the canal, on our way to the pub, I've been miles away, completely immersed in all thoughts of Silas, how his body glistened and writhed in the sauna less than an hour ago.

His deep throaty baritone brakes into my daydream. "This is how I want to do this."

"Hmmm?" I force myself back to reality, breathing in the heady perfume of the dog-daisies and wild garlic growing abundantly along the edge of the towpath.

He's been thoughtful for about ten minutes and it sounds like he's got a 'cunning' plan. "I will ask you a question, and you will answer; but only if you feel comfortable. If I ask the wrong question at the wrong time, tell me and I'll ask another until I ask one that you feel you can answer. Do you think that will work?"

It's a simple approach to a complicated problem. "Yes, I think I can do that, Silas."

I *can* do that. It will prolong the agony somewhat, drag the process out, but the end result will be the same. He'll know and then, *I'll* know... if he can still want me; designer baggage and all!

We chose a table on the periphery of the beer garden, out of earshot of the other patrons. The pub is buzzing, typical of a Sunday afternoon in the countryside. Silas chooses to sit beside me, his hand resting on my thigh, turning his body away from the rest of the customers, shielding me from the crowd, giving me his full attention.

We both have a pint of the guest ale. It's a pleasant hoppy, local brew and it's going down well. Bear is secured, the loop of his lead threaded through the table leg. At least the ducks and swans are safe today.

Eventually, Silas clears his throat. "I'm not sure what to ask, now I've free rein." I just sit and allow him to find a question.

Stroking my leg, he seems to be concentrating on how to approach this. Little does he know the chances of me answering are slim, so I just wait. He seems nervous, I don't know why. I'm shitting myself!

"Okay, I've got one." He clears his throat. "When you left... when you went away, how did you remain hidden? How come they didn't find you?"

Ah, that's a fair question... I can answer this one... I grip his hand for courage and take a cleansing breath.

"Well," I stutter as I recall the horrid events of the day that led to me leaving my home, "the physical leaving part was... difficult." I frown at the painful memory. "I'd already packed my bags, prepared to go but I didn't for a minute think I would ever leave him. I had nowhere to go, you see. Then, that day it all went to shit." There's no other way to call it. It went completely, irrecoverably to shit!

Swallowing, I take another deep breath then a long pull on my pint. "I'll explain the shit part later. But you asked *how* I disappeared... strangely, that was the easy part." He's listening, intently. "The first night, I just checked into a Travelodge. Money wasn't an issue. My Grandmother had left me some cash. Not a huge amount but it was substantial enough, if I was careful." In all honesty, my meagre inheritance literally saved my life, without it, I'm sure I wouldn't be here now. "It's surprising what a bit of hair-dye and some charity shop clothes can camouflage."

"Without the external armour of make-up and designer clothes, I was just another single mum. The plainer I looked, the less attention I attracted. I deliberately put on weight; stopped the personal grooming and became scruffy, indistinct and invisible. It was a brilliant but simple disguise. I just blended in with the crowd."

Pause and breathe Edi – he's all ears, quiet but thoughtful. Keep going!

"Finding somewhere to live was a bit more problematic. I couldn't stay in Manchester that was for certain so, eventually, I moved to The Midlands. I used some of my inheritance to buy a small flat. It wasn't in a great area, but it was cheap and cheerful and for the first time I was free to do as I pleased. That's where we stayed for the first five years. That's where I had David."

I know I've oversimplified, and he'll know too. In truth, the first few months were horrendous; I was in constant fear of being recognised but he doesn't need the gory details, just the facts.

"So, you were pregnant when you left?" He's intrigued.

Summoning more courage, I continue. "Yeah," that was a sad time, "but because I was deliberately getting fatter, I didn't realise it. When I finally did, I didn't dare go to the doctors. I couldn't risk being recognised, so I just ignored it and got on with things." I was stupid, naïve and terrified. "I didn't have any anti-natal appointments and I didn't have any scans, but I knew with absolute certainty I was pregnant… the exact day; *hah…* how's that for stupid?" I laugh in derision at the bitter memory; "even down to the very minute of conception, so I could estimate my due date pretty accurately."

"Jesus!" It's his turn to take a deep draft of beer. Checking over his shoulder to ensure we're still unobserved, he leans closer.

"Yeah, I know, I was foolish." My turn to drink. The beer helps.

"So, what happened next?" It's as if I'm telling a story about a stranger… and he's engrossed.

"Well, I went into labour early. About six weeks early by my reckoning and I immediately regretted not visiting a doctor or hospital. I knew something wasn't right. The pains were excruciating and far too frequent. It was completely different to before… to when I had Lizzy, you know… just so different. My waters broke, but they were pink and bloody. I panicked but luckily, I had a really good neighbour. An older woman who had become a good friend, a bit of a surrogate auntie - She would babysit occasionally when I was working, and if I had an afternoon shift at the shop, she would pick Lizzy up from nursery for me - I managed to knock on her door." I owe Gloria so much, she undoubtedly saved mine and David's lives that day. "She rang for an ambulance and I was rushed into hospital, just in time as it happens. The baby was breach and in distress." It was a frightening time and I shudder at the vivid memory. Silas tenderly places his hand over mine, offering comfort and encouragement. He can see this is difficult for me. "I needed an emergency C-section. When I came out of the anaesthetic, they explained that David was in the special care baby unit. He had some problems because he was so small - breathing difficulties - and he was placed on a ventilator. I was only able to see him from a distance at first. I was too sore to take it all in properly, and he was too poorly for me to hold." Strangely, my scar tissue twinges as if to remind me it's there. I give my tummy a rub.

"Go on, if you want to… take your time," he encourages kindly.

Boosted by his support and sincerity, I press on… "I was distraught. My daughter was placed with foster parents; I was guilt ridden, both about that and the certainty I had caused David's problems because of my selfishness at not visiting a doctor during my pregnancy."

This is hard to talk about but I need to do it… "When I was physically fit enough to go home, I had to leave David in the hospital. He was still too little and needed to be in an incubator. I felt as if I was abandoning my baby. The separation anxiety was overwhelming. I still had no idea that he was Downs; nobody told me, not one nurse or doctor. Not one specialist. I had no idea, he just looked like a perfect little bundle to me." I smile at the vivid recall, the beep, beep, beep of the machines and antiseptic smell of the hospital and the tiny visible shock of red hair. It's as clear now as it was then.

"While Lizzy was at nursery, I visited the hospital. Every day. I expressed milk and watched as he was fed through a tube. I felt helpless, returning home every evening to take care of my other child, before repeating the process all over again the next day. But then, after a couple of weeks, I was allowed to hold him for the first time. It was wonderful... It was only when they unhooked him from all the wires and tubes, I saw his little face fully. I knew instantly he had Downs. It was as clear as could be and, while I was shocked, I was immediately, unconditionally in love with him. He was beautiful."

Hot, scalding, tears are running down my face. It surprises me, I haven't shed a tear for years. I chose to develop an armour. A coping mechanism, so strong that externally I'm almost without emotion. I was happy for people to think I was cold and aloof. It meant they didn't get too close.

Silas remains silent, allowing me to gather myself together. He just cups my cheek tenderly and brushes the tears away with his thumb. It's a comforting gesture. Sniffing, I melt in to his touch. He doesn't speak, just sits, holding my face, staring into my eyes, silently willing me to continue. God, knows what the other customers must be thinking!

Encouraged, I find the strength to carry on. "I loved him, but I couldn't accept him... I was only just nineteen. I still felt like a child myself, despite everything I'd done. I already had one child depending on me and now I had another; one who's problems and needs were considerable. I didn't know what to do, what it meant. I was terrified, overwhelmed by my feelings to think logically. Would you believe, I even considered going back to Manchester?"

I'm sobbing freely now, unable to control my tears, my emotions getting the better of me. "I held him and cared for him.

Fed, changed and sang to him. But deep inside, I was in turmoil, trying to hide my growing anguish from everyone in case they thought I was useless and unable to cope," I snort out a sarcastic laugh at the irony. "I brought him home at six weeks, the day he was due to be born. They gave me some literature about special care babies and told me the health visitor would call on me the following week. I felt so alone."

My voice has reduced to a whisper. "Lizzy was an angel, she loved her little brother unconditionally, which only heightened my misery. I had no idea how I was going to care for this precious little boy. But underneath the worry, my resentment was there too. My feelings were so mixed that I couldn't sleep, couldn't eat. I didn't wash or care for myself. My whole life revolved around my children, and I cared for them as best as I could." I take a deep breath. I need to continue this, no matter how difficult it is. Silas holds my hands in his, giving them a reassuring squeeze. "The health visitor came to visit me the following week. If she was at all shocked by my appearance, she didn't say anything. The baby was thriving. My daughter was surpassing all her milestones, but I was suffering. I know now, it was post-natal depression; but then, I was ignorant, I had no clue."

Inhaling, I count to five as I take a deep cleansing breath. Lifting my head, I look deeply into his troubled eyes, taking solace from what I see there; compassion, understanding, empathy even… I resolve to tell it all. Even the darkest and most difficult part.

I clear my throat and rub my hands over my face, buying some well-needed time.

"We'd been home for about a month. I wasn't coping at all but I struggled on. He wouldn't stop crying. It was relentless, day and night. And I didn't know what to do, how to soothe him, how to help him; this tiny little baby who had been given to *me* to look after." Patting my chest with the palm of my hand in emphasis, I'm conscious my voice has risen. Looking round anxiously, I see a couple of people glancing our way. I dip my head and recompose myself, forcing myself to use a softer tone. "I was at my wits end, desperate, a walking zombie. I was barely functioning. Sleep was impossible, food would choke me so I stopped eating. I don't expect you to understand any of this... I barely understand my actions, now I look back."

My brain is in turmoil with the frantic need to purge itself of my most shameful secrets. I've smashed down the walls of a dam and now I can't stem the flow of words surging from my mouth. I don't expect him to understand, but I realise I'm desperate for his acceptance.

Compelled to continue, I go on... "I *really* didn't know what I was doing. My mind couldn't find a single positive thought; I couldn't see a way through it, this was it for the rest of our lives and I was only *nineteen!*" Repeating it, shaking my head in annoyance at myself; what difference did my age make? I don't know, but I feel the need to stress the point. "My daughter was safe at nursery. I was on auto-pilot. I put him in his cot. As usual he was screaming. I ran a bath. I got in. I took a razorblade and cut my wrist." Closing my eyes at the sickening image, forging forward, I need to finish this. "Gloria, my old neighbour, concerned at David's persistent crying found me; she had a key, so she let herself in. I woke up in hospital... I owe her my life." And David's. Without a shadow of doubt if it hadn't been for Gloria, I wouldn't be here today.

Silas opens his mouth to speak but I hold up my hand to stop him, I'm almost there and I can't stop now...

"They said it was touch and go for a few hours. I had several blood transfusions. The nurses treated me like a pariah. David and my daughter were put into care, but I was oblivious. I was detained under the mental health act. It was only when I was being assessed for release, I eventually received the counselling I so desperately needed. I was given cognitive therapy. I had to attend daily sessions with a specialist. Honestly, it really helped. Gradually, I recovered... though, it took weeks, months even. Once I was discharged from the mental health facility, I was allocated a place in a mother and baby support unit. My daughter remained in care, but they brought her to visit me daily. She would protest so loudly at home time that, eventually, they allowed her to stay with me too".

"We lived there for six months while I recovered and received support in relation to David's downs syndrome. It was the best support I'd ever had. They were truly amazing. Finally, I was given proper advice and the right kind of help. I realised that I wasn't mad, or bad, or crazy, just very, very depressed. It took time, but eventually, we returned to our tiny flat, where we were able to start our little life together as a family." I exhale, the relief is profound. Suddenly I'm much calmer – I'm nearly there for this revelation. Silas holds his tongue, allowing me to finish.

"The bumble bees have a dual purpose. After I'd recovered and could reflect, I needed to have something significant to remind me I'd been down at rock bottom, but I'd got through it. The worker bee is the symbol of Manchester, my city, and resonant for me... hard work and all that... Did you know it's a myth that aerodynamically, they shouldn't be able to fly? There was a study made in the 1930's. Bees actually use a figure of eight motion that gives them lift. Slowed down it looks like they're painting the infinity symbol in the air... though the small bees do need courage. Their resilience just spoke to me, it was the right design for my ink. Not only do they hide my scars, they represent the people who mean the most to me in my life - It's that simple - Mum, Dad, Lizzy, David, Gran and of course, Gloria. And all of them except the children, sadly gone... *all*."

There... it's said. Now he knows. Remaining silent, he takes hold of my wrist and removes my new watch. Tracing his fingers over the delicate tattoo, he touches each bee lightly, before moving on to the next, counting the tiny yellow insects. All the way round my wrist he goes before resting his finger in the gap where the circle doesn't meet. Where his lips have created a purple bruise.

"What does this mean?" he asks softly, curious.

"I think you know," I whisper. "It means there's space for one more significant person in my heart and my life… just one… but that person needs to be… a mighty force to fill that void."

"I'm working on it," is his surprising reply.

"Good…" is mine. I've only known him a week, but I can't imagine not having him around. The revelation both thrills and scares me to death. But I'm very aware he may not have the same feelings for me. Why would he?

"Do you want another drink?" He pulls me back to the present with the bland question. *Do I want another drink?* "Perhaps something stronger?"

"Yeah, yes please. I'd love a whiskey." I may as well. The hard liquor will help soothe my shattered nerves.

"Grouse ok?" he asks as he stands from the bench and picks up our empty pint glasses. Bear sits up expectantly – I'd almost forgotten about him.

"Perfect. Thank you." He knows I'm not just thanking him for the offer of some amber nectar, I'm thanking him for listening and not judging.

Leaning in, he lands an unexpected kiss on my lips. "No worries, Honey-bee… I'll just be a tick." And off he goes, into the pub.

Absentmindedly, I scratch Bear's soft head. He leans against my leg panting gently, his silky fur keeping me warm on one side. The late afternoon air is cooling and I can feel the goose pimples rising on my other leg.

A few minutes later and Silas is back with our drinks. He's succumbed to the hard stuff too. He's also brought us a couple of baguettes, ham for him, cheese for me. It's not a fish finger sandwich, but with the warm crusty bread, local crumbly cheese and homemade chutney, it is a very close second. I tuck in gratefully. Who knew that confessions make you hungry? The bread gives a satisfying crunch as I take a welcome bite.

As the warm afternoon descends into a balmy evening, we sip our drinks and chat, mainly about our likes and dislikes; just two people shooting the breeze. Silas imparts some more details and plans for the business, I tell him more about Lizzy and David. It's a companionable conversation after the intensity of my confession, and is very welcome.

He has a strange ability to make me feel comfortable. By the time we've watched the beautiful sunset and the sky's grown to a dark navy blue, we're swaying and giggling.

With some of my darkest and heaviest secrets released, I feel lighter somehow. The whiskey buzz of our last four drinks has taken the edge off and Silas has tried out some of his cheesy jokes. I suspect they're Sparks' recycled stories and we're definitely more than just tipsy as we sway along the towpath, towards Silas's barn; luckily Bear, loping ahead of us, knows his way home.

Chapter 39

I'm a little out of breath as we reach the front door of the barn. Silas has his arm draped over my shoulder and mine is round his waist, my thumb hooked through his belt loop. The speed of our walk, had our hips bumping together and that in itself, has stolen my breath. Just touching him in this way sets off a craving I've never felt before... ever.

Unlocking the door, Silas flicks on the light, illuminating the downstairs room. Bear cocks his leg on a tree before entering and making a beeline for his bed in the kitchen. Circling three times before settling down, he tucks his head between his paws, huffs once then closes his eyes.

"Well, that's him in bed!" Silas laughs then turns to face me. "Now it's your turn." Scooping me up, I'm chucked unceremoniously over his shoulder yelping, and before I know where I'm, I'm on my way up the stairs.

Opening the bedroom door, he lowers me to my feet, but doesn't stop to take stock or allow me to gather myself. He just grabs my tee-shirt and pulls it off, over my head. I just stand there and let him. He reaches around my back, unclipping and removing my bra - a smile tickles my lips as I recall how he struggled with the front fastener yesterday - taking only the briefest second to glance at my breasts before unzipping my jeans and dragging them down my legs, along with my underwear. The jeans are skinny, so they halt at my ankles. It means he has to kneel and remove my shoes, before finally, he can rip my jeans off and I'm standing stark naked before him.

No words are spoken. None are needed. He just lifts me so that I'm cradled in his arms and takes me to the bed, lying me down before climbing on top of me, fully clothed.

Kneeing my legs apart, he spreads his weight all over me. I can feel the button fly of his jeans hard against my pubic bone.

Bending my knees so my feet are flat on the bed, I cradle him between my thighs, tilting my pelvis so I can rub against the unyielding denim. Silas is just lying over me, gazing into my eyes.

His hands are cupping the sides of my head, his fingers playing with my hair. "I could look at you forever," he sighs. "You are so beautiful. The more I look, the more beautiful you become."

The feeling is mutual. I could say exactly the same about him. He's stunning. I examine his face in minute detail, noticing for the first time he has a mole just under his left eyebrow. More of a freckle really. It isn't prominent, but close up, I can see it. There's a small scar that runs underneath the rim of his lower lip; I hadn't noticed that before either. And his eyes, oh his eyes… this close, they're a molten gold, flecked with chocolate and amber and the tiny crinkles reveal a life spent laughing and smiling. Lifting my hand, I trace my thumb lightly along the scar under his lip.

"I didn't notice this before." Lifting my head, I kiss it lightly.

"Fell off my bike when I was seven. The brake handle caught me; needed four stiches. They called me Indie, for a while after that," he muses.

"Indie?" I don't get it.

"You know, like Indiana Jones… or I should say Harrison Ford. He has that scar on his chin. Look…" He bites his lower lip, stretching the skin so I can see it more clearly. It really does look the same as Harrison Fords. That must be why he preferers the stubble.

"Ahhhh!" I get it now. I'm still grazing myself slowly against his groin. The friction is soothing and I can feel his solid erection beneath his fly.

"I'm still dressed," he announces, as if I don't know.

"You are."

Pushing back, so he's straddling my thighs, he looks down at me in wonder. "You are so beautiful. I don't think I've ever seen a woman so lovely." His hands are warm as they smooth over my torso. He explores every inch of my skin. I should be embarrassed but I'm not.

"Is Bear your guide dog? I ask, smirking. He must be really short sighted if he thinks I'm that good.

"Yeah, where are you...?" He pats around my body as if he's a blind man feeling his way. "Oh, there you are." He tips forward and kisses me softly.

Sitting back, he continues to explore. Following the line of every rib with his fingers, he stops when he finds a mole and kisses it. Satisfied it's received enough attention, he continues his intimate examination. Long dark fingers are tenderly stroking, featherlike in their touch, tracing up the sides of my ribcage.

"Arms above your head," he instructs me caressing the sensitive skin of my armpits, then my underarms, along my forearms and to my hands, ending with my fingertips. Everywhere he touches me, has my skin tingling in response.

Removing his hands from mine, he takes hold of his belt buckle and undoes it. Slowly, without taking his eyes off mine he draws it through the keeper, removing it altogether. He finishes by snapping it out of the belt-loops. The leather cracks like a whip causing my breath to hitch and Silas to smile knowingly.

Bending forward, an unasked question in his eyes, he hovers above me. Gently, he wraps the belt round my wrists. He's still unsure as he loops the loose end around the slatted wooden headboard. I confirm my acceptance with a muted groan. He's sure now, so he quickly ties off the buckle; checking it isn't too tight by running his little finger under the worn leather, in the small space between my wrist and the belt.

447

"Comfortable?" he smirks as I writhe beneath him.

"No…" I tease sulkily.

I'm no longer able to reach his groin to feel the friction because he has moved further down my body, but I still try. Twisting, stretching and turning, heaving his weight around like it's nothing, I'm panting with the effort and in anticipation.

Keeping his eyes locked on mine, he kneels, still straddling my thighs and starts to remove his shirt. One button, then the next, then the next; revealing his magnificent chest inch by beautiful inch. It looks so erotic making me wanton. My desire is building and I feel the hot wetness gathering between my legs. The anticipation is killing me. I can't hold my tongue any longer.

"Silas," I hiss impatiently, through my teeth. I can't take my eyes off him. "Take it off, I want to see you."

Without delay he shrugs off his shirt. Then, expecting him to remove his jeans I'm dumbstruck when he places his large hands over his chest, touching himself, following the same path as he did when he touched me; tracing his muscles, showing off his physique, just for me, taunting me, forcing me to watch him as he pleasures himself. "You like that Honey?" He's moving up and down, undulating with the heaves of my body as I try my best to rub against him.

"Yesses… take it off, take it all off." I demand and he complies.

Unfastening his button fly, he notices a glistening trail on his seam where my juices have left their mark on his jeans. Flattening his hand, he presses over it, cupping himself, gathering my essence. Then, as I stare wantonly, he brings his hand to his mouth and licks straight up the palm. "Mmm, I love the taste of you…" He closes his eyes. Hooking his thumbs into the waistband of his jeans he lowers them down his legs until they're stretched tightly around his thighs. The unyielding denim is stiff and the position in which he's balanced over me has the coarse material digging into my legs, trapping me, holding me down, so I can't move at all.

He's wearing tight, white boxers. Leaning over to the side and stretching one leg, he kicks himself free of his jeans. It's a relief. There's a red band on my thighs, where the pressure has marked my skin. Quickly, he stands to remove his boxers and once he's naked, he crawls back over me and resumes his straddled position. *God!* He looks fucking magnificent. My mouth begins to water.

"Now then, what shall we do?" He folds his arms across his chest and grips his chin between his thumb and forefinger, tilting his head in contemplation as if he's making a crucial decision, unsure where to start. "I know..." he says, to himself, tapping the side of his face with his index finger before stroking it over the scar under his lip. He shifts towards me, crawling over my hips, up my chest until he's hovering above my upper torso. "I'm going to fuck your tits!" He announces with a decisive nod and devilish grin.

"What!" I blurt, kicking my legs on a shocked laugh.

"Yes, I'm going to fuck your tits, then I'm going to eat your sweet, wet, little, cunny, until you squirt all over my face. Then I'm going to fuck it... hard!" He's smug, it's like he has devised a plan of action and is explaining it to a co-conspirator – I suppose he's in a way.

"You're the boss," I whisper with a cheeky grin.

"Yeah, I am. Aren't I the lucky bastard?"

Reaching forward, he tilts his pelvis in my face. If I wasn't trussed up like a medieval sacrifice, I would have his cock in my mouth; but I'm restrained so I can't. He gives me a knowing smile, and I frown at him. Sliding his cock along my breastbone, he makes himself comfortable.

Cupping my tender breasts, he forces them together so they form a pair of soft cushions around his hard dick. His tip pokes out from the top and I can see his stomach tensing as he slides himself, back and forth, through the valley of my cleavage.

"Edi, your tits are so warm and soft. This feels like heaven." I've broken out in a light perspiration. The dampness allows him to glide with ease as he pumps himself, building up a nice level rhythm. "I think I need some lubrication though..." Reaching over into his bedside draw, he pulls out a small travel sized bottle of baby oil. Before I know what's happening, I feel the drip, drip, drip, of the cool aromatic oil on my breasts.

Replacing the oil in the drawer, he resettles himself and pushing my boobs together, he resumes the slick slide through the now well-oiled cleft. He's right, the oil makes it more sensitive and I can feel every vein and ridge as he pumps away freely. His heavy ball sack bumps and grinds along the ridge of my diaphragm; his bristly pubic hair, grazes my chest, setting my nerves tingling and my clit dancing with anticipation.

"Grrr, yeah, Honey-bee." Pump, pump "Yeah." He increases the pressure on my breasts. His big hands are strong, and the vice like grip he has on my boobs is bordering on painful. He watches his glistening, black cock, his hands squeezing my breasts even harder, forcing them together as he tit-wanks himself. My nipples are rigid and screaming out for attention.

"Silas, hard. Squeeze hard," I demand, the sight is thrilling. He looks splendid straddling me, driving his hard, black dick between my soft, pink mounds. He tweaks my nipples between his thumb and forefinger, pinching hard as he glides, back and forth. It doesn't break his rhythm. The harsh treatment of the tender tips, causes the receptors in my groin to twinge in expectation and a trickle of hot fluid leaves my vagina. "Harder," I demand trying to capture that elusive sensation and he doesn't disappoint.

The tight hold he has on my breasts is excruciating, but along with the pain is the erotic image of him working himself up to a huge explosion. The pain becomes pleasurable, building, and the tingling between my legs grows stronger with each squeeze and tweak.

"Fuucckk! Yeah, here it comes, Edi," he yells, and with a final, hard thrust, a fountain of sweet, white, creamy cum erupts from the tip of his dick like a geyser. Spurting into the air, it rains down and covers my chest, my breasts, scorching globules land, dripping onto my face, over my chin, splattering onto my lips.

Greedily, I open my mouth, to catch some of the delicious, salty-sweetness.

"Yeah, take it Honey," he lowers his cock into my mouth so that I can finish the job properly. I suck and lick to my heart's content, my vagina clenching and releasing just at the sheer sounds he's making.

"Mmm, delicious these Mars Bars!" smacking my lips together I joke, as I clean every bit of cum from his mocha skin.

"Really?" he laughs at my cheeky description of his tasty manhood. "I prefer cherry cream drops myself." He's leapt off me and is kneeling between my legs before I can even breathe. Spreading my thighs wide apart. "This one, in particular, is a rare delicacy." Lowering his mouth, he swirls his tongue round the very tip, of my beating clitoris making me flex my hips and cry out. "Mmm, yes, cherry with a hint of honey." Tipping my head back and stretching my neck, I start to groan in ecstasy. He's barely started and I'm already writhing in pleasure.

"Aggh, yes, soooo, *gooood*!" I purr.

"Yes, cherry," … lick … "Honey," … lick… "and cream." His hot tongue plunges deep inside, swirling and lapping at my flowing juices like a connoisseur enjoying a fine wine. "You taste divine, I want to eat you out every day." He forces harder, two fingers spreading the lips of my vulva while his tongue dances and laps at my hot pink flesh. "Honey-bee, feel me, come on, let me hear you." He bites my clit, clamping his teeth round

451

the bud then fluttering his tongue so precisely over the most sensitive part that I cry out.

"Ahhhh…. Yeah, *Oooh!*"

I open my eyes and look down my body. I'm stretched out, every muscle is taught and elongated as I writhe and squirm. My bound wrists are aching and I can't feel my fingers, but the sensation going on down below is so incredible I don't give a dam about my numb arms. "Fuucckk." Unable to stop the filth from coming out of my mouth, I scream demandingly, I want him to fuck me, to violate me, to own me.

I'm beginning to shudder and shake uncontrollably; my climax imminent. Feeling me tense, he knows I'm close so he eases off the pressure and slows his pace until he stops altogether. Lifting his head to give me respite from the intensity, he gently blows a wisp of hot breath directly onto my beating clitoris.

I've recovered a little of my equilibrium. I'm still writhing and panting, but the feeling of imminent explosion has abated slightly. As usual, Silas has perfect timing.

"And back we go," he murmurs, diving straight back into me. After only thirty seconds of relief, he's working me again.

This time he inserts two fingers, hooking them and stroking my inner wall, caressing my G-spot. I lift my hips, trying to escape the pressure, but the tension in my legs and stomach has returned with a vengeance, intensifying the heavy throbbing sensation at the junction of my thighs. Any second now, I'm going to snap.

"Look at that, it's beautiful, so pink and wet." He's so close. "These fingers are fucking you, and I'm going to lick up all that sweet cherry and honey juice, the minute you come." It's filthy talk, sensual and erotic - and fucking amazing. "Come on dirty girl, let's be having you." He rams his fingers high and hard.

"Oooh, Silas, ohmm, I'm coming, Aggh, fingers, gahh, I'm coming!" I warn him, I know this is going to be huge.

"Come on then, what're you waiting for?" He plunges his fingers so deep that I feel his fist against my vulva, then he pumps them; once, twice, three times. He repeats the move again, as he simultaneously clamps his teeth over my clitoris, so sharply it's almost too painful.

That's it, I can't hold on any longer. That last thrust and bite has tipped me over the edge and I'm suddenly free-falling into an abyss of intense pleasure. Oh Lord!! It comes, and comes, and comes. I squirt vaginal juices at the point of release; his loud moans indicate his appreciation and satisfaction as he laps and licks at my river of cum.

The sensitivity is too much. Twisting away I attempt to turn onto my side. Needing to close my legs; needing him to move away from my overused bundle of nerves and allow me to come down. Wrestling against him I start to squirm and moan my discomfort. The muscles in my shoulders are cramping from being locked in one place for so long. I need to move my arms. Now that I've come, all my nerve endings are screaming in protest.

"Silas, please untie me." I croak. He just stays where he is, licking and kissing. "Silas... please, untie me!" panicking at the notion that he might just decide to keep me tethered; I'm ready to kick off big style, when he heaves a huge contented sigh.

Reluctantly, he leaves his position between my thighs and crawls up the bed to sit beside me. He unbuckles my arms in no time at all. My bicep muscles are sore but singing in relief as the blood flows into my forearms and hands. Massaging the life back into my wrists, he smiles as he starts to rub and manipulate my stiff joints. Flexing my fingers and rolling my neck I smile back. "That was unbelievably good," I hum.

"Better?"

"Yes, thank you." I purr like a contented kitten.

"Good!" Before I can say more, I'm flipped over onto my stomach. My hips are lifted so I'm in a downward dog position!

"Ah," I yelp as my face is planted in the soft pillows of his bed. *Slap!* a stinging palm lands on my behind, so swiftly and sharply, I'm not sure if it really happened. *Thwack!* Until it happens again. "Ouch! *What the fuck, Silas!*" I push myself up on all fours, planning to escape from his clutches but I'm restrained and pressed down.

"No, you've been a bad girl, cursing and swearing at me. I think a little spanking will do you good." *Smack, whack, slap!* Three sharp stinging slaps in a row. I don't know whether to be angry or aroused. Then, I feel the head of his huge cock, pressing against my wet slit and I know the answer... arousal has got the better of me.

"Again," I pant, needing to feel the sharp sting. *Slap, slap, slap!!!* Sharper this time "MORE!!" I shout, *where has this desire for pain come from. Thwack, slap, slap!!* "FUCK ME!!" Oh, and he does... The pressure of his enormous erection and the sting from his relentless slapping has me sweating. I lean down and wipe my face over the pillow, drying the trickles of perspiration dripping down my temples. "HARDER!" I yell.

"Jesus, Edi, what's come over you?" *Slam, slam, slam, slam.* He pumps into me with an almost violent force, It's amazing and painful and delicious. "Christ, girl, I can't hold on much longer... do you want it harder?"

"Yesss!" I'm screaming with every blow. "I'm gonna come... Silas... Jeeze... now!" I go limp, dropping forward onto the bed. Silas follows me, his solid chest pressing into my back. The sheer weight of him has the pressure in my groin exploding and I come again. It's a fast fix... not as intense as the last one, but just as pleasurable.

I can't hear myself think; the blood is pounding in my ears so loudly. My heart rate must be up to about a hundred and sixty beats per minute. I may pass out. I'm limp, like a rag doll. All my muscles have turned to jelly and my limbs are far too heavy for me to move them.

I feel, rather than hear Silas' own release, as he pushes one of my legs so it's bent at the knee. He hammers home one last time, filling me up with his cum.

Christ, I can't move. My arse is stinging like a bastard and my vagina is burning from overuse; but good Lord in Heaven, the sensation is one of utter, euphoric rapture. I'm soaring, floating on air, dizzy with the release of both mind and body. I'm cleansed. Silas has replenished my courage to fly.

Chapter 40

A distant buzzing has me stiffening in my semi-conscious state. My ears twitch and I go cold all over. *NO!*

Snapping open my eyes I know a panic attack is imminent. I'm lying on my tummy in a huge bed, tangled and swathed in white and blue linen. The morning sun is forcing distorted shards of yellow light through the slats of the white Venetian blinds. Splicing through the window and onto the bed, they land on my bare skin. One leg is out of the bed and resting on top of the covers. My arms are folded beneath the pillow, my cheek resting on top.

The buzzing stops and relief floods through me. I still haven't moved. I sense shifting and the bed dips. Turning my head to rest my other cheek on the pillow, I find Silas's handsome face looking down at me. He's naked and has a smudge of toothpaste on his bottom lip. "Morning Honey-Bee." He leans down and kisses me on my mouth, sideways. I flip over onto my back and fling my arms round his neck.

"Morning yourself, Boss-man!" I whisper, in what I hope is a seductive voice. Unbelievably, especially after last night's exertions, I feel like I could do with a little morning exercise before work. "Fancy a work-out?" I cheekily grab his dick with my hand, leaving no room for misunderstanding.

"Mmm? Thought you'd never ask." He whips the covers from my naked body and presses me down into the mattress. His hand strokes from my neck, giving my breast a little squeeze on its way to my groin.

He kisses me firmly as he pushes me over so that I'm lying flat, beneath him; the change causing me to lose my grip on his penis. Blindly, I grapple around, seeking it out and eventually he's back in my tight fist. Tenderly, I start to stroke him, encouraging him to grow wider and longer while he gently plays with my clit, flicking and rubbing. I'm wet now so he inserts a finger. "This is a nice surprise." He kisses my mouth.

"Why, Sir? I gasp, "if you will parade around with your goods on display, it would be impolite not to sample them," I mumble through his lips.

"Well, I'd better not disappoint then." He rolls on top and enters me with one graceful, swift thrust. "Jesus, that feels good," he whispers, drawing back and plunging in again. "Are you okay?"

"Yes, I'm amazing…. It feels perfect." It really does. I thought I would be tender, but I'm not. I lift my legs and wrap them round his neat waist.

"Not sore?" *Thrust.*

"No." *Tilt   .*

"No aches or pains?" *Thrust.*

"Ahh, No!" *Rock.*

"You, sure?" *Swivel and thrust.*

"Sssss! yesss! Aghhh!" *Tilt, pull.*

"Okay, Honey-Bee. Let's rock this joint." *Bang, slam, thrust,* "Aghhh, yeah, c'mon, fuckin' yeah!"

He rolls us so I'm on top. Bracing my arms on his chest, I rock my hips back and forth as he bucks his hips underneath me. I sit like a champion dressage rider, circling my hips, lifting and dropping, a perfect rising trot!

Steadily I'm increasing my pace as he tightly grips the cheeks of my arse. Tipping forward, I dangle my breasts in his face placing my hands on the bed beside his head. My hair tumbles around his face like a veil. He takes the hint and wraps his luscious lips round one nipple while squeezing the other tightly in his hand. Raising up, I slam down on him, I can feel him so deeply.

Sitting back up, I support my weight by leaning on his chest and change position, planting my feet flat on the bed either side of his hips, so I'm squatting over him. Hovering above him I widen my stance to give myself more balance. Bracing my thigh muscles, I rise and fall, up and down. From this angle, the view is amazing. I can see his massive cock sliding in and out of my slippery channel. I'm worshiping him with my body.

"Fucking hell... look at that. Oh man, Christ, Edi, look at how deep I am."

He's watching as I bounce up and down on his dick. He can see himself disappear; one second immersed balls deep, then, sliding out, right to the tip, before gliding back inside.

He's pulsing against me. He's ready to come, but I'm not so I stop to shift position again.

"Hey!" he protests, unsure of what I'm doing.

"Hold your horses, mister!" I turn my back on him and re-squat, taking a reverse cow-girl position. Now he has a view of my arse and back.

This position is a bit trickier, so I gently grasp hold of his dick, and guide him inside, before bracing my hands on his knees.

Tipping forward, I lift my arse so that I can feel the head of his cock, just inside, then I lower. "Yee-ha!" I call, the cow-girl in me is coming out to play.

"Fucking hell, Jesus, Edi, I can see myself being swallowed. Your arse is amazing," *Slap!* He's completely unable to resist the opportunity of a quick smack of my bottom!

I start to move in earnest now. I'm getting close and I'm determined to come, but to achieve detonation in this position it calls for some additional clitoral stimulation.

Descending hard, I impale myself and stay put. "Silas, I need to touch myself."

Placing my fingers on my clitoris, I start to rub and flick; but I'm soon forced to stop when he sits up, his chest colliding with my back. I'm now sitting astride his lap, kneeling across his thighs, with him buried deep inside me. "I think I'll do that if you don't mind…"

Removing my hand, he replaces it with his own, wrapping the other arm round my waist to support me. Giving him control, I reach my arms back over my shoulders, grasping him around his neck. His lips latch on to my throat beneath my ear, sending shivers through my whole being. His fingers begin a delectable dance over my clit, and I start to grind myself onto him.

Slowly at first. Rotating my hips in a seductive sensuous rhythm. He's so deep, even the smallest of movements could have me tipping over the edge.

"You nearly there, Honey?" he mutters in my ear. All I can do is groan and rise and fall. "Tell me, you're nearly there, Bee."

"I'm nearly there," I pant, God, I'm close…

Then it happens. He ripples his fingers and flicks his hips and I come. Clenching and trembling in release.

"Silas! Yes, oh, yes, Si…" I breathe out his name. I could say it forever. It trips of my tongue like a prayer. A prayer I want to repeat morning, noon and night!

"Edi… My Edi… my Honey-bee… God, woman… I'm getting addicted to you… you're gonna be bad for my health." He's said that before, but this time it seems to have more meaning. "I can't get enough. I can't seem to get close enough or deep enough. Are you okay?" He helps me off his lap and turns me to face him. There's some concern on his face and I'm not sure I like it.

"Yeah, yes, I'm fine. Why wouldn't I be?" I feel a bit self-conscious. I'm aware he hasn't come.

"I… you… I don't know… I feel weird. Ignore me, I'm saying stupid shit." Stupid shit indeed! I shut my mouth before I say the stupid shit that is buzzing around in *my* head. "You need to know, that so far, you've surprised me at every turn. I want to tell you something but I don't want you to take it the wrong way. Just listen a minute." He swallows, organizing his thoughts. "I've had a lot of sex." *Brilliant, just what I wanted to hear!* He must sense my recoil because he lifts a finger, "Just hear me out, please. I've had a lot of sex, but I've *never* experienced sex like I have with you. It's incredible. Every time you amaze me. Every time, is like the first time. It's a revelation. I've never come so hard, or so often in one session."

"Err, thank you... I guess." I sound distinctly ungrateful. And, I'm aware that he still hasn't come! "It's nice to finally know I'm good in bed. Should I add it to my C.V?" I snip. There's no humour in my voice, even though I was aiming for it.

"Fuck, no! I didn't mean it that way. Jesus, Edi. What I'm trying very badly to say is, I really like you. I like you a lot and I'm terrified you don't like me in the same way."

"I like you in the same way," I answer quietly. *I like you so much!*

"Really? You really like me that much?" The relief in his voice is tangible.

"I like you that much." I can't say it any more, otherwise I might use the 'L' word and that wouldn't be good. "I've told you. You make me come. Sex with you is an education... a revelation. I'm learning to love my body and what it can do... but I only want to learn, with you."

Climbing off the bed, I walk into the bathroom. Some distance between us is probably a good idea at this point in time. Turning on the shower, I hear him follow me in. No distance between us then! "Do you want to shower with me?" Turning, to face him, I notice, he's still hard.

"Yes," Is his simple answer. Stepping into me, he wraps me in his arms and walks me into the scalding stream of water.

We stand under the hot jets for ages, just kissing, not fondling, or groping, just holding each other and kissing. Long, lingering, exploring, loving kisses. This has a deeper meaning than all the incredible sex. This feels significant. It's engrossing, consuming and right.

By the time we break away from each other, our skin is pruned and wrinkled. We haven't washed, or shampooed or conditioned, we've just stood under the water and kissed. My lips feel swollen, my neck is aching from tilting it back, my heart is hammering and my eyes are weeping. Thankfully, the shower is hiding my tears.

I look at him and he looks at me. I've no idea what this is or where this is going, but I've as much chance of stopping it as a butterfly does halting a stampeding elephant.

Chapter 41

We give the black transit van parked on the kerb outside the gate a wide birth. It's so close to the entrance Silas has to swerve around it.

"Pillock!" he curses as he drives into the car park.

We all have a stupidly busy day ahead. I have two people coming in for interviews and Silas has an internal flight to Manchester to pick up a client, then deliver him to Heathrow before he returns this evening. Christina is up to her eyes, juggling arrangements for a promotional gala evening in honour of our new client - I'm not looking forward to that - I'll have to think of an excuse to get out of it. I also need to check in with the girls and David. Yes, I've a busy week coming up!

Silas parks up, then leans over and kisses me hard on the mouth. "I'll see you later. I should be back before five, but it depends on the flight plans."

He climbs out of the car and let's Bear out of the back. I jump out too and reach into the back seat for my lap top bag just as a bright flash lights up the sky. It's gone in a split second and the sky looks clear; just white fluffy clouds. There's been no storm warning, but I vow to check the forecast when I get inside; it wouldn't be good news for the flights today if I've misread the weather reports.

"I'll check for storms," I say as I stride off in the direction of the office. Silas pivots on the spot, holds his arms out to the side, palms up, he shrugs at me, looking up at the sky with a quizzical expression on his face. "Lightning," I explain. He shakes his head. He obviously missed it, but it wouldn't do for him to be flying into a headlong squall.

"Bear, come." He turns, Bear trotting at his heels towards the hangar.

I watch him go, he has such a strong purposeful stride. I'm smug in the knowledge it is me that's put the spring in his step this morning.

My office looks the same as it did when I left it yesterday; boxes of paraphernalia on my desk and all my books stacked in a pile, waiting to be packed.

"What went on here then?" I jump, as Christina comes barrelling in and lands her arse heavily in one of my easy chairs.

"Misunderstanding." It's the only explanation she's getting this morning.

"Lovers tiff?" she asks, cheekily. But the sarcasm is only half-hearted, she seems a bit preoccupied.

"Something like that, but it was nothing... we're good." My tongue is going to turn black and fall out any minute but I couldn't stand having to spill my guts again so I allow the little white lie to stand.

"Good to know... do you want a coffee before we start the day? I'm buying." She heaves herself off the chair and heads out to the kitchen.

"Yeah, be there in a sec,'" I call to her retreating back. Bear enters my office and sneaks under my desk; sulking, by the look of things. I understand why when Silas follows him in, dressed in his pilot's uniform. He looks edible. "It's like Piccadilly Circus in here this morning." I smile as I walk over and give him a peck on the cheek.

"I'm in the dog house." He leans into my peck and nods in the direction of Bear at the same time. "Literally!" The only bit of him that is visible is his tail and it isn't wagging.

"Oh dear... I'll Baby-Bear sit, don't worry. If it's any consolation, I like the uniform." I raise my eyebrows suggestively making him laugh.

Jiggling my mouse, to wake up my lap top, I toggle to the weather site. "Well, it must have been a fluke." He looks at me in utter confusion, so I elaborate. "That lightning... because there's no sign of a storm. You should be good to depart in an hour."

I make to leave the office, but without warning I'm snatched back and drawn tightly into his arms. "Oh!" My back collides his chest so I'm melded against him. There's no escape. Snaking his arms tightly round my midriff, he bends his knees so that he can thrust his hips into me. A rod of iron pokes against my bottom. Burying his nose in my hair he inhales deeply; all I can do is dissolve into him and soak up the attention.

"I'll miss you," he whispers quietly. "You'll need to wait here until I get back." Nuzzling my ear, he lowers his voice and takes my lobe in his teeth before murmuring, "No car!" Feeling his lips this close to my ear makes me shiver. This isn't the place or time to be getting horny.

"My car's outside," I remind him.

"*Was* outside; Sparks has taken it for a service... My request. He'll drop it at the apartment later."

"Ah, your master plan has worked, Boss-man!" I giggle, swivelling in his embrace so I'm facing him. Kissing his nose once, I stretch sideways, managing to scoop my scheduler and pen from my desk. "Although, I was *very* impressed with your acquisition yesterday. That *was* masterful." I purr against his lips. "Now, let me go so I can have coffee with your ex-wife and compare notes!"

The look of horror that crosses his face is hilarious and in a fit of disbelief, he releases me from his arms. "'*J*'-for joke, Silas..." I'm still laughing as I walk into the kitchen, where Christina is sat with two steaming mugs of coffee and her work diary, ready for our weekly planning meeting.

"Aww! Gosh, sorry... I'm so, tired! She yawns loudly as I plonk myself down in the adjacent chair. It's only now I notice she isn't her usual immaculate self.

"Burning the candle at both ends?" I open my diary to Monday and smooth down the page.

"You could say that," she winks at me opening her own diary so we can synchronise. "I went on a date. It was disastrous."

"Oh?" I don't know why that surprises me; she's an absolute bombshell and I'm sure she has men tumbling all over themselves to spend time in her company. "That's a shame... Umm, sorry to hear that it didn't go well." I frown at my ineptitude. I don't really know what the etiquette is when you're talking with your 'potential' boyfriend's ex-wife about her disastrous date.

She adds a spoon of sugar to her coffee and stirs. "Yeah, he didn't have much conversation. Thankfully, he was okay in the sack, so that made up for it!" Finally, she flashes her mischievous smile.

"*Christina!*" Oh, she's a pistol... I'm stunned but I can't help but laugh.

"What? Oh, *come* on... It's not as if you and himself, haven't been fucking like mink all weekend! I can tell by the look on the smug bastard's face. He's like the cat that got the cream."

"*Christina!*" I gasp again incredulously, this time with embarrassment. I don't know what else to say, so I say nothing.

Sipping her coffee, she observes me closely over the rim of her mug. "I told you he was good, didn't I?" Cheekily tilting her shoulders in a semblance of a sexy jiggle, she blows the steam off her coffee. She's an absolute nightmare! How mortifying. "Oh, get over it already!" The mug is placed on the table as she takes a sincerer tone. "Honestly, sweetheart... I'm completely fine with it. Seriously, Edi, I mean it."

Taking my hand across the table, she gives it a squeeze. "*Lor-Lummy!* that's all water under the leaky bridge. It's long gone, we're so done – honestly!" My face must be a picture. "I can tell he's smitten. I couldn't be happier for you both. C'mon, let's get this week planned so I can go and collapse in my office and pretend to be working."

After giving me one last squeeze, she removes her hand from mine and refocuses. "Now then… what's on the horizon this week?" Swiftly she turns her attention to the planner, picks up her pen and just like that, she's switched to her business-head.

Thankful the personal discussion appears to be over, I pick up my own pen and focus my attention on the real reason for our meeting. With our heads down, we spend a constructive hour planning the rest of the week, then on to the staff interviews. I love this job much more than I had ever anticipated.

*

The first candidate I interviewed was a bit of a let-down. Though her CV was impressive, her interview lacked both knowledge and enthusiasm. I won't be offering her a position. Dragging the answers out of her was like pulling teeth and I could swear there was a whiff of weed about her.

The second candidate however, was perfect. She was young and didn't have as much experience as the first candidate, but what she lacked in knowledge she more than made up for in desire and enthusiasm. She was bubbly and keen. We hit is off right away and the fact her previous employer gave a glowing reference didn't hurt.

Following a brief discussion with Christina - who tells me she trusts my judgement and if I'm happy, then so is she - I decide I will offer Susan Smith the position of Finance Manager. She should fit in really well with the rest of the team.

The bland name doesn't suit her effervescent personality, she made an instant impression. On appearance alone, Susan would be hard for anyone to forget. She's an amazon! A complete stunner, aged twenty-six with a shiny black bob and is probably over six feet tall in her stacked baby pink platforms, tight black top and short, floral rah-rah skirt; she looks hip, fresh and edgy and is very, very tall! Why is everyone so much taller than me?

With my final decision made, I call her at four o'clock and offer her the job. The scream she bellows down the phone confirms her excitement. She's delighted and I can't help laughing along with her and joining in her glee. Susan says she can start on Monday, so Monday it is.

Satisfied with my success on making my first appointment, I crack on. Ploughing through even more C. V.'s, I still have two more candidates to see for the finance admin role and then there's the HR position to fill. Christina has mentioned a possible I.T. position too. The remaining two applicants will be coming in tomorrow and Wednesday. Hopefully, by next week we will have a full team on board and the upstairs office will be buzzing with activity. Things are really coming together and I'm thoroughly satisfied with my progress today.

Silas is back. It's five-thirty and I'm starving. Bear has sulked most of the day, but now he's bounding around like a puppy.

"Honey, I'm home!" Silas calls as he strolls into my office and gives me a warm bear-hug. "Hmm, I really missed you." He kisses the top of my head and holds me close. I could get use to this attention. "Shall we go?"

"Yeah, just let me pack up and I'll be with you in a sec."

"I'm parched, while you do that, I'll get a drink. I'm a bit dehydrated. Do you want anything?" he asks as he walks out of my office.

"No, I'm good thank you."

My office phone starts to ring. Checking the time, I contemplate letting it go to answerphone, but manners get the better of me and I decide to answer. "Good evening, Royal Tudor Charters, how may I help you?"

"Hello, may I speak to Ms Sykes please." I don't recognise the voice. "This is Ms Sykes, speaking."

"Meredith, I'm Sam Hall from the Daily Mail, can you confirm you were at the Paris Fashion Week closing party on Saturday night?" The probing voice punches its question like a fist, knocking the wind out of me. "Meredith, it is Meredith Frost, isn't it? It is you. You were spotted at Paris fashion week. Can you confirm the rumour you will be appearing alongside Lynda Summers in a celebrity calendar? Are you prepared to tell me your story?" The persistent voice is firing rapid questions like a Gatling gun. I'm stunned into panicked silence.

Horrified, I drop the receiver, fumbling to place it back into the cradle.

How did they find me?

I stand, staring at the phone as if it's just burned me; my hands over my mouth stifling a scream. Panic rises and I begin to shake.

How the hell did they find me?

Hearing a noise, I spin on the spot, expecting to see an army of reporters at my office door but it is only Silas on his way back with a bottle of water he's bought from the vending machine in the foyer.

"What's up?" He takes in my distressed state in an instant, just as my phone begins to ring again making me leap about nine feet into the air. I stare at the phone, willing it to stop. Silas strides over and lifts the receiver.

"No... leave..." but I'm too slow.

"Tudor," he answers curtly, giving me a '*what?*' look.

His eyebrows rise as the voice on the other end starts to bark in his ear. I can't hear any actual words, but I've a good idea.

"Who is this?" Silas yells down the phone. The voice remains the same, steady and probing, rehearsed questions of an accomplished reporter. "There's no one here of that name. Clearly, you have the wrong information." He slams the phone down and stares in fury at my horrified face. "Bear, come. C'mon, were leaving." He grabs my hand and drags me out of the office, not waiting to see if Bear is following us. Without a word he leads me along the quiet corridor.

"Silas, wait, please can you slow down."

Completely ignoring my plea, he keeps up the pace. I jog to keep up with him. Through the reception area we go and out into the main foyer. Only then does he stop and speak to me, placing his hands on my shoulders and whirling me to face him.

"Stay here. I'll pull the car up as close as I can to the doors." He disappears outside. I stand, holding on to Bear. I'm quaking with nerves and feeling utterly foolish. I'm a grown woman, I should be able to deal with this but my thoughts keep returning to the sly voice on the phone. How dare they think they can intrude into my life. Bear, clearly sensing my distress, leans his soft body against my leg to offer support.

The roar of the car engine breaks into my trance and a moment later, Silas pulls up outside the main doors. Quickly and without thinking I exit the building and dive into the passenger seat.

Silas opens his door and Bear leaps in; his huge paws landing on Silas's lap before he squirms into the back, snaking through the gap between the front seats. In about five seconds flat, Silas has the doors closed and centrally locked. The clutch screams in protest as the car is slammed into first gear and we're zooming out of the electric gates and down the lane. I feel like a bank robber making my escape with the getaway driver.

"You okay?" It's the first time he's spoken since we left the office.

"Yeah." I breathe. "You?" I sit side-on, staring at his lovely profile. He looks concerned.

"Yeah, I'm fine. I'm more bothered about you." He's glancing in his rear-view mirror. *Are we being followed?* "You're coming home with me. I don't want you on your own with those scumbags snooping around."

"Okay... but what about my clothes and stuff?" It's a stupid question but, what about my clothes?

"I'll ask Tia to bring some over. Don't worry. She's discreet." He sounds as if he's already planned it all.

"Okay." I mumble again. I've gone cold and I'm shivering. "Oh, God... I'll need to speak to the Beeches... To Lizzy... Jesus, Si... What am I gonna to do?" I'm freaking out, my brain is running in overdrive.

"Shhh, relax, Honey-bee. At the moment they're only fishing. It would seem your lovely *'friend'* Lynda has been busy shooting her mouth off. But we knew that didn't we?"

"Yeah, I suppose we did." I knew she'd be trouble as soon as I bumped into her on Saturday.

"But there's no concrete evidence, no photos. Try and keep calm. I'll look after you, Honey."

The thought of him looking after me gives me a warm comforting feeling; perhaps not enough to completely relax me, but enough to think I can cope with the impending shitstorm!

We drive through the outskirts of the village and into the lush greenery of the Surrey countryside. As the shops and houses morph into fields and hedgerows I begin to calm. And when the barn comes into sight, my breathing begins to slow, returning to normal.

Silas skids to a halt on the gravel driveway, scattering the stone chippings across the yard. As soon as he opens the car door, Bear leaps out but I stay put, frozen in place as if I need permission to move. Silas collects me from my side of the car and leads me into the house, closing the door behind us, locking the intruding world outside.

Chapter 42

The trill of the land line startles me out of my trancelike state. Silas marches into the kitchen, choosing to take the call out of my hearing. I stand like a spare part in the hallway, not really knowing what to do. I think I'm a bit shell-shocked.

"Tudor?" is the only word I can hear; his voice is muffled and distant. Within seconds, he's back. That was a really quick call. "Tia has brought your clothes. They should be in the bedroom." I'm still frozen with shock and disbelief. "Edi, did you hear me? I said, Tia has left you clothes in the bedroom. My bedroom."

"Err, yer... yes, I can't... yes, thank you..." I stammer. My mouth isn't working and my speech is slurred. "So, so bad... Silas, I don't... can't..." My legs buckle, unable to support my weight any longer, I collapse to the floor. Silas is beside me in an instant, lifting me to my feet and supporting my weight. "I'm so sorry." It's all I can say. I repeat the words, over and over; *the* one word I can't abide from others is the only word that will come, but it doesn't seem enough. "I'm so sorry, Silas."

When I wake, it's dark. Silas is lying by my side, his bent arm supporting his head. Fully alert, his shimmering dark eyes are awash with concern and worry. "How're you feeling?" he asks, softly.

"I'm okay, I think." Mentally, I check my vital signs. My body is relaxed and warm, no shakes, no headache. I register that I'm enveloped in a patchwork quilt. Yeah, I think I'm okay. "Yes, I'm alright. How long was I out?"

"About two hours. Is this normal?" Stroking my hair from my face, his voice is soft and tinged with concern.

"It's happened before, but not for ages. I think it's my body's way of dealing, you know, with stress." I don't move, just lying still and allowing my equilibrium to reset.

"Edi, you scared the ever-loving shit out of me..." The veil of anxiety that was shrouding his face a moment ago has lifted slightly with the apparent improvement in my wellbeing. "Well, I'm pleased you're back." Relieved, he kisses me, and a warm glow permeates my skin. "Very pleased you're back." He kisses me again, this time the kiss is firmer, fuelled by his growing passion. His mouth is hot and damp, his tongue tentatively seeks out mine as if he needs assurance, I'm willing.

Sensing hesitation, I urge him on, kissing him back furiously, forcing my mouth to his with an unyielding urgency I've never felt before. For a fraction of a second, he seems to re-evaluate. And I half expect him to call a halt, but then, completely unable to hold back, he loses all sense of restraint. His kiss becomes filled with the ravenous hunger of a starving man. I'm immediately awakened, the adrenalin from earlier, returning with such vengeance, a deluge of desire rages through me. Flinging my arms around his neck, I match his fierceness; a feverish demonstration of my growing need, I have to have him... now if not sooner!

Barely coherent, I pant, my demand into his face... "Silas, this is completely inappropriate, I know, but I really want you to take my mind away from all of this. You have to make love to me. I need you to make love to me." My fingers tracing his face. "Please. Make it go away... make the world go away for a while...?" not knowing how else to phrase it. The need to immerse myself in him, the thought of just him and me, of nothing but the two of us, in the throes of passion, is the only escape from this burgeoning nightmare.

"You're sure?" He whispers into my mouth.

"Silas, I was never surer... *please*...take me..."

473

"Then if you're sure, your wish is my command."

There's no need for me to say it twice. His kiss becomes consuming, my response, frantic. Desperate for that sweet, sweet oblivion, I grapple at his clothing, dragging his tee-shirt over his head, grasping for his belt, the desperate desire to have him naked and fucking me is unbearable, I'm incensed.

"Slow down, Edi. We'll get there." He takes my wrists and places my hands by my sides, winning control. Slowing my urgent need, he rises leaving the bed.

Untangling me from my hiding place beneath the quilt, I'm lifted from the comfort of the mattress and placed on my feet. Curling my toes in the tufts of the soft woollen carpet, I stare at him, waiting his next move; anticipation of what's to come is building in me, it's alive, a growing flame.

Holding me in place with just his eyes he forces me to remain still as he commences to strip me, relieving me of my restrictive clothing. His skilful fingers quickly undo the buttons on my blouse, my bra is dropped to the floor. Unzipping my skirt, he allows it to fall, the silky material brushes over my hips before it lands, puddling on the floor, circling my ankles. Fleetingly, he allows himself a salacious look up and down my body before tugging my knickers down my thighs, indicating for me to step out of them.

Within no time, I'm completely naked before him. Oddly, there's no flush of shame or embarrassment, just a sensation of complete liberation. Delicious tingles travel through my body as my skin heats in response to his molten stare. Adrenalin courses through my system, intensifying my desire, fuelling my ravenous need for him to bury himself deep within me. I'm greedy for him.

Turning his back to me, he opens his wardrobe and starts to rummage. I'm instantly curious; here I am, naked and wanting and he's having a clear out? *What's he doing?*

I don't have to wait long for him to reveal the mystery. When he faces me, he's holding a box. I recognise it instantly. It's the same as the box that held my new shoes, only this one is a different colour.

"Sit," he points to the bed and I sit. "These are for you. Ever since I saw you in the black ones on Saturday, I've wanted to see you in the red."

I don't speak. Watching him kneeling before me, he removes the stunning red heels from the box. They're similar to the black ones, but these are more of a sandal, strappy and high with a tassel lace tie.

First my right foot, then my left. The shoes are guided onto my feet and the laces tied with care.

"There..." Silas kneels back and admires his handiwork. There's no point in protesting that he shouldn't have bought them. I'll be ignored and scolded, so I accept the gift without complaint. They're simply beautiful. Stretching out my leg, I admire their stunning beauty as I seductively lean back on my hands and watch his face.

"Thank you; I love them..." I purr, skimming my toe up and down his chest, settling with my foot on his shoulder. This allows him a full provocative view of my most intimate area. I'm totally naked, except for the red C.F.M. shoes and there's absolutely no subtlety or room for misunderstanding; quite blatantly, I want sex... and I want it now!

Removing my foot from his shoulder, he gracefully rises to his feet. "Come with me." His voice is more of a growl and I follow like an automaton, a willing puppet, red shoes, naked body...

He walks me out of the bedroom and down the stairs. Wondering where we're going, I'm soon put out of my misery when I'm led outside and into the rear garden. The moon is bright and full. It's a gloriously sultry summer evening, warm and balmy with a light, fresh breeze. The feel of the night air on my skin, a sensual caress.

Silas draws me towards him and I'm turned to face the overgrown garden. Now, instead of him leading me, I'm made to walk in front. He guides the way gently, holding my upper arms with his strong hands, steering me through the garden, along an invisible pathway.

I sense his eyes roving all over my skin. I can only imagine what I must look like from behind, my creamy skin illuminated by the pale moon, my loose hair billowing around my slender shoulders. The steeple height of the red heels has my buttocks clenching taught. My shoulder blades are being drawn together by the pressure of his hands on my upper arms.

Treading carefully, so as not to trip, I watch where I place my feet, pushing out my chest, so my breasts to gently undulate with each step, my full hips swaying as I pace in a slow, seductive rhythm. Unhurriedly, we progress across the garden and into the wooded area behind the house.

Once there, he guides me towards a majestic copper beech tree. "Wait there," he says, his voice sounds strangely wraithlike in the open night air. I stand and wait, watching as he removes his remaining items of clothing. Finally, there we stand; a modern-day Adam and Eve beneath the imposing copper beech, in the dark moonlit woodland.

"Stand here," he motions to the base of the tree. I comply, manoeuvring into my designated spot. Anticipation is making my breath catch, my limbs tremble. "Now, lean your back against the tree and support yourself with your arms. I'm not in the mood to take prisoners tonight." Again, I comply. Desire has flooded my system and the need for him has overridden any other conscious thought. "Ready?" he asks.

"You know I'm ready." My voice is husky with want. I spread my legs, planting my come-fuck-me shoes hip-distance apart and start to touch myself; it's as if I'm possessed by the shameless spirit of a woodland dryad.

My sex is soaked and glistening. Trailing my fingers to my core I circle them a few times across my pulsing opening. Enjoying the tingling sensation, I coat my fingers with my warm, glossy essence before trailing them back up the centre of my body and into my mouth. Silas just stands, transfixed, watching as I wantonly, seductively, lick and suck my sticky fingers clean.

Unable to control his need any longer, he lunges towards me, crashing his body into mine and pressing me with force against the unyielding bark of the tree.

"Ooh!" The severity of the collision knocks the wind right out of me, but I don't care.

"Grrr." Grasping my thighs, he boosts me up and off my feet, my arms drape over his shoulders grappling for purchase. My thighs automatically encircling his neat waist, crossing my ankles at the small of his back. I hear him groan in pleasure when the heel of my shoe, jabs at his firm glutes.

"Mm," I'm open and ready and I can't wait any longer. "Now, Silas, now… fuck me, take me away from reality." There will be no need to beg; he's with me.

Rearing back, his grip on my thighs tighten and he drives forward, slamming into me, brutally, untamed, no holds barred.

We're wild, ferocious animals. Mating like two savage beasts; fucking and howling into the night like nocturnal creatures, fiercely clawing at each other.

I bite his neck, he squeezes my hips, I dig my nails in to his shoulders, he gnaws on my nipple. I scream his name, he howls mine at the moon, like a feral wolf. I scratch and pummel his back in urgency, he pistons his groin into me like a rutting stallion.

We're unrestrained in our mindless passion. It's crazy, hard, violent, uninhibited and it's fucking incredible.

"Oh Goddd!" Tears of desperation are streaming from my eyes. Barely able to catch a breath, I scream in agony and ecstasy as he repeatedly ploughs into me. The jagged splinters from the bark pierce my skin, grazing my shoulder blades, but I don't care, it only fuels my desire.

"Grrr, yeah... yesss!" he hisses as he loses himself to the moment.

Our hearts are drumming in complete synchronicity now, our sweaty bodies smashing together in a relentless rhythm; but still we go on. Unable to get close enough, unable to get deep enough, seeking that all-consuming depth of penetration, that indelible connection we both need to grasp fulfilment.

"Oh... Silas... *please...* "

Harder and harder he thrusts, deeper and deeper he goes, my legs are cramping, my thighs stiffening in spasm. I'm rigid, tilting my head back. The orgasm, when it hits me, is a tsunami of sensation. I howl my release at the night sky, again and again, and again. He joins me in my elation, our voices reverberating through the trees, our overwhelming, animalistic urge to copulate, unable to extinguish the fire.

Without slowing, or uncoupling, we start over, his dick remains rigid, even though he has just come. He drives into me, I grapple, clinging on to his slippery sweat riddled skin, swathing my limbs and body, round his hard contours.

We're entwined like the virulent ivy that climbs, trails and creeps over the branches and twigs of the copper beech we cling to. We're a helix of tendrils and limbs, unable to stop but yet, too spent to continue.

We're unstoppable, becoming one flesh, bonded bone and blood; life contained in our own aura, our own plain of existence, oblivious to the outside world. Just us. Two pure, luminous, beings fusing into one whole.

"Silas, please," my voice is hoarse from screaming, my limbs are weakening. I've no idea how he's maintaining this relentless assault. His eyes are blank as he continues to pound into me over and over. "Silas," I plead, willing him to hear me. He does, my voice breaks through his trans - like state, drawing him back to the present.

Gradually he begins to slow his pace. Burying his head in my neck, he slows his powerful thrusting until it becomes a gentle rhythmic pumping.

As the frantic fucking gives way to gentle lovemaking my legs relax, and my body responds in the only way it knows how…and with that relaxation, my orgasm finally arrives, wave after shimmering wave of sheer unadulterated ecstasy.

Silas explodes, filling me completely, hot cum shooting inside me, drenching me, soothing me. There's so much it leaks out dripping onto the forest floor between his bare feet.

The finality of the detonation causes us both to collapse in a heap. Silas drops to his knees taking me with him, my back scrapes against the rough bark as we land at the base of the tree, totally spent, exhausted, the raging inferno extinguished at last.

I don't know how long we remain entwined, nestled in the tree roots, but eventually I feel Silas move. Standing, he leaves his clothes where they're and gathers me in his arms.

My back feels raw. It stings, but not so bad that I can't stand it. He carries me back inside, up the stairs; once again locking the world outside as we enter the bathroom. Idly I notice he has left a trail muddy footprints on the cream stair carpet.

Gently lowered to my feet I'm encouraged to sit on the edge of the bath. Silas kneels before me and removes my sandals.

"I like your shoes." His cheeky grin is infectious.

"I'm pleased to hear it… they're my favourite pair." I sass back at him. "But I prefer to do this with bare feet…" Softly, I run my toes up the length of his semi-hard cock.

There's a glistening film of cum coating him, so my toes glide easily along his hardening length. The incredulous look he gives me is comical. "Are you trying to give me a heart attack?" Batting my exploring toes away from his now solid length, he picks up my shoes and places them outside the bathroom door before returning and flicking on the shower.

Through all of this, my admiring eyes are hypnotised by the bounce of his huge jutting dick as it bobs and weaves with each movement and step.

"Tsk…" He tuts at me and shakes his head in mock despair. "You're insatiable…" Weaving his fingers through my hair, he tucks a strand behind my ear before cupping my face. Tilting my chin, my greedy eyes have no option but to leave his beautiful manhood and land on his beautiful face. "I've created a monster… come on, let's shower."

"Yes, let's." I sigh, dreamily.

In the shower I have an odd sensation of deja-vu, as we repeat everything, we did this morning. Standing under the powerful jets, we all but dissolve into the warmth of the flowing water, clinging on to each other like life would end if we let go. Kissing, silently caressing, washing, cleansing, loving. No words are needed, no confirmation required.

Once cleansed and dry, we enter the bedroom and crawl beneath the blue and white linen sheets. He envelops me in his arms where I lie, contented and spent.

"Good night, Honey-bee." Kissing my temple, he snuggles against me.

"Goodnight, Boss-man," I whisper, but my eyes are already closed, my tired body sinking into the soft mattress. If I never wake up again, this is how I want to spend eternity; enfolded, completely in the strong arms of the man I love.

There, I've admitted it. If this isn't love, I don't know what is. Together, we welcome the darkness and oblivion of an undisturbed sleep.

Chapter 43

Tuesday morning dawns. It is raining and dull but I feel bright and alive. My back aches a bit, some bruising I think, but I would do it all again in a heartbeat. Silas lies beside me, sleeping the sleep of the innocent! The thought makes me smile. You could never call him innocent! My dark prince, my dusky saviour, my beautiful boss-man, my lover.

"Silas, hey, handsome. It's morning, time to get up sleepy head. C'mon Boss-man." Leaning over him, I whisper softly in his ear rocking his shoulder gently, encouraging him out of his slumber. "Hey, big man. Wakey, wakey."

He moves so quickly, reminiscent of a pouncing tiger. Within a split second, I'm grabbed and pinned to the bed. His weight is evenly spread, but he's still a heavy sod and it steals my breath for a moment. It's clear that I really need to work on my evasion tactics, I'm rubbish at escapology. "We need to get up," I huff as I force him off of me, pushing with all my might to heave his solid mass away so I can wriggle out from beneath him.

Frowning but ever the gentleman, he relents. "Are you bossing the Boss-man?" he asks with a smirk. Grudgingly, I kick my way out of the tangle of sheets and climb out of bed.

Ha... as if I could boss him around! "Now, Silas. Get up." He huffs like a stroppy adolescent as he looks at the time. When it registers, he too climbs out of bed and starts the laborious routine of getting ready for work.

Sipping coffee and eating toast in the cosy country kitchen is my new favourite thing. It follows closely to watching him shower and of course getting dressed. It's almost as erotic as watching him getting undressed... Mmm Silas, undressed!

Bear has been let out to do his business and is now chomping on his breakfast. The metal name-tag on his collar clinks against the ceramic dog bowl as he devours his biscuits. All too soon he's finished and licking his lips forlornly. I'm treated to the full-on puppy-dog eye experience as he sits and looks expectantly at my piece of toast.

Checking Silas is otherwise engaged at the cooker, I press my finger to my lips, indicating that he should keep schtum and then toss him the last corner of my toast. Bear leaps and snatches it out of the air in one fluid movement, then gobbles it down as if he's never been fed.

"I saw that!" Silas's back is turned, so he's reacting on instinct. *Eyes in the back of his head.* Bear slinks off guiltily and lies on the rug in the lounge. "Would you like some eggs?" Silas asks, his back still turned towards me.

I'm sat, daydreaming, admiring his well-defined shoulders, narrow waist and tight buttocks... even dressed in his smart charcoal grey work pants and crisp white tailored shirt, there's no hiding his muscular physique. I think I might be drooling as I gape, swinging my legs.

"No, thanks. The toast was enough. Is there any more coffee in the pot?"

"Yeah, help yourself. Can you top mine up please?" Silas tips the scrambled eggs onto his plate and drops the pan into the sink, where it hisses as it cools.

Slipping off my stool, I slope over to the worktop beside the sink, passing Silas on the way to where the expensive coffee machine is simmering invitingly - pausing only to stroke the palm of my hand over his fine behind as I pass by.

Removing two fresh mugs from the mug-tree and pouring us each another cup and gaze through the window at the lush garden. It's more of a small copse really, and the tightly knit woodland ensures sanctuary from the outside world.

483

"Did you pick up your clothes this morning?" I ask, as I sip my steaming brew.

"Yeah, when I let the hound out." He shovels eggs into his mouth and takes a bite of his own toast. Cheekily, I open my mouth like a baby bird, begging for some of his eggs. He obliges, giving me his last forkful. "I thought you didn't want any?"

"I didn't but yours looked so nice. Yum…thank you!" They're really good.

Bear has crept back into the kitchen, unable to resist the aroma of Silas's breakfast. "Sneak!" He pitches his last piece of toast at Bear, who takes it as forgiveness and once again leaps into the air snatching the flying crust before it can land on the floor.

We ride to the office in a heightened state of awareness, on the lookout for low lying journalists and photographers. We don't see anything suspicious, but the phone calls yesterday really shook me up. They shouldn't really, I'm being stupidly paranoid. I'm not an interesting story… this is so silly.

Pulling my phone from my bag, I quickly text the girls, I can't believe it's been over a week since we spoke. I'll need to ring them later tonight, so I let Lizzy know to expect my call.

"I'll need to visit David this week." I haven't seen him since last Wednesday and that was only a flying visit. He gets so engrossed in his life at the Beeches he hardly ever rings me.

"Why don't we go together?" Silas smiles at me. "We can take them out for dinner. There's a nice restaurant nearby."

"Oh, yes, I think David would love that." Silas doesn't miss my frown at an uncertain thought.

"Penny for them?" he muses.

"I was just thinking. Shouldn't we ask Wendy to come too? I mean, she's David's girlfriend," they're a couple after all.

Rummaging in my bag I find my sunglasses; the sun is really low this morning.

"Yeah, good idea. You ring David later and let him know. How about Friday? Nice way to end the week." He's enthusiastic.

I slip my shades on, relax back into my seat and enjoy the lovely scenery. "Cool, I'll do it this afternoon."

When we pull into the airfield car park the tatty black transit from yesterday is still parked next to the fence. I'm vaguely wondering if it's been dumped, when two men, dressed in scruffy jeans and dog-eared leather jackets, jump out of a sliding panel door.

"Meredith! This way. Meredith!" One of them is up against the fence, poking the lens of his camera through the gap, the other one is waiving his arm above his head, holding a pen and in the other hand he has a notepad. "Meredith Frost... can you confirm that you will be joining Lynda Summers, for a reunion photo shoot? Have you anything to say to your husband? Where have you been hiding? Do you have a comment about your new relationship?"

I'm stunned, paralysed with fear, unable to move, frozen like a statue staring at the pantomime unfurling on the other side of the fence. The scumbag of a photographer is snapping away, flashes popping into my face, take after, take after take. *Shit!!*

A flurry of black and tan fur rockets past me with a cacophony of growls and barks. Bear has gone berserk, launching himself from the car and galloping towards the perimeter fence, teeth bared, snarling and snapping like a rabid beast.

Before I can react, my arm is seized and I'm spun around, my chest colliding with a hard mass of solid muscle; Silas grabs and hoists me clean off my feet, charging into the foyer.

Outside, all Holy Hell is breaking loose. The terrified paparazzi, clamour and yell, diving and scrambling for the

485

relative safety of the transit, in an attempt to escape Bears' unbridled fury.

The next thing I know, I'm watching in suspended disbelief from inside the foyer, as an equally furious Sparks and Spanners appear from the aircraft hangar... in the fire engine! They speed towards the fence, unravelling the hose as they go. It's a well-rehearsed safety procedure and they take no time in dousing the reporters and their van with the full powered, relentless force of the water cannon! It's complete anarchy.

Thoroughly soaked to the skin and screaming blue, bloody murder about damaged cameras, ferocious guard dogs and illegal use of fire safety equipment, the two paparazzi, leap back into their battered van - which is now sporting some rather impressive dents from the pressure of the water – and start the reluctant engine. Performing a two wheeled U-turn, they rev off down the road, just as Christina's Mercedes is driving up the lane.

Silas is still laughing as I turn to look at him. I can't believe it. The Papers are on to me and he finds all this entertaining?

"What?" He looks at me with a big shit eating grin on his face. "Aw, come on, Edi. They deserved it." Turning on my furious heels, I stomp off in the direction of my office. "Edi, come on... it was a bit of fun," he calls after me.

"What the *fuck* is going on?" Christina enters the foyer. Clearly, she's taken in the fire engine, the hose, the soaked driveway, the mad dog and Silas! Equally clearly, she's not the least bit impressed.

"Ask your ex-husband!!" I yell over my shoulder – I'm not impressed either! "He's the one that set the Chuckle Brothers loose!"

"Well?" she demands as I slam my office door.

Jesus, talk about childish behaviour! Now they've a brilliant story about being attacked by a vicious dog while they were hosed down like hippies at a 60's peace rally; and all because they were seeking out the *'Ice Queen.'* Christ, tomorrows papers will be full of it!

Needing some urgent damage control, I decide I must speak to Lizzy sooner rather than later. She needs to be warned. I'll also need to speak to Mark at the Beeches and explain what's going on, just in case he picks up the paper. Then, I need to speak to Christina.

After tomorrow, I doubt that my future at RTC will be very secure. Bobby will see the papers and he will know where I am. Now he's working exclusively with RTC, I'm sure his influence will ensure I'm dismissed forthwith. My immediate priority is protecting the children. Bobby mustn't ever know about them, especially David.

Burying my face in my hands, I'm seething in anger at my stupidity; the irony of the ridiculous, chain of events that brought me to this horrendous position. Nearly twenty years! Twenty *fucking* years... wiped out... just like that. My privacy that I worked so assiduously to protect is gone, just because I attended one *fucking* party. Just because I met someone and thought I would be safe having a life! God, I'm so stupid. When will I learn? Why ever would I believe I could have a life for myself?

I should've stayed anonymous, remained invisible, that way at least Lizzy and David would be protected, but *oh, no!* I had to have a career, a life of my own... what a self-centred idiot I've been.

I need to think, but I can't. I'm disjointed and befuddled. I've been out of the spotlight for so long, I don't know how to handle the intrusions. Moreover, I'm terrified of what will happen once I'm confronted with Bobby. I could lose my job. No, I *will* lose my job. No doubt about that; it's a foregone conclusion. I'll have nowhere to live. I'll have to move David. Lizzy will be followed.

Oh Jesus, God!! What a frigging mess.

In my panicked state, I don't hear Silas and Christina enter my office until they're standing right in front of me. Christina takes a chair moving it round so she's sitting beside me. Silas just stands like a schoolboy who's in trouble with the head-mistress.

Placing a comforting arm round my shoulder, Christina bends forward so we're eye to eye. "Edi, this isn't your fault." She's being so kind. It brings a lump to my throat. "Look, Silas has explained. So, you have a past... so what? These people... these scumbags, they can't harm you. Your stronger than that. Look..." sighing, she glances at Silas for moral support. Silas comes around to my side of the desk and kneels on the floor before me, taking hold of my trembling hands.

"Honey-bee... look at me. They've gone. What's the worst that can happen eh?" He's contrite, Christina is nodding her agreement but I can't share their confidence...

"Oh, I don't know... let's think about it shall we." Defiantly I count off all the things that could happen on my fingers like I'm making a list! "My daughter will be hounded and stalked. My son will be exposed. They'll find out about my new job. Your business will be put under the spotlight, you'll lose customers. I'll be pursued, so will you and you." I nod at each of them in turn emphasizing my point. "Every aspect of your lives will change. People you don't know will tell stories about you. Your private lives will become public knowledge." They flash each other a nervous glance at that revelation... "your divorce, your working relationship. My relationship with Silas; you have no idea how these people can twist things. My old pictures will be all over the news again, my children will see how sordid my life was. And they will dig up every little bit of dirt they can find from the past twenty years and everyone will know about me."

Utterly distraught, I look beseechingly at Silas; pleading with my eyes, willing him to understand. He does, I think. His dark hooded eyes, so recently sparking with mirth are now filled with apprehension. They drift to my watch, his hand and fingers proactively circling my wrist.

Yes, now you get it!

"Edi…" Christina starts but can't find the words. She stands and gives me a hug. "Don't give up. Don't let them win. You will think of something. You're a smart woman." She looks directly at Silas. "I'll speak to you later," she scolds ominously, and with that she leaves my office. Silas remains on the floor holding my hand.

"She's right you know," he whispers. "You are smart. Why not turn this to your advantage? There must be a way of putting the ball in your court, you just need to find it." Maybe he's right. Perhaps there's a way round it but at the moment, what I need more than anything is damage control.

Pulling myself together, prompt action is required. "Will you come with me tonight to see David? After today, I don't think it can wait until Friday".

Lizzy is in the States, so she's safe at the moment but I'll need to speak to her sooner rather than later. I just need the children safe. Since my 'accident' practical solutions have always been my way of coping in a crisis. Think of the worst possible thing that can happen and mitigate from there. Currently, the worst thing would be for them to find out about David and approach The Beeches for a story or pictures.

Yes, I'll start with David, then Lizzy… I should make a list and work through it. Past situations have forced me to think on my feet. Christina's words are resounding in my head. I *can* and *will* think of something, some way to bend this to my advantage. I am a smart woman. After all, I stayed out of the lime-light for twenty years. Perhaps it's time to tell my side of the story? Suddenly a raft of ideas is forming, some I dismiss and some I file away for later use. Silas's voice jolts me out of my thoughts.

"Yes, yes of course I'll come," he says. "Please tell me that you aren't thinking of running away. You have us on your side now. Both of us, me and Christina... and you know what a force of nature she can be," he says as he stands up. "Speaking of which, I think I need to go and talk to her." Bending, then folding his arms around me as I remain seated, he hugs me tightly. "The guys said to tell you 'sorry' for the Billy Smart's Circus performance out there."

Despite my mood, I can't help a little laugh at the image of the two journalists, reeling in the jets of the water cannon. Serves them right, *scroaty* little toe-rags.

"Silas, I don't want to leave. I'm so grateful for what you and Christina have done for me. But, seriously, if this is going to cause you problems, I'd rather go now, before..." I want to say, before I fall too deeply, but I think it's too late for that.

"Before... what? Don't you think I know? I feel the same. I could no more let you go now, than fly to the moon on a broomstick. Silly, beautiful, amazing girl... we need to embrace these feelings, not fight against them." He lifts me to my feet and draws me close, engulfing me in his arms and squeezing tightly. "I never knew what it was like to need someone; to want to spend every second of every waking and sleeping moment with that one special person... until I met you, I had no idea. I can't lose you now I've found you. This isn't just infatuation. It isn't just sex. It isn't just a flash in the pan... I think this is it... I think I've found the one... and I think; no, I know, it's you."

His sincere words floor me, knock me sideways. I didn't expect it from him, even though I feel it too, deeply inside myself. Every time we're together, it is like we're two halves of the same person. In truth, I felt it the first moment I saw him, standing there, looking critically at the unsightly splodge of mayo on my black trousers. I hug his waist tightly, not sure what to say.

490

"Ditto!" The feeling is mutual. It's far too soon to unleash the 'L' word, but it is simmering on my tongue, threatening to leap out of my mouth in an unguarded moment. It's been just over a week; my world has been completely turned on its head and I don't want it to topple back.

"We'll think of something… but for now, Ms Sykes, we all have work to do, so cheer the fuck up," he scolds me, bringing me back to earth.

"Okay, Boss-man. Get me a coffee…" He does.

Chapter 44

After work, we don't go back to the barn. Instead, we leave Bear with Christina and drive over to The Beeches. The sooner I see David, the better. I'm still on high alert, looking out for black transit vans and scummy-looking little men with cameras.

By the time we arrive, it's tea-time. There are a couple of cars in the car park, but I recognise them as belonging to the staff. The only other vehicle is The Beeches mini-bus. We park alongside it.

After signing in we go in search of our respective boys. Unsurprisingly, we find them sat together with Wendy at a table in the conservatory.

They're having what looks like a very posh afternoon tea. Complete with chintzy patterned china cups and saucers, a delicate, three-tiered cake stand is loaded with cream cakes, mini trifles and small, triangular-cut sandwiches. I notice wryly, that the sandwiches have been disregarded, in favour of the cakes and deserts. That's David, all over. Sweet over savoury every time!

Nic is the first to notice us. He looks up at Silas. He doesn't smile but he becomes more animated in his movements, rising from the table so suddenly he knocks his cup over, the remaining dregs of tea spilling into the saucer.

Noticing the sudden movement, David also looks up from his supper. His reaction is the polar opposite of Nic's. His smile is huge and he gives me a wave as he gracefully leaves the table. Increasing his speed, he strides purposefully to where I'm waiting and lifts me off my feet with an almighty bear-hug.

"Mummy!" Whirling me round, he places me back on my feet and gives me a big sloppy kiss. My beloved boy. "We've had tea but there's is still some left if you want some."

"That would be lovely, darling." Taking a moment to glance at Wendy, I notice she's also smiling. *Phew!*

"Wendy, will you get some more cups for Mum and Nic's dad please?" David asks and she delightedly obeys.

"Yes, of course. Please won't you join us for some tea?" Politeness personified, her manners are impeccable. I'm reminded of the prim middle-class couple I met last time I was here, she's certainly a credit to her mum and dad. Judging by her warm nature, there's more of her dad in her than her stiff upper lip mum. Wendy motions we should take the remaining two seats at their table before scuttling off in the direction of the kitchen, presumably to collect the additional cups.

If David finds it at all strange Silas and I arrived together, he doesn't show it.

"Here mum, you sit here." David indicates to my place. Nic is following behind us. He has Silas by the hand and is leading him to the table. "Nic, your dad can sit next to my mum..." David gives Nic a cheeky grin. I get the feeling he's playing matchmaker! Seizing this as the ideal opportunity I dive in.

"David, it's funny you should mention that... you know I have a new job?" Removing my jacket, I hang it on the back of my seat.

Wendy is back and has placed the clean cups and saucers in front of us. She commences pouring out two cups of tea. "Would you like milk and sugar?" she asks. The perfect hostess. Pride wells in David's face.

"Just milk please," Silas and I chorus together.

Wendy nods and adds milk to the cups. Job done, she takes her place beside David, offering him a demure smile before picking up her own cup and saucer and sipping her tea.

"Is your new job good mum?" David pulls the conversation back on track.

"Yes, it's wonderful actually." Stealing a glance at Silas, I see his small nod of encouragement. "As a matter of fact," I continue now everyone is settled. "would you believe that Silas is my new boss. Isn't that a coincidence?" Picking up my cup to give the message time to sink in, I take a welcome sip of steaming tea.

For a couple of seconds, David's eyebrows pucker with a puzzled frown, but it's only fleeting and before long he's smiling broadly, revealing the small gap between his two front teeth, his cry of joy filling the room.

"Wow! Mum, that's great. You really work with Nic's dad?" Silas nods at him in confirmation. "I hope you are enjoying your new job mum... Nic, did you hear that? My mum is working for your dad. Isn't that funny?" Keen as ever to involve Nic in the conversation, David aims his response directly at him.

Nic shrugs his shoulders and tilts his head to one side, towards his dad. The resemblance between them is striking, now they're sat side by side. I don't know how it didn't register with me before.

Silas absentmindedly leans his own head over so that his temple and Nic's temple meet in a light knock. It's an intimate moment between father and son and I suspect it's more meaning behind it than the simple gesture would betray. Dominic just bears his usual blank expression - I don't know how much of the conversation he understands - but Wendy is mirroring David in rapt delight. Straightening up, Silas squeezes Nic's hand briefly before continuing.

"It's wonderful to be working with your mum, David." Leaning over he adds in a conspiratorial stage-whisper, "between you, me and the gatepost she's loving it!" Flicking mischievous eyes my way, his lopsided grin does nothing to disguise the double meaning; causing a pink flush to heat my cheeks and a delicious ripple of desire zaps my centre. Silas picks up on my embarrassment but continues anyway... "In-fact, she's loving it so much that I'm going to ask her to go to dinner with me.

494

Perhaps even on a date... what do you think guys?" Silas conspires with the boys, man-to-man, as if they're his best buddies and he needs their advice on the best way to handle this. I lean back and look at him, in mock horror, going along with the façade. But David isn't fooled one bit. Giving me the fish eye, he's suspicious.

"Do you want to go on a date with him?" he nods over, indicating Silas.

"*David!*" Taken aback by his rudeness, I admonish his disrespectful tone. I understand he's being protective, which supposedly is a good thing, but it doesn't mean he can be impolite.

"Sorry..." David mumbles, abashed.

Nic suddenly stands up. Placing a hand on Silas's shoulder, he still doesn't speak, but he sways from foot to foot, agitated, looking at me with that completely blank expression of his. *Oh, God, is this getting out of hand?*

"It's okay mate..." Silas places a hand over Nic's reassuringly. "It was mum's idea. Mum and Edi, are really great friends. They get along famously."

Nic immediately sits back down and starts to rock, back and forth in his chair. In deep contemplation, he stares at his tea cup for a few seconds, before picking it up and holding it out towards Wendy, who willingly obliges, filling it with tea, milk and two sugars. Nic puts the cup in his saucer and commences stirring it, careful not to slop it over the sides before picking up the cup and taking a huge gulp of tea.

Silas turns to face his son, ensuring he has his full attention, he removes the cup from Nic's fumbling fingers and replaces it on the saucer before explaining further. "Hey Kiddo, listen to me... Mum really likes Edi. She wanted to come with us today, but she's been so busy with work and she needed a little rest; but she told me to tell you that she'll be over tomorrow evening. Is that okay, Kiddo?" He leans in so close to Nic that their noses are almost touching, making fixed, solid eye contact, ensuring Nic understands the message. Silas obviously loves his son very much; he understands and anticipates his moods and reactions as if it's second nature. "She's tired, but she's babysitting Bear for me tonight." At the mention of Bear, Nic ceases his rocking and just stares at the table.

"Berrr." It's quiet, but just about audible. There's comfort in the sound. Nic clearly loves Bear.

"He's big." We all turn at the sound of the new voice. Wendy's opinion of Bear is not clear, other than she finds him big! But, the sudden rush of affection I feel for her is palpable. She has helped diffuse what could easily have become a volatile situation with just two words and a swift change of subject.

David still seems unsure though, I can tell by the way he keeps glancing between Silas and me. However, Wendy surprises me further when she takes my hand across the table and in a loud whisper, shyly offers her opinion. "If he asks you, I think you should go on a date... he's cute!"

There's a clunking noise and a rattle of crockery as, jumping back in her seat, she narrows her eyes at David, giving him a withering look Lizzy would be proud of. I think he has booted her under the table! "Stop flirting with Nic's dad!" Yes, it's as I thought; there's a touch of the green-eyed monster making its presence felt.

Ignoring all the date chat, Silas replies directly to Wendy... "he's big, but he's very gentle," confusing everybody by picking up the conversation as if there wasn't any interruption at all. Silas chooses this moment to play his trump-card. "If you like, we can all go to the pub on Friday and he can come with us. What do you think?" Glancing round the table at everyone expectantly, he's so encouraging.

"Berrr. Pubbb. Yesss," Nic is keen. He's rocking again, but this time it is a bit quicker; a little more positive.

"Yes, please, Nic's dad!" So is Wendy. She claps her hands together in glee.

It would seem that Silas has hit the jackpot with that suggestion. Everyone is enthusiastic about visiting the local and the prospect of some pub grub.

"On your date with my mum?" Yes, the thought of going to the pub has worked like a charm with my boy. David has changed his tune and is beside himself, grinning from ear to ear impishly. "We can be the chaperones." Laughing now, he springs up and gives me a hug. "We'll make sure that you have a good time and that Mr Nic's dad behaves like a gentleman!"

Oh, my lord!

I'm blushing like a teenager at the thought of 'Silas behaving.' I can't look him in the eye! Then I realise David is speaking from experience; he and Wendy have a chaperone when they go out together. It makes complete sense to him we should too and I love him all the more for being protective.

"Davey, if I'm going on a date with your mum, I think you can call me Silas. Mr Tudor makes me feel really old and Mr Nic's dad is too much of a mouth full."

"But you *are* really old; like my mum." Oh goodness, David's filter's broken in all the excitement... but I suppose to him, we are really old!

"David, don't be cheeky! I'm sure *Silas* will be a complete gentleman, but having you all there will make me feel so much safer." In an effort to soften my scolding I give him a swift kiss on the cheek. I wink at Silas, who lifts his eyebrows in surprise; giving me such a smouldering look, I have to distract myself with some cake.

"Well, you know what they say… many a good tune is played on an old fiddle!" His suggestive comment goes right over their heads.

However, Wendy finds this hilarious and is laughing like a drain at Silas. "My mum and dad are *really* old. Older than you even," she chuckles. "My dad can't play the fiddle…" David folds his arms and shakes his head at her levity.

You want to listen to yourself, my boy before you cast judgement!

Now the news of Silas and my budding relationship has been, sort of, semi-broken, the conversation becomes much easier and we chat away for about half an hour, sipping tea, deftly eating our way through the remaining curly sandwiches.

By seven-thirty, people are drifting out of the conservatory, clearing plates, generally tidying up when Mark makes his appearance. He starts to herd a few of the remaining stragglers into the TV lounge. It's movie night and noticing our presence, he gives a little nod in the general direction of his office, indicating he could do with a quick word.

"David. I need to speak to Mark, but I'll see you on Friday… for our date okay?" I add quietly.

"I love you mum," he whispers so only I can hear.

"And I love you lots, David," I whisper back. It's a hint at our little family ritual…

David's cheeky smile is infectious as, breaking away from me he calls over his shoulder, "but, I love you more than Jelly Tots!"

"I love you more than Rainbow Drops."

"And I love you more than Cocoa Pops!" Laughing, he takes Wendy by the hand. Together they wander into the TV lounge.

"It's Frozen, tonight." Wendy waves at me in utter delight. "It's my favourite film. I know all the songs." David pulls her into the room, desperate to find a seat before the film starts. "See you on Friday," she calls over her shoulder.

Silas looks a little bemused at our ricochet of '*I love yous.*' "It's a family thing," I shrug at him.

He either gets it or he doesn't. The fact is, *we* get it and that's all that matters.

As if to prove his point, Nic leans into Silas; his form of a hug, though he doesn't use his arms. "Pubbb. Berrr. Bye," he says, then trots off, half jogging after David and Wendy.

"That was relatively painless..." Silas announces. "Mind you... I didn't really know what to expect. Lucky for you, you'll have three chaperones on Friday," his eyebrows jiggle suggestively.

"Lucky me!" I grin back. "Now for the hard part."

Mark is in his office, tucking into a huge slice of left over coffee and walnut cake as we enter.

"Sorry, just couldn't resist." He chomps. "It's nice to see you both." Indicating the chairs in front of his desk, we sit, side by side.

When Silas takes hold of my hand, Mark stops chewing, the cake hovering in front of his mouth, his eyes flicking between us, the question clear on his face. Slowly, he places the cake on his plate and reclines back in his chair wiping the crumbs from his fingers.

I've seen this pose before, usually when he's contemplating a situation; just as now. "Ah!" he exclaims. "Am I to understand, that you are here to..." He waits for one of us to speak.

"Yes and no," Silas says before I can stop him. "Yes, we've just let the kids know that we want to start seeing each other...

they're okay with it, before you ask. But the real reason is more serious and possibly more incendiary than that."

Incendiary... that's a good choice of word, I couldn't have put it better myself.

Hoping Silas will take the lead, I keep my mouth firmly closed, mentally wishing he would break the bad news to Mark, but he doesn't. Instead, just inclining his head in Marks direction, he's right, it is up to me.

Mark sits waiting patiently, as is his wont, reclining back in his chair, his big hands clasped loosely over his barrel chest. Eyebrows raised in expectation, alternating questioning glances between Silas and me, eventually he breaks the awkward silence. "I'm all ears... fire away."

Biting the bullet, I take a deep breath. "Mark, I'm really sorry, but I might have caused you some potential issues." It's not a great start, but it gets his full attention. Silas squeezes my hand in encouragement. "There's been some... *developments* in the last couple of days that may cause you some trouble." I'm waffling... not getting to the point. The truth is, I don't know how to get to the bloody point! "How can I put this?"

"How about, you take a deep breath, and blurt it out? It seems to work for the kids. I'm pretty un-shockable, you know. People do tend to 'blurt' a lot around here."

Noticing a cake crumb on his shirt, he flicks it off before unclasping his hands, giving me his full focus, the warmth of his smile signifying his un-shockability and relaxed nature.

Clearing my throat, I inhale, here goes nothing. "I've been found by the Paparazzi, and they took photos of me. They might put something in the paper. I needed to warn you, in case you see it and realise it's me. You can't let David see it." I blurt as instructed.

Mark looks at me quizzically. "You've been found? What does that mean?" Mark, doesn't know me or my history, so this is difficult.

Turning to Silas, needing an injection of moral support and inspiration, I'm relieved to see his steady reassuring gaze. There's a little tension in the line of his jaw, but it isn't showing in the rest of his face. Nodding his encouragement, indicating I'm doing just fine, he urges me to continue. So, I do... "It's all to do with my past. It is stupidly irrelevant really. But... well..." *Here goes nothing.* "I'm Meredith Frost... *The Ice Queen.*"

I've admitted it now. Never in a million years, did I think I would be saying that again!

Mark's very quiet, even for him. Silas doesn't move but I feel his grip on my hand tighten when he registers Mark's passing glance at my chest. It's fleeting, but he did it, as if he needed to confirm what I'm saying. The brief scrutiny makes me squirm with self-consciousness.

Secretly, I wanted him not to know me; to be oblivious to the name and to who Meredith Frost was, but I'm being delusional. I don't want him to recognise or remember the headlines; but it's apparent I'm hoping for the impossible, because it's crystal clear from his demeanour, he does indeed remember and recognises me.

I'm bitterly disappointed by his reaction, I thought he was better than that. We sit in silence for a couple of minutes while Mark digests my bomb-shell.

"Well, err, that's quite a... a... revelation." Sitting up straighter in his chair he smooths the creases in his shirt. "I must say, I didn't see that one coming... though now you mention it..." He's stumbling over his words. I can tell he's embarrassed for me and doesn't really know what to say, or how to handle this situation for the best.

Eventually, he regains some of his professional composure and looks me squarely in the eyes. "Edi... your secret's safe with us." His voice is soft, reassuring even. Though I can't forget his initial response, I might be able to forgive, if he proves he can be trusted. "Please, forgive me. It's a shock. Not that I don't think you're beautiful... you are..." He's blushing at his own ineptitude, it's amusing... "but I honestly, wouldn't have recognised you had you not told me." His professional manner keeps slipping. It's with some difficulty he manages to continue. "I... you... I have to tell you I had the biggest crush on you when I was younger. I had all your posters in my room... and, until this moment, I had no idea."

He's flushed and spluttering like a schoolboy. Nervously, he looks at Silas, who in turn is bristling with every inappropriate word Mark utters.

"Ummm..." I feel sick with embarrassment and humiliation. The last thing I need is for my son's carer to tell me I was his schoolboy wet dream!

Sensing my growing distress, Silas jumps in to the conversation. "Yes, well... we can all say that, I'm sure. You were no different to any boy of the same age. But the fact is Edi has lived out of the public eye for years. She's raised her family, earned her degree and secured her new career."

His jaw is ticking fiercely; teeth grinding, he's stern, the coldness in his eyes when speaking to Mark is chilling. Unblinking, he just stares Mark down delivering his lecture. "At last she has a life of her own. Unfortunately, there's been ... shall we say... a slight setback."

Slight setback! More like an almighty landslide!

Turning to face me, his demeanour softens as he continues, "it's all my fault. We were in Paris at the weekend, and she was recognised. The lid is ready to be blown off this powder-keg."

Refocussing on Mark, he becomes more determined. "Look, Mark, you really need to be on our side here... we're only at the beginning of this huge shit-storm. If we can't get a handle on this before it grows legs, Edi's life will be splattered all over the news and papers again."

I've no idea how many adjectives and similes he just used in that one sentence, but it was a pretty accurate description of this whole disastrous situation. But there's just one thing that's entirely inaccurate with his statement, I won't allow him to shoulder the blame for all this... this is all *my* responsibility.

"Silas, this isn't your fault. It's me, I'm entirely to blame. I should have been honest with you and Christina right from the get go." I can see that now. "I've been an idiot. I let my guard down and now I've dragged you all into my mess. Mark, don't for a minute think he's in any way to blame. This was all my own doing. I've caused all this by being selfish and naïve." I don't want Mark to think that way of Silas.

Silas carries on, ignoring my outburst. "Regardless as to who is or isn't at fault here, the potential for damage doesn't bear thinking about. No-one knows about David, or The Beeches, or *me*, or Nic but they soon will. We need your assurance, to be ready when they come snooping." Silas has put it in a nut-shell. Mark needs to be equipped to deflect any interested parties that might seek out a cheap-thrill story.

Mark has taken to Silas's stern mood well. After his initial reaction to my news, he's absorbed everything Silas has said and is once again the consummate professional.

"What can I do? Tell me and I'll do it." He's passionately protective of all his charges at The Beeches, so that was a good tactic by Silas. I'm relieved by Mark's reaction.

"As yet, we don't exactly know what their approach will be. Until this morning, they were just angling based on hearsay; but today, they came to the airfield fully armed and dangerous. They

503

took some pictures when we weren't expecting it. It's possible they might be in tomorrow's papers. To be honest, we're erring on the side of caution at this point. It could be something of nothing... there may be no interest at all in the story and everything may just blow over; but we'd rather be safe than sorry.

Silas picks up his glass and takes a long pull of water. Clearing his throat, he looks at me before he takes it upon himself to continue. "However, there's a bigger problem. A major potential issue is Edi's Ex; wherever he's. The papers will be looking for him for a comment. The more we keep a lid on all this the better for all concerned. Edi's ex doesn't know anything yet... though I'm sure by tomorrow he will."

"Mark, he doesn't know about David," leaning forward, I interject, forcing my point. "I mean, he knows about Lizzy - he's her dad, but he hasn't seen her for years - but he never knew about David. And David doesn't know about him either. He's never asked about him. He knows he has the same dad as his sister, but as far as he's concerned, he was never in the picture. It's only ever been the three of us." It's only now I can see how this could play out and I'm beginning to panic again.

Silas places a protective arm around my shoulder to calm me. Mark's face is a picture of worry and concern.

"Mark, there's a definite possibility tomorrow they will run a story in the paper. If you see it, please could you try and keep it away from David and Nic?" Silas asks.

"Yes, *God,* yes, of course I will. You have my word." Leaning towards me, he sounds sincere enough. "Edi, Seriously, my priority is the same as yours, keeping David and his friends safe. I'll do everything in my power to protect him... them!" He looks at us both in turn. "You two are amazing. You have managed to find each other in spite of all this and seem committed and strong. I'll hold the fort here. You do what you need to do to get through this. Whatever you decide, it will be the right thing... trust yourselves." He stands to see us out.

"If you don't mind me asking..." anticipating his question, Silas smiles and shakes his hand as he confirms.

"Christina, knows everything - and she's okay with it. She blames me for this latest mess though, as is her wont!" Placing his arm securely round my shoulder, he guides me through the office door.

Within a few minutes, I'm sitting quietly in the passenger seat, mulling over our conversation with Mark. He said to do '*the right thing*'... but what is the right thing? We drive home in the dark, back to Silas's barn and the quiet security of the secluded woodland. I feel exhausted. I need to think, but my brain isn't cooperating.

We arrive back so suddenly it's as if we were teleported. I missed the whole journey. It's pitch black – no stars tonight and the security light doesn't come on as we get out of the car.

"Hmmm? A bulb must have blown," Silas announces unsurely, reaching up and tapping the milky coloured glass on the front of the motion sensor. But I don't miss his cautious glance around the yard; he's looking for something but I don't know what.

A light breeze ruffles the hair round my shoulders, causing me to shudder and I've an uncomfortable feeling I'm being watched. We're in the middle of nowhere and I know we weren't followed either this afternoon or tonight. Silas clearly takes home security seriously and is fiercely protective of his privacy.

"Don't worry about it," he says, as if reading my mind. "You'll be safe here with me." Guiding me indoors, he takes one last lingering look around the garden before following me inside and locking the door on the outside world. "I'll check it in the morning."

Kicking off my shoes where I stand, I drop my bag on the floor. Silas swiftly picks it up and hangs it in the cloakroom. My shoes are dropped neatly onto the shoe rack. I would have left them where they were.

"Drink?" Silas asks.

"Please," I answer as I traipse into the living room.

Chapter 45

Collapsing onto the sofa, I'm too tired to move, I flop down onto the soft overstuffed cushions and lie there like a sack of potatoes. I'm musing over what to do if all hell breaks loose when a large bag of crisps fly's over my head, landing in my lap, making me jump.

"Stop overthinking it." Silas skirts the edge of the sofa, carrying two glasses in one hand and a bottle of scotch in the other. Sitting down beside me he places the glasses on the coffee table, unscrews the cap, and pours us each a three-finger measure of his favourite 12-year-old Lagavulin, single malt.

Picking up a glass he hands it to me, then using the remote control, switches on the TV. Flicking through the channels he finds what he's looking for, his eyes fill with mischief as he turns his grinning face to mine.

"What?" I pause, the rim of my glass just skimming my lips.

"It's movie night... *'Let it go... let it go!'*" he sings to me. I roll my eyes and take a sip of the warming amber liquid. "Seriously, Edi... just for tonight try to let it go. It might not be as bad as it seems. Mark's right. We'll think of something."

Turning up the volume, we sit and watch *'Frozen'* like a couple of kids. It's the first time I've watched it and I'm really enjoying it. I can tell Silas has already seen it, probably several times before with Nic, he seems to know where all the songs fit and hums along to many of them. It's endearing.

As he sits engrossed in the movie, I take the time to admire his handsome profile. I can't believe I've only known him for just over a week; it feels like he's been part of my life forever.

My mobile phone starts to ring; picking it up from where it is nestled beside the empty crisp packet, I slide to answer. "Hello?" I didn't notice the display.

"Hi, Edi, is that you?" It's Sammy, calling from the States. She sounds unusually harassed, which is so different from her usual come day-go day persona.

"Hi, sweetie, yes, yes it's me!" Nodding at Silas that I won't be long, I stand and walk over to the window. Silas mouths *'Do you want me to pause this?'* I shake my head in decline... *'No, it's okay'*. "How are you getting on... are you still in Washington?" The night sky is still black, but for the odd passing car, illuminating the hedges at the bottom of the driveway.

"No, no... we moved on to Baltimore for a bit of *'Hairspray'* love and now were making our way to Philadelphia... for some *'Freedom'*. It's a bit back to front, but it's working out okay... but that's not why I'm phoning."

That statement has me instantly on guard. "Oh?" What's going on?

She hesitates, as if she's not too sure how to phrase it. "Listen... Lizzy had a weird phone call today and she's a bit freaked out. That's why I'm calling you." *Oh crap, no!* "Some bloke claiming to be from *The Globe* newspaper. Asking questions about *you!* It was all a bit *Steve Strange*."

Shit! "Is she there, Sammy?"

"No, she's got a date... don't sweat it though, it's okay. Just one of the students we've sort of kinda, been travelling with. They've gone for burgers. I didn't want to go and play gooseberry fool." *Since when, it's never bothered her before?* "And anyway, I wanted to call you before she got back... what's going on Edi? It all sounds a bit odd." *Ah, that's the real reason...*

"Oh Sammy, it's all got a bit... complicated. I don't want her speaking to anybody until I can explain things. Can you just tell her I'm dealing with it and she should just... deny everything... tell her not to get involved in conversation, especially with journalists until I speak to her. Can you do that, please?"

"Yeah, okay… keep your hair on!"

"Oh Sammy, it's such a mess! I've fucked up big style, but I promise I'll sort it. I can't say any more, but I'll speak to Lizzy and explain everything, then she can tell you. Just… keep safe… okay?"

"Yeah, okay… Are you sure *you're* okay though? You sound a bit freaky-deaky."

"I'm fine. Silas is looking after me…" I'll distract her with gossip.

"Ahh, yes, the mysterious Sirius… I mean *Silas*. He sounds interesting. Got any juicy goss' for me?" It worked.

"No, no, you're far too young and innocent to hear about that!" It would only make her curly hair curl even more!

"You've got to be kidding me! I need deet's. C'mon Edi, spill the beans!"

"No, no, that's for another day. Look, can you ask Lizzy to call me tomorrow? Hopefully, it's something or nothing, but I'd like her to be pre-warned just in case… and remember… *don't speak to anyone!* Okay?"

"Yeah, okay. Spoilsport. Love ya loads!"

"Love you too. More than Jelly Tots…bye," I hear her laugh at the familiar retort.

"Hershey Kisses," she replies and the phone goes dead.

"What was all that about?" The credits are rolling on the film and Silas has turned the volume down so we can only just hear the closing music.

"Oh, just Sammy. Lizzy has received a phone call today from someone fishing for information about me. I can't believe they've found her number. They must have done some serious digging around. The bastards… they don't give up do they?" I flop back on the sofa and toss my phone onto the coffee table.

"They're only doing their job." Silas leans over and pulls me down so I'm on top of him. We both lounge on the plush settee like beached whales. "Besides, they won't find anything. There's nothing to find... is there?" He gets a double chin squashing his head down so he can look at me.

"No, nothing. Just a boring, student life and boring mum stuff. Lizzy must be curious though. Weird blokes phoning asking random questions about her mum. She knows bits, but not everything. I'll need to do some serious explaining tomorrow."

I push up so I'm straddling his hips and he can see me properly. Idly, I start to unbutton his shirt. I'm in serious need of some distraction. "You know, I think I'm going to need a bit of relaxation before I go to bed." Buttons undone, I spread his shirt open, exposing the fine planes of his chest and detailed abs.

Softly tracing my finger down the centre of his chest I let it fall into his belly button, before continuing the line of descent along the track of downy hair that disappears beneath his waistband.

"Hmmm, do you now? Do your worst Honey-bee..." He flexes his arms over his head giving me full access to his chest and body. "Take what you need, I'll not stop you."

I don't need a second invitation. My deft fingers quickly have his belt open. The zip fly of his jeans swiftly follows. Lifting my weight off him, just enough to allow me to pull his jeans down below his hips, I tug impatiently at his boxers. "Someone's in a hurry," he smirks, tilting his hips just enough for me so I can better expose him.

Once his boxers are nestled in the crumpled folds of his jeans, I lean back so I can admire him in all of his masculine glory. He could be a model in an exotic magazine, only better, because he's real and not airbrushed.

He just reclines there, thick arms stretched back over the side arm of the sofa, his shirt sleeves pulled tight over his flexed biceps. His white shirt hangs open, pooling round his ribcage and his beautiful, black cock rests on his taught stomach; his jeans and boxers pulled down, exposing just enough of his solid, muscular thighs to tantalise and send a flush of desire surging through me. Man, he looks deadly. Lord, what a picture of perfection he's.

"What now?" he asks me. *What now indeed?*

Unspeaking, I rise and step off the sofa. Holding his gaze, I rummage underneath my skirt and slide my knickers down my legs, stepping out of them I leave them on the floor, before climbing back onto the sofa and straddling his hips. He remains still, observing me, watching in silence as I take what I so desperately need.

Gently, I reach under my skirt, which is now shielding both my modesty and his cock. Letting my fingers feel their way, I find what I'm looking for and lift it from its resting place on his stomach, so it is upright and rigid. Inching forward, I hover myself over his massive erection, keeping my eyes on his. His expression doesn't change, though I notice a tensing of his jaw, as he clenches his teeth together when I touch him.

Hovering above him, I tease myself, flicking his cock over my throbbing clitoris a few times, soaking up the wetness, making him sticky with my juices. My body is veiled by the silky material of my skirt, neither of us can see what I'm doing.

Unable to wait any longer, I guide his broad, wet head to my opening, rocking my hips, getting him in just the right place before... *SLAM!* I drop all of my weight down in one swift motion. Lowering so quickly, that it knocks the breath out of us both. I feel like I've impaled myself on an iron post. There's pain, but it hurts so good!

"*Jesus... fuck!*" The curses fly out of his mouth as I swiftly lift and lower, pounding down and grinding hard, forcing my clitoris against his pubic bone to ensure maximum friction. "Fuck, yeah!" Unable to restrain himself, his arms come around me, his

511

hands cupping my buttocks under my skirt and teasing them apart, widening my opening so he can slide in and out easier. "Faster," he demands, raising me up and hauling me back down heavily, precisely.

"Owww!" It hurts, he's so deep I can feel the head of his penis grazing my cervix. "Fuck me, faster," jack-knifing effortlessly, he sits up, so quickly our chests collide.

Swiftly he turns the tables, tipping me backwards so he's now on top and in control. Lifting my leg so it rests on the back of the sofa, he places his hand on my inside thigh, pushing my legs wider and him deeper. "Christ, I can't get in deep enough... fuck Edi, you're amazing. Your sweet pussy is so fucking tight. Are you okay Honey-Bee?"

"Yesss... oh Silas, yes... fuck me. Hard, please." I need to be pounded, banged, fucked 'till I'm sore. I love the ferocity of his lovemaking and surprisingly, I'm learning I enjoy a bit of pain with my pleasure. "Harder, *HARDER!*" I'm screaming now. If he had neighbours, they'd think I was being murdered.

Suddenly he pulls out, leaving me hanging. Before I know what is happening, my skirt and his jeans are on the floor and I'm being bent over the arm of the sofa, my arse is in the air, my legs spread wide apart. There's no preamble or gentleness. Before I can protest, he's back inside me and pounding away, drilling into me at a ferocious pace.

My lower stomach is wedged into the arm of the sofa, his weight forcing me against the unyielding frame. It's painful, but the building pressure generated by this position has me gripping onto him like a vice. It's oh, so good.

"Ah, ah, gahh!" I grunt with each punishing drive.

Placing his hands under my thighs, he lifts me, tilting me forward and widening my legs further so I've no option but to bend my knees and curl my legs round him in reverse. I lower my hands to the floor to support my weight and prevent myself from falling to the ground.

I'm now in a precarious handstand pose, over the arm of the couch, with Silas kneeling on the cushion behind me. This new arrangement gives him even more access to my body. Reaching beneath me and using both his thumbs, he starts a brutal assault on my clitoris. Rubbing hard vibrating circles, it does the trick and I'm immediately trying to close my legs, battling to hold my imminent climax at bay but in this position, it's impossible.

"Come on, Edi. I know it's there, fucking come off..." *Flick, squeeze rub, slam!* He's being rough, and I love it. "Fucking come... now!" he demands coarsely, and I've no option but to do as I'm bid. I explode, throbbing, gripping on to his length, sucking him in so that with each pound he goes deeper.

The pain is exquisite! I can feel my vagina contracting; the now familiar female ejaculate running down my legs as I squirt my vaginal juices all over his massive cock. Capturing the deluge, he wipes his wet hands down the backs of my legs, sharing my wetness with me.

I know he's yet to come, so I'm a little surprised when he once again pulls out. My surprise doesn't last long. I'm flipped over and my back is lowered onto the sofa cushion, my legs hanging off the end. Kneeling before me, he lifts my legs and drapes them over his shoulders then buries his tongue deep inside me.

My orgasm is still throbbing away and the ministrations of his mouth soon has me writhing in pleasure once again. Just as it hits me, he pulls back, rises to his knees and drives deep inside with a grunt.

"Huh! Grr, gahh, fuck, You. Are. Fucking. Amazing! Come, now!"

Once again, I'm a slave to his demand and I come all over him. This time he joins me in my euphoria. I feel his hot cum soaking my insides, scalding me, pumping me full to the brim. When he pulls out, my vagina contracts so violently that his semen squirts out of me and coats his flexing stomach.

We're both panting, soaked in cum and sweat, totally spent and it's fucking wonderful. My sex is sore, tight and tender. It will sting like a bitch when I pee, I know it!

"Up you get." He assists me to my feet. I'm a bit wobbly but I think I can manage the stairs.

"Thank you." Flinging my arms round his neck, I give him the first kiss of the evening. It is deep and passionate and I want it to go on forever, but I need sleep.

Leaning back, I almost tumble, but Silas catches me. Lifting me off my feet, he carries me like a small child, up the stairs and lays me on the bed.

Removing my remaining clothes, then his own, he tucks us in and flicks off the light. If I die in the night, I will die a very happy, contented, woman.

Chapter 46

I'm rudely woken from my blissful slumber by an almighty crash. It's still dark, so it can't be morning. Silas is sat bolt upright beside me, the duvet pooling round his waist. Noticing I'm awake, he places his finger to his lush lips... *hush*... I need to be quiet.

Flinging himself free of the quilt, he stalks silently over to the window, as naked as a jaybird. Even in my anxious state, I can appreciate his statuesque physique.

Tilting the blinds slightly ajar, he peers out. Panic is mounting within my chest and my heart is letting me know something isn't quite right. Unsure of what I'm doing, but aware I need to be as close to him as possible, I leave the bed and join him at the window.

"What do you think it was?" I whisper quietly. Peering out between the blinds, I can see nothing but the dark green of the front garden. The Range Rover is where we left it on the gravel driveway. The trees are swaying in the night breeze but otherwise, there's no movement.

"Not, sure... it could be a fox or a badger." He's staring deeply into the night, trying to focus on what might be out there. "If Bear were here, he'd be going nuts by now..."

The crash comes again, only this time it's followed by an animal like wail. "I think it's a fox," he states as the wail comes again. "Yeah, it sounds like a fox. It's probably tipped the dustbin over or something." I'm not convinced. The foxes I've heard have a strange, high pitched barking yowl. This sounds more like a strangled cat.

"Could it be a cat?" I ask, still whispering.

"Perhaps... I'll check tomorrow. I'm not going outside now."

Reclosing the blinds to the eerie night we clamber back into bed, snuggling down and drawing the duvet round us. Silas pulls me close, enveloping me in his arms so I'm swathed safely against his hard body. He rests his cheek on the top of my head, and I burrow tightly into him, relishing the contact.

Gradually, his breathing regulates and mine falls into the same steady rhythm. Soothed and comfortable, I'm asleep in ten seconds.

I dream of foxes chasing cats who are chasing badgers. Blinding flashes of bright iridescent lightening augments the madcap scene causing the images to morph into a relief of monochromic black and white. Whirling and cartwheeling, their crazy chase speeds round and round, creating a staccato cinematic image like something from an old black and white, Mack Sennett movie. In my dream, the lightening is interspaced with odd crashes of thunder sounding like bin lids being smashed together. They beat a steady rhythm as the group of strange animals chase each other round and round the garden – my dreams are so vivid and bizarre lately!

As morning finally dawns, we both stretch awake. I take a '*Jack Reacher*' shower and in less than six minutes, I'm back in the bedroom, sat drying my hair as Silas comes back in with two steaming mugs of tea.

"It was definitely a fox. There's far too much mess for it to have been a cat and I think a badger would have made more. I've scooped it all back in the bin now." He hands me my mug and goes into the bathroom. "It wouldn't have happened if the hound had been here." He's missing Bear. I smile fondly at his flippant description of his constant companion. *Hound indeed!*

Driving to the office is uneventful. The roads are uncharacteristically quiet for once.

"I'll need to check on my car later today. If I leave it stationary much longer it won't start," I muse. The old BMW has seen me through a lot of years and has proved to be a good workhorse. But I'm under no illusions; it needs plenty of TLC to keep it going these days.

"No worries. I told you, Sparks has given it a good going over; It'll be fine. Anyway, you were supposed to be getting a car with the job; I'll chase Christina on that."

"No rush..." I'm sentimentally attached to my rusty-bucket.

We turn into the car park and park up. Bear is sat on-guard, waiting in his usual spot by the window in the foyer. On seeing Silas, he stands and starts to wag his tail. I can see his mouth moving in a familiar silent bark. As we approach the automatic doors, Christina rushes out to meet us. She looks flustered and she never looks flustered.

"Come inside quickly, both of you." Grabbing Silas by the arm, she drags him in. I follow on his heels. We're almost frog-marched to her office in double quick time. Her door is slammed shut and we're stood, bewildered, wondering what on earth has caused her distress.

We soon find out. Marching round her desk, she picks up the morning paper and flings it towards us. There, on the front page, is a huge picture of me. I'm stood, clearly visible through the open panels of the vertical blinds at the bedroom window of Silas's converted barn. Naked from the waist up, tits on display and a look of concern on my face, gazing out into the night! *Fuck!* ... This was taken last night! The headline reads:

MEREDITH FROST – THE RETURN OF THE ICE QUEEN!

The sub-text states:

'Once the most sought-after glamour model in the business, Meredith Frost, AKA the 'Ice Queen', so called because of her cold demeanour, looks anything but chilly as she appears at the window of her new lover's home.

Frost triggered a media sensation when she vanished more than nineteen years ago. Speculation was rife that her husband and manager, Bobby Price; Now a renowned Celebrity Agent, was culpable for her sudden disappearance; though it was later confirmed she had simply dropped out of public life, choosing to hide away from the spot light.

However, an unexpected appearance at Paris Fashion week on Saturday has sent the media world into a frenzy once again.

Rumour has it that Meredith, is set to resurrect her lucrative modelling career. As the photograph reveals, not much has changed for this natural beauty. This reporter can confirm after nearly twenty years away from the spotlight, the lovely Meredith has not lost any of her considerable charms. As the saying goes – the camera never lies.

The questions remain; where has she been and what has she been doing? Moreover, what will Bobby Price make of the reappearance of The Ice Queen? For more pictures, turn to page fourteen.

I can't believe what I'm seeing. My hands fly to my mouth as I try to supress the shocked cry that is desperate to escape. Silas is silent as he slowly flicks to page fourteen.

Unable to look, I keep my eyes trained directly on him, watching for a reaction and totally terrified of what might actually be there, in the papers for all the world to see. Silently I pray that his face will tell me… it doesn't let me down.

The searing flash of pain that crosses his handsome face is swiftly followed by a look of pure anger, his features eventually settle on blind, seething, fury.

I can't bare it. I've done this… me… nobody else. This is all my fault. I've brought this hideousness to their door… me. I should have stayed away and got a little job where I would be able to remain anonymous. This whole thing is because of my stupid selfishness. I deserve everything I get…

"*Jesus…*" His shoulders are shaking as he looms menacingly over the newspaper. His arms are braced and ramrod straight. His hands are flat on the desk as, with head bowed, he effectively shields my view of the double page centre spread. The sheer power radiating from the vibrations wracking his rigid form cause the desk to judder and creak under the unyielding weight of his barely controlled rage. "*Fucking hell…*" I've no idea what's in there and I daren't look. Christina stands frozen in time, like a statue. She's as pale as a ghost. Clearly troubled, I can almost hear her thoughts.

Christina ignores me and aims her reproachful stare directly at Silas. Eventually he lifts he head, locking eyes with hers. They just stare blankly at each other, their expressions stony and emotionless. I've no idea what is passing between them but something is and it's very disconcerting.

Eventually, Christina speaks for the first time in minutes. Her tone is icy and completely uncharacteristic.

"Can this be fixed?"

"There's no damage done," Silas' voice holds exactly the same tone as Christina's and it scares me.

"*No damage!* Christ, Silas. Your picture is all over the papers…"

Wait, surely, she means *my* picture?

"This could be catastrophic… you know, that don't you?"

"I said, there's no damage done… I'll sort it."

I've no idea what they're talking about, but clearly my exposure by the media and the link to their business has caused this unforgiveable upset. I should leave now and just disappear again before it gets any worse for them. It's apparent now that the noise last night wasn't a fox, or a badger or a cat! *No,* it was a fucking weasel; a skunk in human clothing, a snake in the grass! The worst kind of predator imaginable. A privacy invading, unscrupulous, corrupt, mindless, thoughtless, uncaring scumbag. The lowest of the low, sleaziest bastard on the planet... a tabloid journalist!

"Silas, this is serious... if we've been exposed... just sort it."

"Christ, for the last time..." Shaking his head, whatever is going on between them has been complicated by the appearance of these pictures. Silas turns away from Christina and focuses his gaze on me, his eyes soften in sympathy as he looks at me. The tension in his shoulders begins to lessen.

"I'm so sorry!"

His voice is a hoarse whisper. The declaration is so quiet I hardly hear it. "Edi, I really am so, so sorry!" I can't cope with empty remorse. I know, he's sorry. Sorry that he can't carry on with me; Sorry that it's finished, sorry that I've caused all this upset and that he'll sacrifice me for his own sanity. I've been on the receiving end of false guilt before; I'm not stupid, I know how this works. It needs to end and *he's* sorry...

Stealing my resolve, I make a snap decision. "I'll go. I didn't mean to cause all this trouble." My voice is cold and remarkably steady. *The Ice Queen* has made her appearance after all.

"NO!" The ferocity of his shout makes me jump. Standing from his hunched position over the desk, he whirls round, shocking me with his ire. "No... No, Edi, you don't understand. *I'm sorry!*"

Now I'm totally confused. I look up at Christina, hoping to see something in her face that will help me to understand... I see something, but it isn't what I expect. Her eyes are filled with tears and she's looking at me with utter sadness. *What's going on?*

Realisation hits me like a thunder-clap. It's the photographs on page fourteen. Seized with sheer panic I understand immediately.

Oh no! They've managed to find Lizzy, so they must have found David. *Oh God!* I feel ill. Lizzy's safely hidden in the States - for now, at least - away from the lenses of prying photographers, but David... and Nic... *Oh no! Lord help me.* I've exposed them to the press! In a fit of sheer panic, I snatch the offending newspaper from under Silas' nose.

The images confronting me are grainy and in shadow. My initial thought is one of relief, they aren't of David.

My subsequent thought is one of unmitigated horror. These pictures are of me... and Silas... we're naked... against a tree, partially secluded by shadowy, leafy shrubs and trees in the wooded area at the rear of his property.

Suddenly I'm in freefall, my stomach lurches at the sight of the horrendous images. I feel sick and bile rises in my throat.

"Catch her..." Christina calls, just a split second too late as my body crumbles in a heap so I'm kneeling on the floor.

Oh Jesus, this is even worse than I could imagine!

I feel large hands lift me and place me on a chair. I've not fainted, it's just my legs won't hold my bodyweight any longer. Silas drops into a crouch by my side, but I brush him away. I need to look... need to see.

Forcing myself to stand, I lean over the desk bracing my arms as if in parody of Silas's earlier pose.

The incriminating pictures are of poor quality, obviously the result of being taken through a long-distance lens. They've been crudely censored - for what it's worth. Certain areas have been pixilated out, but it's crystal clear, even to a blind person, we're in the midst of passion.

In one image my head is tipped back, my mouth open in a silent cry, my eyes are rolling in my head. I can almost hear my scream of ecstasy ringing through the trees. My legs are wrapped around Silas's waist; ankles tightly crossed. My C.F.M. shoes jump right off the page, loud and proud. You can even make out the indentations in his shoulders where my fingers are gripping so tightly as he pounds into me.

The image is explicit; pornographic even. I don't know how they got away with printing it in a daily paper. Only the inferiority of the exposure and the distance at which it was taken offer us some small amount of modesty. But it's is still possible to make out the distinctive shape of Silas's tight buttocks, even with the added pixilation.

The caption below the photograph reads:

Meredith and her lover perform outdoors for the cameras.

Scanning my eyes across the page, I take in the next image. It was taken on the same night. In this picture, we're on the woodland floor, Silas has his back against the copper beech and I'm straddled across his lap, kissing him. Our post-coital bliss is evident.

This caption says:

Meredith and her man enjoy an intimate moment.

It's like watching a slow-motion car accident; I don't want to look, but I'm unable to look away. The next picture shows me at the air field, the morning the paparazzi ambushed us. I look terrified and bewildered, the focus of the shot is Bear, he's in full flight, leaping at the camera and snarling like a wild wolf, fangs bared, spittle flying.

They've surpassed themselves with this caption:

Meredith's 'Hound from Hell' – Rabid dog attacks photographers.

Un-fucking-believable!! And they don't stop there. Oh no… The next picture is an old one. A posed photograph, from my glamour modelling days. In fact, I think it is the last ever photoshoot before my disappearance. Then there are a couple more from last night. A close up of my face as I stare out of the window, and one of Silas, his stunning face in full view.

"No damage..." jabbing her polished finger at the picture of his face. "This is clearly you..." she hisses at him. "This..." *tap-tap with her finger.* "could cause us untold damage..." Dropping heavily in her seat, she glares at him, then me.

"Edi, this isn't about you. Believe me." *Not about me...?* "Seriously, this is much more... complicated..." Staring at Silas, her tears finally dried and her composure gathered, she gives him her stoniest glare. "Fix it."

I look at Silas in utter confusion. My mind is whirling with questions. He's incredibly tense, his anger is barely contained.

"I'm so sorry Edi," he whispers.

I hold up my hand, palm facing him. I don't want to hear sorry. My anger is rising too and I can do without grand gestures.

Clearly exasperated with all the drama, Christina tsks him loudly. She's getting cross now. "Silas, for Christ's sake... are you a complete imbecile? What were you thinking? Why the fuck did you insist on indulging in this stupid fantasy? Outside!! For fucks sake!" Christina's indignation is resonant in her tone. Her voice pierces the quiet. She's as mad as all Holy Hell.

"I wasn't thinking. I was in the moment." He keeps his eyes turned to me, accepting his bollocking meekly.

"Jesus, '*In the moment*! *In the fucking moment!!* Jesus H. Christ! The hell you were. You can frigging-well say that again. Will you never *bleeding* learn? You. Stupid. Idiotic. Bastard!" Her language is filthy and littered with curses. She certainly has an extensive vocabulary where profanities are concerned. Exhaling her derision Christina visibly collects her rage as she looks at me. "Edi, apologies are not enough. This is diabolical and we're totally to blame."

No, no, she's wrong - this is nothing to do with them... I know it's my fault. I'm so confused, I don't even know what the hell I'm feeling.

I look down at the pictures. The old photograph leaps out at me more than the others. Perhaps because it's in colour, whereas the others are in black and white.

I point at the photograph. The hideousness of that day plunders my mind and I feel the pressing need to explain... "Look, can you see that? There's a bruise here." I trace my finger over the image. Half an inch below my left collarbone, it's just possible to discern the hint of a shadow. The light make-up barely conceals the outline.

Silas and Christina observe in silence as I quietly disparage the old photograph. "And here." Again, I trace the faint track of faded red on my arm.

To me, it's obviously a set of finger marks. If I concentrate, I can still feel the pinch of them. "And here." This time, there's no denying the fading bluish shadow on my ribs, just beneath my right breast. And on the breast, itself, is a livid half-moon shape, just above the nipple... a bite mark.

The room is silent, apart from the sound of Silas's increasingly heavy breathing and the ticking of the office clock. I can't remove my eyes from the old photograph. The more I look at it, the more it looks like a picture of a battered wife. How could anybody miss the signs? Perhaps it's my eyes playing tricks on me or the fact I know the truth behind the image.

"I was still bleeding when this picture was taken." Seemingly, I'm talking to myself now, remembering the incident as if it were yesterday. "I miscarried after this beating." My voice has taken on a flat tone. Christina gasps in utter shock at the revelation. "Bobby, made me cover up the bruises and get on with the photo shoot." Dropping my hand to my side, I keep staring at the sickening images.

"*What?*" Silas is incredulous. He really can't comprehend what I'm saying.

"It was nothing new. The only difference was I had just lost a baby."

I'm numb. Christina is stunned into silence. Her barracking of Silas pales into insignificance compared to this new disclosure from my past. Silas on the other hand is pulsating with supressed anger.

"I think I need to sit down." I feel queasy, faint. I drop back into the leather chair, folding inwards on myself.

Silas drops into the other and Christina lifts her eyes towards the ceiling before shaking her head and dropping them back down. We all just sit there, numbly, staring at the sick images, not knowing what to do or say.

Sensing that something is wrong, Bear lays his head on my knee, offering his own form of comfort. I'd forgotten he was in the room. Even with his soft, warm fur touching my legs I still start to shiver. I'm cold and can't seem to pull myself together. My teeth are chattering and my body is shot through with an uncontrollable fit of trembling shakes.

Concerned at my sudden collapse, Christina stands from her chair and drapes a cashmere throw round my shoulders, shifting Bear out of the way so she can get to me. "You need to take her home... NOW!" She points a well-manicured nail at Silas. "She's going into shock."

"I need a drink," I mumble, barely coherent.

Spurred into action by my odd request, Christina pulls a bottle of whiskey out of her desk cupboard and takes three glasses from the water tray. Pouring us all a hefty half tumbler, she hands them round. I knock mine back in one go. It burns my throat and heats my stomach but my shakes subside a little as the soft fabric of the cashmere shawl warms my freezing skin. But Christina is correct, I need to get out of here.

"Silas, can you take me back to the apartment please." My voice is still flat and emotionless. I'm flat and emotionless.

"Yes, we'll go now." He hasn't drunk his whiskey, so I pick it up and slug it back. Perhaps if I get plastered, I'll feel better.

"Be careful," Christina warns. Again, I get the feeling she's talking about something other than the incriminating pictures.

"I will…" Silas answers, equally cryptically. But I'm too far gone to care.

Chapter 47

I don't remember getting into the car, or any part of the drive home, or the journey into the apartment, or getting into bed. It all just happened. Now I'm lying numbly under the duvet in the luxurious bedroom, my scattered wits, reeling with all sorts of possible scenarios. What should I do? Leave and hide or stay and fight? I know what would be the easiest, but easy doesn't mean it's the right thing to do.

'There's always something you can do, and whatever you do will be the right thing.' Mark's parting words from yesterday echo through my brain. But there are too many burning questions, too many people who can get hurt and too many secrets that have the potential to destroy too many lives…

But what about David? What about Lizzy? What's going to happen when I face Bobby again? What about Silas and Christina and their business? What about me? Dare I even ask that?

This was supposed to be a new beginning. The start of a new life for the children. But instead, all I've managed to do is fall heavily for my boss, upset his ex-wife, screw up their business and rake up my sordid past. I've well and truly fucked everything up. *Well done Edi!*

As I lie in the warm, cosy comfort and luxury of the huge bed, I allow the tears to flow freely for the first time in years, unbidden I sob and sob. Shaking, breath restricting, choking, wracking, howling hysterical tears. I cover my face with my hands and release all the pent-up anger, shame and fear.

After about half an hour, my sobs have turned to dry, hacking heaves and my face feels swollen and puffy from the reservoir of tears I've shed. Untangling myself from the relative security of the warm duvet, I drop my heavy feet to the floor. There's a weight to my body I don't recognise. I'm sluggish and listless but my mind is made up. I can't stay.

Automatically, I begin to gather my belongings. Opening the wardrobe, I stare at my work clothes, they look like charity-shop cast-offs hanging sparsely in the vast closet. My two posh dresses are swathed sarcastically in plastic covers, a mockery of designer clothing I no longer possess. The sight of the green dress grips at my heart – casting a memory of a wonderful night in Paris – I can't take it with me. Dragging just my jeans, leggings and tee-shirts from the wardrobe, I close the door on the rest - I don't need them anymore.

What meagre possessions I own - there aren't many - I stuff haphazardly into my holdall. It takes barely minutes. Leaving my new watch on the bedside table, I run my fingers over the tell-tale ridges on my scarred wrist, tracing the outline of the small courageous flying insects and counting them all. I remind myself why I have them as I scribble a quick note for Silas.

'Silas, thank you for everything. The short time we had was wonderful– but I can't stay. Please apologise to Christina, I didn't mean to cause so much trouble. Edi.'

And that's it. Once again, I'm running away from a situation of my own making.

In the kitchen, the beautiful peonies that were so fresh and vibrant just a week ago have wilted. Pale pink and white petals are shed like so many fallen tears, scattered over the worktop, some are even on the tiled floor.

I take one last look at the luxurious apartment that has been my home for just two short weeks. So much has happened, so many good things, it feels like I've lived here for a lifetime. Switching off the light and setting the alarm, I gently close the front door and head out into the dark foreboding night.

In the car park my trusty, rusty, old BMW is sat waiting. After dumping my bags on the back seat, I climb in and turn the key;

I've absolutely no idea where I'm going but I know for certain I can't stay.

Rubbing my face with my dry hands, I breathe deeply, then exhale a slow stream of air. "Right Edi, where to?" I cough to clear my throat and sniff back my resolve as I shift the car into gear.

Even after nineteen years, I own next to nothing. All of my possessions are on the back seat of my car or in storage, but I'm reassured my children are safe. I need to get away, to plan and to start afresh.

Irritated, I wipe my face, dashing away the boiling tears that just won't abate.

I'm leaving him. I don't want to but there's no option. This time it's different, this time the man I'm leaving is different. This time the man is good and kind and loving. This time I'm leaving to protect him from me, not the other way around. He doesn't deserve this. It's time to go.

In a painful sardonic imitation of that fateful night, nineteen years ago I turn the car into the road, I look left and right without a clue where I'm going or what I'm going to do.

I'm leaving... the unwelcome phrase keeps screaming in my head... I'm leaving... *him*... unable to supress them, I allow the tears to flow properly.

Freely sobbing into the night, I drive away, reminded of the juddering, hiccoughing crying Lizzy made that horrible night so long ago, only this time, the tears are mine.

As if, to rub salt into the raw, gaping wound a song comes on the radio. A hurtful, scornful and familiar reminder that there's no escaping my past. Shaking my head, I laugh disdainfully at the irony of the lyrics that are so relevant to my life, they could have been written especially for me.

"Another ditch in the road... keep moving...

Another stop sign… keep moving on,

And the years fly by so fast…

You wonder how you're gonna get through."

My mind's so scrambled, it won't settle on one single, sensible thought. All logic has deserted me. Every streetlight and traffic light I pass, works like a remote switch; each one triggering yet another random collection of conscious arguments that insist on zapping through my synapses like electric shocks.

Bombarded with conflicting thoughts I can't desconnect, I weigh up my options. I ran away once. I disappeared once. I can do it again… and then what? How will I start again? How will I be able to forget him? He's filled my mind and ignited a flame I thought was extinguished long ago. But I've no other options…

This isn't just about me… It never really was…I drive on into the relentless night…

To be continued……

Find out what happens to Edi and Silas in the next book:

Courage to Fall

It's taken eighteen years for Edi Sykes to finally get her act together.

Now, at the age of thirty-six, she has a hard-earned degree and for the first time in her life is preparing to do something entirely for herself.

A new opportunity in a private air and logistics company holds exciting prospects and offers the chance of a brighter future.

However, when Edi comes face to face with her new boss, she's unexpectedly smitten by the moodily enigmatic Silas Tudor.

Silas is hard to resist, and he makes it clear that his interest in Edi goes far beyond that of an employee/employer relationship.

But Edi has secrets and things aren't always what they seem. After years of keeping a low profile, of staying under the radar, of no dating and certainly no male attention, Edi struggles with the flood of unfamiliar feelings rushing to the surface, threatening to turn her safe little world upside-down.

Should she throw caution to the wind? Should she risk exposing everything and embark on a relationship with this man? Should she have courage to fly?

Sometimes we need to spread our wings,
Sometimes we need to trust our hearts and take a leap of faith,
Sometimes we need the courage to fly...

Printed in Great Britain
by Amazon

62102336R00317